# THE BROADVIEW
## *Introduction to*
# Literature

## *Short Fiction*

# THE BROADVIEW
## *Introduction to*
# Literature

## *Short Fiction*

### Second Edition

*General Editors*
Lisa Chalykoff
Neta Gordon
Paul Lumsden

broadview press

BROADVIEW PRESS – www.broadviewpress.com
Peterborough, Ontario, Canada

Founded in 1985, Broadview Press remains a wholly independent publishing house. Broadview's focus is on academic publishing; our titles are accessible to university and college students as well as scholars and general readers. With over 600 titles in print, Broadview has become a leading international publisher in the humanities, with world-wide distribution. Broadview is committed to environmentally responsible publishing and fair business practices.

**Library and Archives Canada Cataloguing in Publication**

The Broadview introduction to literature, short fiction / general editors, Lisa Chalykoff, Neta Gordon, Paul Lumsden. — Second edition.

Also published as 1 section in The Broadview introduction to literature.
Includes bibliographical references and index.
ISBN 978-1-55481-403-9 (softcover)

1. Short stories. 2. Short stories, English. I. Chalykoff, Lisa, editor II. Gordon, Neta, 1971-, editor III. Lumsden, Paul, 1961-, editor IV. Title: Short fiction. V. Title: Introduction to literature, short fiction.

PN6120.2.B75 2018          808.83'1          C2018-901773-2


*Broadview Press handles its own distribution in North America:*
PO Box 1243, Peterborough, Ontario K9J 7H5, Canada
555 Riverwalk Parkway, Tonawanda, NY 14150, USA
Tel: (705) 743-8990; Fax: (705) 743-8353
email: customerservice@broadviewpress.com

Distribution is handled by Eurospan Group in the UK, Europe, Central Asia, Middle East, Africa, India, Southeast Asia, Central America, South America, and the Caribbean. Distribution is handled by Footprint Books in Australia and New Zealand.

Broadview Press acknowledges the financial support of the Government of Canada through the Canada Book Fund for our publishing activities.

Canada

Interior design and typeset by Eileen Eckert
Cover design by Michel Vrana

PRINTED IN CANADA

# Contributors to *The Broadview Introduction to Literature*

| | |
|---|---|
| Managing Editor | Marjorie Mather |
| Managing Editor, First Edition | Don LePan |
| Developmental and Textual Editor | Laura Buzzard |
| Editorial Coordinator | Tara Bodie |
| | |
| Contributing Editors and Translators | Lisa Chalykoff |
| | Neta Gordon |
| | Ian Johnston |
| | David Swain |
| | |
| Contributing Writers | Laura Buzzard |
| | Andrew Reszitnyk |
| | Paul Johnston Byrne |
| | Tara Bodie |

Editorial Contributors

| | |
|---|---|
| Tara Bodie | Bryanne Manveiler |
| Alicia Christianson | Amanda Mullen |
| Joel DeShaye | Virginia Philipson |
| Victoria Duncan | Anja Pujic |
| Rose Eckert-Jantzie | David Ross |
| Emily Farrell | Nora Ruddock |
| Travis Grant | Kate Sinclair |
| Karim Lalani | Jack Skeffington |
| Phil Laven | Helena Snopek |
| Kellen Loewen | Kaitlyn Till |
| Melissa MacAulay | Morgan Tunzelmann |

## PRODUCTION

| | |
|---|---|
| PRODUCTION COORDINATOR: | Tara Lowes |
| PROOFREADERS: | Joe Davies |
| | Judith Earnshaw |
| | Michel Pharand |
| DESIGN AND TYPESETTING: | Eileen Eckert |
| PERMISSIONS COORDINATOR: | Merilee Atos |
| COVER DESIGN: | Michel Vrana |

# Contents

# Preface

On hearing that Broadview was planning a new anthology designed to provide an overview of literature at the first-year level, more than a few people expressed surprise. What could a new anthology have to offer that really is different—that gives something new and valuable to academics and students alike? We hope that you will find your own answers to that question once you have looked through this volume. Certainly our intent has been to offer something that is in many ways different. We have brought fresh eyes to the process of choosing a table of contents; from Ama Ata Aidoo's "The Message" to John Gauld's "Freyfaxi," you'll find selections here that have not been widely anthologized elsewhere. You'll also find more visual material than in competing anthologies—including author-illustrated works such as Alasdair Gray's "The Star" and graphic literature such as Anders Nilsen's "Towards a Conceptual Framework."

Not everything about *The Broadview Introduction to Literature* is entirely new, of course. Many of the selections will, we hope, be familiar to instructors; as to which of the "old chestnuts" continue to work well in a teaching context, we have in large part been guided by the advice provided to us by academics at a variety of institutions across Canada. But even where familiar authors and selections are concerned, we think you'll find quite a bit here that is different. We have worked hard to pitch both the author introductions and the explanatory notes at a consistent level throughout—and, in both introductions and notes, to give students more by way of background.

For the second edition, we wanted to keep the same balance of fresh and familiar texts while making the anthology as a whole more contemporary and relevant. We have added more literature from the last twenty years in all genres, with a particular focus on contemporary Canadian writers; more world literature, both in English and in translation; more literature by Indigenous writers; more science fiction; and more graphic and illustrated literature.

Finally, you'll find fresh material posted on the companion website associated with the anthology. The site <http://sites.broadviewpress.com/BIL/> features additional material on many literary sub-genres and movements; material on writing essays about literature—and on referencing and citation; a much fuller glossary of literary terms than it is possible to include in these pages; self-test quizzes on the information provided in the introductions to the various genres; and several additional selections that we were unable to find space for in the bound book. Those looking to explore the borders of short fiction may find further examples of long short stories (or short novels) on the website—including Kafka's "Metamorphosis," Conrad's "The Secret Sharer," and Joyce's "The Dead." All are introduced and annotated according to the same principles and presented in the same format as the selections in the bound-book anthology. Those wishing to go beyond these choices for fiction—or for drama—may assign any one of the more than 300 volumes in the acclaimed Broadview Editions series, and we can arrange to have that volume bundled together with the bound-book anthology in a shrink-wrapped package, at little or no additional charge to the student.

Any of the genre volumes of the anthology may also be bundled together in special-price shrink-wrapped packages; whatever genres your course covers, and whatever works you would like to cover within those genres, we will do our best to put together a package that will suit your needs. (Instructors should note that, in addition to the main companion website of materials that may be of interest both to students and to instructors, we have posted instructor-related materials on a separate website.)

I do hope you will like what you see—and I hope as well that you will be in touch with any questions or suggestions; we will always be on the lookout for good ideas as to what we should add to the anthology's companion website—and/or for what we should look to include in the next edition of *The Broadview Introduction to Literature.*

[D.L., M.M.]

# Acknowledgements

The General Editors, managing editors, and all of us at Broadview owe a debt of gratitude to the academics who have offered assistance and feedback at various stages of the project:

Thomas Allen
Rhonda Anderson
Trevor Arkell
Veronica Austen
John Ball
David Bentley
Gregory Betts
Shashi Bhat
Linda Van Netten Blimke
Nicholas Bradley
Chris Bundock
Hilary Clark
David Clark
Jocelyn Coates
Richard Cole
Alison Conway
David Creelman
Heidi J. Tiedemann Darroch
Carrie Dawson
Celeste Daphne Derksen
Joel DeShaye
Lorraine DiCicco
Kerry Doyle
Monique Dumontet
Christopher Fanning
Sarah Fanning
Michelle Faubert
Triny Finlay
Rebecca Gagan
Jay Gamble
Dana Hansen

Alexander Hart
Ceilidh Hart
Linda Harwood
Chandra Hodgson
Kathryn Holland
Ashton Howley
Renee Hulan
Kathleen James-Cavan
Karl Jirgens
Michelle Jordan
Diana Frances Lobb
Kathryn MacLennan
Shelley Mahoney
Rohan Maitzen
Laura Manning
Joanna Mansbridge
Mark McDayter
Lindsey McMaster
Susan McNeill-Bindon
Alexis McQuigge
Craig Melhoff
Bob Mills
Stephanie Morley
Maureen Moynagh
Andrew Murray
Russell Perkin
Allan Pero
Mike Perschon
John Pope
Phyllis Rozendal
Cory Rushton

Laura Schechter

Stephen Schryer

Peter Slade

Marjorie Stone

Marc Thackray

Daniel Tysdal

Molly Wallace

David Watt

Nanci White

David Wilson

Dorothy Woodman

Gena Zuroski-Jenkins

# The Study of Literature

The Nobel prize-winning physicist Paul Dirac reportedly said, "The aim of science is to make difficult things understandable in a simple way; the aim of poetry is to state simple things in an incomprehensible way." More recently, noted Language poet Charles Bernstein—whose work typically challenges the limits of simple comprehension—published the poem "Thank you for saying thank you," in which he explicitly takes up the issue of how poetry "states" things:

> This is a totally
> accessible poem.
> There is nothing
> in this poem
> that is in any
> way difficult.
> All the words
> are simple &
> to the point.

Though Bernstein's work is undoubtedly meant to register as ironic, both his poem and Dirac's comment draw attention to the idea that literature uses language in a peculiar way, and that one of the most fundamental questions readers of literature must ask themselves is: "How is this said?" Or—with apologies to Dirac—the question might be: "How do the language choices in this text make a seemingly simple thing—for example, a statement about love, or family, or justice, or grief—not incomprehensible, but rather more than just something simple?"

Another way of approaching the question of how literature works is to consider the way this anthology of literature is organized around the idea of genre, with texts chosen and categorized according to the way they fit into the classifications of poetry, short fiction, drama, and literary non-fiction. One way of organizing an introductory anthology of literature is the historical, in which selections are sorted from oldest to most recent, usually grouped together according to what have become acknowledged as distinctive historical periods of literary output. Another is the topical or thematic, in which historically and generically diverse selections are grouped together according to subject matter, so that students may compare differing attitudes toward, for example, gender relations, personal loss, particular historical events, or the process of growing up. The decision by an editor of an anthology—or the instructor of a course—to select one organizing principle over another is not arbitrary, but reflects a choice in terms of teaching students how to approach the reading of literature. In very simple terms, one might regard the three options thus: the historical configuration emphasizes discovering the "what" and "when" of literature—what is the body of written work that has come to be considered "literature" (especially in terms of tracing the outlines of a national literature), and when were examples from this distinguished corpus written? The thematic configuration emphasizes sorting through the "why" of literature—why do writers turn to literature to work through complex ideas, and what can we make of our complex responses to differing, often competing, stances on various topics? The generic configuration, finally, emphasizes the "how" of literature—how is the text put together? What are its working parts? How does an attention to the formal attributes of a literary piece help the reader understand the way it achieves its intellectual and emotional—its more than just simple—effects?

What do literary critics mean when they refer to genre? The word was introduced into the English language sometime in the late eighteenth century, borrowed from the French word *genre*, which means "kind" or "style" of art, as when the British agricultural reformer Arthur Young refers in his travel narratives to the "genre" of Dutch painting, which he finds wanting in comparison to the work of the Italian masters. We can look back further to the Latin root *genus*, or even the Greek γένος (*génos*), a term which also refers to the idea of a distinct family or clan; thus, the notion of "kind" might helpfully be thought of as a way of thinking about resemblances, relationships, and keys to recognition among the literary genres. Another helpful analogy is the way biologists have taken up the term *genus* as part of the taxonomy of organisms. The term *genus felis*, for example, refers to a particular order of small cats, including such species as the domestic cat (*felis catus*) and the wildcat (*felis silvestris*); both species share common generic attributes, such as a similar size and a preferred diet of small rodents. For biologists and literary critics alike, the concept of genus or genre, respectively, is used to group things together according to a system of shared, identifiable features, with both terms allowing for the idea that larger groupings can be further broken down into even more specific ones (thus we can refer to the various breeds of domestic cats, or the distinctions among the Petrarchan, Shakespearean, and Spenserian sonnets).

Biologists tend to use the word "characteristics" to designate the features of a genus; literary critics, on the other hand, make use of the word "convention," a somewhat more complicated term. Like *characteristics*, the term *conventions* refers to distinguishing elements of a genre, which is why the study of literature requires a thorough understanding of the specialized descriptive vocabulary used to discuss such elements as a text's metre, its narrative point of view, its use of figurative language, etc. The introductions to each section of this anthology will draw attention to this specialized vocabulary, and students will also want to refer to the extensive glossary of literary terms located at the end of the anthology. The idea of convention, though, has additional conceptual importance relating to the way texts are built to be read. While a domestic cat is simply born with retractable claws and a taste for mice, a literary text is constructed, written in a particular way, often with the aim of eliciting a particular response from a reader. The word convention, in this sense, harks back to the legal concept of agreement, so that when writers make use of conventions associated with a genre, they set up a kind of contract with the reader whereby the reader has a sense of what to expect from the text. For example: when the first five minutes of a film include a long shot of the Pentagon, along with a few quickly edited shots of grim-looking military personnel moving quickly through underground hallways, and perhaps a shot of someone in a dark suit yelling into a cellphone, "Operation Silvestris has been aborted!" the audience understands that they are in for some sort of political thriller. They need not know anything about the details of Operation Silvestris to make this interpretive leap, as the presence of a few conventions of the political thriller (the shot of the Pentagon, the phrase "Operation [blank] has been aborted!") are enough to provide the general outline of a contract entered into between film and audience. Likewise, recognizing that a poem has 14 lines and makes use of a rhyming couplet at the end will provide knowledgeable readers of literature with an inkling as to what they should expect, as these readers will be familiar with the structural conventions of the Shakespearean sonnet.

Whereas a legal contract is a fairly straightforward affair—it outlines the terms of agreement for both sides and more or less explicitly refers to the penalties for undermining those terms—the contract between text and reader is multifaceted. One of the most fascinating things about the way writers make use of literary convention is that the terms of agreement are constantly subject to further consideration, thoughtful challenge, or outright derision. Thus, when the speaker of Shakespeare's sonnet 130 refers to his lady's "dun" breasts and "reek[ing]" breath, the point is not to insult his mistress, or even to admire her in a new, more realistic way; rather, the point is to ridicule the way other poets slavishly adhere to the convention that sonnets glorify a woman's beauty, comparing her eyes to the sun and her breath to the smell of roses. This reading is available for the reader who knows that by the time

Shakespeare decided to try his hand at the genre, translations and imitations of the Petrarchan sonnet had been circulating at the Elizabethan court for many decades. Like organisms, or even laws, conventions of literature evolve over time as writers seek to rethink the rules of the form they wish to explore. The speaker in Lillian Allen's "One Poem Town," warns an imaginary writer: "keep it kool! kool! kool! / on the page / 'cause, if yu bring one in / any other way / we'll shoot you with metaphors." Here, Allen—a writer of experimental poetry—both shows and reflects on the way the conventions of genre can create a set of expectations about what constitutes "proper" literature, and how those expectations can be tested.

Is it somehow problematic to inquire too tenaciously into the working parts of a literary text? Does one risk undermining the emotional force of a poem, the sharp wit of a play, or the exciting plot of an adventure tale if one pays too much attention to seemingly mundane issues of plot structure or metre? To paraphrase a common grievance of the distressed student: by examining the way literature works, are we, somehow, just wrecking it? These questions might, paradoxically, recall Dirac's complaint that literature makes simple things incomprehensible: while we know that literature can manage to communicate difficult notions, making what is mysterious more comprehensible, it is often difficult to articulate or make a viable argument about how it does so. By paying attention to the way a text is built and to the way an author constructs his or her end of the contract, the reader can begin to understand and respond explicitly to the question of how literature produces its particular effects.

Consider the following two textual excerpts:

> Come live with me and be my love,
> And we will all the pleasures prove.
> (Christopher Marlowe, 1590)

> Boom, boom, boom, let's go back to my room,
> And we can do it all night, and you can make me feel right.
> (Paul Lekakis, 1987)

Based on a quick reading, which excerpt is more appropriate for inclusion in a Valentine's Day card? A poll of employees at Hallmark, not to mention the millions of folks invested in the idea that Valentine's Day is a celebration of romance, would likely make an overwhelming case for the Marlowe excerpt. But why? Answering that question might involve a methodological inquiry into how each excerpt produces a particular response, one which might be broken down into five stages:

**Level One: Evaluation—Do I like this text? What is my gut reaction to it?**
No doubt, most students of literature have heard an instructor proclaim, with
more or less vitriol, "It doesn't matter if you like the poem/story/play! This
is a literature class, not a book club!" And, while it is true that the evaluative
response does not constitute an adequate final critical response to a text, it's
important to acknowledge one's first reaction. After all, the point of literature
is to produce an effect, sometimes an extreme response. When a text seems
confusing, or hilarious, or provocative, or thrilling, it prompts questions: How
are such effects produced using mere words in particular combinations? Why
would an author want to generate feelings of confusion, hilarity, provocation,
etc.? How am I—the reader—being positioned on the other end of such effects?

**Level Two: Interpretation—What is the text about?** This is a trickier level
of reading than it might seem. Students sometimes think, mistakenly, that
all literature—and especially poetry—is "open to interpretation," and that all
interpretations are therefore correct. This line of thinking leads to snap, top-
down interpretations, in which the general "mood" of the text is felt at a gut
level (see above), and the ensuing reading of the poem is wrangled into shape
to match that feeling. It is sometimes helpful to think about interpretation
as a kind of translation, as in the way those who work at the United Nations
translating talking points from Arabic to Russian are called "interpreters."
Though no translation is flawless, the goal of simultaneous translation is to
get as close as possible to the meaning of the original. Thus, an interpretation
should be thought of as a carefully paraphrased summary or, for particularly
dense works, a line by line explication of the literary text, both of which may
require several rereadings and some meticulous use of a dictionary. As with
reading for evaluation, reading for interpretation can help generate useful critical questions, such as: How does the way this text is written affect my attitude
toward the subject matter? What is the point of all the fancy language, which
makes this text more or less difficult to interpret? Now that I've figured out
what this text is about—at least in terms of its subject matter—can I begin to
determine what sorts of themes are being tackled?

A note about the distinction between subject matter and **theme**: while
these terms are sometimes used interchangeably, the notion of theme differs
from subject matter in that it implies an idea about or attitude toward the
subject matter. A good rule of thumb to remember is that theme can never be
summed up in just one word (so, there is no such thing as the theme of "Love"
or "Family" or "Women"). Whereas the subject matter of Shakespeare's sonnet
"Shall I compare thee to a summer's day" is admiration or the nature of beauty,

one theme of the poem, arguably, is that the beloved's good qualities are best made apparent in poetry, and that art is superior to nature. Another theme of the poem, arguably, is that the admiration of youth is best accomplished by someone older. Thus, identifying a text's subject matter via interpretation aims to pinpoint a general topic, while the process of contemplating a text's theme is open to elaboration and argumentation.

**Level Three: Description—What does the text look like, at least at first glance? Can you give a quick account of its basic formal features?** At this level of reading, one starts to think about how a text is built, especially in terms of basic generic features. For example, are we dealing with poetry? Short fiction? Drama? If poetry, can we identify a sub-genre the text fits into—for instance, the sonnet, the ode, or the elegy—and can we begin to assess whether the author is following or challenging conventions associated with that genre? Of course, answering these questions requires prior knowledge of what, for example, a conventional ode is supposed to look like, which is why the student of literature must have a thorough understanding of the specific terminology associated with the discipline. At this level of reading, one might also begin to think about and do some preliminary research on when and where the text was written, so that the issues of literary history and cultural context are broached; likewise, one might begin to think about who is writing the poem, as the matter of the author's societal position might prove a fruitful avenue for further investigation. Thus, a consequent objective at this level of reading is to map the terrain of inquiry, establishing some general facts about the text as building blocks that underpin critical analysis.

**Level Four: Analysis—How are particular formal features working, especially as they interact with content?** The word analysis comes from the Greek terms ανά- (ana-), meaning "throughout," and λνέιν (lysis), meaning "to loose." Thus, the procedure for analysis involves taking a text and shaking it apart in order to see more clearly all its particular bits and pieces. This level of reading is akin to putting a text under a microscope. First, one has to identify individual formal features of the text. Then one needs to consider how all the parts fit together. It is at this level that one's knowledge of generic conventions and particular literary techniques—the way figurative language works, the ways in which rhythm and rhyme affect our response to language, the way plotting and point of view can be handled, and so on—is crucial. It may be the case that not everything one notices will find its way into an essay. But the goal at this level of reading should be to notice as much as possible (and it is usually when working at this level that an instructor will be accused of "reading too much into a text," as if that image of a moth beating its wings against a window means nothing more than that the moth is trapped, and that it just happens to have been included in a work). Careful analysis shows that nothing in a text "just happens" to be there. A text is constructed out of special uses of language that beg to be "read into." Reading at this level takes time and a certain amount of expertise so as to tease out how the work is built and begin to understand the connections between form and content.

**Level Five: Critical Analysis—How do the formal elements of a literary work connect with what the work has to say to the reader?** It is at this level of reading that one begins to make an argument, to develop a thesis. In order to construct a viable thesis, one needs to answer a question, perhaps one of the questions that arose at an earlier level of reading. For example, why does this poem, which seems on the surface to be about love, make use of so many images that have to do with science? What is up with this narrator, who seems to be addressing another character without in any way identifying who he is speaking to? What is significant about the fact that the climax of this play hangs on the matter of whether a guy is willing to sell a portrait? It is at this level of reading, rather than at the level of interpretation, that the literary critic is able to flex his or her creative muscles, as a text poses any number of viable questions and suggests any number of viable arguments. Note, however, that the key word here is "viable." In order to make an argument—in order to convincingly answer a question posed—one must have the textual evidence to make the case, evidence that has been gleaned through careful, meticulous, and thoughtful reading.

Returning now to the two texts, let's see if we can come up with one viable argument as to why Marlowe's text seems more likely to show up in a Valentine's Day card, going through each level of reading to build the foundation—the case—for making that argument.

**Level One: Evaluation.** At first glance, the Marlowe text just seems more romantic than the Lekakis text: it uses flowery words and has a nice flow to it, while the phrase "do it all night" is kind of blunt and unromantic. On a gut level, one might feel that a Valentine's Day card should avoid such blunt language (although this gut reaction might suggest a first useful research question: why should romance be associated with flowery language rather than blunt expressions?).

Moving on to **Level Two: Interpretation.** Well, the Lekakis text is certainly the more straightforward one when it comes to interpretation, though one has to know that the phrase "do it" refers to having sex as opposed to some other activity (and it is interesting to note that even in the more straightforward text, the author has used a common euphemism). The phrase "Boom boom boom" seems to be untranslatable, which begs the question of why the author used it. Is the phrase still meaningful, even if it's just a series of sounds?

As for the Marlowe text, a careful paraphrase would go something like this: "Move in with me and be my lover, and we can enjoy all kinds of pleasures together." Hmmm—wait a minute: what does the author mean by "pleasures"? Eating good food? Playing card games? Though the word is arguably vague, the references in the first line to moving in together and love make it pretty clear that "pleasures" is another euphemism for having sex (though perhaps a more elegant one than "doing it").

If both texts can be interpreted similarly—both are the words of a would-be lover trying to convince the object of his/her affection to have sex—why does it matter which phrase ends up in a Valentine's Day card? What are the significant differences between each text that cause them to generate distinct gut responses?

**Level Three: Description.** The Marlowe text, at least this piece of it, is a **couplet**, written in iambic **tetrameter** (or eight syllables in each line that follow the rhythmic pattern of unstressed/stressed). The language is flowery, or, to use a slightly more technical phrase, the **diction** is elevated, which means that this is not the way people normally talk in everyday life. In fact, there seems to have been a lot of attention paid to making the words sound pleasing to the ear, through patterns of rhythm and rhyme, and also through patterns of alliteration in the consonants (of the soft "l" sound in the first line, and then of powerful plosives at the end of the second).

The Lekakis text also makes use of rhyme, but in a different way: each line includes an **internal rhyme**, so that "boom" rhymes with "room" and "night" rhymes with "right." The rhythmic pattern is harder to make sense of, as there is a different number of syllables in each line and a lot of short, sharp words that undermine a sing-song effect. The sound effects of the text are comparatively harsher than in the Marlowe text, with many "b" and "k" and "t" sounds.

The Marlowe text was written in the 1590s, while the Lekakis text is a popular dance song from the 1980s; it might be interesting to follow up on the distinct cultural contexts out of which each work emerges. It might also be interesting to examine how each text thematizes the subject of having sex: whereas the Marlowe text seems to promote the attitude that the "pleasures" of sex should be tried out (to "prove" in sixteenth-century English meant to test or to try out) within the context of "living with" someone, or that love and sex go hand-in-hand, the Lekakis text seems to suggest that even sex on one "night" in someone's "room" can make one feel "right." Or, good sex has nothing at all to do with love.

Because these texts are so short and are fairly simple, much of the work of **Level Four: Analysis** has already been touched on. A closer inspection of the use of rhyme and **alliteration** in the Marlowe text demonstrates the way the poem insists on the idea that love can be "proved" by sex, while the internal rhyming of the words "me," "be," and "we" further indicates a strong emphasis on how the joining of two people represents a significant change. The use of elevated diction is consistent, suggesting that discussions of love and sex are worthy of serious consideration.

As for the Lekakis text, a major point to analyze is the phrase "Boom boom boom." Is this **onomatopoeia**? If so, what "sense" is the sound trying to express? The sound of sex? If so, what kind of sex are we talking about here? Or is it the sound of something else, perhaps dancing (as is suggested by the cultural context out of which the text emerges)? Maybe the phrase is simply meant to express excitement? What do we make of the plain speech the text employs? Does the use of such diction debase notions of sex, or is it simply more candid about the way sex and love might be separated?

As you can see, the level of **Critical Analysis**, or argument, is quickly and organically developing. If the research question one decides on is, What is interesting about the distinct way each text thematizes the relationship between love and sex?, a viable argument, based on evidence gleaned from close reading, might be: "Whereas Marlowe's text suggests that the pleasures of sex are best discovered within the context of a stable, long-term relationship, the text by Lekakis asserts that sex can be enjoyed in and of itself, undermining the importance of the long-term relationship." One might take this argument further. Why is what you have noted significant or particularly interesting? A possible answer to that question—and an even more sophisticated thesis—might be: "Thus, while the Lekakis text is, on the surface, less romantic, its attitude toward sex is much less confining than the attitude presented in Marlowe's text." Or, one might pursue an entirely different argument: "Whereas Marlowe's text indicates that sex is to be enjoyed mutually by two people, the Lekakis text implies that sex is something one 'does' to another person. Further, it implies that sex is a fairly meaningless and potentially aggressive activity."

The above description of the steps taken toward critical analysis shows how students of literature are meant to approach the works they read. What the description does not convey is why one would bother to make the effort at all, or why the process of critical literary analysis is thought to be a meaningful activity. In order to answer that question, it is helpful to consider how the discipline of literary studies came to be considered a worthwhile course of study for university and college students.

The history of literary studies is both very old and, in terms of the study of English literature, very fresh. In the fifth century, Martianus Capella wrote the allegory *De nuptiis Philologiae et Mercurii* ("The Marriage of Philology and Mercury"), in which he described the seven pillars of learning: grammar, dialectic, rhetoric, geometry, arithmetic, astronomy, and musical harmony. Collectively, such subjects came to be referred to as the liberal arts; as such, they were taken up by many of the high medieval universities as constituting the core curriculum. During the Early Modern period, the study of the so-called *trivium* (grammar, dialectic, rhetoric) was transformed to include the critical analysis of classical texts, i.e., the study of literature. As universities throughout Europe, and later in North America, proliferated and flourished between the sixteenth and nineteenth centuries, the focus remained on classical texts. As Gerald Graff explains, "In theory, the study of Greek and Latin was supposed to inspire the student with the nobility of his cultural heritage." (Somewhat paradoxically, classical texts were studied primarily in terms of their language use as opposed to their literary quality, perhaps because no one read or spoke Greek or Latin outside the classroom.) Until the late nineteenth century, the university system did not consider literary works written in English (or French or German or Italian) to be worthy of rigorous study, but only of *appreciation*. As Terry Eagleton notes in *Literary Theory: An Introduction*, the reading of works of English Literature was thought best left to working-class men, who might attend book clubs or public lectures, and to women; it was "a convenient sort of non-subject to palm off on the ladies, who were in any case excluded from science and the professions." It was only in the early twentieth century—hundreds of years after the founding of the great European universities—that literature came to be taken seriously as a university or college subject.

Over the past century and more, the discipline of literary studies has undergone a number of shifts. In the very early twentieth century, literature was studied largely for the way in which it embodied cultural tradition; one would learn something about being American or British by reading so-called great works of literature. (As British subjects, Canadians were also taught what it was to be a part of the British tradition.) By mid-century the focus had shifted to the aesthetic properties of the work itself. This fresh approach was known as Formalism and/or the New Criticism. Its proponents advocated paying close attention to literary form—in some cases, for an almost scientific approach to close reading. They tended to de-emphasize authorial biography and literary history. The influence of this approach continues to be felt in university and college classrooms (giving rise to such things as, for example, courses organized around the concept of literary genre). But it is important to keep in mind here that the emphasis on form—on generic conventions, on literary terminology, on the aesthetic as opposed to the cultural, philosophical, or moral qualities of literature—is not the only way to approach the study of literature, but was, rather, institutionalized as the best, most scholarly way. The work of close reading and producing literary criticism is not in any way "natural," but is how the study of literature has been "disciplined"; thus the student in a literature classroom should not feel discouraged if the initial steps of learning what it is he or she is supposed to be doing are challenging or seem strange.

The most recent important shift to have occurred in the "disciplining" of literary studies was the rise in the 1960s and 1970s of what became known as "literary theory." There is not room enough here to adequately elucidate the range of theories that have been introduced into literary studies, but a crude comparison between how emerging methods were set in opposition to New Criticism (which is itself a type of literary theory) may be useful. John Crowe Ransom's *The World's Body*—a sort of manifesto for New Criticism—argues that the work of the literary critic must strenuously avoid, among other things, "Any other special studies which deal with some abstract or prose content taken out of the work ... [such as] Chaucer's command of medieval sciences ... [or] Shakespeare's understanding of the law." In other words, the New Critic should focus solely on the text itself. In contrast, those today who make use of such theoretical frameworks as New Historicism, Gender Studies, or Postcolonial Studies will strenuously *embrace* all manner of "special studies" in order to consider how the text interacts with context. As Anne Stevens points out in *Literary Theory and Criticism*, "A cornerstone of literary theory is a belief in the cultural construction of knowledge . . . literary theory gives you a way to step back and think about the constructedness of culture and reflect upon your own preconceptions." For the student of literature trying to work out how to answer the question: "Why is what I have noticed in the text significant?", literary theory provides an extensive set of vocabularies and methodologies. For example: a New Historicist or a Marxist approach might help a student inquire into how a particular poem illuminates historical notions of class divisions. A Gender Studies approach might be useful for an examination of what a particular play can tell us about changing conceptions of masculinity. A Semiotic approach might consider the complex set of meaning systems gestured toward in the image of a police uniform described in a science fiction story. And, though it might seem that the focus on form that so defines the New Critical approach becomes irrelevant once Literary Theory arrives on the disciplinary scene, the fact is that most field practitioners (i.e., writers of literary criticism) still depend heavily on the tools of close reading; formal analysis becomes the foundation on which a more theoretical analysis is built.

Thus, we might consider a sixth level of reading: advanced critical analysis. At this level the stakes are raised as arguments about why a text's formal construction is meaningful are set within a larger conceptual framework. The work of advanced critical analysis requires that the literary critic think about and research whatever conceptual framework is being pursued. For example, after noticing that the Marlowe text and the Lekakis text are written about 400 years apart, one might further research cultural attitudes toward sex in the two time periods to come up with another, even more sophisticated, layer of argumentation, one which would not only provide insight into two literary texts, but show how the comparative analysis of such texts tells us something about how viewpoints on sex have shifted. Or, after noticing that both texts are written by male authors, one might further research and consider what they reveal about masculine approaches to sex and seduction. Or, after discovering that Marlowe's poem follows the conventions of **pastoral** poetry, or that "Boom boom boom, let's go back to my room" became popular within the LGBT community, one might contemplate and develop an argument about the implications of the way sex is idealized and/or becomes part of a complex cultural fantasy. Or, after discovering that Marlowe presented homoerotic material frequently in his other writing (in his poem "Hero and Leander," for example, he writes of one of the male protagonists that "in his looks were all that men desire"), one might inquire into the ways in which the author's or narrator's sexual orientation may or may not be relevant to a discussion of a love poem. To put it bluntly (and anachronistically), does it matter if Marlowe was gay?

Because the reading of literature entails a painstaking, thoughtful interaction with some of the most multifaceted, evocative, and provocative uses of language humans have produced, thinking about such work critically may tell us something about what it means to be human.

[N.G.]

# Short Fiction

## History

It's hard to imagine a time when people didn't tell stories. There is something close-to-magical about their capacity to capture and transport us. The Cherokee-Greek author Thomas King makes an even bolder claim about stories in his 2003 Lecture Series, *The Truth about Stories*, when he declares, "the truth about stories is that that's all we are." Although this may sound extreme, King has a point: stories are indeed a key way we root ourselves to the past and establish our identities in the present. King, for example, shares an "Earth Diver" story, which is a kind of story that has been passed orally between First Nations for millennia to explain not only how the earth came to be, but the relationships between the various beings who make up the world. As he points out, Earth Diver stories are an oral version of the more general origin story, and all people have these. King illustrates how his Earth Diver story, for example, is both similar to and different from the earliest books of the Bible. These stories, credited to Moses and dating back to around 400 BCE, also explain how the world came to be (in Genesis) and how the Jewish people escaped slavery (in Exodus). Every culture, like most families and most individuals, has its foundational stories, stories that are used to establish origins and explain what makes us who we are.

The short stories collected here are a modern incarnation of this fundamental story-telling impulse, one with a history that is both shorter and more culturally specific than that of the origin story. The short story—if we understand it as a genre of prose fiction that authors have been conscious of producing and consciously trying to understand—came into being quite rapidly in the nineteenth century, in both America and Europe, with writers such as Washington Irving, Nathaniel Hawthorne, and Edgar Allan Poe (in America), and Honoré de Balzac, Anton Chekhov, and E.T.A. Hoffmann (in Europe). Why would this genre have come into being so suddenly in both America and Europe? For one thing, more and more people were learning to read, and were reading for pleasure; not surprisingly, easily accessible and affordable forms of writing, such as newspapers and magazines, rose to feed this new readership's hunger. The short story was ideally suited to these venues: it is compact, discrete, and entertaining. This history reflects the fact that short fiction is a dynamic literary form, one that quickly echoes social and cultural change.

The flexibility of short fiction may also explain why this genre has, from its earliest years, accommodated so many literary styles and forms of experimentation. In the early 1800s Hoffmann used it as a means of giving expression to surrealism—a movement that sought to channel the unconscious mind, with its myriad images and seemingly nonsensical connections. The modernists Virginia Woolf and Katherine Mansfield both used short fiction to express the modernist's fascination with human consciousness, making a close study of the many levels of perception—conscious, unconscious, sensual, emotional—in a style of writing that sought to capture the full "stream" of human consciousness, as the philosopher William James put it (see "The Garden Party" and "Kew Gardens" for examples of this form of writing). The American writer Edgar Allan Poe used short fiction to bring forth some of the darkest elements and impulses of the human mind, anticipating Freud's theories of guilt and the unconscious in ways that lead quite rapidly to the flourishing traditions of the mystery and the psychological thriller (see "The Black Cat" for a macabre study of psychological guilt). Another field of literature with deep roots in short fiction is regionalism, a kind of writing that focuses on the particular characteristics of a place and the human culture it helps shape. Some of the best-loved examples of literary regionalism are short stories; William Faulkner's "A Rose for Emily" and Alistair MacLeod's "As Birds Bring Forth the Sun" are two excellent examples. Authors have also used this genre to think through and ask us to imagine worlds other than our own—a kind of writing broadly termed speculative fiction. We include several examples here: Ursula K. Le Guin's "The Ones Who Walk Away from Omelas," Octavia Butler's "Speech Sounds," Eden Robinson's "Terminal Avenue," and Leanne Betasamosake Simpson's "Big Water" all imagine alternate worlds in ways that encourage us to view our own worlds anew, and often in newly-critical ways.

## Short Fiction: Some Defining Characteristics

No one has ever fixed on a tidy definition of short fiction (or the novel), and this is largely because of the genre's diversity. The only characteristics a piece of writing *must* have to be classified as short fiction are the two captured in its name: it must be relatively *short*, and it must be *fiction*.

How short is short? There is no rule for this, but there is a great rule of thumb, one that Poe introduced in his review of Hawthorne's *Twice-Told Tales* in the genre's early days: one of the quintessential features of short fiction is that readers can consume it in a single sitting; if we can't read a story all at once (barring breaks to answer the telephone or make a cup of tea), then it isn't really a short story: it's moving toward the novella or, more typically, the novel. The longest story we've included here is Rohinton Mistry's "Squatter," at about 10,000 words. To represent the other extreme, sometimes called microfiction, we've included James Kelman's "Acid," which comes in at just under 150 words.

The brevity of short fiction also helps to explain what many—including Poe—see as another key characteristic of a successful short story: that it possess a certain singularity of purpose. Poe thought that a proper short story should be crafted from its first sentence to create a very specific effect on the reader. As he put it back in 1842,

> A skilful literary artist has constructed a tale. If wise, he has not fashioned his thoughts to accommodate his incidents; but having conceived, with deliberate care, a certain unique or single effect to be wrought out, he then invents such incidents—he then combines such events as may best aid him in establishing this preconceived effect. If his very initial sentence tend [sic] not to the out-bringing of this effect, then he has failed in his first step. In the whole composition there should be no word written, of which the tendency, direct or indirect, is not to the one pre-established design.

These days few would claim that *all* short story writers begin with an effect they want to create and then choose characters, events, and language to bring it about. And we're certainly less preoccupied with an author's intentions these days than people were back in Poe's time (critics now being more likely to think of a text as a thing with a life of its own that extends beyond the author's thoughts about it). But there is something in Poe's statement that remains as true today as it was then: good short stories tend to have a relatively tight focus. While a novel can develop many characters and include many plot lines, the brevity of the short story encourages a much tidier approach. To give just one example, many short stories focus on the development of a single human relationship over time; in this collection, Edith Wharton's "Atrophy," Raymond Carver's "Cathedral," William Trevor's "Folie à Deux," Emma Donoghue's "Seven Pictures Not Taken," Jhumpa Lahiri's "Interpreter of Maladies," Michael Christie's "The Extra," and Madeleine Thien's "Simple Recipes" all have a human relationship at their centre.

Yet my characterization of these stories as being about a specific relationship is an act of critical judgement: there is always more than one way to articulate the focus of a story. Such efforts are attempts to isolate a central theme in a work, a **theme** being an abstract concept that is made concrete in fiction through characters, actions, images, dialogue, etc. In order to be fully developed, however, a theme must go beyond naming the concept (e.g., "love") and assert what the work is saying about it (e.g., "love hurts"). Though some themes are more central than others, it's important to note that no work of literature has just one. To illustrate this, let's take another look at two of the stories mentioned above. While many might argue that the haunting nature of early relationships is central to "Folie à Deux," others might well prioritize themes relating to guilt, isolation, or the connections between human and non-human animals; all four concepts are being explored through event, character, and image. Similarly, while Raymond Carver certainly explores the dynamic nature of human relationships in the way he relates the three characters in "Cathedral," he's also using characters, events, and images to ask us to think about jealousy, disability, communication, and prejudice, for instance. In sum, though short stories often gain some of their elegance and artistic unity through a singularity of focus, the business of articulating this focus very quickly moves us from description to thematic analysis.

We've now considered some of the ways the "short" of "short fiction" gives this genre certain distinctive characteristics. The "fiction" element of "short fiction" clearly isn't as important in trying to understand the distinctive features of this genre—novels are fiction, too. But the fictional element is at least as important in helping us understand how short stories create meaning and inspire responses in readers. A key element in almost all prose **fiction**, whether we're dealing with a novel or a short story, is that it tells a story, and an invented one at that. For many years fictional narratives were defined in opposition to non-fictional narratives: while fiction tells us made-up stories, the theory went, non-fiction is based on real historical events. Over the last few decades, literary critics and historians alike have become more aware of how much is shared by fictional and non-fictional narratives: for example, both rely on the author's imagination to select, arrange, and prioritize events and the "characters" who enact them in very particular ways. In other words, there is much invention at play in any narrative, whether based on real or made-up events. The line separating the fictional and the non-fictional is one that continues to be questioned and debated by theorists, critics, and writers of our own day. Here we include two works that purposefully trouble the line between fiction and non-fiction, and in both, the non-fictional content comes from the writers' own lives. Ali Smith highlights the challenge to fiction she poses right in her title: "True Short Story" presents a collage of narratives, autobiographical, historical, and mythic, which are only minimally stitched together via shared theme and image. Somewhat differently, in "Towards a Conceptual Framework for Understanding Your Relationship to the Entire Universe in Four Simple Diagrams," Anders Nilsen presents what he calls a "universal memoir" that takes events from his own life and situates them within an imaginative, graphic context that asks some fascinating questions about where a life begins and ends. Both of these works make bold use of form to draw attention to the various parts that compose their totalities, and in so doing, both Smith and Nilsen encourage us to go beyond simply absorbing stories, and to think about how they are made.

## Making Short Stories: The Selection and Manipulation of Events

Most of us have probably encountered friends who aren't particularly good storytellers; maybe they leave out necessary details or, conversely, ramble on at such length that we lose interest in the story. Short story writers need many of the same skills as those of us who can spin a good tale orally. They need to be particularly adept at two things: selecting which events to include and ordering them in a way that sparks and sustains a reader's interest.

Over the years authors and scholars have developed a number of terms and distinctions to name the ways writers organize narratives. For example, novelist E.M. Forster came up with the useful distinction between **story** and **plot** to help us think about how we use time to organize narrative information: while a story is the chronological unfolding of the events that compose a narrative, the plot is the result of an author's manipulation of these events. Thus we say that the events of a narrative are *plotted*. Sometimes the plot follows the chronological order of the story. This is the case in Katherine Mansfield's "The Garden Party": we follow the day's happenings as they unfold, beginning with breakfast and preparations for the party, proceeding to the party itself (which gets quite brief treatment, interestingly), and ending with Laura's evening trip to the grieving widow (notice how wonderfully the fading of day coincides with the darkening of mood here). In contrast, Madeleine Thien's "Simple Recipes" veers dramatically from chronological ordering: our narrator moves us repeatedly between her present position as an adult and her memories of childhood events. Such plotting almost always emphasizes causality—it uses the past to in some way *explain* the present. Such causation can be established very suddenly, to great dramatic effect. This is the case in Thien's story, where it isn't until the final paragraphs that we learn of the father's present state, and the state of the narrator's feelings for him; these final bits of narrative information enable a sudden realization that these two people are as they are because of the past we've just been told about: these past events have had profound consequences for both of them.

Another effect that can be created by manipulating the order in which we receive information is **suspense**, our anticipation of an outcome of events. Think of how Flannery O'Connor's "A Good Man Is Hard to Find" pulls readers along by first presenting The Misfit as a notorious figure in the newspaper—hardly more than an idea, really—and slowly but surely drawing him closer and closer into the lives of the Grandmother and her family. As is often the case, ambiguity is a key ingredient in the creation of suspense here: it's our uncertainty, first about the identity of the stranger—*is* he The Misfit? No, surely not—and then about the nature of this man's character—just how good or bad a man is he? Would he do that? No, surely not—that propels us forward in anticipation that answers will be given.

A field of literary criticism called narratology has developed a number of useful terms for naming particular ways that authors organize and present the events in a narrative. **Analepsis**, for example, is a shift backward in time (a technique also known as a flashback) and is routinely used by short story writers to create history for characters and events. Emma Donoghue makes very artful use of analepsis in "Seven Pictures Not Taken," a story in which our narrator very purposefully selects seven moments, via specific images, over the course of a relationship. The story is composed entirely of instances of analepsis, in other words. What we learn of our narrator we learn through her selection and description of the images and through her decision to imagine her past in this way (what can we infer about a character who chooses to imagine the past as a series of separate photographs, Donoghue seems to be asking us). **Prolepsis**—a sudden movement ahead to future time, also known as a flashforward—is used less frequently in short fiction. We see an interesting example of it in Eden Robinson's "Terminal Avenue": as the narrator describes the family's last potlatch on Monkey Beach, this voice states, "This will happen in four hours when they land." In this seemingly simple statement we in fact see analepsis and prolepsis combined—we're being given a flashforward within a memory. Here Robinson provides a great illustration of the paradox that, while it's sometimes complex to clearly express how time is manipulated in narratives, such shifts in time are a simple facet of life: the human mind is wonderfully adept at roving back and forth through time, putting events together for itself.

Sometimes authors choose to embed one story within another, thus creating what is called an **embedded narrative**: a story within a story. Rohinton Mistry's "Squatter" is an embedded narrative: what we encounter in the story is an unidentified narrator telling us the story of Nariman Hansotia, who is himself telling various stories, but centrally the story of the migrant Sarosh, to the boys of Firozsha Baag (an apartment complex in Mumbai). As this description illustrates, embedded narratives are more structurally complex, and this complexity can create certain effects. For example, embedding one narrative within another inevitably makes storytelling itself a theme worth thinking about. Embedding one narrative within another can also reveal information about character: in "Squatter," for instance, we might well ask ourselves why the narrator didn't just take over the telling of Sarosh's stories for himself: why give Nariman such pride of place? If you were to read the full collection from which "Squatter" is taken—*Tales from Firozsha Baag*—you would learn that our narrator is in fact a man named Kersi, who was once one of the boys whom Nariman Hansotia delighted with his tales. Thus the fact that Kersi, our narrator, chooses to weave Nariman's storytelling so closely within his own might suggest, for example, his desire to honour his mentor, thereby lending a story that uses comedy to advance a biting critique of racism a gentle emotional warmth.

## Freytag's Pyramid

Another tool that can enhance our ability to stand back from a story and see how authors distribute narrative information and tension levels to create a good story is **Freytag's Pyramid**. This tool was invented by German novelist and playwright Gustav Freytag to analyze the classical, five-act plays from ancient Greece and Renaissance England in the late nineteenth century. However, these days Freytag's Pyramid is just as commonly used to analyze short fiction. The tool was invented when Freytag noticed that many of the classical plays he studied arranged narrative events in a similar way, which he sought to systematize in his "pyramid." The five stages he named correspond to the five acts in many classical plays. Not all short stories—or for that matter, plays—include the five parts and, even when they do, they're sometimes not so tidily or discretely arranged as they used to be. However, Freytag's Pyramid is useful precisely because it gives us a model to apply: whether a short story conforms to the five stages or not, examining its structure against this standard allows us to gain some critical distance from the plotting of events: we can begin to step back from the work and see the choices that have gone into crafting the story.

The five stages Freytag identified were, first, **exposition**, in which some context is established and the conflict that will be examined and resolved in some way over the course of the work is introduced. Second comes the **rising action** in which both the conflict and the central characters are more thoroughly developed; third is the **climax**, which can be understood in a couple of ways: it can be the moment of highest drama or tension in a work or, slightly differently, the moment that marks a turning point in the protagonist's life. Fourth comes what Freytag called the **falling action**, where the conflict between protagonist and antagonist is resolved; this often involves a moment of tension during which the protagonist is again tested or altered, though not so dramatically as in the climax. Finally, the fifth element is the **dénouement**, wherein events are concluded.

Stories conform to the expectations of Freytag's Pyramid to differing degrees. A short story that is well served by Freytag's schema is Achebe's "Dead Men's Path." There isn't any right way of drawing the lines between the five stages, but thinking about how to do so nicely opens up the story. One possibility is to say the exposition begins with our introduction to Michael Obi, a young teacher known to be an "outspoken" champion of the new ways, who has arrived to run the "unprogressive" Ndume Central school, and ends when we learn of Michael and Nancy's plans to make the school "*modern* and delightful," inside and out (p. 134). The rising action, in which the characters and conflict come into clearer focus, would then begin when we learn about the existence of the "dead men's path," and of Michael's decision to seal it off (p. 135). From here, the tension rises quickly: the climax might well be the uncomfortable meeting between Michael and the village priest, who arrives to reach a compromise—which Obi refuses—and leaves with the ominous statement, "I have no more words" (p. 136). The consequences of Obi's actions become clear when a village woman dies in childbirth and Michael awakens to find his school a shambles; this interval would then constitute the falling action in that the priest's authority seems to have been affirmed over that of Michael (and thus the conflict between protagonist and antagonist is resolved). At this point, there is only the dénouement left: Achebe uses his final sentence to establish the rich irony that Michael, having taken on the agenda of the colonial powers, is condemned for exercising these powers too crudely.

You may well have different ideas about where to draw the lines between these five stages, particularly in a story such as "Dead Men's Path," where there is a progressive stepping up of tension rather than a sudden leap. The very process of drawing these lines asks us to consider many questions, such as whether Michael's authority is lost when his school is destroyed (which represents his authority over the villagers), or when he is reprimanded by the "white" Supervisor (which represents his authority within the colonial administration). And this is precisely why Freytag's Pyramid is such a useful analytic tool: it sparks thought, and often debate. Moreover, there are certainly cases in which we could argue convincingly that stories lack some of the elements. For example, stories that conclude with a shocking sudden event—known as an "O. Henry" or a "surprise ending"—such as Faulkner's "A Rose for Emily" and Kate Chopin's "The Story of an Hour," could be said to lack both falling action and dénouement: the narrative simply ends with the disclosure of a climactic revelation or event. Alternatively, we might interpret the sudden mention of the odour of decay in "A Rose for Emily" as the climax, which would make the powerful final image we are left with both falling action and dénouement. Similarly, we might argue that "The Story of an Hour" reaches its climax not with the surprising arrival, but with that moment of resolution within the mind of the wife, when she recognizes and embraces her freedom. The point of Freytag's Pyramid is not so much to label the parts of a story as it is to enable us to stand back and recognize that there are discernible stages in the plotting of events, the development of character, and the distribution of narrative tension.

## Character and Characterization

There is perhaps no feature of storytelling that more powerfully draws us into a narrative than character: the simple fact is that we human beings find each other (and ourselves) endlessly interesting. Fiction, whether of the long or short variety, gives us an opportunity to indulge and indeed examine this interest. The development of literary characters is quite sensibly termed **characterization**. And for all the power that characters have to pull us out of ourselves, to pull us into stories, and to make us care about the figments of someone else's imagination, they are constructed with surprisingly few tools. Characters are developed in three basic ways: through narrative description (which can include suggestive physical description as well as direct statements about character), through actions (including dialogue) that implicitly suggest traits, and by giving us access to characters' feelings and thought processes.

The basic vocabulary surrounding character is quite simple: characters are said to be **round** when they have enough complexity to give them a three-dimensional likeness to human beings; characters are said to be **flat** when they lack such complexity. It's important to bear in mind that these aren't evaluative terms: flat characters are not inferior to or less useful than round characters; rather, these character types serve different purposes. The characters in fables, for example, are *necessarily* flat because it is their task to stand in for or symbolize things. Had Aesop given his tortoise complexity, the additional traits would only have lessened his capacity both to oppose the hare and stand in for the benefits of slow and steady work. And it isn't just fables that require flat characters to achieve their ends: many short stories require them as well: think of Thomas King's "A Short History of Indians in Canada" and Le Guin's "The Ones Who Walk Away from Omelas": as in Aesop's fable, the flat characters in these stories do the work of standing in for certain social categories. Giving them idiosyncratic characteristics would only detract from their ability to do this work.

One other distinction commonly used to categorize characters is stasis versus dynamism. While **static characters** (whether round or flat) remain essentially unchanged over the course of a work, **dynamic characters** undergo some kind of development, either experiencing a shift in character or revealing new dimensions of their character as the narrative unfolds (it's not always easy to distinguish between these two processes). Static characters can be round or flat: for instance, Flora from Alice Munro's "Friend of My Youth" seems to be a round character since she reveals a number of interesting traits (we might think of cheerfulness, adaptability, competence, fierce independence, a seemingly forgiving nature, patience, and industriousness). And you might say it's the very consistency of these traits in the face of such a remarkable series of life events that makes Flora so compelling a character: we keep waiting for the emotional calculus to complete itself, for some hint of bitterness or anger to come into view—for her to *become* a dynamic character. But does she? In fact, as the story proceeds, Flora's status as a character comes to the fore as the narrator offers different ways Flora's actions might be interpreted and contemplates the varying motivations we might have for "reading" her one way or another.

## Setting

Because the events in stories have to occur somewhere, it is inevitable that all fiction has a setting or, more often than not, settings. While this is also the case with drama, it's not with poetry: for example, a lyric can articulate ideas and feelings without specifying a locale. Fiction writers are a little freer to imagine setting than playwrights since they're not constrained by the need to choose settings that can be physically created on a stage. Given this freedom, it's not surprising that writers of short and long fiction craft all kinds of imaginary geographies, which achieve a variety of ends.

The most basic of these ends is to help create a convincing fictional world. This aim is a constant regardless of whether authors are attempting to construct a world that resembles one that exists or has existed or are seeking to create a world that is different from our own. There are no rules about how much description is necessary to establish setting, or how this material should be incorporated into a story; but more often than not authors avoid overt, sustained descriptions of setting and instead delineate it gradually through the use of small, seemingly unnecessary details. It's typically the accumulation of details that allows the reader's imagination to create the locations in which actions occur.

Yet the work accomplished by setting goes well beyond the creation of a convincing fictional world. It also does tremendous work of other sorts, in echoing theme, shaping character, establishing mood, and creating symbols, for example. Take Alistair MacLeod's decision to begin "As Birds Bring Forth the Sun" with the vague claim, "Once there was a family with a highland name who lived beside the sea" (p. 158). Although the narrator might have begun by telling us where and when this tale is set, he withholds these details, as well as his own personal connection to the story. Not only does this withholding of information help to create a mood of mystery and even tension in the story, it also helps to develop our narrator's character by revealing his own desire to maintain the mythic qualities of this family story. This is one example of the general fact that authors choose the details of their imaginary geographies carefully, often making them accomplish multiple tasks. Think, for instance, of Joyce's decision in "Araby" to describe the street where the neighbourhood children play as "blind." How might we link this word choice with themes or the development of our narrator's character? Similarly, the house in Poe's "The Black Cat" accomplishes some great work in creating symbols: as our narrator falls further and further from his better nature, so his home undergoes a parallel degradation; in the end, the ugly secret in his heart seems to be disturbingly paralleled by the ugly secret in the cellar. In contrast, in Munro's "Friend of My Youth" it's the stability of Flora's house, echoing the stability and indeed stasis of her own life, that seems to give it symbolic qualities. Not only do the two sides of the house echo the contrasting lives of its inhabitants, they also serve as a social statement that the outside world reads and interprets. In all of these cases setting helps to contribute to mood, whether through the choice of the adjective "blind" or through the use of strong images, of a house quite literally divided in Munro, or of a house undergoing a process of decay in Poe. Setting works so effectively to create mood and echo theme because it gives expression to the fact that we can never neutrally view or inhabit the places we interact with: our geographies are always, to some extent, emotional geographies. Fiction highlights and intensifies this fact, allowing us to savour it and, if we look closely into the matter, interrogate it.

## Point of View and Narration

All short fiction comes from a certain **point of view**, a very roomy expression that generally refers to the perspective from which a story is told. This includes both the kind of narrator an author utilizes and, more challengingly, the narrator's attitude toward events and characters.

The vast majority of short stories utilize either a first- or a third-person narrator (there are examples of second-person narration, but they are relatively rare). In the case of **third-person narration**, we usually don't know the identity of the narrator, who refers to all characters in the third person ("he," "she," "Peter," etc.) but generally makes no reference to him or herself (indeed, it's only the demands of English that require us to ascribe a sex to such anonymous voices). The opposite is true of a **first-person narrator** (sometimes also called a **character narrator**): we typically do know the narrator's identity, and such a voice tends to refer to him or herself in the first person ("I").

So long as a writer is using the realist style, only omniscient narrators can exhibit the power called **omniscience**. We know we have an **omniscient narrator** when we are given access to the thoughts and feelings of different characters as well as the details of their past and even future lives. Sometimes it is only one or two characters whose inner worlds we gain access to—this is called **limited omniscience**. Perhaps not surprisingly, omniscient narrators often give priority to the thoughts of the protagonist, as in Chinua Achebe's "Dead Men's Path." Lahiri's "Interpreter of Maladies" is an interesting example insofar as we only have access to Mr. Kapasi's thoughts and feelings for the majority of the story, yet near the end, we are given a sudden, quite substantial glimpse into Mina Das's mind and past, which suddenly transforms our knowledge of her and casts almost all of the actions and relationships we thought we knew in a different light.

Determining the narrator's attitude toward events may sometimes be a real challenge for readers. This is especially the case with third-person narrators, who are often imagined to be objective purveyors of information. Though we have little choice but to take the basic facts delivered by third-person narrators as truthful, we should be alert for signs of the particular attitudes such narrators exhibit toward characters and events. As an example, consider Mansfield's "The Garden Party," where some close reading reveals that the narrator gives more sympathetic treatment to Laura, who is initially horrified to carry on with the party after learning of the neighbour's death, than to her sisters or mother, who show impatience with Laura's sensitivity. Notice, for instance, how the narrator's final comment undermines Jose's words as she responds to Laura's horror at continuing with plans for the party:

> "If you're going to stop a band playing every time someone has an accident, you'll lead a very strenuous life. I'm every bit as sorry about it as you. I feel just as sympathetic." Her eyes hardened.

The narrator's decision to add that last sentence—"Her eyes hardened"—suggests that this voice isn't simply describing the characters and events (which it is indeed doing): it's also revealing a certain attitude toward them. Jose's eyes could have "glazed over" or "stared at her sister" rather than "harden," a term that so efficiently suggests her lack of sympathy and the fact that she is not "every bit as sorry" about the man's death as is Laura.

Many readers have an easier time discerning the narrator's attitude toward characters and events in the case of first-person narratives; this is perhaps because there is no guise of objectivity clinging to first-person narrators: it is clear that all of our information is being filtered through a consciousness that has its own particular way of viewing the world. As readers, our task is to try to discern how events and characters might appear to us were we able to correct for the narrator's biases. Sometimes this is relatively easy: in "Cathedral," for instance, Carver makes use of a male narrator whose prejudices toward and jealousy of Robert, his wife's blind friend, are difficult to miss. Such prejudices mean that, when it comes to assessing our narrator's view of characters and events, we must account for the effects of an **unreliable narrator**, a narrator whose understandings or information may be called into question.

## Free Indirect Discourse

Though authors have to make decisions about what kind of narrator to use, a specific style of writing, known as **free indirect discourse**, represents something of a middle ground between first- and third-person narration. Developed by nineteenth-century authors (from Jane Austen through to Gustave Flaubert and Anton Chekhov), this style of writing allows an author to imbue a third-person perspective with some of the characteristics of first-person writing. Flaubert inspired moral outrage for his use of free indirect discourse to give expression to Emma Bovary's adulterous desires precisely because this style of writing makes it difficult to discern whether the ideas we are reading are those of the narrator or those of the character being described by the narrator. Flaubert's reading public objected to this ambiguity, believing that it was the narrator's duty to unequivocally condemn Emma's unfaithfulness. Happily for us, this style of writing has long outlasted Flaubert's initial experimentation and is widely found in third-person writing today. Edith Wharton makes fine use of free indirect discourse to sketch out Nora Frenway's thoughts about her own adulterous desires in "Atrophy":

> Not that she was a woman to be awed by the conventions. She knew she wasn't. She had always taken their measure, smiled at them—and conformed. On account of poor George Frenway, to begin with. Her husband, in a sense, was a man to be pitied; his weak health, his bad temper, his unsatisfied vanity, all made him a rather forlornly comic figure. But it was chiefly on account of the two children that she had always resisted the temptation to do anything reckless. The least self-betrayal would have been the end of everything. Too many eyes were watching her, and her husband's family was so strong, so united—when there was anybody for them to hate—and at all times so influential, that she would have been defeated at every point, and her husband would have kept the children.
>
> At the mere thought she felt herself on the brink of an abyss.

Though the **voice** delivering these words to us is clearly that of the narrator—Nora is referred to as "she," not "I"—it is difficult to determine whether we are accessing Nora's thoughts or the knowledge and opinions of the omniscient narrator. Once we reach the first sentence of the second paragraph—"At the mere thought she felt herself on the brink of an abyss"—we receive confirmation that at least those ideas coming to us near the end of the first paragraph must have originated in Nora's mind. But ambiguity remains regarding the earlier statements. Also note the stylistic advantages that come from free indirect discourse: Wharton varies the rhythm of some of her sentences to *suggest* that we are accessing Nora's thought processes. Intentionally ungrammatical "run-on" sentences (or comma splices) are often used in free indirect discourse, as are double dashes—the purpose being to try to capture the somewhat chaotic flow of human thought. Here we seem to see Nora adjust her initial claim that the family is united, to the more precise and critical idea that they are united "when there was anybody for them to hate." When we think to ourselves (as opposed to when we write for others), our ideas are often refined through such gradual processes of self-correction and adjustment.

## Metafiction

**Metafiction** is writing that draws a reader's attention to the fact that he or she is engaged in the process of reading a piece of writing. It's best understood in opposition to the specific style of writing known as realism. When successful, realism induces what is sometimes called the realist illusion, an expression for that delightful way in which a story can allow us to lose awareness of the fact that we are reading, thus enabling us to fall into the textual world the author has created for us. A key characteristic of metafiction is that it disrupts the realist illusion and renders us self-conscious readers.

Readers have differing degrees of sensitivity to metafiction; however, some forms are unmistakable and virtually unavoidable, as when an author refers to the story we are reading. Ali Smith provides an example of this at the end of "True Short Story" when she tells us that "this story was written in discussion with my friend Kasia." This reference to the production of the very story we are reading cannot help but draw most readers out of the realist illusion and make us conscious of the fact that we are reading a constructed piece of writing. In a piece of fiction called "True Short Story" about a woman with a friend named Kasia, this metafictional reference to how the story was made in consultation with Kasia is but one of several ways Smith is encouraging us to think about the relationship between fiction and non-fiction, between story and autobiography, between literature and life. Metafiction often encourages us to remove our gaze from the work we are reading and think about it within a larger context, as Smith does here.

A second means by which authors encourage self-consciousness in read-ers is by making reference to some facet of literature. Smith's story, which we could describe as intensely metafictional, provides two good examples of this technique: first, she ends her story by listing ideas about short fiction expressed by no less than 13 writers; second, she has two men and two women discuss the difference between the novel and the short story within the story itself. Mistry also makes storytelling itself a theme in "Squatter" both by creating an embedded narrative (see "Making Short Stories: The Selection and Manipula-tion of Events" above) and, more boldly, by crafting a character, Jehangir, who discusses the literary styles and techniques (such as humour) used by Nariman, one of the two storytellers we encounter. Margaret Atwood gives us another variation on this kind of metafiction in "Happy Endings" when she discusses endings and plots, even referring in one instance to a weak point in her own story's plotting. Reading a story that itself talks about weak plotting or the use of humour in stories makes many readers conscious of what they themselves are reading and of how it is plotted or makes use of humour, for example. This is one of metafiction's most common impacts: it alters our perspective on the story, encouraging us to regard it more analytically.

Some forms of metafiction are more subtle and might easily be missed by even careful readers. This is the case when authors purposefully disregard literary conventions: if a reader isn't aware of the conventions themselves, they can't be expected to notice an author manipulating them. And this explains one of the great pleasures of learning about literature: it gives us access to a code of conventions authors have relied on to make meaning. When an author alters a literary convention, readers "in the know" become alert to this and start thinking about why he or she might have made this gesture. Microfiction provides an interesting example of this. A reader new to short fiction might read Kelman's "Acid" and think, "this is a very short short story indeed," and have it end there. But for readers familiar with this field's history, microfic-tion's very minimalism might well prompt questions, such as, "Is this a short story?" This question might, in turn, provoke others about the nature of short fiction: "How *do* we define short fiction?" "Which characteristics are necessary and which are merely optional?" These questions, in short, demonstrate that we have been rendered self-conscious readers and have shifted from merely reading the work in front of us to analyzing it.

There is nothing new about metafiction. A famous example is found in Chaucer's medieval verse narrative "Troilus and Criseyde." In his Epilogue, Chaucer addresses the text itself, saying "go litel book," and expresses his hopes that it won't be misunderstood by the world. However, metafiction has become much more popular and experimental since the 1970s and is now a significant component of contemporary fiction, short and long. The question of why authors wish to break the realist illusion and render us self-conscious readers is a complex and difficult one, but one that deserves at least brief consideration here. Some see the popularity of metafiction as an inevitable consequence of the fact that readers are highly literate these days and can become bored by a given set of literary conventions. By definition, conventions become familiar, and they can begin to strike readers as tired and trite. Authors seek to **defamiliarize** fiction—to make that which was familiar *unfamiliar* and fresh—by breaking rules and pushing boundaries. New forms of metafiction come along to renew the literary genre and for a time seem fresh, exciting, challenging. We see Murakami's efforts to refresh the love story in "On Seeing the 100% Perfect Girl One Beautiful April Morning": on the one hand, this story challenges the suspension of disbelief requisite to most stories about romantic love, while on the other, it manifests some of the love story's most cherished ideals: the genre's conventions exist in a bracing state of tension.

A final point: just because a work is broadly classified as realist does not mean that it is devoid of metafictional elements. Coady's "Hellgoing," for example, is a story that is realist in virtually all regards, but could well take a metafictional turn were readers to focus their attention on the theme of storytelling, and more specifically on the protagonist's efforts to manipulate the story of her visit home to best suit her audience of women friends (an effort that becomes more noticeable as we sense how poorly the brother conforms to the pattern of gender relations the group seeks to affirm). Munro's "Friend of My Youth" invites a similar metafictional turn when the narrator veers from her task of narrating the story of Flora for us and begins to consider the differing ways she and her mother interpreted these characters, and indeed, the motivations they had for "reading" these people in different ways. Both of these stories are gently encouraging us to think about how the past is made into a story, about the multiple ways the past can be narrated, about the impossibility of a definitive version of events—more generally, about how life is turned into history. These are some of the many ways authors use small stories to ask rather large questions about neutrality, authority, and history. However briefly, these examples suggest the role metafictional elements can play in making us more critical readers. Many have argued that the rise of metafiction reflects the needs of our own times: in a world in which so many competing interests seek to convince us of the truth of their claims, or to destabilize the possibility of truth, people need critical skills. Metafiction provides a means by which authors can tell a good story, one that can even move us emotionally, while also offering readers the opportunity to deepen their thinking about story, history, and truth.

[L.C.]

# Edgar Allan Poe
1809–1849

Designed to produce an atmosphere of terror by laying open to the reader the realm of the irrational, the uncanny, and the macabre, the Gothic tales of Edgar Allan Poe haunt the outskirts of the mind long after the last page is turned. In the "strange medium of his works," Robert Louis Stevenson detected "a certain jarring note, a taint of something that we do not care to dwell upon or find a name for." Poe returns to this nameless "something" again and again in stories like "The Pit and the Pendulum" (1842), "The Tell-Tale Heart" (1843), and "The Black Cat" (1843).

However one defines the "suggestive indefinitiveness" at the core of his most characteristic tales—a fascination with death, the iron grip of the past, or what Poe called "the human thirst for self-torture" perhaps come close— its presence reflects his pursuit of "a unity of effect or impression," a quality he considered the form of short fiction uniquely well suited to support. Poe held that the very brevity of the tale enlarges its power: because such works may be read at a sitting, the soul of the reader is fully at the writer's control, with neither weariness nor distraction to compromise the totality of the effect. But if the compactness of the tale allows the writer to realize "the fulness [sic] of his intention," it also demands perfect craft: for Poe, every word must advance "the one pre-established design."

Although Poe was among the first major theorists of the modern short story, his fictional practice has always been controversial, particularly among fellow American writers. Some object to his baroque prose and highly wrought formalism; others dismiss him as a hack who, having spent much of his life in poverty, indulged a lurid sensationalism in the hope of securing a wider readership. But as D.H. Lawrence observed, Poe was above all "an adventurer into vaults and cellars and horrible underground passages of the human soul," an author who not only founded detective fiction but who invested familiar forms with enormous power and psychological complexity.

## The Black Cat

For the most wild, yet most homely narrative which I am about to pen, I neither expect nor solicit belief. Mad indeed would I be to expect it, in a case where my very senses reject their own evidence. Yet, mad am I not—and very surely do I not dream. But to-morrow I die, and to-day I would unburden my soul. My immediate purpose is to place before the world, plainly, succinctly, and without comment, a series of mere household events. In their consequences, these events have terrified—have tortured—have destroyed me. Yet I will not attempt to expound them. To me, they have presented little but Horror—to many they will seem less terrible than *barroques*.[1] Hereafter, perhaps, some intellect may be found which will reduce my phantasm[2] to the common-place—some intellect more calm, more logical, and far less excitable than my own, which will perceive, in the circumstances I detail with awe, nothing more than an ordinary succession of very natural causes and effects.

From my infancy I was noted for the docility and humanity of my disposition. My tenderness of heart was even so conspicuous as to make me the jest of my companions. I was especially fond of animals, and was indulged by my parents with a great variety of pets. With these I spent most of my time, and never was so happy as when feeding and caressing them. This peculiarity of character grew with my growth, and in my manhood, I derived from it one of my principal sources of pleasure. To those who have cherished an affection for a faithful and sagacious dog, I need hardly be at the trouble of explaining the nature or the intensity of the gratification thus derivable. There is something in the unselfish and self-sacrificing love of a brute, which goes directly to the heart of him who has had frequent occasion to test the paltry friendship and gossamer fidelity of mere *Man*.

I married early, and was happy to find in my wife a disposition not uncongenial with my own. Observing my partiality for domestic pets, she lost no opportunity of procuring those of the most agreeable kind. We had birds, gold-fish, a fine dog, rabbits, a small monkey, and *a cat*.

This latter was a remarkably large and beautiful animal, entirely black, and sagacious to an astonishing degree. In speaking of his intelligence, my wife, who at heart was not a little tinctured with superstition, made frequent allusion to the ancient popular notion, which regarded all black cats as witches in disguise. Not that she was ever *serious* upon this point—and I mention the matter at all for no better reason than that it happens, just now, to be remembered.

Pluto[3]—this was the cat's name—was my favourite pet and playmate. I alone fed him, and he attended me wherever I went about the house. It was even with difficulty that I could prevent him from following me through the streets.

Our friendship lasted, in this manner, for several years, during which my general temperament and character—through the instrumentality of the Fiend Intemperance[4]—had (I blush to confess it) experienced a radical alteration for the worse. I grew, day by day, more moody, more irritable, more regardless of the feelings of others. I suffered myself to use intemperate language to my

---

1    *barroques* French: weird, strange.
2    *phantasm* Delusion or frightening apparition.
3    *Pluto* In classical mythology, Pluto is the lord of the underworld.
4    *Fiend Intemperance* The narrator demonizes the excessive consumption of alcohol.

wife. At length, I even offered her personal violence. My pets, of course, were made to feel the change in my disposition. I not only neglected, but ill-used them. For Pluto, however, I still retained sufficient regard to restrain me from maltreating him, as I made no scruple of maltreating the rabbits, the monkey, or even the dog, when by accident, or through affection, they came in my way. But my disease grew upon me—for what disease is like Alcohol!—and at length even Pluto, who was now becoming old, and consequently somewhat peevish—even Pluto began to experience the effects of my ill temper.

One night, returning home, much intoxicated, from one of my haunts about town, I fancied that the cat avoided my presence. I seized him; when, in his fright at my violence, he inflicted a slight wound upon my hand with his teeth. The fury of a demon instantly possessed me. I knew myself no longer. My original soul seemed, at once, to take its flight from my body and a more than fiendish malevolence, gin-nurtured, thrilled every fibre of my frame. I took from my waistcoat-pocket a pen-knife, opened it, grasped the poor beast by the throat, and deliberately cut one of its eyes from the socket! I blush, I burn, I shudder, while I pen the damnable atrocity.

When reason returned with the morning—when I had slept off the fumes of the night's debauch—I experienced a sentiment half of horror, half of remorse, for the crime of which I had been guilty; but it was, at best, a feeble and equivocal feeling, and the soul remained untouched. I again plunged into excess, and soon drowned in wine all memory of the deed.

In the meantime the cat slowly recovered. The socket of the lost eye presented, it is true, a frightful appearance, but he no longer appeared to suffer any pain. He went about the house as usual, but, as might be expected, fled in extreme terror at my approach. I had so much of my old heart left, as to be at first grieved by this evident dislike on the part of a creature which had once so loved me. But this feeling soon gave place to irritation. And then came, as if to my final and irrevocable overthrow, the spirit of PERVERSENESS. Of this spirit philosophy takes no account. Yet I am not more sure that my soul lives, than I am that perverseness is one of the primitive impulses of the human heart—one of the indivisible primary faculties, or sentiments, which give direction to the character of Man. Who has not, a hundred times, found himself committing a vile or a silly action, for no other reason than because he knows he should not? Have we not a perpetual inclination, in the teeth of our best judgment, to violate that which is *Law*, merely because we understand it to be such? This spirit of perverseness, I say, came to my final overthrow. It was this unfathomable longing of the soul *to vex itself*—to offer violence to its own nature—to do wrong for the wrong's sake only—that urged me to continue and finally to consummate the injury I had inflicted upon the unoffending brute. One morning, in cool blood, I slipped a noose about its neck and hung it to the limb of a tree;—hung it with the tears streaming from my eyes, and with the bitterest remorse at my heart;—hung it *because* I knew that it had loved me, and *because* I felt it had given me no reason of offence;—hung it *because* I knew that in so doing I was committing a sin—a deadly sin that would so jeopardize my immortal soul as to place it—if such a thing were possible—even beyond the reach of the infinite mercy of the Most Merciful and Most Terrible God.

On the night of the day on which this cruel deed was done, I was aroused from sleep by the cry of fire. The curtains of my bed were in flames. The whole house was blazing. It was with great difficulty that my wife, a servant, and myself, made our escape from the conflagration.[1] The destruction was complete. My entire worldly wealth was swallowed up, and I resigned myself thenceforward to despair.

I am above the weakness of seeking to establish a sequence of cause and effect, between the disaster and the atrocity. But I am detailing a chain of facts—and wish not to leave even a possible link imperfect. On the day succeeding the fire, I visited the ruins. The walls, with one exception, had fallen in. This exception was found in a compartment wall, not very thick, which stood about the middle of the house, and against which had rested the head of my bed. The plastering had here, in great measure, resisted the action of the fire—a fact which I attributed to its having been recently spread. About this wall a dense crowd were collected, and many persons seemed to be examining a particular portion of it with very minute and eager attention. The words "strange!" "singular!" and other similar expressions, excited my curiosity. I approached and saw, as if graven in *bas relief*[2] upon the white surface, the figure of a gigantic *cat*. The impression was given with an accuracy truly marvellous. There was a rope about the animal's neck.

When I first beheld this apparition—for I could scarcely regard it as less—my wonder and my terror were extreme. But at length reflection came to my aid. The cat, I remembered, had been hung in a garden adjacent to the house. Upon the alarm of fire, this garden had been immediately filled by the crowd—by some one of whom the animal must have been cut from the tree and thrown, through an open window, into my chamber. This had probably been done with the view of arousing me from sleep. The falling of other walls had compressed the victim of my cruelty into the substance of the freshly-spread plaster; the lime of which, with the flames, and the *ammonia* from the carcass, had then accomplished the portraiture as I saw it.

---

1    *conflagration* Destructive fire.
2    *bas relief* Relief sculpture characterized by slightly raised features that project from a flat background.

Although I thus readily accounted to my reason, if not altogether to my conscience, for the startling fact just detailed, it did not the less fail to make a deep impression upon my fancy. For months I could not rid myself of the phantasm of the cat; and, during this period, there came back into my spirit a half-sentiment that seemed, but was not, remorse. I went so far as to regret the loss of the animal, and to look about me, among the vile haunts which I now habitually frequented, for another pet of the same species, and of somewhat similar appearance, with which to supply its place.

One night as I sat, half stupefied, in a den of more than infamy, my attention was suddenly drawn to some black object, reposing upon the head of one of the immense hogsheads[1] of Gin, or of Rum, which constituted the chief furniture of the apartment. I had been looking steadily at the top of this hogshead for some minutes, and what now caused me surprise was the fact that I had not sooner perceived the object thereupon. I approached it, and touched it with my hand. It was a black cat—a very large one—fully as large as Pluto, and closely resembling him in every respect but one. Pluto had not a white hair upon any portion of his body; but this cat had a large, although indefinite splotch of white, covering nearly the whole region of the breast. Upon my touching him, he immediately arose, purred loudly, rubbed against my hand, and appeared delighted with my notice. This, then, was the very creature of which I was in search. I at once offered to purchase it of the landlord; but this person made no claim to it—knew nothing of it—had never seen it before.

I continued my caresses, and, when I prepared to go home, the animal evinced a disposition to accompany me. I permitted it to do so; occasionally stooping and patting it as I proceeded. When it reached the house it domesticated itself at once, and became immediately a great favourite with my wife.

For my own part, I soon found a dislike to it arising within me. This was just the reverse of what I had anticipated; but—I know not how or why it was—its evident fondness for myself rather disgusted and annoyed. By slow degrees, these feelings of disgust and annoyance rose into the bitterness of hatred. I avoided the creature; a certain sense of shame, and the remembrance of my former deed of cruelty, preventing me from physically abusing it. I did not, for some weeks, strike, or otherwise violently ill use it; but gradually—very gradually—I came to look upon it with unutterable loathing, and to flee silently from its odious presence, as from the breath of a pestilence.

What added, no doubt, to my hatred of the beast, was the discovery, on the morning after I brought it home, that, like Pluto, it also had been deprived of one of its eyes. This circumstance, however, only endeared it to my wife, who, as I have already said, possessed, in a high degree, that humanity of feel-

---

1    *hogsheads* Casks.

ing which had once been my distinguishing trait, and the source of many of my simplest and purest pleasures.

With my aversion to this cat, however, its partiality for myself seemed to increase. It followed my footsteps with a pertinacity which it would be difficult to make the reader comprehend. Whenever I sat, it would crouch beneath my chair, or spring upon my knees, covering me with its loathsome caresses. If I arose to walk it would get between my feet and thus nearly throw me down, or, fastening its long and sharp claws in my dress, clamber, in this manner, to my breast. At such times, although I longed to destroy it with a blow, I was yet withheld from so doing, partly by a memory of my former crime, but chiefly—let me confess it at once—by absolute dread of the beast.

This dread was not exactly a dread of physical evil—and yet I should be at a loss how otherwise to define it. I am almost ashamed to own—yes, even in this felon's cell, I am almost ashamed to own—that the terror and horror with which the animal inspired me, had been heightened by one of the merest chimaeras[1] it would be possible to conceive. My wife had called my attention, more than once, to the character of the mark of white hair, of which I have spoken, and which constituted the sole visible difference between the strange beast and the one I had destroyed. The reader will remember that this mark, although large, had been originally very indefinite; but, by slow degrees—degrees nearly imperceptible, and which for a long time my Reason struggled to reject as fanciful—it had, at length, assumed a rigorous distinctness of outline. It was now the representation of an object that I shudder to name—and for this, above all, I loathed, and dreaded, and would have rid myself of the monster *had I dared*—it was now, I say, the image of a hideous—of a ghastly thing—of the GALLOWS!—oh, mournful and terrible engine of Horror and of Crime—of Agony and of Death!

And now was I indeed wretched beyond the wretchedness of mere Humanity. And a brute beast—whose fellow I had contemptuously destroyed—*a brute beast* to work out for *me*—for me a man, fashioned in the image of the High God—so much of insufferable woe! Alas! neither by day nor by night knew I the blessing of Rest any more! During the former the creature left me no moment alone; and, in the latter, I started, hourly, from dreams of unutterable fear, to find the hot breath of *the thing* upon my face, and its vast weight—an incarnate Night-Mare that I had no power to shake off—incumbent eternally upon my *heart*!

Beneath the pressure of torments such as these, the feeble remnant of the good within me succumbed. Evil thoughts became my sole intimates—the darkest and most evil of thoughts. The moodiness of my usual temper in-

---

1    *chimaeras* Illusory or monstrous things.

creased to hatred of all things and of all mankind; while, from the sudden, frequent, and ungovernable outbursts of a fury to which I now blindly abandoned myself, my uncomplaining wife, alas! was the most usual and the most patient of sufferers.

One day she accompanied me, upon some household errand, into the cellar of the old building which our poverty compelled us to inhabit. The cat followed me down the steep stairs, and, nearly throwing me headlong, exasperated me to madness. Uplifting an axe, and forgetting, in my wrath, the childish dread which had hitherto stayed my hand, I aimed a blow at the animal which, of course, would have proved instantly fatal had it descended as I wished. But this blow was arrested by the hand of my wife. Goaded, by the interference, into a rage more than demoniacal, I withdrew my arm from her grasp and buried the axe in her brain. She fell dead upon the spot, without a groan.

This hideous murder accomplished, I set myself forthwith, and with entire deliberation, to the task of concealing the body. I knew that I could not remove it from the house, either by day or by night, without the risk of being observed by the neighbours. Many projects entered my mind. At one period I thought of cutting the corpse into minute fragments, and destroying them by fire. At another, I resolved to dig a grave for it in the floor of the cellar. Again, I deliberated about casting it in the well in the yard—about packing it in a box, as if merchandize, with the usual arrangements, and so getting a porter to take it from the house. Finally I hit upon what I considered a far better expedient than either of these. I determined to wall it up in the cellar—as the monks of the middle ages are recorded to have walled up their victims.

For a purpose such as this the cellar was well adapted. Its walls were loosely constructed, and had lately been plastered throughout with a rough plaster, which the dampness of the atmosphere had prevented from hardening. Moreover, in one of the walls was a projection, caused by a false chimney, or fireplace, that had been filled up, and made to resemble the rest of the cellar. I made no doubt that I could readily displace the bricks at this point, insert the corpse, and wall the whole up as before, so that no eye could detect any thing suspicious. And in this calculation I was not deceived. By means of a crow-bar I easily dislodged the bricks, and, having carefully deposited the body against the inner wall, I propped it in that position, while, with little trouble, I re-laid the whole structure as it originally stood. Having procured mortar, sand, and hair,[1] with every possible precaution, I prepared a plaster which could not be distinguished from the old, and with this I very carefully went over the new brickwork. When I had finished, I felt satisfied that all was right. The wall did

---

1    *hair* The addition of animal hair to mortar increases its durability.

not present the slightest appearance of having been disturbed. The rubbish on the floor was picked up with the minutest care. I looked around triumphantly, and said to myself—"Here at least, then, my labour has not been in vain."

My next step was to look for the beast which had been the cause of so much wretchedness; for I had, at length, firmly resolved to put it to death. Had I been able to meet with it, at the moment, there could have been no doubt of its fate; but it appeared that the crafty animal had been alarmed at the violence of my previous anger, and forbore to present itself in my present mood. It is impossible to describe, or to imagine, the deep, the blissful sense of relief which the absence of the detested creature occasioned in my bosom. It did not make its appearance during the night—and thus for one night at least, since its introduction into the house, I soundly and tranquilly slept; aye, slept even with the burden of murder upon my soul!

The second and the third day passed, and still my tormentor came not. Once again I breathed as a freeman. The monster, in terror, had fled the premises forever! I should behold it no more! My happiness was supreme! The guilt of my dark deed disturbed me but little. Some few inquiries had been made, but these had been readily answered. Even a search had been instituted—but of course nothing was to be discovered. I looked upon my future felicity as secured.

Upon the fourth day of the assassination, a party of the police came, very unexpectedly, into the house, and proceeded again to make rigorous investigation of the premises. Secure, however, in the inscrutability of my place of concealment, I felt no embarrassment whatever. The officers bade me accompany them in their search. They left no nook or corner unexplored. At length, for the third or fourth time, they descended into the cellar. I quivered not in a muscle. My heart beat calmly as that of one who slumbers in innocence. I walked the cellar from end to end. I folded my arms upon my bosom, and roamed easily to and fro. The police were thoroughly satisfied and prepared to depart. The glee at my heart was too strong to be restrained. I burned to say if but one word, by way of triumph, and to render doubly sure their assurance of my guiltlessness.

"Gentlemen," I said at last, as the party ascended the steps, "I delight to have allayed your suspicions. I wish you all health, and a little more courtesy. By the bye, gentlemen, this—this is a very well constructed house." [In the rabid desire to say something easily, I scarcely knew what I uttered at all.]—"I may say an *excellently* well constructed house. These walls—are you going, gentlemen?—these walls are solidly put together"; and here, through the mere phrenzy of bravado, I rapped heavily, with a cane which I held in my hand, upon that very portion of the brick-work behind which stood the corpse of the wife of my bosom.

But may God shield and deliver me from the fangs of the Arch-Fiend! No sooner had the reverberation of my blows sunk into silence, than I was answered by a voice from within the tomb!—by a cry, at first muffled and broken, like the sobbing of a child, and then quickly swelling into one long, loud, and continuous scream, utterly anomalous and inhuman—a howl—a wailing shriek, half of horror and half of triumph, such as might have arisen only out of hell, conjointly from the throats of the dammed in their agony and of the demons that exult in the damnation.

Of my own thoughts it is folly to speak. Swooning, I staggered to the opposite wall. For one instant the party upon the stairs remained motionless, through extremity of terror and of awe. In the next, a dozen stout arms were toiling at the wall. It fell bodily. The corpse, already greatly decayed and clotted with gore, stood erect before the eyes of the spectators. Upon its head, with red extended mouth and solitary eye of fire, sat the hideous beast whose craft had seduced me into murder, and whose informing voice had consigned me to the hangman. I had walled the monster up within the tomb!

—1843

# Kate Chopin
1850–1904

Kate Chopin became a writer late in life, beginning her career only after the death of her husband in 1882. The short stories and two published novels of this writer of the American South were often considered transgressive in her day, addressing the subjects of race and class, marriage and divorce, sexuality, and female autonomy. Through her provocative writing, Chopin sought to expose the nature of truth as tied to the limited perspective of the individual, showing that, in her words, "truth rests upon a shifting basis and is apt to be kaleidoscopic."

The controversy that Chopin's ideas incited is perhaps best exemplified by the reception of her most recognized work, *The Awakening* (1899). The novel, which depicts one woman's sensual awakening and her defiance of societal expectations of women, received high praise from a few reviewers, but a larger number dismissed it as "morbid," "sordid," and "sex fiction." It took scholars roughly 50 years after Chopin's death to acknowledge *The Awakening* as a novel of enduring importance—a work of historical value for its critical engagement with the role of women at the turn of the nineteenth century, but also a work that would continue to resonate for generations of readers.

Like *The Awakening*, "The Story of an Hour," first published in the December 1894 issue of *Vogue*, probes the marked tension between what Chopin referred to as the "outward existence which conforms, [and] the inward life which questions."

# The Story of an Hour

Knowing that Mrs. Mallard was afflicted with a heart trouble, great care was taken to break to her as gently as possible the news of her husband's death.

It was her sister Josephine who told her, in broken sentences; veiled hints that revealed in half concealing. Her husband's friend Richards was there, too, near her. It was he who had been in the newspaper office when intelligence of the railroad disaster was received, with Brently Mallard's name leading the list of "killed." He had only taken the time to assure himself of its truth by a second telegram, and had hastened to forestall any less careful, less tender friend in bearing the sad message.

She did not hear the story as many women have heard the same, with a paralyzed inability to accept its significance. She wept at once, with sudden, wild abandonment, in her sister's arms. When the storm of grief had spent itself she went away to her room alone. She would have no one follow her.

There stood, facing the open window, a comfortable, roomy armchair. Into this she sank, pressed down by a physical exhaustion that haunted her body and seemed to reach into her soul.

She could see in the open square before her house the tops of trees that were all aquiver with the new spring life. The delicious breath of rain was in the air. In the street below a peddler was crying his wares. The notes of a distant song which someone was singing reached her faintly, and countless sparrows were twittering in the eaves.

There were patches of blue sky showing here and there through the clouds that had met and piled one above the other in the west facing her window.

She sat with her head thrown back upon the cushion of the chair, quite motionless, except when a sob came up into her throat and shook her, as a child who has cried itself to sleep continues to sob in its dreams.

She was young, with a fair, calm face, whose lines bespoke repression and even a certain strength. But now there was a dull stare in her eyes, whose gaze was fixed away off yonder on one of those patches of blue sky. It was not a glance of reflection, but rather indicated a suspension of intelligent thought.

There was something coming to her and she was waiting for it, fearfully. What was it? She did not know; it was too subtle and elusive to name. But she felt it, creeping out of the sky, reaching toward her through the sounds, the scents, the colour that filled the air.

Now her bosom rose and fell tumultuously. She was beginning to recognize this thing that was approaching to possess her, and she was striving to beat it back with her will—as powerless as her two white slender hands would have been.

When she abandoned herself a little whispered word escaped her slightly parted lips. She said it over and over under her breath: "free, free, free!" The vacant stare and the look of terror that had followed it went from her eyes. They stayed keen and bright. Her pulses beat fast, and the coursing blood warmed and relaxed every inch of her body.

She did not stop to ask if it were or were not a monstrous joy that held her. A clear and exalted perception enabled her to dismiss the suggestion as trivial.

She knew that she would weep again when she saw the kind, tender hands folded in death; the face that had never looked save with love upon her, fixed and grey and dead. But she saw beyond that bitter moment a long procession of years to come that would belong to her absolutely. And she opened and spread her arms out to them in welcome.

There would be no one to live for her during those coming years; she would live for herself. There would be no powerful will bending hers in that blind persistence with which men and women believe they have a right to impose a private will upon a fellow-creature. A kind intention or a cruel intention made the act seem no less a crime as she looked upon it in that brief moment of illumination.

And yet she had loved him—sometimes. Often she had not. What did it matter! What could love, the unsolved mystery, count for in face of this possession of self-assertion which she suddenly recognized as the strongest impulse of her being!

"Free! Body and soul free!" she kept whispering.

Josephine was kneeling before the closed door with her lips to the keyhole, imploring for admission. "Louise, open the door! I beg; open the door—you will make yourself ill. What are you doing, Louise? For heaven's sake open the door."

"Go away. I am not making myself ill." No; she was drinking in a very elixir of life through that open window.

Her fancy was running riot along those days ahead of her. Spring days, and summer days, and all sorts of days that would be her own. She breathed a quick prayer that life might be long. It was only yesterday she had thought with a shudder that life might be long.

She arose at length and opened the door to her sister's importunities. There was a feverish triumph in her eyes, and she carried herself unwittingly like a goddess of Victory. She clasped her sister's waist, and together they descended the stairs. Richards stood waiting for them at the bottom.

Some one was opening the front door with a latchkey. It was Brently Mallard who entered, a little travel-stained, composedly carrying his grip-sack and umbrella. He had been far from the scene of accident, and did not even know there had been one. He stood amazed at Josephine's piercing cry; at Richards' quick motion to screen him from the view of his wife.

But Richards was too late.

When the doctors came they said she had died of heart disease—of joy that kills.

—1894

# Charlotte Perkins Gilman
1860–1935

Charlotte Perkins Gilman was born into a family prominent for activism and reform; her great-aunt was Harriet Beecher Stowe, author of *Uncle Tom's Cabin*. As a young woman she embraced the idea that a single woman could be a useful member of society and she resolved to dedicate her life to her work. Circumstances intervened, however: she fell in love, married, and plunged into a severe depression after the birth of her only child in 1885. She received treatment from the "nerve doctor" S. Weir Mitchell, who prescribed his famous "rest cure"—isolation, quiet domesticity, and abstention from intellectual endeavours—which greatly worsened her condition. In 1892, she published the short story "The Yellow Wallpaper," in which the protagonist is treated according to similar principles.

By this time, Gilman had left her husband, moved to California, and began again to work outside the home, forging a career as a feminist writer and lecturer. She won admiration from women reformers such as Jane Addams (1860–1935) and Elizabeth Cady Stanton (1815–1902). Her non-fiction work *Women and Economics* (1898) was a bestseller. From 1909 to 1916, she wrote for and edited her own magazine, *The Forerunner*; in 1915, the magazine serialized her novel *Herland*, about a utopia populated solely by women. In a statement that she made about the composition of "The Yellow Wallpaper," Gilman expressed the belief that informed all of her writing: "Work, in which is joy and growth and service, without which one is a pauper and a parasite," was essential for women.

## The Yellow Wallpaper

It is very seldom that mere ordinary people like John and myself secure ancestral halls for the summer.

A colonial mansion, a hereditary estate, I would say a haunted house and reach the height of romantic felicity—but that would be asking too much of fate!

Still I will proudly declare that there is something queer about it.

Else, why should it be let so cheaply? And why have stood so long untenanted?

John laughs at me, of course, but one expects that.

John is practical in the extreme. He has no patience with faith, an intense horror of superstition, and he scoffs openly at any talk of things not to be felt and seen and put down in figures.

John is a physician, and *perhaps*—(I would not say it to a living soul, of course, but this is dead paper and a great relief to my mind)—*perhaps* that is one reason I do not get well faster.

You see, he does not believe I am sick! And what can one do?

If a physician of high standing, and one's own husband, assures friends and relatives that there is really nothing the matter with one but temporary nervous depression—a slight hysterical tendency—what is one to do?

My brother is also a physician, and also of high standing, and he says the same thing.

So I take phosphates or phosphites—whichever it is—and tonics, and air and exercise, and journeys, and am absolutely forbidden to "work" until I am well again.

Personally, I disagree with their ideas.

Personally, I believe that congenial work, with excitement and change, would do me good.

But what is one to do?

I did write for a while in spite of them, but it *does* exhaust me a good deal—having to be so sly about it, or else meet with heavy opposition.

I sometimes fancy that in my condition, if I had less opposition and more society and stimulus—but John says the very worst thing I can do is to think about my condition, and I confess it always makes me feel bad.

So I will let it alone and talk about the house.

The most beautiful place! It is quite alone, standing well back from the road, quite three miles from the village. It makes me think of English places that you read about, for there are hedges and walls and gates that lock, and lots of separate little houses for the gardeners and people.

There is a *delicious* garden! I never saw such a garden—large and shady, full of box-bordered paths, and lined with long grape-covered arbours with seats under them.

There were greenhouses, but they are all broken now.

There was some legal trouble, I believe, something about the heirs and co-heirs; anyhow, the place has been empty for years.

That spoils my ghostliness, I am afraid, but I don't care—there is something strange about the house—I can feel it.

I even said so to John one moonlight evening, but he said what I felt was a draught, and shut the window.

I get unreasonably angry with John sometimes. I'm sure I never used to be so sensitive. I think it is due to this nervous condition.

But John says if I feel so, I shall neglect proper self-control; so I take pains to control myself—before him, at least, and that makes me very tired.

I don't like our room a bit. I wanted one downstairs that opened on the piazza and had roses all over the window, and such pretty old-fashioned chintz hangings! But John would not hear of it.

He said there was only one window and not room for two beds, and no near room for him if he took another.

He is very careful and loving, and hardly lets me stir without special direction.

I have a schedule prescription for each hour in the day; he takes all care from me, and so I feel basely ungrateful not to value it more.

He said we came here solely on my account, that I was to have perfect rest and all the air I could get. "Your exercise depends on your strength, my dear," said he, "and your food somewhat on your appetite; but air you can absorb all the time." So we took the nursery at the top of the house.

It is a big, airy room, the whole floor nearly, with windows that look all ways, and air and sunshine galore. It was nursery first and then playroom and gymnasium, I should judge; for the windows are barred for little children, and there are rings and things in the walls.

The paint and paper look as if a boys' school had used it. It is stripped off—the paper—in great patches all around the head of my bed, about as far as I can reach, and in a great place on the other side of the room low down. I never saw a worse paper in my life. One of those sprawling flamboyant patterns committing every artistic sin.

It is dull enough to confuse the eye in following, pronounced enough to constantly irritate and provoke study, and when you follow the lame uncertain curves for a little distance they suddenly commit suicide—plunge off at outrageous angles, destroy themselves in unheard-of contradictions.

The colour is repellent, almost revolting; a smouldering unclean yellow, strangely faded by the slow-turning sunlight. It is a dull yet lurid orange in some places, a sickly sulphur tint in others.

No wonder the children hated it! I should hate it myself if I had to live in this room long.

There comes John, and I must put this away—he hates to have me write a word.

We have been here two weeks, and I haven't felt like writing before, since that first day.

I am sitting by the window now, up in this atrocious nursery, and there is nothing to hinder my writing as much as I please, save lack of strength.

John is away all day, and even some nights when his cases are serious.

I am glad my case is not serious!

But these nervous troubles are dreadfully depressing.

John does not know how much I really suffer. He knows there is no reason to suffer, and that satisfies him.

Of course it is only nervousness. It does weigh on me so not to do my duty in any way!

I mean to be such a help to John, such a real rest and comfort, and here I am a comparative burden already!

Nobody would believe what an effort it is to do what little I am able—to dress and entertain, and order things.

It is fortunate Mary is so good with the baby. Such a dear baby!

And yet I *cannot* be with him, it makes me so nervous.

I suppose John never was nervous in his life. He laughs at me so about this wallpaper!

At first he meant to repaper the room, but afterwards he said that I was letting it get the better of me, and that nothing was worse for a nervous patient than to give way to such fancies.

He said that after the wallpaper was changed it would be the heavy bedstead, and then the barred windows, and then that gate at the head of the stairs, and so on.

"You know the place is doing you good," he said, "and really, dear, I don't care to renovate the house just for a three months' rental."

"Then do let us go downstairs," I said. "There are such pretty rooms there."

Then he took me in his arms and called me a blessed little goose, and said he would go down cellar, if I wished, and have it whitewashed into the bargain.

But he is right enough about the beds and windows and things.

It is as airy and comfortable a room as anyone need wish, and, of course, I would not be so silly as to make him uncomfortable just for a whim.

I'm really getting quite fond of the big room, all but that horrid paper.

Out of one window I can see the garden—those mysterious deep-shaded arbours, the riotous old-fashioned flowers, and bushes and gnarly trees.

Out of another I get a lovely view of the bay and a little private wharf belonging to the estate. There is a beautiful shaded lane that runs down there from the house. I always fancy I see people walking in these numerous paths and arbours, but John has cautioned me not to give way to fancy in the least. He says that with my imaginative power and habit of story-making, a nervous weakness like mine is sure to lead to all manner of excited fancies, and that I ought to use my will and good sense to check the tendency. So I try.

I think sometimes that if I were only well enough to write a little it would relieve the press of ideas and rest me.

But I find I get pretty tired when I try.

It is so discouraging not to have any advice and companionship about my work. When I get really well, John says we will ask Cousin Henry and Julia down for a long visit; but he says he would as soon put fireworks in my pillow-case as to let me have those stimulating people about now.

I wish I could get well faster.

But I must not think about that. This paper looks to me as if it *knew* what a vicious influence it had!

There is a recurrent spot where the pattern lolls like a broken neck and two bulbous eyes stare at you upside down.

I get positively angry with the impertinence of it and the everlastingness. Up and down and sideways they crawl, and those absurd unblinking eyes are everywhere. There is one place where two breadths didn't match, and the eyes go all up and down the line, one a little higher than the other.

I never saw so much expression in an inanimate thing before, and we all know how much expression they have! I used to lie awake as a child and get more entertainment and terror out of blank walls and plain furniture than most children could find in a toy-store.

I remember what a kindly wink the knobs of our big old bureau used to have, and there was one chair that always seemed like a strong friend.

I used to feel that if any of the other things looked too fierce I could always hop into that chair and be safe.

The furniture in this room is no worse than inharmonious, however, for we had to bring it all from downstairs. I suppose when this was used as a playroom they had to take the nursery things out, and no wonder! I never saw such ravages as the children have made here.

The wallpaper, as I said before, is torn off in spots, and it sticketh closer than a brother[1]—they must have had perseverance as well as hatred.

Then the floor is scratched and gouged and splintered, the plaster itself is dug out here and there, and this great heavy bed which is all we found in the room, looks as if it had been through the wars.

But I don't mind it a bit—only the paper.

There comes John's sister. Such a dear girl as she is, and so careful of me! I must not let her find me writing.

She is a perfect and enthusiastic housekeeper, and hopes for no better profession. I verily believe she thinks it is the writing which made me sick!

But I can write when she is out, and see her a long way off from these windows.

---

1    *sticketh ... brother* From Proverbs 18.24.

There is one that commands the road, a lovely shaded winding road, and one that just looks off over the country. A lovely country, too, full of great elms and velvet meadows.

This wallpaper has a kind of sub-pattern in a different shade, a particularly irritating one, for you can only see it in certain lights, and not clearly then.

But in the places where it isn't faded and where the sun is just so—I can see a strange, provoking, formless sort of figure that seems to skulk about behind that silly and conspicuous front design.

There's sister on the stairs!

Well, the Fourth of July is over! The people are all gone, and I am tired out. John thought it might do me good to see a little company, so we just had Mother and Nellie and the children down for a week.

Of course I didn't do a thing. Jennie sees to everything now.

But it tired me all the same.

John says if I don't pick up faster he shall send me to Weir Mitchell in the fall.

But I don't want to go there at all. I had a friend who was in his hands once, and she says he is just like John and my brother, only more so!

Besides, it is such an undertaking to go so far.

I don't feel as if it was worthwhile to turn my hand over for anything, and I'm getting dreadfully fretful and querulous.

I cry at nothing, and cry most of the time.

Of course I don't when John is here, or anybody else, but when I am alone.

And I am alone a good deal just now. John is kept in town very often by serious cases, and Jennie is good and lets me alone when I want her to.

So I walk a little in the garden or down that lovely lane, sit on the porch under the roses, and lie down up here a good deal.

I'm getting really fond of the room in spite of the wallpaper. Perhaps because of the wallpaper.

It dwells in my mind so!

I lie here on this great immovable bed—it is nailed down, I believe—and follow that pattern about by the hour. It is as good as gymnastics, I assure you. I start, we'll say, at the bottom, down in the corner over there where it has not been touched, and I determine for the thousandth time that I *will* follow that pointless pattern to some sort of conclusion.

I know a little of the principle of design, and I know this thing was not arranged on any laws of radiation, or alternation, or repetition, or symmetry, or anything else that I ever heard of.

It is repeated, of course, by the breadths, but not otherwise.

Looked at in one way, each breadth stands alone; the bloated curves and flourishes—a kind of "debased Romanesque" with delirium tremens[1]—go waddling up and down in isolated columns of fatuity.

But, on the other hand, they connect diagonally, and the sprawling outlines run off in great slanting waves of optic horror, like a lot of wallowing sea-weeds in full chase.

The whole thing goes horizontally, too, at least it seems so, and I exhaust myself trying to distinguish the order of its going in that direction.

They have used a horizontal breadth for a frieze, and that adds wonderfully to the confusion.

There is one end of the room where it is almost intact, and there, when the crosslights fade and the low sun shines directly upon it, I can almost fancy radiation after all—the interminable grotesque seems to form around a common centre and rush off in headlong plunges of equal distraction.

It makes me tired to follow it. I will take a nap, I guess.

I don't know why I should write this.

I don't want to.

I don't feel able.

And I know John would think it absurd. But I *must* say what I feel and think in some way—it is such a relief!

But the effort is getting to be greater than the relief.

Half the time now I am awfully lazy, and lie down ever so much.

John says I mustn't lose my strength, and has me take cod liver oil and lots of tonics and things, to say nothing of the ale and wine and rare meat.

Dear John! He loves me very dearly, and hates to have me sick. I tried to have a real earnest reasonable talk with him the other day, and tell him how I wish he would let me go and make a visit to Cousin Henry and Julia.

But he said I wasn't able to go, nor able to stand it after I got there; and I did not make out a very good case for myself, for I was crying before I had finished.

It is getting to be a great effort for me to think straight. Just this nervous weakness, I suppose.

And dear John gathered me up in his arms, and just carried me upstairs and laid me on the bed, and sat by me and read to me till it tired my head.

He said I was his darling and his comfort and all he had, and that I must take care of myself for his sake, and keep well.

---

1   *Romanesque* Medieval architectural style involving columns and round arches similar to those found in Roman architecture; *delirium tremens* Condition resulting from extreme alcohol withdrawal; its symptoms include tremors, hallucinations, and random physical movements.

He says no one but myself can help me out of it, that I must use my will and self-control and not let any silly fancies run away with me.

There's one comfort—the baby is well and happy, and does not have to occupy this nursery with the horrid wallpaper.

If we had not used it, that blessed child would have! What a fortunate escape! Why, I wouldn't have a child of mine, an impressionable little thing, live in such a room for worlds.

I never thought of it before, but it is lucky that John kept me here after all, I can stand it so much easier than a baby, you see.

Of course I never mention it to them any more—I am too wise—but I keep watch for it all the same.

There are things in that paper that nobody knows about but me, or ever will.

Behind that outside pattern the dim shapes get clearer every day.

It is always the same shape, only very numerous.

And it is like a woman stooping down and creeping about behind that pattern. I don't like it a bit. I wonder—I begin to think—I wish John would take me away from here!

It is so hard to talk with John about my case, because he is so wise, and because he loves me so.

But I tried it last night.

It was moonlight. The moon shines in all around just as the sun does.

I hate to see it sometimes, it creeps so slowly, and always comes in by one window or another.

John was asleep and I hated to waken him, so I kept still and watched the moonlight on that undulating wallpaper till I felt creepy.

The faint figure behind seemed to shake the pattern, just as if she wanted to get out.

I got up softly and went to feel and see if the paper *did* move, and when I came back John was awake.

"What is it, little girl?" he said. "Don't go walking about like that—you'll get cold."

I thought it was a good time to talk, so I told him that I really was not gaining here, and that I wished he would take me away.

"Why, darling!" said he. "Our lease will be up in three weeks, and I can't see how to leave before.

"The repairs are not done at home, and I cannot possibly leave town just now. Of course if you were in any danger, I could and would, but you really are better, dear, whether you can see it or not. I am a doctor, dear, and I know.

You are gaining flesh and colour, your appetite is better, I feel really much easier about you."

"I don't weigh a bit more," said I, "nor as much; and my appetite may be better in the evening when you are here but it is worse in the morning when you are away!"

"Bless her little heart!" said he with a big hug. "She shall be as sick as she pleases! But now let's improve the shining hours[1] by going to sleep, and talk about it in the morning!"

"And you won't go away?" I asked gloomily.

"Why, how can I, dear? It is only three weeks more and then we will take a nice little trip of a few days while Jennie is getting the house ready. Really, dear, you are better!"

"Better in body perhaps—" I began, and stopped short, for he sat up straight and looked at me with such a stern, reproachful look that I could not say another word.

"My darling," said he, "I beg of you, for my sake and for our child's sake, as well as your own, that you will never for one instant let that idea enter your mind! There is nothing so dangerous, so fascinating, to a temperament like yours. It is a false and foolish fancy. Can you not trust me as a physician when I tell you so?"

So of course I said no more on that score, and we went to sleep before long. He thought I was asleep first, but I wasn't, and lay there for hours trying to decide whether that front pattern and the back pattern really did move together or separately.

On a pattern like this, by daylight, there is a lack of sequence, a defiance of law, that is a constant irritant to a normal mind.

The colour is hideous enough, and unreliable enough, and infuriating enough, but the pattern is torturing.

You think you have mastered it, but just as you get well under way in following, it turns a back-somersault and there you are. It slaps you in the face, knocks you down, and tramples upon you. It is like a bad dream.

The outside pattern is a florid arabesque,[2] reminding one of a fungus. If you can imagine a toadstool in joints, an interminable string of toadstools, budding and sprouting in endless convolutions—why, that is something like it.

That is, sometimes!

---

1    *improve the ... hours* See Isaac Watts's popular children's poem "Against Idleness and Mischief" (1715): "How doth the little busy bee / Improve each shining hour."

2    *arabesque* Complex decorative design.

There is one marked peculiarity about this paper, a thing nobody seems to notice but myself, and that is that it changes as the light changes.

When the sun shoots in through the east window—I always watch for that first long, straight ray—it changes so quickly that I never can quite believe it.

That is why I watch it always.

By moonlight—the moon shines in all night when there is a moon—I wouldn't know it was the same paper.

At night in any kind of light, in twilight, candlelight, lamplight, and worst of all by moonlight, it becomes bars! The outside pattern, I mean, and the woman behind it is as plain as can be.

I didn't realize for a long time what the thing was that showed behind, that dim sub-pattern, but now I am quite sure it is a woman.

By daylight she is subdued, quiet. I fancy it is the pattern that keeps her so still. It is so puzzling. It keeps me quiet by the hour.

I lie down ever so much now. John says it is good for me, and to sleep all I can.

Indeed he started the habit by making me lie down for an hour after each meal.

It is a very bad habit I am convinced, for you see, I don't sleep.

And that cultivates deceit, for I don't tell them I'm awake—O no!

The fact is I am getting a little afraid of John.

He seems very queer sometimes, and even Jennie has an inexplicable look.

It strikes me occasionally, just as a scientific hypothesis, that perhaps it is the paper!

I have watched John when he did not know I was looking, and come into the room suddenly on the most innocent excuses, and I've caught him several times *looking at the paper*! And Jennie too. I caught Jennie with her hand on it once.

She didn't know I was in the room, and when I asked her in a quiet, a very quiet voice, with the most restrained manner possible, what she was doing with the paper—she turned around as if she had been caught stealing, and looked quite angry—asked me why I should frighten her so!

Then she said that the paper stained everything it touched, that she had found yellow smooches on all my clothes and John's, and she wished we would be more careful!

Did not that sound innocent? But I know she was studying that pattern, and I am determined that nobody shall find it out but myself!

Life is very much more exciting now than it used to be. You see I have something more to expect, to look forward to, to watch. I really do eat better, and am more quiet than I was.

John is so pleased to see me improve! He laughed a little the other day, and said I seemed to be flourishing in spite of my wallpaper.

I turned it off with a laugh. I had no intention of telling him it was *because* of the wallpaper—he would make fun of me. He might even want to take me away.

I don't want to leave now until I have found it out. There is a week more, and I think that will be enough.

I'm feeling so much better!

I don't sleep much at night, for it is so interesting to watch developments; but I sleep a good deal during the daytime.

In the daytime it is tiresome and perplexing.

There are always new shoots on the fungus, and new shades of yellow all over it. I cannot keep count of them, though I have tried conscientiously.

It is the strangest yellow, that wallpaper! It makes me think of all the yellow things I ever saw—not beautiful ones like buttercups, but old, foul, bad yellow things.

But there is something else about that paper—the smell! I noticed it the moment we came into the room, but with so much air and sun it was not bad. Now we have had a week of fog and rain, and whether the windows are open or not, the smell is here.

It creeps all over the house.

I find it hovering in the dining-room, skulking in the parlour, hiding in the hall, lying in wait for me on the stairs.

It gets into my hair.

Even when I go to ride, if I turn my head suddenly and surprise it—there is that smell!

Such a peculiar odour, too! I have spent hours in trying to analyze it, to find what it smelled like.

It is not bad—at first—and very gentle, but quite the subtlest, most enduring odour I ever met.

In this damp weather it is awful, I wake up in the night and find it hanging over me.

It used to disturb me at first. I thought seriously of burning the house—to reach the smell.

But now I am used to it. The only thing I can think of that it is like is the *colour* of the paper! A yellow smell.

There is a very funny mark on this wall, low down, near the mopboard. A streak that runs round the room. It goes behind every piece of furniture, except the bed, a long, straight, even *smooch*, as if it had been rubbed over and over.

I wonder how it was done and who did it, and what they did it for. Round and round and round—round and round and round—it makes me dizzy!

I really have discovered something at last.

Through watching so much at night, when it changes so, I have finally found out.

The front pattern *does* move—and no wonder! The woman behind shakes it!

Sometimes I think there are a great many women behind, and sometimes only one, and she crawls around fast, and her crawling shakes it all over.

Then in the very bright spots she keeps still, and in the very shady spots she just takes hold of the bars and shakes them hard.

And she is all the time trying to climb through. But nobody could climb through that pattern—it strangles so; I think that is why it has so many heads.

They get through, and then the pattern strangles them off and turns them upside down, and makes their eyes white!

If those heads were covered or taken off it would not be half so bad.

I think that woman gets out in the daytime!

And I'll tell you why—privately—I've seen her!

I can see her out of every one of my windows!

It is the same woman, I know, for she is always creeping, and most women do not creep by daylight.

I see her in that long shaded lane, creeping up and down. I see her in those dark grape arbours, creeping all around the garden.

I see her on that long road under the trees, creeping along, and when a carriage comes she hides under the blackberry vines.

I don't blame her a bit. It must be very humiliating to be caught creeping by daylight!

I always lock the door when I creep by daylight. I can't do it at night, for I know John would suspect something at once.

And John is so queer now that I don't want to irritate him. I wish he would take another room! Besides, I don't want anybody to get that woman out at night but myself.

I often wonder if I could see her out of all the windows at once.

But, turn as fast as I can, I can only see out of one at one time.

And though I always see her, she *may* be able to creep faster than I can turn! I have watched her sometimes away off in the open country, creeping as fast as a cloud shadow in a wind.

If only that top pattern could be gotten off from the under one! I mean to try it, little by little.

I have found out another funny thing, but I shan't tell it this time! It does not do to trust people too much.

There are only two more days to get this paper off, and I believe John is beginning to notice. I don't like the look in his eyes.

And I heard him ask Jennie a lot of professional questions about me. She had a very good report to give.

She said I slept a good deal in the daytime.

John knows I don't sleep very well at night, for all I'm so quiet!

He asked me all sorts of questions, too, and pretended to be very loving and kind.

As if I couldn't see through him!

Still, I don't wonder he acts so, sleeping under this paper for three months.

It only interests me, but I feel sure John and Jennie are affected by it.

Hurrah! This is the last day, but it is enough. John is to stay in town over night, and won't be out until this evening.

Jennie wanted to sleep with me—the sly thing; but I told her I should undoubtedly rest better for a night all alone.

That was clever, for really I wasn't alone a bit! As soon as it was moonlight and that poor thing began to crawl and shake the pattern, I got up and ran to help her.

I pulled and she shook, I shook and she pulled, and before morning we had peeled off yards of that paper.

A strip about as high as my head and half around the room.

And then when the sun came and that awful pattern began to laugh at me, I declared I would finish it today!

We go away tomorrow, and they are moving all my furniture down again to leave things as they were before.

Jennie looked at the wall in amazement, but I told her merrily that I did it out of pure spite at the vicious thing.

She laughed and said she wouldn't mind doing it herself, but I must not get tired.

How she betrayed herself that time!

But I am here, and no person touches this paper but Me—not *alive*!

She tried to get me out of the room—it was too patent! But I said it was so quiet and empty and clean now that I believed I would lie down again and sleep all I could; and not to wake me even for dinner—I would call when I woke.

So now she is gone, and the servants are gone, and the things are gone, and there is nothing left but that great bedstead nailed down, with the canvas mattress we found on it.

We shall sleep downstairs tonight, and take the boat home tomorrow.

I quite enjoy the room, now it is bare again.

How those children did tear about here!

This bedstead is fairly gnawed!

But I must get to work.

I have locked the door and thrown the key down into the front path.

I don't want to go out, and I don't want to have anybody come in, till John comes.

I want to astonish him.

I've got a rope up here that even Jennie did not find. If that woman does get out, and tries to get away, I can tie her!

But I forgot I could not reach far without anything to stand on!

This bed will *not* move!

I tried to lift and push it until I was lame, and then I got so angry I bit off a little piece at one corner—but it hurt my teeth.

Then I peeled off all the paper I could reach standing on the floor. It sticks horribly and the pattern just enjoys it! All those strangled heads and bulbous eyes and waddling fungus growths just shriek with derision!

I am getting angry enough to do something desperate. To jump out of the window would be admirable exercise, but the bars are too strong even to try.

Besides I wouldn't do it. Of course not. I know well enough that a step like that is improper and might be misconstrued.

I don't like to *look* out of the windows even—there are so many of those creeping women, and they creep so fast.

I wonder if they all come out of that wallpaper as I did?

But I am securely fastened now by my well-hidden rope—you don't get me out in the road there!

I suppose I shall have to get back behind the pattern when it comes night, and that is hard!

It is so pleasant to be out in this great room and creep around as I please!

I don't want to go outside. I won't, even if Jennie asks me to.

For outside you have to creep on the ground, and everything is green instead of yellow.

But here I can creep smoothly on the floor, and my shoulder just fits in that long smooch around the wall, so I cannot lose my way.

Why there's John at the door!

It is no use, young man, you can't open it!

How he does call and pound!

Now he's crying to Jennie for an axe.

It would be a shame to break down that beautiful door!

"John dear!" said I in the gentlest voice. "The key is down by the front steps, under a plantain leaf!"

That silenced him for a few moments.

Then he said—very quietly indeed, "Open the door, my darling!"

"I can't," said I. "The key is down by the front door under a plantain leaf!"

And then I said it again, several times, very gently and slowly, and said it so often that he had to go and see, and he got it of course, and came in. He stopped short by the door.

"What is the matter?" he cried. "For God's sake, what are you doing!"

I kept on creeping just the same, but I looked at him over my shoulder.

"I've got out at last," said I, "in spite of you and Jane! And I've pulled off most of the paper, so you can't put me back!"

Now why should that man have fainted? But he did, and right across my path by the wall, so that I had to creep over him every time!

—1892

# *Edith Wharton*

## 1862–1937

Edith Wharton was born in New York into a life of wealth and privilege, but, from an early age, she perceived that her peers, particularly women, were imprisoned by the social constraints of her class. Her novels and short stories would become known for their keen, often satiric observation of social mores—especially those of the high society world of her youth—and the ways in which those mores complicated and stifled the lives of her characters. As the novelist Francine Prose has said, "no one has written more incisively not just about a historical period and a particular social milieu but about something more timeless—the ardor with which we flee and return to the prison of conditioning and convenience."

Like most girls of her class, Wharton was educated at home by governesses, but she augmented her education by reading widely. As she reveals in her autobiography, *A Backward Glance*, she also loved "making up" stories and began to write when very young, even though her family disapproved of the activity as beneath her class—"something between a black art and a form of manual labor." In fact, she was so strapped for writing paper she was often reduced to using the wrapping from packages for her compositions. In 1879, *The Atlantic Monthly* published some of her poems; 25 novels, 86 short stories, and numerous works of non-fiction were to follow, with her 1920 novel, *The Age of Innocence*, winning a Pulitzer Prize.

By 1913, Wharton had moved permanently to France and, like her good friend, the writer Henry James (1843–1916), she capitalized on her knowledge of the differences between American and European society to write novels like *The Custom of the Country* (1913) with settings on both sides of the Atlantic.

# Atrophy

1

Nora Frenway settled down furtively in her corner of the Pullman[1] and, as the express plunged out of the Grand Central Station, wondered at herself for being where she was. The porter came along. "Ticket?" "Westover." She had instinctively lowered her voice and glanced about her. But neither the porter nor her nearest neighbours—fortunately none of them known to her—seemed in the least surprised or interested by the statement that she was travelling to Westover.

---

1    *Pullman* Luxurious railway carriage.

Yet what an earth-shaking announcement it was! Not that she cared, now; not that anything mattered except the one overwhelming fact which had convulsed her life, hurled her out of her easy velvet-lined rut, and flung her thus naked to the public scrutiny.... Cautiously, again, she glanced about her to make doubly sure that there was no one, absolutely no one, in the Pullman whom she knew by sight.

Her life had been so carefully guarded, so inwardly conventional in a world where all the outer conventions were tottering, that no one had ever known she had a lover. No one—of that she was absolutely sure. All the circumstances of the case had made it necessary that she should conceal her real life—her only real life—from everyone about her; from her half-invalid irascible husband, his prying envious sisters, and the terrible monumental old chieftainess, her mother-in-law, before whom all the family quailed and humbugged and fibbed and fawned.

What nonsense to pretend that nowadays, even in big cities, in the world's greatest social centres, the severe old-fashioned standards had given place to tolerance, laxity and ease! You took up the morning paper, and you read of girl bandits, movie-star divorces, "hold-ups" at balls, murder and suicide and elopement, and a general welter of disjointed disconnected impulses and appetites; then you turned your eyes onto your own daily life, and found yourself as cribbed and cabined, as beset by vigilant family eyes, observant friends, all sorts of embodied standards, as any white-muslin novel heroine of the 'sixties![1]

In a different way, of course. To the casual eye Mrs. Frenway herself might have seemed as free as any of the young married women of her group. Poker playing, smoking, cocktail drinking, dancing, painting, short skirts, bobbed hair and the rest—when had these been denied to her? If by any outward sign she had differed too markedly from her kind—lengthened her skirts, refused to play for money, let her hair grow, or ceased to make-up—her husband would have been the first to notice it, and to say: "Are you ill? What's the matter? How queer you look! What's the sense of making yourself conspicuous?" For he and his kind had adopted all the old inhibitions and sanctions, blindly transferring them to a new ritual, as the receptive Romans did when strange gods were brought into their temples....

The train had escaped from the ugly fringes of the city, and the soft spring landscape was gliding past her: glimpses of green lawns, budding hedges, pretty irregular roofs, and miles and miles of alluring tarred roads slipping away into

---

1    *white-muslin ... 'sixties* Refers to the 1860s trend of the sensation novel, characterized by lurid plots involving crime and shocking family secrets. Among the most popular of these novels was Wilkie Collins's *The Woman in White* (1860), in which the title character is unjustly committed to an asylum.

mystery. How often she had dreamed of dashing off down an unknown road with Christopher!

Not that she was a woman to be awed by the conventions. She knew she wasn't. She had always taken their measure, smiled at them—and conformed. On account of poor George Frenway, to begin with. Her husband, in a sense, was a man to be pitied; his weak health, his bad temper, his unsatisfied vanity, all made him a rather forlornly comic figure. But it was chiefly on account of the two children that she had always resisted the temptation to do anything reckless. The least self-betrayal would have been the end of everything. Too many eyes were watching her, and her husband's family was so strong, so united—when there was anybody for them to hate—and at all times so influential, that she would have been defeated at every point, and her husband would have kept the children.

At the mere thought she felt herself on the brink of an abyss. "The children are my religion," she had once said to herself; and she had no other.

Yet here she was on her way to Westover.... Oh, what did it matter now? That was the worst of it—it was too late for anything between her and Christopher to matter! She was sure he was dying. The way in which his cousin, Gladys Brincker, had blurted it out the day before at Kate Salmer's dance: "You didn't know—poor Kit?[1] Thought you and he were such pals! Yes, awfully bad, I'm afraid. Return of the old trouble! I know there've been two consultations—they had Knowlton down. They say there's not much hope; and nobody but that forlorn frightened Jane mounting guard...."

Poor Christopher! His sister Jane Aldis, Nora suspected, forlorn and frightened as she was, had played in his life a part nearly as dominant as Frenway and the children in Nora's. Loyally, Christopher always pretended that she didn't; talked of her indulgently as "poor Jenny." But didn't she, Nora, always think of her husband as "poor George"? Jane Aldis, of course, was much less self-assertive, less demanding, than George Frenway; but perhaps for that very reason she would appeal all the more to a man's compassion. And somehow, under her unobtrusive air, Nora had—on the rare occasions when they met—imagined that Miss Aldis was watching and drawing her inferences. But then Nora always felt, where Christopher was concerned, as if her breast were a pane of glass through which her trembling palpitating heart could be seen as plainly as holy viscera in a reliquary. Her sober after-thought was that Jane Aldis was just a dowdy self-effacing old maid whose life was filled to the brim by looking over the Westover place for her brother, and seeing that the fires were lit and the rooms full of flowers when he brought down his friends for a week-end.

---

1   *Kit* Short for Christopher.

Ah, how often he had said to Nora: "If I could have you to myself for a week-end at Westover"—quite as if it were the easiest thing imaginable, as far as his arrangements were concerned! And they had even pretended to discuss how it could be done. But somehow she fancied he said it because he knew that the plan, for her, was about as feasible as a week-end in the moon. And in reality her only visits to Westover had been made in the company of her husband, and that of other friends, two or three times, at the beginning.... For after that she wouldn't. It was three years now since she had been there.

Gladys Brincker, in speaking of Christopher's illness, had looked at Nora queerly, as though suspecting something. But no—what nonsense! No one had ever suspected Nora Frenway. Didn't she know what her friends said of her? "Nora? No more temperament than a lamp-post. Always buried in her books.... Never very attractive to men, in spite of her looks." Hadn't she said that of other women, who perhaps, in secret, like herself...?

The train was slowing down as it approached a station. She sat up with a jerk and looked at her wrist-watch. It was half-past two, the station was Ockham; the next would be Westover. In less than an hour she would be under his roof, Jane Aldis would be receiving her in that low panelled room full of books, and she would be saying—what would she be saying?

She had gone over their conversation so often that she knew not only her own part in it but Miss Aldis's by heart. The first moments would of course be painful, difficult; but then a great wave of emotion, breaking down the barriers between the two anxious women, would fling them together. She wouldn't have to say much, to explain; Miss Aldis would just take her by the hand and lead her upstairs to the room.

That room! She shut her eyes, and remembered other rooms where she and he had been together in their joy and their strength.... No, not that; she must not think of that now. For the man she had met in those other rooms was dying; the man she was going to was someone so different from that other man that it was like a profanation to associate their images.... And yet the man she was going to was her own Christopher, the one who had lived in her soul; and how his soul must be needing hers, now that it hung alone on the dark brink! As if anything else mattered at such a moment! She neither thought nor cared what Jane Aldis might say or suspect; she wouldn't have cared if the Pullman had been full of prying acquaintances, or if George and all George's family had got in at that last station.

She wouldn't have cared a fig for any of them. Yet at the same moment she remembered having felt glad that her old governess, whom she used to go and see twice a year, lived at Ockham—so that if George did begin to ask questions, she could always say: "Yes, I went to see poor old Fraulein; she's absolutely crippled now. I shall have to get her a Bath chair.[1] Could you get me a catalogue of prices?" There wasn't a precaution she hadn't thought of—and now she was ready to scatter them all to the winds....

Westover—"Junction!"

She started up and pushed her way out of the train. All the people seemed to be obstructing her, putting bags and suit-cases in her way. And the express stopped for only two minutes. Suppose she should be carried on to Albany?

Westover Junction was a growing place, and she was fairly sure there would be a taxi at the station. There was one—she just managed to get to it ahead of a travelling man with a sample case and a new straw hat. As she opened the door a smell of damp hay and bad tobacco greeted her. She sprang in and gasped: "To Oakfield. You know? Mr. Aldis's place near Westover."

## 2

It began exactly as she had expected. A surprised parlour maid—why surprised?—showed her into the low panelled room that was so full of his presence, his books, his pipes, his terrier dozing on the shabby rug. The parlour maid said she would go and see if Miss Aldis could come down. Nora wanted to ask if she were with her brother—and how he was. But she found herself unable to speak the words. She was afraid her voice might tremble. And why should she question the parlour maid, when in a moment, she hoped, she was to see Miss Aldis?

The woman moved away with a hushed step—the step which denotes illness in the house. She did not immediately return, and the interval of waiting in that room, so strange yet so intimately known, was a new torture to Nora. It was unlike anything she had imagined. The writing table with his scattered pens and letters was more than she could bear. His dog looked at her amicably from the hearth, but made no advances; and though she longed to stroke him, to let her hand rest where Christopher's had rested, she dared not for fear he should bark and disturb the peculiar hush of that dumb watchful house. She stood in the window and looked out at the budding shrubs and the bulbs pushing up through the swollen earth.

"This way, please."

Her heart gave a plunge. Was the woman actually taking her upstairs to his room? Her eyes filled, she felt herself swept forward on a great wave of passion and anguish.... But she was only being led across the hall into a stiff lifeless drawing-room—the kind that bachelors get an upholsterer to do for them, and then turn their backs on forever. The chairs and sofas looked at her with an undisguised hostility, and then resumed the moping expression

---

1    *Bath chair* Wheelchair.

common to furniture in unfrequented rooms. Even the spring sun slanting in through the windows on the pale marquetry of a useless table seemed to bring no heat or light with it.

The rush of emotion subsided, leaving in Nora a sense of emptiness and apprehension. Supposing Jane Aldis should look at her with the cold eyes of this resentful room? She began to wish she had been friendlier and more cordial to Jane Aldis in the past. In her intense desire to conceal from everyone the tie between herself and Christopher she had avoided all show of interest in his family; and perhaps, as she now saw, excited curiosity by her very affectation of indifference.

No doubt it would have been more politic to establish an intimacy with Jane Aldis; and today, how much easier and more natural her position would have been! Instead of groping about—as she was again doing—for an explanation of her visit, she could have said: "My dear, I came to see if there was anything in the world I could do to help you."

She heard a hesitating step in the hall—a hushed step like a parlour maid's—and saw Miss Aldis pause near the half-open door. How old she had grown since their last meeting! Her hair, untidily pinned up, was grey and lanky. Her eyelids, always reddish, were swollen and heavy, her face sallow with anxiety and fatigue. It was odd to have feared so defenceless an adversary. Nora, for an instant, had the impression that Miss Aldis had wavered in the hall to catch a glimpse of her, take the measure of the situation. But perhaps she had only stopped to push back a strand of hair as she passed in front of a mirror.

"Mrs. Frenway—how good of you!" She spoke in a cool detached voice, as if her real self were elsewhere and she were simply an automaton wound up to repeat the familiar forms of hospitality. "Do sit down," she said.

She pushed forward one of the sulky arm-chairs, and Nora seated herself stiffly, her hand-bag clutched on her knee, in the self-conscious attitude of a country caller.

"I came——"

"So good of you," Miss Aldis repeated. "I had no idea you were in this part of the world. Not the slightest."

Was it a lead she was giving? Or did she know everything, and wish to extend to her visitor the decent shelter of a pretext? Or was she really so stupid—

"You're staying with the Brinckers, I suppose. Or the Northrups? I remember the last time you came to lunch here you motored over with Mr. Frenway from the Northrups'. That must have been two years ago, wasn't it?" She put the question with an almost sprightly show of interest.

"No—three years," said Nora mechanically.

"Was it? As long ago as that? Yes—you're right. That was the year we moved the big fern-leaved beech. I remember Mr. Frenway was interested in tree moving, and I took him out to show him where the tree had come from. He IS interested in tree moving, isn't he?"

"Oh, yes; very much."

"We had those wonderful experts down to do it. 'Tree doctors,' they call themselves. They have special appliances, you know. The tree is growing better than it did before they moved it. But I suppose you've done a great deal of transplanting on Long Island."

"Yes. My husband does a good deal of transplanting."

"So you've come over from the Northrups'? I didn't even know they were down at Maybrook yet. I see so few people."

"No; not from the Northrups'."

"Oh—the Brinckers'? Hal Brincker was here yesterday, but he didn't tell me you were staying there."

Nora hesitated. "No. The fact is, I have an old governess who lives at Ockham. I go to see her sometimes. And so I came on to Westover——" She paused, and Miss Aldis interrogated her brightly: "Yes?" as if prompting her in a lesson she was repeating.

"Because I saw Gladys Brincker the other day, and she told me that your brother was ill."

"Oh." Miss Aldis gave the syllable its full weight, and set a full stop after it. Her eyebrows went up, as if in a faint surprise. The silent room seemed to close in on the two speakers, listening. A resuscitated fly buzzed against the sunny window pane. "Yes; he's ill," she conceded at length.

"I'm so sorry; I ... he has been ... such a friend of ours ... so long...."

"Yes; I've often heard him speak of you and Mr. Frenway." Another full stop sealed this announcement. ("No, she knows nothing," Nora thought.) "I remember his telling me that he thought a great deal of Mr. Frenway's advice about moving trees. But then you see our soil is so different from yours. I suppose Mr. Frenway has had your soil analyzed?"

"Yes; I think he has."

"Christopher's always been a great gardener."

"I hope he's not—not very ill? Gladys seemed to be afraid——"

"Illness is always something to be afraid of, isn't it?"

"But you're not—I mean, not anxious ... not seriously?"

"It's so kind of you to ask. The doctors seem to think there's no particular change since yesterday."

"And yesterday?"

"Well, yesterday they seemed to think there might be."

"A change, you mean?"

"Well, yes."

"A change—I hope for the better?"

"They said they weren't sure; they couldn't say."

The fly's buzzing had become so insistent in the still room that it seemed to be going on inside of Nora's head, and in the confusion of sound she found it more and more difficult to regain a lead in the conversation. And the minutes were slipping by, and upstairs the man she loved was lying. It was absurd and lamentable to make a pretense of keeping up this twaddle. She would cut through it, no matter how.

"I suppose you've had—a consultation?"

"Oh, yes; Dr. Knowlton's been down twice."

"And what does he——"

"Well; he seems to agree with the others."

There was another pause, and then Miss Aldis glanced out of the window. "Why, who's that driving up?" she enquired. "Oh, it's your taxi, I suppose, coming up the drive."

"Yes, I got out at the gate." She dared not add: "For fear the noise might disturb him."

"I hope you had no difficulty in finding a taxi at the Junction?"

"Oh, no; I had no difficulty."

"I think it was so kind of you to come—not even knowing whether you'd find a carriage to bring you out all this way. And I know how busy you are. There's always so much going on in town, isn't there, even at this time of year?"

"Yes; I suppose so. But your brother——"

"Oh, of course my brother won't be up to any sort of gaiety; not for a long time."

"A long time; no. But you do hope——"

"I think everybody about a sick bed ought to hope, don't you?"

"Yes; but I mean——"

Nora stood up suddenly, her brain whirling. Was it possible that she and that woman had sat thus facing each other for half an hour, piling up this conversational rubbish, while upstairs, out of sight, the truth, the meaning of their two lives hung on the frail thread of one man's intermittent pulse? She could not imagine why she felt so powerless and baffled. What had a woman who was young and handsome and beloved to fear from a dowdy and insignificant old maid? Why, the antagonism that these very graces and superiorities would create in the other's breast, especially if she knew they were all spent in charming the being on whom her life depended. Weak in herself, but powerful from her circumstances, she stood at bay on the ruins of all that Nora had ever loved. "How she must hate me—and I never thought of it," mused Nora, who had imagined that she had thought of everything where her relation to her lover was concerned. Well, it was too late now to remedy her omission; but at least she must assert herself, must say something to save the precious minutes that remained and break through the stifling web of platitudes which her enemy's tremulous hand was weaving around her.

"Miss Aldis—I must tell you—I came to see——"

"How he was? So very friendly of you. He would appreciate it, I know. Christopher is so devoted to his friends."

"But you'll—you'll tell him that I——"

"Of course. That you came on purpose to ask about him. As soon as he's a little bit stronger."

"But I mean—now?"

"Tell him now that you called to enquire? How good of you to think of that too! Perhaps tomorrow morning, if he's feeling a little bit brighter...."

Nora felt her lips drying as if a hot wind had parched them. They would hardly move. "But now—now—today." Her voice sank to a whisper as she added: "Isn't he conscious?"

"Oh, yes; he's conscious; he's perfectly conscious." Miss Aldis emphasized this with another of her long pauses. "He shall certainly be told that you called." Suddenly she too got up from her seat and moved toward the window. "I must seem dreadfully inhospitable, not even offering you a cup of tea. But the fact is, perhaps I ought to tell you—if you're thinking of getting back to Ockham this afternoon there's only one train that stops at the Junction after three o'clock." She pulled out an old-fashioned enamelled watch with a wreath of roses about the dial, and turned almost apologetically to Mrs. Frenway. "You ought to be at the station by four o'clock at the latest; and with one of those old Junction taxis.... I'm so sorry; I know I must appear to be driving you away." A wan smile drew up her pale lips.

Nora knew just how long the drive from Westover Junction had taken, and understood that she was being delicately dismissed. Dismissed from life—from hope—even from the dear anguish of filling her eyes for the last time with the face which was the one face in the world to her! ("But then she does know everything," she thought.)

"I mustn't make you miss your train, you know."

"Miss Aldis, is he—has he seen any one?" Nora hazarded in a painful whisper.

"Seen any one? Well, there've been all the doctors—five of them! And then the nurses. Oh, but you mean friends, of course. Naturally." She seemed to reflect. "Hal Brincker, yes; he saw our cousin Hal yesterday—but not for very long."

Hal Brincker! Nora knew what Christopher thought of his Brincker cousins—blighting bores, one and all of them, he always said. And in the extremity of his illness the one person privileged to see him had been—Hal Brincker! Nora's eyes filled; she had to turn them away for a moment from Miss Aldis's timid inexorable face.

"But today?" she finally brought out.

"No. Today he hasn't seen any one; not yet." The two women stood and looked at each other; then Miss Aldis glanced uncertainly about the room. "But couldn't I—Yes, I ought at least to have asked if you won't have a cup of tea. So stupid of me! There might still be time. I never take tea myself." Once more she referred anxiously to her watch. "The water is sure to be boiling, because the nurses' tea is just being taken up. If you'll excuse me a moment I'll go and see."

"Oh, no, no!" Nora drew in a quick sob. "How can you?... I mean, I don't want any...."

Miss Aldis looked relieved. "Then I shall be quite sure that you won't reach the station too late." She waited again, and then held out a long stony hand. "So kind—I shall never forget your kindness. Coming all this way, when you might so easily have telephoned from town. Do please tell Mr. Frenway how I appreciated it. You will remember to tell him, won't you? He sent me such an interesting collection of pamphlets about tree moving. I should like him to know how much I feel his kindness in letting you come." She paused again, and pulled in her lips so that they became a narrow thread, a mere line drawn across her face by a ruler. "But, no; I won't trouble you; I'll write to thank him myself." Her hand ran out to an electric bell on the nearest table. It shrilled through the silence, and the parlour maid appeared with a stage-like promptness.

"The taxi, please? Mrs. Frenway's taxi."

The room became silent again. Nora thought: "Yes; she knows everything." Miss Aldis peeped for the third time at her watch, and then uttered a slight unmeaning laugh. The blue-bottle banged against the window, and once more it seemed to Nora that its sonorities were reverberating inside her head. They were deafeningly mingled there with the explosion of the taxi's reluctant starting-up and its convulsed halt at the front door. The driver sounded his horn as if to summon her.

"He's afraid too that you'll be late!" Miss Aldis smiled.

The smooth slippery floor of the hall seemed to Nora to extend away in front of her for miles. At its far end she saw a little tunnel of light, a miniature maid, a toy taxi. Somehow she managed to travel the distance that separated her from them, though her bones ached with weariness, and at every step she seemed to be lifting a leaden weight. The taxi was close to her now, its door open, she was getting in. The same smell of damp hay and bad tobacco greeted her. She saw her hostess standing on the threshold. "To the Junction, driver—back to the Junction," she heard Miss Aldis say. The taxi began to roll toward the gate. As it moved away Nora heard Miss Aldis calling: "I'll be sure to write and thank Mr. Frenway."

—1927

# James Joyce
1882–1941

James Joyce was born in Dublin, and although he left the city for good in 1904, it provided the background for all his major works. His best-known novel, *Ulysses* (1922), describes a day in the life of three of the city's inhabitants, with the various incidents paralleling episodes from Homer's *Odyssey*. It is written in an intricately constructed combination of literary styles, including long sections of stream-of-consciousness narration.

Joyce and Nora Barnacle, a woman whom he met on a Dublin street and who would become his wife and lifelong companion, lived in Trieste, Zurich, and Paris, where Joyce made his living by teaching English. In 1914, the modernist poet Ezra Pound arranged for Joyce's autobiographical novel *A Portrait of the Artist as a Young Man* to be serialized in *The Egoist*, a British magazine. The same year, Joyce's collection of short stories, *Dubliners*, was published. In each story, the protagonist experiences what Joyce called an "epiphany," a moment of revelation that he described as "a sudden spiritual manifestation, whether in the vulgarity of speech or of gesture or in a memorable phase of the mind itself."

Shortly after, Joyce began work on *Ulysses*. In 1918, *The Egoist* and an American magazine, *The Little Review*, began serializing the work, but charges that passages were obscene led to the suspension of serialization. Joyce is said to have retorted, "If *Ulysses* isn't fit to read, life isn't fit to live." It was finally published in book form in Paris in 1922.

By this time, friends and admirers were supporting Joyce financially, allowing him to concentrate on his writing; he began work on his last book, *Finnegans Wake*, an extremely complex work of dream imaginings and linguistic invention, which was published in 1939.

# Araby[1]

North Richmond Street, being blind,[2] was a quiet street except at the hour when the Christian Brothers' School set the boys free. An uninhabited house of two storeys stood at the blind end, detached from its neighbours in a square ground. The other houses of the street, conscious of decent lives within them, gazed at one another with brown imperturbable faces.

The former tenant of our house, a priest, had died in the back drawing-room. Air, musty from having been long enclosed, hung in all the rooms, and

---

1    *Araby* Charity bazaar held in Dublin in 1894; it was advertised as a "grand, Oriental fête."
2    *being blind* I.e., being a dead-end street.

the waste room behind the kitchen was littered with old useless papers. Among these I found a few paper-covered books, the pages of which were curled and damp: *The Abbot*, by Walter Scott, *The Devout Communicant* and *The Memoirs of Vidocq*.[1] I liked the last best because its leaves were yellow. The wild garden behind the house contained a central apple-tree and a few straggling bushes under one of which I found the late tenant's rusty bicycle-pump. He had been a very charitable priest; in his will he had left all his money to institutions and the furniture of his house to his sister.

When the short days of winter came dusk fell before we had well eaten our dinners. When we met in the street the houses had grown sombre. The space of sky above us was the colour of ever-changing violet and towards it the lamps of the street lifted their feeble lanterns. The cold air stung us and we played till our bodies glowed. Our shouts echoed in the silent street. The career of our play brought us through the dark muddy lanes behind the houses where we ran the gantlet of the rough tribes from the cottages, to the back doors of the dark dripping gardens where odours arose from the ash-pits, to the dark odorous stables where a coachman smoothed and combed the horse or shook music from the buckled harness. When we returned to the street light from the kitchen windows had filled the areas.[2] If my uncle was seen turning the corner we hid in the shadow until we had seen him safely housed. Or if Mangan's sister came out on the doorstep to call her brother in to his tea we watched her from our shadow peer up and down the street. We waited to see whether she would remain or go in and, if she remained, we left our shadow and walked up to Mangan's steps resignedly. She was waiting for us, her figure defined by the light from the half-opened door. Her brother always teased her before he obeyed and I stood by the railings looking at her. Her dress swung as she moved her body and the soft rope of her hair tossed from side to side.

Every morning I lay on the floor in the front parlour watching her door. The blind was pulled down to within an inch of the sash so that I could not be seen. When she came out on the doorstep my heart leaped. I ran to the hall, seized my books and followed her. I kept her brown figure always in my eye and, when we came near the point at which our ways diverged, I quickened my pace and passed her. This happened morning after morning. I had never spoken to her, except for a few casual words, and yet her name was like a summons to all my foolish blood.

---

1    *The Abbot* 1820 historical novel by Sir Walter Scott about Mary, Queen of Scots; *The Devout Communicant* Title common to several nineteenth-century religious tracts; *The Memoirs of Vidocq* Autobiography of François Vidocq, a nineteenth-century Parisian criminal turned police detective.

2    *areas* Spaces between the railings and the fronts of houses, below street level.

Her image accompanied me even in places the most hostile to romance. On Saturday evenings when my aunt went marketing I had to go to carry some of the parcels. We walked through the flaring streets, jostled by drunken men and bargaining women, amid the curses of labourers, the shrill litanies of shop-boys who stood on guard by the barrels of pigs' cheeks, the nasal chanting of street-singers, who sang a *come-all-you* about O'Donovan Rossa,[1] or a ballad about the troubles in our native land. These noises converged in a single sensation of life for me: I imagined that I bore my chalice safely through a throng of foes. Her name sprang to my lips at moments in strange prayers and praises which I myself did not understand. My eyes were often full of tears (I could not tell why) and at times a flood from my heart seemed to pour itself out into my bosom. I thought little of the future. I did not know whether I would ever speak to her or not or, if I spoke to her, how I could tell her of my confused adoration. But my body was like a harp and her words and gestures were like fingers running upon the wires.

One evening I went into the back drawing-room in which the priest had died. It was a dark rainy evening and there was no sound in the house. Through one of the broken panes I heard the rain impinge upon the earth, the fine incessant needles of water playing in the sodden beds. Some distant lamp or lighted window gleamed below me. I was thankful that I could see so little. All my senses seemed to desire to veil themselves and, feeling that I was about to slip from them, I pressed the palms of my hands together until they trembled, murmuring: *O love! O love!* many times.

At last she spoke to me. When she addressed the first words to me I was so confused that I did not know what to answer. She asked me was I going to *Araby.* I forget whether I answered yes or no. It would be a splendid bazaar, she said; she would love to go.

—And why can't you? I asked.

While she spoke she turned a silver bracelet round and round her wrist. She could not go, she said, because there would be a retreat that week in her convent.[2] Her brother and two other boys were fighting for their caps and I was alone at the railings. She held one of the spikes, bowing her head towards me. The light from the lamp opposite our door caught the white curve of her neck, lit up her hair that rested there and, falling, lit up the hand upon the railing. It fell over one side of her dress and caught the white border of a petticoat, just visible as she stood at ease.

—It's well for you, she said.

---

1    *come-all-you* Ballad, so called because many ballads started with this phrase; *O'Donovan Rossa* Jeremiah O'Donovan Rossa (1831–1915), an activist for Irish independence.
2    *convent* I.e., convent school.

—If I go, I said, I will bring you something.

What innumerable follies laid waste my waking and sleeping thoughts after that evening! I wished to annihilate the tedious intervening days. I chafed against the work of school. At night in my bedroom and by day in the class-room her image came between me and the page I strove to read. The syllables of the word *Araby* were called to me through the silence in which my soul luxuriated and cast an Eastern enchantment over me. I asked for leave to go to the bazaar on Saturday night. My aunt was surprised and hoped it was not some Freemason[1] affair. I answered few questions in class. I watched my master's face pass from amiability to sternness; he hoped I was not beginning to idle. I could not call my wandering thoughts together. I had hardly any patience with the serious work of life which, now that it stood between me and my desire, seemed to me child's play, ugly monotonous child's play.

On Saturday morning I reminded my uncle that I wished to go to the bazaar in the evening. He was fussing at the hallstand, looking for the hat-brush, and answered me curtly:

—Yes, boy, I know.

As he was in the hall I could not go into the front parlour and lie at the window. I left the house in bad humour and walked slowly towards the school. The air was pitilessly raw and already my heart misgave me.

When I came home to dinner my uncle had not yet been home. Still it was early. I sat staring at the clock for some time and, when its ticking began to irritate me, I left the room. I mounted the staircase and gained the upper part of the house. The high cold empty gloomy rooms liberated me and I went from room to room singing. From the front window I saw my companions playing below in the street. Their cries reached me weakened and indistinct and, leaning my forehead against the cool glass, I looked over at the dark house where she lived. I may have stood there for an hour, seeing nothing but the brown-clad figure cast by my imagination, touched discreetly by the lamplight at the curved neck, at the hand upon the railings and at the border below the dress.

When I came downstairs again I found Mrs. Mercer sitting at the fire. She was an old garrulous woman, a pawnbroker's widow, who collected used stamps for some pious purpose. I had to endure the gossip of the tea-table. The meal was prolonged beyond an hour and still my uncle did not come. Mrs. Mercer stood up to go: she was sorry she couldn't wait any longer, but it was after eight o'clock and she did not like to be out late, as the night air was bad for her. When she had gone I began to walk up and down the room, clenching my fists. My aunt said:

---

1    *Freemason* In reference to the Freemasons, a secret society believed by many in Ireland to be anti-Catholic.

—I'm afraid you may put off your bazaar for this night of Our Lord.

At nine o'clock I heard my uncle's latchkey in the halldoor. I heard him talking to himself and heard the hallstand rocking when it had received the weight of his overcoat. I could interpret these signs. When he was midway through his dinner I asked him to give me the money to go to the bazaar. He had forgotten.

—The people are in bed and after their first sleep now, he said.

I did not smile. My aunt said to him energetically:

—Can't you give him the money and let him go? You've kept him late enough as it is.

My uncle said he was very sorry he had forgotten. He said he believed in the old saying: *All work and no play makes Jack a dull boy.* He asked where I was going and, when I had told him a second time he asked me did I know *The Arab's Farewell to his Steed.*[1] When I left the kitchen he was about to recite the opening lines of the piece to my aunt.

I held a florin tightly in my hand as I strode down Buckingham Street towards the station. The sight of the streets thronged with buyers and glaring with gas recalled to me the purpose of my journey. I took my seat in a third-class carriage of a deserted train. After an intolerable delay the train moved out of the station slowly. It crept onward among ruinous houses and over the twinkling river. At Westland Row Station a crowd of people pressed to the carriage doors; but the porters moved them back, saying that it was a special train for the bazaar. I remained alone in the bare carriage. In a few minutes the train drew up beside an improvised wooden platform. I passed out on to the road and saw by the lighted dial of a clock that it was ten minutes to ten. In front of me was a large building which displayed the magical name.

I could not find any sixpenny entrance and, fearing that the bazaar would be closed, I passed in quickly through a turnstile, handing a shilling to a weary-looking man. I found myself in a big hall girdled at half its height by a gallery. Nearly all the stalls were closed and the greater part of the hall was in darkness. I recognized a silence like that which pervades a church after a service. I walked into the centre of the bazaar timidly. A few people were gathered about the stalls which were still open. Before a curtain, over which the words *Café Chantant* were written in coloured lamps, two men were counting money on a salver.[2] I listened to the fall of the coins.

Remembering with difficulty why I had come I went over to one of the stalls and examined porcelain vases and flowered tea-sets. At the door of the

---

1    *The Arab's … his Steed* Popular Romantic poem by Caroline Norton (1808–77).
2    *Café Chantant* Café that provides musical entertainment; *salver* Tray.

stall a young lady was talking and laughing with two young gentlemen. I remarked their English accents and listened vaguely to their conversation.

—O, I never said such a thing!

—O, but you did!

—O, but I didn't!

—Didn't she say that?

—Yes. I heard her.

—O, there's a ... fib!

Observing me the young lady came over and asked me did I wish to buy anything. The tone of her voice was not encouraging; she seemed to have spoken to me out of a sense of duty. I looked humbly at the great jars that stood like eastern guards at either side of the dark entrance to the stall and murmured:

—No, thank you.

The young lady changed the position of one of the vases and went back to the two young men. They began to talk of the same subject. Once or twice the young lady glanced at me over her shoulder.

I lingered before her stall, though I knew my stay was useless, to make my interest in her wares seem the more real. Then I turned away slowly and walked down the middle of the bazaar. I allowed the two pennies to fall against the sixpence in my pocket. I heard a voice call from one end of the gallery that the light was out. The upper part of the hall was now completely dark.

Gazing up into the darkness I saw myself as a creature driven and derided by vanity; and my eyes burned with anguish and anger.

—1914

# Eveline

She sat at the window watching the evening invade the avenue. Her head was leaned against the window curtains and in her nostrils was the odour of dusty cretonne.[1] She was tired.

Few people passed. The man out of the last house passed on his way home; she heard his footsteps clacking along the concrete pavement and afterwards crunching on the cinder path before the new red houses. One time there used to be a field there in which they used to play every evening with other people's children. Then a man from Belfast bought the field and built houses in it—not like their little brown houses but bright brick houses with shining roofs. The children of the avenue used to play together in that field—the Devines, the Waters, the Dunns, little Keogh the cripple, she and her brothers and sisters.

---

1    *cretonne* Thick cotton fabric often used for chair coverings or curtains.

Ernest, however, never played: he was too grown up. Her father used often to hunt them in out of the field with his blackthorn stick; but usually little Keogh used to keep *nix*[1] and call out when he saw her father coming. Still they seemed to have been rather happy then. Her father was not so bad then; and besides, her mother was alive. That was a long time ago; she and her brothers and sisters were all grown up; her mother was dead. Tizzie Dunn was dead, too, and the Waters had gone back to England. Everything changes. Now she was going to go away like the others, to leave her home.

Home! She looked round the room, reviewing all its familiar objects which she had dusted once a week for so many years, wondering where on earth all the dust came from. Perhaps she would never see again those familiar objects from which she had never dreamed of being divided. And yet during all those years she had never found out the name of the priest whose yellowing photograph hung on the wall above the broken harmonium beside the coloured print of the promises made to Blessed Margaret Mary Alacoque.[2] He had been a school friend of her father. Whenever he showed the photograph to a visitor her father used to pass it with a casual word:

—He is in Melbourne now.

She had consented to go away, to leave her home. Was that wise? She tried to weigh each side of the question. In her home anyway she had shelter and food; she had those whom she had known all her life about her. Of course she had to work hard both in the house and at business. What would they say of her in the Stores when they found out that she had run away with a fellow? Say she was a fool, perhaps; and her place would be filled up by advertisement. Miss Gavan would be glad. She had always had an edge on her, especially whenever there were people listening.

—Miss Hill, don't you see these ladies are waiting?

—Look lively, Miss Hill, please.

She would not cry many tears at leaving the Stores.

But in her new home, in a distant unknown country, it would not be like that. Then she would be married—she, Eveline. People would treat her with respect then. She would not be treated as her mother had been. Even now, though she was over nineteen, she sometimes felt herself in danger of her father's violence. She knew it was that that had given her the palpitations. When they were growing up he had never gone for her, like he used to go for Harry and Ernest, because she was a girl; but latterly he had begun to threaten her and say what he would do to her only for her dead mother's sake. And

---

1    *keep nix* Keep watch.

2    *harmonium* Reed instrument similar to an organ; *Blessed Margaret Mary Alacoque* Marguerite Marie Alacoque (1647–90), a French Catholic nun and religious mystic who had visions of Christ. She was made a saint in 1920.

now she had nobody to protect her. Ernest was dead and Harry, who was in the church decorating business, was nearly always down somewhere in the country. Besides, the invariable squabble for money on Saturday nights had begun to weary her unspeakably. She always gave her entire wages—seven shillings—and Harry always sent up what he could but the trouble was to get any money from her father. He said she used to squander the money, that she had no head, that he wasn't going to give her his hard-earned money to throw about the streets, and much more, for he was usually fairly bad of a Saturday night. In the end he would give her the money and ask her had she any intention of buying Sunday's dinner. Then she had to rush out as quickly as she could and do her marketing, holding her black leather purse tightly in her hand as she elbowed her way through the crowds and returning home late under her load of provisions. She had hard work to keep the house together and to see that the two young children who had been left to her charge went to school regularly and got their meals regularly. It was hard work—a hard life—but now that she was about to leave it she did not find it a wholly undesirable life.

She was about to explore another life with Frank. Frank was very kind, manly, open-hearted. She was to go away with him by the night-boat to be his wife and to live with him in Buenos Ayres where he had a home waiting for her. How well she remembered the first time she had seen him; he was lodging in a house on the main road where she used to visit. It seemed a few weeks ago. He was standing at the gate, his peaked cap pushed back on his head and his hair tumbled forward over a face of bronze. Then they had come to know each other. He used to meet her outside the Stores every evening and see her home. He took her to see *The Bohemian Girl*[1] and she felt elated as she sat in an unaccustomed part of the theatre with him. He was awfully fond of music and sang a little. People knew that they were courting and, when he sang about the lass that loves a sailor, she always felt pleasantly confused. He used to call her Poppens out of fun. First of all it had been an excitement for her to have a fellow and then she had begun to like him. He had tales of distant countries. He had started as a deck boy at a pound a month on a ship of the Allan Line[2] going out to Canada. He told her the names of the ships he had been on and the names of the different services. He had sailed through the Straits of Magellan and he told her stories of the terrible Patagonians.[3] He

1    *The Bohemian Girl* 1843 opera by Irish composer Michael Balfe.
2    *Allan Line* Steamship company that made weekly sailings between Liverpool and western Canada via South America.
3    *Straits of Magellan* Sea route near the tip of South America; *terrible Patagonians* Refers either to the strong, unpredictable Patagonian winds in the Strait of Magellan, or to a group of South American natives that early explorers had claimed were giants. By the beginning of the nineteenth century, this rumour was discredited.

had fallen on his feet in Buenos Ayres, he said, and had come over to the old country just for a holiday. Of course, her father had found out the affair and had forbidden her to have anything to say to him.

—I know these sailor chaps, he said.

One day he had quarrelled with Frank and after that she had to meet her lover secretly.

The evening deepened in the avenue. The white of two letters in her lap grew indistinct. One was to Harry; the other was to her father. Ernest had been her favourite but she liked Harry too. Her father was becoming old lately, she noticed; he would miss her. Sometimes he could be very nice. Not long before, when she had been laid up for a day, he had read her out a ghost story and made toast for her at the fire. Another day, when their mother was alive, they had all gone for a picnic to the Hill of Howth.[1] She remembered her father putting on her mother's bonnet to make the children laugh.

Her time was running out but she continued to sit by the window, leaning her head against the window curtain, inhaling the odour of dusty cretonne. Down far in the avenue she could hear a street organ playing. She knew the air. Strange that it should come that very night to remind her of the promise to her mother, her promise to keep the home together as long as she could. She remembered the last night of her mother's illness; she was again in the close dark room at the other side of the hall and outside she heard a melancholy air of Italy. The organ-player had been ordered to go away and given sixpence. She remembered her father strutting back into the sickroom saying:

—Damned Italians! coming over here!

As she mused the pitiful vision of her mother's life laid its spell on the very quick of her being—that life of commonplace sacrifices closing in final craziness. She trembled as she heard again her mother's voice saying constantly with foolish insistence:

—Derevaun Seraun! Derevaun Seraun![2]

She stood up in a sudden impulse of terror. Escape! She must escape! Frank would save her. He would give her life, perhaps love, too. But she wanted to live. Why should she be unhappy? She had a right to happiness. Frank would take her in his arms, fold her in his arms. He would save her.

She stood among the swaying crowd in the station at the North Wall. He held her hand and she knew that he was speaking to her, saying something about the passage over and over again. The station was full of soldiers with brown

---

1   *Hill of Howth*  Hill located northeast of Dublin, on the Howth peninsula.
2   *Derevaun … Seraun!*  The meaning of this phrase is uncertain; it may be garbled Irish or simply gibberish.

baggages. Through the wide doors of the sheds she caught a glimpse of the black mass of the boat, lying in beside the quay wall, with illumined portholes. She answered nothing. She felt her cheek pale and cold and, out of a maze of distress, she prayed to God to direct her, to show her what was her duty. The boat blew a long mournful whistle into the mist. If she went, to-morrow she would be on the sea with Frank, steaming towards Buenos Ayres. Their passage had been booked. Could she still draw back after all he had done for her? Her distress awoke a nausea in her body and she kept moving her lips in silent fervent prayer.

A bell clanged upon her heart. She felt him seize her hand:

—Come!

All the seas of the world tumbled about her heart. He was drawing her into them: he would drown her. She gripped with both hands at the iron railing.

—Come!

No! No! No! It was impossible. Her hands clutched the iron in frenzy. Amid the seas she sent a cry of anguish!

—Eveline! Evvy!

He rushed beyond the barrier and called to her to follow. He was shouted at to go on but he still called to her. She set her white face to him, passive, like a helpless animal. Her eyes gave him no sign of love or farewell or recognition.

—1914

# *Virginia Woolf*
1882–1941

It is no accident that the life of Virginia Woolf, one of the most innovative writers of the twentieth century, coincides very nearly with the emergence and flourishing of literary modernism. Many of her highly experimental novels—notably *Mrs Dalloway* (1925), *To the Lighthouse* (1927), and *The Waves* (1931)—are key landmarks in the modernist revolt against conventional modes of literary representation. In contrast to what she described as the superficial, "materialist" fixation of Edwardian novelists on external details, Woolf set out to convey the essence of lived experience, the incessant influx of impressions—"trivial, fantastic, evanescent, or engraved with the sharpness of steel"—that stream through and light up the mind from moment to crowded moment with all manner of fugitive, seemingly random images, thoughts, feelings, memories, and associations.

For Woolf, life does not form an orderly, linear chronicle of events, like "a series of gig lamps symmetrically arranged." Rather, "life is a luminous halo, a semi-transparent envelope surrounding us from the beginning of consciousness to the end." In order to faithfully render some semblance of this "uncircumscribed spirit," Woolf followed writers like James Joyce in developing a fluid stream-of-consciousness technique that subordinates the action of plot to the subjective interplay of perception, recollection, emotion, and understanding. This essentially lyrical method is used to great effect in stories like "Kew Gardens" (1919).

The circumstances of Woolf's own life were often deeply troubled. Although born into an illustrious British family with an impressive literary pedigree, Woolf received no formal education, an injustice that occupies a central place in much of her social and political writing. The loss of her parents and several siblings exacted a heavy emotional and psychological toll, and periodic fits of mental instability and depression ultimately led her to suicide. But though her hauntingly beautiful, intricately crafted novels and stories are written in a predominantly elegiac key, they also explore the rich multiplicity of connections between individuals, memories, and moments in time that persist across the years.

*Vanessa Bell, woodcut illustration for "Kew Gardens," 1919. Vanessa Bell was Virginia Woolf's sister and fellow member of the Bloomsbury Group, a social circle of talented avant-garde writers, artists, and intellectuals that flourished in London in the first half of the twentieth century. Best known as a post-impressionist painter, Bell was also a designer, and she produced book covers and illustrations for Hogarth Press, the publishing house Virginia Woolf operated with her husband. The above illustration appeared in a Hogarth Press edition of "Kew Gardens."*

# Kew Gardens[1]

From the oval-shaped flower-bed there rose perhaps a hundred stalks spreading into heart-shaped or tongue-shaped leaves half way up and unfurling at the tip red or blue or yellow petals marked with spots of colour raised upon the surface; and from the red, blue or yellow gloom of the throat emerged a straight bar, rough with gold dust and slightly clubbed at the end. The petals were voluminous enough to be stirred by the summer breeze, and when they moved, the red, blue, and yellow lights passed one over the other, staining an inch of the brown earth beneath with a spot of the most intricate colour. The light fell either upon the smooth grey back of a pebble, or the shell of a snail with its brown circular veins, or, falling into a raindrop, it expanded with such intensity of red, blue, and yellow the thin walls of water that one expected them to burst and disappear. Instead, the drop was left in a second silver grey once more, and the light now settled upon the flesh of a leaf, revealing the branching thread of fibre beneath the surface, and again it moved on and spread its illumination in the vast green spaces beneath the dome of the heart-shaped and tongue-shaped leaves. Then the breeze stirred rather more briskly overhead and the colour was flashed into the air above, into the eyes of the men and women who walk in Kew Gardens in July.

The figures of these men and women straggled past the flower-bed with a curiously irregular movement not unlike that of the white and blue butterflies who crossed the turf in zig-zag flights from bed to bed. The man was about six inches in front of the woman, strolling carelessly, while she bore on with greater purpose, only turning her head now and then to see that the children were not too far behind. The man kept this distance in front of the woman purposely, though perhaps unconsciously, for he wanted to go on with his thoughts.

"Fifteen years ago I came here with Lily," he thought. "We sat somewhere over there by a lake, and I begged her to marry me all through the hot afternoon. How the dragon-fly kept circling round us: how clearly I see the dragon-fly and her shoe with the square silver buckle at the toe. All the time I spoke I saw her shoe and when it moved impatiently I knew without looking up what she was going to say: the whole of her seemed to be in her shoe. And my love, my desire, were in the dragon-fly; for some reason I thought that if it settled there, on that leaf, the broad one with the red flower in the middle of it, if the dragonfly settled on the leaf she would say 'Yes' at once. But the dragon-fly went round and round: it never settled anywhere—of course not,

---

1    *Kew Gardens* Royal Botanic Gardens in Kew, a district of Greater London.

happily not, or I shouldn't be walking here with Eleanor and the children—Tell me, Eleanor, d'you ever think of the past?"

"Why do you ask, Simon?"

"Because I've been thinking of the past. I've been thinking of Lily, the woman I might have married ... Well, why are you silent? Do you mind my thinking of the past?"

"Why should I mind, Simon? Doesn't one always think of the past, in a garden with men and women lying under the trees? Aren't they one's past, all that remains of it, those men and women, those ghosts lying under the trees ... one's happiness, one's reality?"

"For me, a square silver shoe-buckle and a dragon-fly—"

"For me, a kiss. Imagine six little girls sitting before their easels twenty years ago, down by the side of a lake, painting the water-lilies, the first red water-lilies I'd ever seen. And suddenly a kiss, there on the back of my neck. And my hand shook all the afternoon so that I couldn't paint. I took out my watch and marked the hour when I would allow myself to think of the kiss for five minutes only—it was so precious—the kiss of an old grey-haired woman with a wart on her nose, the mother of all my kisses all my life. Come Caroline, come Hubert."

They walked on past the flower-bed, now walking four abreast, and soon diminished in size among the trees and looked half transparent as the sunlight and shade swam over their backs in large trembling irregular patches.

In the oval flower-bed the snail, whose shell had been stained red, blue, and yellow for the space of two minutes or so, now appeared to be moving very slightly in its shell, and next began to labour over the crumbs of loose earth which broke away and rolled down as it passed over them. It appeared to have a definite goal in front of it, differing in this respect from the singular high-stepping angular green insect who attempted to cross in front of it, and waited for a second with its antennae trembling as if in deliberation, and then stepped off as rapidly and strangely in the opposite direction. Brown cliffs with deep green lakes in the hollows, flat blade-like trees that waved from root to tip, round boulders of grey stone, vast crumpled surfaces of a thin crackling texture—all these objects lay across the snail's progress between one stalk and another to his goal. Before he had decided whether to circumvent the arched tent of a dead leaf or to breast it there came past the bed the feet of other human beings.

This time they were both men. The younger of the two wore an expression of perhaps unnatural calm; he raised his eyes and fixed them very steadily in front of him while his companion spoke, and directly his companion had done speaking he looked on the ground again and sometimes opened his lips only after a long pause and sometimes did not open them at all. The elder man had a curiously uneven and shaky method of walking, jerking his hand forward and throwing up his head abruptly, rather in the manner of an impatient carriage horse tired of waiting outside a house; but in the man these gestures were irresolute and pointless. He talked almost incessantly; he smiled to himself and again began to talk, as if the smile had been an answer. He was talking about spirits—the spirits of the dead, who, according to him, were even now telling him all sorts of odd things about their experiences in Heaven.

"Heaven was known to the ancients as Thessaly, William, and now, with this war,[1] the spirit matter is rolling between the hills like thunder." He paused, seemed to listen, smiled, jerked his head and continued:—

"You have a small electric battery and a piece of rubber to insulate the wire—isolate?—insulate?—well, we'll skip the details, no good going into details that wouldn't be understood—and in short the little machine stands in any convenient position by the head of the bed, we will say, on a neat mahogany stand. All arrangements being properly fixed by workmen under my direction, the widow applies her ear and summons the spirit by sign as agreed. Women! Widows! Women in black—"

Here he seemed to have caught sight of a woman's dress in the distance, which in the shade looked a purple black. He took off his hat, placed his hand upon his heart, and hurried towards her muttering and gesticulating feverishly. But William caught him by the sleeve and touched a flower with the tip of his walking-stick in order to divert the old man's attention. After looking at it for a moment in some confusion the old man bent his ear to it and seemed to answer a voice speaking from it, for he began talking about the forests of Uruguay which he had visited hundreds of years ago in company with the most beautiful young woman in Europe. He could be heard murmuring about forests of Uruguay blanketed with the wax petals of tropical roses, nightingales, sea beaches, mermaids and women drowned at sea, as he suffered himself to be moved on by William, upon whose face the look of stoical patience grew slowly deeper and deeper.

Following his steps so closely as to be slightly puzzled by his gestures came two elderly women of the lower middle class, one stout and ponderous, the other rosy-cheeked and nimble. Like most people of their station[2] they were frankly fascinated by any signs of eccentricity betokening a disordered brain, especially in the well-to-do; but they were too far off to be certain whether the gestures were merely eccentric or genuinely mad. After they had scrutinized the

---

1    *Thessaly* Region of ancient Greece; a large, fertile plain surrounded by mountains; *this war* I.e., World War I (1914–18).
2    *their station* I.e., their position in English society.

old man's back in silence for a moment and given each other a queer, sly look, they went on energetically piecing together their very complicated dialogue:

"Nell, Bert, Lot, Cess, Phil, Pa, he says, I says, she says, I says, I says, I says—"

"My Bert, Sis, Bill, Grandad, the old man, sugar,
  Sugar, flour, kippers, greens
  Sugar, sugar, sugar."

The ponderous woman looked through the pattern of falling words at the flowers standing cool, firm and upright in the earth, with a curious expression. She saw them as a sleeper waking from a heavy sleep sees a brass candlestick reflecting the light in an unfamiliar way, and closes his eyes and opens them, and seeing the brass candlestick again, finally starts broad awake and stares at the candlestick with all his powers. So the heavy woman came to a standstill opposite the oval-shaped flower-bed, and ceased even to pretend to listen to what the other woman was saying. She stood there letting the words fall over her, swaying the top part of her body slowly backwards and forwards, looking at the flowers. Then she suggested that they should find a seat and have their tea.

The snail had now considered every possible method of reaching his goal without going round the dead leaf or climbing over it. Let alone the effort needed for climbing a leaf, he was doubtful whether the thin texture which vibrated with such an alarming crackle when touched even by the tip of his horns would bear his weight; and this determined him finally to creep beneath it, for there was a point where the leaf curved high enough from the ground to admit him. He had just inserted his head in the opening and was taking stock of the high brown roof and was getting used to the cool brown light when two other people came past outside on the turf. This time they were both young, a young man and a young woman. They were both in the prime of youth, or even in that season which precedes the prime of youth, the season before the smooth pink folds of the flower have burst their gummy case, when the wings of the butterfly, though fully grown, are motionless in the sun.

"Lucky it isn't Friday," he observed.

"Why? D'you believe in luck?"

"They make you pay sixpence on Friday."

"What's sixpence anyway? Isn't it worth sixpence?"

"What's 'it'—what do you mean by 'it'?"

"O anything —I mean—you know what I mean."

Long pauses came between each of these remarks: they were uttered in toneless and monotonous voices. The couple stood still on the edge of the flower-bed, and together pressed the end of her parasol deep down into the soft earth. The action and the fact that his hand rested on the top of hers expressed their feelings in a strange way, as these short insignificant words also expressed something, words with short wings for their heavy body of meaning, inadequate to carry them far and thus alighting awkwardly upon the very common objects that surrounded them and were to their inexperienced touch so massive: but who knows (so they thought as they pressed the parasol into the earth) what precipices aren't concealed in them, or what slopes of ice don't shine in the sun on the other side? Who knows? Who has ever seen this before? Even when she wondered what sort of tea they gave you at Kew, he felt that something loomed up behind her words, and stood vast and solid behind them; and the mist very slowly rose and uncovered—O Heavens,—what were those shapes?—little white tables, and waitresses who looked first at her and then at him; and there was a bill that he would pay with a real two shilling piece, and it was real, all real, he assured himself, fingering the coin in his pocket, real to everyone except to him and to her; even to him it began to seem real; and then—but it was too exciting to stand and think any longer, and he pulled the parasol out of the earth with a jerk and was impatient to find the place where one had tea with other people, like other people.

"Come along, Trissie; it's time we had our tea."

"Wherever does one have one's tea?" she asked with the oddest thrill of excitement in her voice, looking vaguely round and letting herself be drawn on down the grass path, trailing her parasol, turning her head this way and that way, forgetting her tea, wishing to go down there and then down there, remembering orchids and cranes among wild flowers, a Chinese pagoda and a crimson-crested bird; but he bore her on.

Thus one couple after another with much the same irregular and aimless movement passed the flower-bed and were enveloped in layer after layer of green-blue vapour, in which at first their bodies had substance and a dash of colour, but later both substance and colour dissolved in the green-blue atmosphere. How hot it was! So hot that even the thrush chose to hop, like a mechanical bird, in the shadow of the flowers, with long pauses between one movement and the next; instead of rambling vaguely the white butterflies danced one above another, making with their white shifting flakes the outline of a shattered marble column above the tallest flowers; the glass roofs of the palm house shone as if a whole market full of shiny green umbrellas had opened in the sun; and in the drone of the aeroplane the voice of the summer sky murmured its fierce soul. Yellow and black, pink and snow white, shapes of all these colours, men, women, and children, were spotted for a second upon the horizon, and then, seeing the breadth of yellow that lay upon the grass, they wavered and sought shade beneath the trees, dissolving like drops of water in the yellow and green atmosphere, staining it faintly with red and blue. It seemed as if all gross and heavy bodies had sunk down in the heat motionless and lay huddled upon the ground, but their voices went wavering from them as if they were flames lolling from the thick waxen bodies of candles. Voices, yes, voices, wordless voices, breaking the silence suddenly with such depth of content-ment, such passion of desire, or, in the voices of children, such freshness of surprise; breaking the silence? But there was no silence; all the time the motor omnibuses were turning their wheels and changing their gear; like a vast nest of Chinese boxes[1] all of wrought steel turning ceaselessly one within another the city murmured; on the top of which the voices cried aloud and the petals of myriads of flowers flashed their colours into the air.

—1919, 1921

---

1    *Chinese boxes* Boxes that fit inside one another.

# *Katherine Mansfield*
## 1888–1923

In her short life, Katherine Mansfield managed to secure a reputation as one of the world's most gifted writers of short fiction. Her later stories in particular are important for their experimentation with style and atmosphere; instead of a conventional storyline, these stories present a series of loosely linked moments, portraying the small details of human life as a means of illuminating a specific character at a specific point of crisis or epiphany. Through such small details, Mansfield addresses grand themes such as the evolution of the self and the reality of death. Malcolm Cowley, a contemporary of Mansfield, wrote that her stories "have a thesis: namely, that life is a very wonderful spectacle, but disagreeable for the actors."

Born as Kathleen Mansfield Beauchamp in Wellington, New Zealand, in 1908 Mansfield moved permanently to Europe, where she could live the bohemian life she craved. In London, she cultivated several close—if sometimes tumultuous—friendships within literary circles, most notably with D.H. Lawrence, Virginia Woolf, and Aldous Huxley.

Mansfield grieved profoundly when her youngest brother Leslie was killed in 1915 as a soldier in France. In an effort to console herself she began writing stories about her childhood in New Zealand; thus began her most productive and successful period as a writer. Her long story *Prelude*, first published by Woolf's Hogarth Press in 1918, draws on her memories of New Zealand, as do several of her other stories, some of which return to the characters she introduces in *Prelude*. *Prelude* was reprinted in *Bliss and Other Stories* (1920); this and her following collection, *The Garden Party and Other Stories* (1922), established her importance as a modernist writer.

Troubled by ill health for most of her adult life, Mansfield died of tuberculosis at 34. After her death, her husband John Middleton Murry published two more collections of her stories, as well as editions of her poems, journals, and letters; her letters in particular are valued almost as highly as her short stories for their wit, perceptiveness, and sincerity.

# The Garden Party

And after all the weather was ideal. They could not have had a more perfect day for a garden party if they had ordered it. Windless, warm, the sky without a cloud. Only the blue was veiled with a haze of light gold, as it is sometimes in early summer. The gardener had been up since dawn, mowing the lawns and sweeping them, until the grass and the dark flat rosettes where the daisy plants had been seemed to shine. As for the roses, you could not help feeling they understood that roses are the only flowers that impress people at garden parties; the only flowers that everybody is certain of knowing. Hundreds, yes, literally hundreds, had come out in a single night; the green bushes bowed down as though they had been visited by archangels.

Breakfast was not yet over before the men came to put up the marquee.[1]

"Where do you want the marquee put, mother?"

"My dear child, it's no use asking me. I'm determined to leave everything to you children this year. Forget I am your mother. Treat me as an honoured guest."

But Meg could not possibly go and supervise the men. She had washed her hair before breakfast, and she sat drinking her coffee in a green turban, with a dark wet curl stamped on each cheek. Jose, the butterfly, always came down in a silk petticoat and a kimono jacket.

"You'll have to go, Laura, you're the artistic one."

Away Laura flew, still holding her piece of bread-and-butter. It's so delicious to have an excuse for eating out of doors and, besides, she loved having to arrange things; she always felt she could do it so much better than anybody else.

Four men in their shirt-sleeves stood grouped together on the garden path. They carried staves[2] covered with rolls of canvas, and they had big tool-bags slung on their backs. They looked impressive. Laura wished now that she was not holding that piece of bread-and-butter, but there was nowhere to put it, and she couldn't possibly throw it away. She blushed and tried to look severe and even a little bit short-sighted as she came up to them.

"Good morning," she said, copying her mother's voice. But that sounded so fearfully affected that she was ashamed, and stammered like a little girl, "Oh—er—have you come—is it about the marquee?"

"That's right, miss," said the tallest of the men, a lanky, freckled fellow, and he shifted his tool-bag, knocked back his straw hat, and smiled down at her. "That's about it."

His smile was so easy, so friendly, that Laura recovered. What nice eyes he had, small, but such a dark blue! And now she looked at the others, they were smiling too. "Cheer up, we won't bite," their smile seemed to say. How very nice workmen were! And what a beautiful morning! She mustn't mention the morning; she must be businesslike. The marquee.

"Well, what about the lily-lawn? Would that do?"

And she pointed to the lily-lawn with the hand that didn't hold the bread-and-butter. They turned, they stared in the direction. A little fat chap thrust out his underlip, and the tall fellow frowned.

---

1  *marquee* Tent.
2  *staves* Rods.

"I don't fancy it," said he. "Not conspicuous enough. You see, with a thing like a marquee," and he turned to Laura in his easy way, "you want to put it somewhere where it'll give you a bang slap in the eye, if you follow me."

Laura's upbringing made her wonder for a moment whether it was quite respectful of a workman to talk to her of bangs slap in the eye. But she did quite follow him.

"A corner of the tennis court," she suggested. "But the band's going to be in one corner."

"H'm, going to have a band, are you?" said another of the workmen. He was pale. He had a haggard look as his dark eyes scanned the tennis court. What was he thinking?

"Only a very small band," said Laura gently. Perhaps he wouldn't mind so much if the band was quite small. But the tall fellow interrupted.

"Look here, miss, that's the place. Against those trees. Over there. That'll do fine."

Against the karakas. Then the karaka trees would be hidden. And they were so lovely, with their broad, gleaming leaves, and their clusters of yellow fruit. They were like trees you imagined growing up on a desert island, proud, solitary, lifting their leaves and fruits to the sun in a kind of silent splendour. Must they be hidden by a marquee?

They must. Already the men had shouldered their staves and were making for the place. Only the tall fellow was left. He bent down, pinched a sprig of lavender, put his thumb and forefinger to his nose and snuffed up the smell. When Laura saw that gesture she forgot all about the karakas in her wonder at him caring for things like that—caring for the smell of lavender. How many men that she knew would have done such a thing. *Oh, how extraordinarily nice workmen were*, she thought. Why couldn't she have workmen for friends rather than the silly boys she danced with and who came to Sunday night supper? She would get on much better with men like these.

It's all the fault, she decided, as the tall fellow drew something on the back of an envelope, something that was to be looped up or left to hang, of these absurd class distinctions. Well, for her part, she didn't feel them. Not a bit, not an atom.... And now there came the chock-chock of wooden hammers. Someone whistled, someone sang out, "Are you right there, matey?" "Matey!" The friendliness of it, the—the—Just to prove how happy she was, just to show the tall fellow how at home she felt, and how she despised stupid conventions, Laura took a big bite of her bread-and-butter as she stared at the little drawing. She felt just like a work-girl.

"Laura, Laura, where are you? Telephone, Laura!" a voice cried from the house.

"Coming!" Away she skimmed, over the lawn, up the path, up the steps, across the veranda, and into the porch. In the hall her father and Laurie were brushing their hats ready to go to the office.

"I say, Laura," said Laurie very fast, "you might just give a squiz[1] at my coat before this afternoon. See if it wants pressing."

"I will," said she. Suddenly she couldn't stop herself. She ran at Laurie and gave him a small, quick squeeze. "Oh, I do love parties, don't you?" gasped Laura.

"Ra-ther," said Laurie's warm, boyish voice, and he squeezed his sister too, and gave her a gentle push. "Dash off to the telephone, old girl."

The telephone. "Yes, yes; oh yes. Kitty? Good morning, dear. Come to lunch? Do, dear. Delighted of course. It will only be a very scratch[2] meal—just the sandwich crusts and broken meringue-shells and what's left over. Yes, isn't it a perfect morning? Your white? Oh, I certainly should. One moment—hold the line. Mother's calling." And Laura sat back. "What, mother? Can't hear."

Mrs. Sheridan's voice floated down the stairs. "Tell her to wear that sweet hat she had on last Sunday."

"Mother says you're to wear that *sweet* hat you had on last Sunday. Good. One o'clock. Bye-bye."

Laura put back the receiver, flung her arms over her head, took a deep breath, stretched, and let them fall. "Huh," she sighed, and the moment after the sigh she sat up quickly. She was still, listening. All the doors in the house seemed to be open. The house was alive with soft, quick steps and running voices. The green baize door[3] that led to the kitchen regions swung open and shut with a muffled thud. And now there came a long, chuckling absurd sound. It was the heavy piano being moved on its stiff castors. But the air! If you stopped to notice, was the air always like this? Little faint winds were playing chase in at the tops of the windows, out at the doors. And there were two tiny spots of sun, one on the inkpot, one on a silver photograph frame, playing too. Darling little spots. Especially the one on the inkpot lid. It was quite warm. A warm little silver star. She could have kissed it.

The front door bell pealed, and there sounded the rustle of Sadie's print skirt on the stairs. A man's voice murmured; Sadie answered, careless, "I'm sure I don't know. Wait. I'll ask Mrs. Sheridan."

"What is it, Sadie?" Laura came into the hall.

"It's the florist, Miss Laura."

---

1   *squiz* New Zealand slang: a quick, close look.

2   *scratch* Quickly thrown together.

3   *green baize door* Swinging door that separated the servants' quarters from the rest of the house. Baize, a felt-like fabric, was often tacked to the inside of doors to insulate against noise.

It was, indeed. There, just inside the door, stood a wide, shallow tray full of pots of pink lilies. No other kind. Nothing but lilies—canna lilies, big pink flowers, wide open, radiant, almost frighteningly alive on bright crimson stems.

"O-oh, Sadie!" said Laura, and the sound was like a little moan. She crouched down as if to warm herself at that blaze of lilies; she felt they were in her fingers, on her lips, growing in her breast.

"It's some mistake," she said faintly. "Nobody ever ordered so many. Sadie, go and find mother."

But at that moment Mrs. Sheridan joined them.

"It's quite right," she said calmly. "Yes, I ordered them. Aren't they lovely?" She pressed Laura's arm. "I was passing the shop yesterday, and I saw them in the window, and I suddenly thought for once in my life I shall have enough canna lilies. The garden party will be a good excuse."

"But I thought you said you didn't mean to interfere," said Laura. Sadie had gone. The florist's man was still outside at his van. She put her arm round her mother's neck and gently, very gently, she bit her mother's ear.

"My darling child, you wouldn't like a logical mother, would you? Don't do that. Here's the man."

He carried more lilies still, another whole tray.

"Bank them up, just inside the door, on both sides of the porch, please," said Mrs. Sheridan. "Don't you agree, Laura?"

"Oh, I *do*, mother."

In the drawing room Meg, Jose, and good little Hans had at last succeeded in moving the piano.

"Now, if we put this chesterfield against the wall and move everything out of the room except the chairs, don't you think?"

"Quite."

"Hans, move these tables into the smoking room, and bring a sweeper to take these marks off the carpet and—one moment, Hans—" Jose loved giving orders to the servants, and they loved obeying her. She always made them feel they were taking part in some drama. "Tell Mother and Miss Laura to come here at once."

"Very good, Miss Jose."

She turned to Meg. "I want to hear what the piano sounds like, just in case I'm asked to sing this afternoon. Let's try over 'This Life is Weary'."

*Pom!* Ta-ta-ta *Tee*-ta! The piano burst out so passionately that Jose's face changed. She clasped her hands. She looked mournfully and enigmatically at her mother and Laura as they came in.

This Life is *Wee*-ary,
A Tear—a Sigh.

A Love that *Chan*-ges,
    This Life is *Wee*-ary,
A Tear—a Sigh.
A Love that *Chan*-ges,
And then ... Good-bye!

But at the word "Good-bye", and although the piano sounded more desperate than ever, her face broke into a brilliant, dreadfully unsympathetic smile.

"Aren't I in good voice, mummy?" she beamed.

This Life is *Wee*-ary,
Hope comes to Die,
A Dream—a *Wa*-kening.

But now Sadie interrupted them. "What is it, Sadie?"

"If you please, m'm, cook says have you got the flags for the sandwiches?"

"The flags for the sandwiches, Sadie?" echoed Mrs. Sheridan dreamily. And the children knew by her face that she hadn't got them. "Let me see." And she said to Sadie firmly, "Tell cook I'll let her have them in ten minutes."

Sadie went.

"Now, Laura," said her mother quickly, "come with me into the smoking room. I've got the names somewhere on the back of an envelope. You'll have to write them out for me. Meg, go upstairs this minute and take that wet thing off your head. Jose, run and finish dressing this instant. Do you hear me, children, or shall I have to tell your father when he comes home tonight? And—and, Jose, pacify cook if you do go into the kitchen, will you? I'm terrified of her this morning."

The envelope was found at last behind the dining-room clock, though how it had got there Mrs. Sheridan could not imagine.

"One of you children must have stolen it out of my bag, because I remember vividly—cream-cheese and lemon-curd. Have you done that?"

"Yes."

"Egg and—" Mrs. Sheridan held the envelope away from her. "It looks like mice. It can't be mice, can it?"

"Olive, pet," said Laura, looking over her shoulder.

"Yes, of course, olive. What a horrible combination it sounds. Egg and olive."

They were finished at last, and Laura took them off to the kitchen. She found Jose there pacifying the cook, who did not look at all terrifying.

"I have never seen such exquisite sandwiches," said Jose's rapturous voice. "How many kinds did you say there were, cook? Fifteen?"

"Fifteen, Miss Jose."

"Well, cook, I congratulate you."

Cook swept up crusts with the long sandwich knife, and smiled broadly.

"Godber's has come," announced Sadie, issuing out of the pantry. She had seen the man pass the window.

That meant that cream puffs had come. Godber's were famous for their cream puffs. Nobody ever thought of making them at home.

"Bring them in and put them on the table, my girl," ordered cook.

Sadie brought them in and went back to the door. Of course Laura and Jose were far too grown-up to really care about such things. All the same, they couldn't help agreeing that the puffs looked very attractive. Very. Cook began arranging them, shaking off the extra icing sugar.

"Don't they carry one back to all one's parties?" said Laura.

"I suppose they do," said practical Jose, who never liked to be carried back. "They look beautifully light and feathery, I must say."

"Have one each, my dears," said cook in her comfortable voice. "Yer ma won't know."

Oh, impossible. Fancy cream puffs so soon after breakfast. The very idea made one shudder. All the same, two minutes later Jose and Laura were licking their fingers with that absorbed inward look that only comes from whipped cream.

"Let's go into the garden, out by the back way," suggested Laura. "I want to see how the men are getting on with the marquee. They're such awfully nice men."

But the back door was blocked by cook, Sadie, Godber's man and Hans. Something had happened.

"Tuk-tuk-tuk," clucked cook like an agitated hen. Sadie had her hand clapped to her cheek as though she had a toothache. Hans's face was screwed up in the effort to understand. Only Godber's man seemed to be enjoying himself; it was his story.

"What's the matter? What happened?"

"There's been a horrible accident," said cook. "A man killed."

"A man killed! Where? How? When?"

But Godber's man wasn't going to have his story snatched from under his very nose.

"Know those little cottages just below here, miss?" Know them? Of course, she knew them. "Well, there's a young chap living there, name of *Scott*, a carter.[1] His horse shied at a traction-engine,[2] corner of Hawke Street this morning, and he was thrown out on the back of his head. Killed."

---

1    *carter* Driver of a horse-drawn vehicle used to transport goods.

2    *traction-engine* Steam locomotive used on roads.

"Dead!" Laura stared at Godber's man.

"Dead when they picked him up," said Godber's man with relish. "They were taking the body home as I come up here." And he said to the cook, "He's left a wife and five little ones."

"Jose, come here." Laura caught hold of her sister's sleeve and dragged her through the kitchen to the other side of the green baize door. There she paused and leaned against it. "Jose!" she said, horrified, "however are we going to stop everything?"

"Stop everything, Laura!" cried Jose in astonishment. "What do you mean?"

"Stop the garden party, of course." Why did Jose pretend?

But Jose was still more amazed. "Stop the garden party? My dear Laura, don't be so absurd. Of course we can't do anything of the kind. Nobody expects us to. Don't be so extravagant."

"But we can't possibly have a garden party with a man dead just outside the front gate."

That really was extravagant, for the little cottages were in a lane to themselves at the very bottom of a steep rise that led up to the house. A broad road ran between. True, they were far too near. They were the greatest possible eyesore and they had no right to be in that neighbourhood at all. They were little mean dwellings painted a chocolate brown. In the garden patches there was nothing but cabbage stalks, sick hens and tomato cans. The very smoke coming out of their chimneys was poverty-stricken. Little rags and shreds of smoke, so unlike the great silvery plumes that uncurled from the Sheridans' chimneys. Washerwomen lived in the lane and sweeps and a cobbler and a man whose house-front was studded all over with minute bird-cages. Children swarmed. When the Sheridans were little they were forbidden to set foot there because of the revolting language and of what they might catch. But since they were grown up, Laura and Laurie on their prowls sometimes walked through. It was disgusting and sordid. They came out with a shudder. But still one must go everywhere; one must see everything. So through they went.

"And just think of what the band would sound like to that poor woman," said Laura.

"Oh, Laura!" Jose began to be seriously annoyed. "If you're going to stop a band playing every time someone has an accident, you'll lead a very strenuous life. I'm every bit as sorry about it as you. I feel just as sympathetic." Her eyes hardened. She looked at her sister just as she used to when they were little and fighting together. "You won't bring a drunken workman back to life by being sentimental," she said softly.

"Drunk! Who said he was drunk?" Laura turned furiously on Jose. She said just as they had used to say on those occasions, "I'm going straight up to tell mother."

"Do, dear," cooed Jose.

"Mother, can I come into your room?" Laura turned the big glass door-knob.

"Of course, child. Why, what's the matter? What's given you such a co-lour?" And Mrs. Sheridan turned round from her dressing-table. She was trying on a new hat.

"Mother, a man's been killed," began Laura.

"*Not* in the garden?" interrupted her mother.

"No, no!"

"Oh, what a fright you gave me!" Mrs. Sheridan sighed with relief, and took off the big hat and held it on her knees.

"But listen, mother," said Laura. Breathless, half-choking, she told the dreadful story. "Of course, we can't have our party, can we?" she pleaded. "The band and everybody arriving. They'd hear us, mother; they're nearly neighbours!"

To Laura's astonishment her mother behaved just like Jose; it was harder to bear because she seemed amused. She refused to take Laura seriously. "But, my dear child, use your common sense. It's only by accident we've heard of it. If someone had died there normally—and I can't understand how they keep alive in those poky little holes—we should still be having our party, shouldn't we?"

Laura had to say "yes" to that, but she felt it was all wrong. She sat down on her mother's sofa and pinched the cushion frill.

"Mother, isn't it really terribly heartless of us?" she asked.

"Darling!" Mrs. Sheridan got up and came over to her, carrying the hat. Before Laura could stop her she had popped it on. "My child!" said her mother, "the hat is yours. It's made for you. It's much too young for me. I have never seen you look such a picture. Look at yourself!" And she held up her hand-mirror.

"But, mother," Laura began again. She couldn't look at herself; she turned aside.

This time Mrs. Sheridan lost patience just as Jose had done.

"You are being very absurd, Laura," she said coldly. "People like that don't expect sacrifices from us. And it's not very sympathetic to spoil everybody's enjoyment as you're doing now."

"I don't understand," said Laura, and she walked quickly out of the room into her own bedroom. There, quite by chance, the first thing she saw was this charming girl in the mirror, in her black hat trimmed with gold daisies and a long black velvet ribbon. Never had she imagined she could look like that. Is mother right? she thought. And now she hoped her mother was right. Am I being extravagant? Perhaps it was extravagant. Just for a moment she had another glimpse of that poor woman and those little children, and the body being carried into the house. But it all seemed blurred, unreal, like a picture in the newspaper. I'll remember it again after the party's over, she decided. And somehow that seemed quite the best plan....

Lunch was over by half-past one. By half-past two they were all ready for the fray. The green-coated band had arrived and was established in a corner of the tennis court.

"My dear!" trilled Kitty Maitland, "aren't they too like frogs for words? You ought to have arranged them round the pond with the conductor in the middle on a leaf."

Laurie arrived and hailed them on his way to dress. At the sight of him Laura remembered the accident again. She wanted to tell him. If Laurie agreed with the others, then it was bound to be all right. And she followed him into the hall.

"Laurie!"

"Hallo!" He was halfway upstairs, but when he turned round and saw Laura he suddenly puffed out his cheeks and goggled his eyes at her. "My word, Laura! You do look stunning," said Laurie. "What an absolutely topping hat!"

Laura said faintly "Is it?" and smiled up at Laurie, and didn't tell him after all.

Soon after that people began coming in streams. The band struck up; the hired waiters ran from the house to the marquee. Wherever you looked there were couples strolling, bending to the flowers, greeting, moving on over the lawn. They were like bright birds that had alighted in the Sheridans' garden for this one afternoon, on their way to—where? Ah, what happiness it is to be with people who all are happy, to press hands, press cheeks, smile into eyes.

"Darling Laura, how well you look!"

"What a becoming hat, child!"

"Laura, you look quite Spanish. I've never seen you look so striking."

And Laura, glowing, answered softly, "Have you had tea? Won't you have an ice? The passion-fruit ices really are rather special." She ran to her father and begged him: "Daddy darling, can't the band have something to drink?"

And the perfect afternoon slowly ripened, slowly faded, slowly its petals closed.

"Never a more delightful garden party ..." "The greatest success ..." "Quite the most ..."

Laura helped her mother with the good-byes. They stood side by side on the porch till it was all over.

"All over, all over, thank heaven," said Mrs. Sheridan. "Round up the others, Laura. Let's go and have some fresh coffee. I'm exhausted. Yes, it's been very successful. But oh, these parties, these parties! Why will you children insist on giving parties!" And they all of them sat down in the deserted marquee.

"Have a sandwich, daddy dear. I wrote the flag."

"Thanks." Mr. Sheridan took a bite and the sandwich was gone. He took another. "I suppose you didn't hear of a beastly accident that happened today?" he said.

"My dear," said Mrs. Sheridan, holding up her hand, "we did. It nearly ruined the party. Laura insisted we should put it off."

"Oh, mother!" Laura didn't want to be teased about it.

"It was a horrible affair all the same," said Mr. Sheridan. "The chap was married too. Lived just below in the lane, and leaves a wife and half a dozen kiddies, so they say."

An awkward little silence fell. Mrs. Sheridan fidgeted with her cup. Really, it was very tactless of father....

Suddenly she looked up. There on the table were all those sandwiches, cakes, puffs, all uneaten, all going to be wasted. She had one of her brilliant ideas.

"I know," she said. "Let's make up a basket. Let's send that poor creature some of this perfectly good food. At any rate, it will be the greatest treat for the children. Don't you agree? And she's sure to have neighbours calling in and so on. What a point to have it all ready prepared. Laura!" She jumped up. "Get me the big basket out of the stairs cupboard."

"But, mother, do you really think it's a good idea?" said Laura.

Again, how curious, she seemed to be different from them all. To take scraps from their party. Would the poor woman really like that?

"Of course! What's the matter with you today? An hour or two ago you were insisting on us being sympathetic."

Oh well! Laura ran for the basket. It was filled, it was now heaped by her mother.

"Take it yourself, darling," said she. "Run down just as you are. No, wait, take the arum lilies too. People of that class are so impressed by arum lilies."

"The stems will ruin her lace frock," said practical Jose.

So they would. Just in time. "Only the basket, then. And, Laura!"—her mother followed her out of the marquee—"don't on any account—"

"What, mother?"

No, better not put such ideas into the child's head! "Nothing! Run along."

It was just growing dusky as Laura shut their garden gates. A big dog ran by like a shadow. The road gleamed white, and down below in the hollow the little cottages were in deep shade. How quiet it seemed after the afternoon. Here she was going down the hill to somewhere where a man lay dead, and she couldn't realize it. Why couldn't she? She stopped a minute. And it seemed to her that kisses, voices, tinkling spoons, laughter, the smell of crushed grass were somehow inside her. She had no room for anything else. How strange!

She looked up at the pale sky, and all she thought was, "Yes, it was the most successful party."

Now the broad road was crossed. The lane began, smoky and dark. Women in shawls and men's tweed caps hurried by. Men hung over the palings; the children played in the doorways. A low hum came from the mean little cottages. In some of them there was a flicker of light, and a shadow, crab-like, moved across the window. Laura bent her head and hurried on. She wished now she had put on a coat. How her frock shone! And the big hat with the velvet streamer—if only it was another hat! Were the people looking at her? They must be. It was a mistake to have come; she knew all along it was a mistake. Should she go back even now?

No, too late. This was the house. It must be. A dark knot of people stood outside. Beside the gate an old, old woman with a crutch sat in a chair, watching. She had her feet on a newspaper. The voices stopped as Laura drew near. The group parted. It was as though she was expected, as though they had known she was coming here.

Laura was terribly nervous. Tossing the velvet ribbon over her shoulder, she said to a woman standing by, "Is this Mrs. Scott's house?" and the woman, smiling queerly, said, "It is, my lass."

Oh, to be away from this! She actually said, "Help me, God," as she walked up the tiny path and knocked. To be away from those staring eyes, or to be covered up in anything, one of those women's shawls even. I'll just leave the basket and go, she decided. I shan't even wait for it to be emptied.

Then the door opened. A little woman in black showed in the gloom.

Laura said, "Are you Mrs. Scott?" But to her horror the woman answered, "Walk in, please, miss," and she was shut in the passage.

"No," said Laura, "I don't want to come in. I only want to leave this basket. Mother sent—"

The little woman in the gloomy passage seemed not to have heard her. "Step this way, please, miss," she said in an oily voice, and Laura followed her.

She found herself in a wretched little low kitchen, lighted by a smoky lamp. There was a woman sitting before the fire.

"Em," said the little creature who had let her in. "Em! It's a young lady." She turned to Laura. She said meaningly, "I'm 'er sister, miss. You'll excuse 'er, won't you?"

"Oh, but of course!" said Laura. "Please, please don't disturb her. I—I only want to leave—"

But at that moment the woman at the fire turned round. Her face, puffed up, red, with swollen eyes and swollen lips, looked terrible. She seemed as though she couldn't understand why Laura was there. What did it mean? Why was this stranger standing in the kitchen with a basket? What was it all about? And the poor face puckered up again.

"All right, my dear," said the other. "I'll thenk the young lady."

And again she began, "You'll excuse her, miss, I'm sure," and her face, swollen too, tried an oily smile.

Laura only wanted to get out, to get away. She was back in the passage. The door opened. She walked straight through into the bedroom where the dead man was lying.

"You'd like a look at 'im, wouldn't you?" said Em's sister, and she brushed past Laura over to the bed. "Don't be afraid, my lass,"—and now her voice sounded fond and sly, and fondly she drew down the sheet—"'e looks a picture. There's nothing to show. Come along, my dear."

Laura came.

There lay a young man, fast asleep—sleeping so soundly, so deeply, that he was far, far away from them both. Oh, so remote, so peaceful. He was dreaming. Never wake him up again. His head was sunk in the pillows, his eyes were closed; they were blind under the closed eyelids. He was given up to his dream. What did garden parties and baskets and lace frocks matter to him? He was far from all those things. He was wonderful, beautiful. While they were laughing and while the band was playing, this marvel had come to the lane. Happy ... happy.... All is well, said that sleeping face. This is just as it should be. I am content.

But all the same you had to cry, and she couldn't go out of the room without saying something to him. Laura gave a loud childish sob.

"Forgive my hat," she said.

And this time she didn't wait for Em's sister. She found her way out of the door, down the path, past all those dark people. At the corner of the lane she met Laurie.

He stepped out of the shadow. "Is that you, Laura?"

"Yes."

"Mother was getting anxious. Was it all right?"

"Yes, quite. Oh, Laurie!" She took his arm, she pressed up against him.

"I say, you're not crying, are you?" asked her brother.

Laura shook her head. She was.

Laurie put his arm round her shoulder. "Don't cry," he said in his warm, loving voice. "Was it awful?"

"No," sobbed Laura. "It was simply marvellous. But, Laurie—" She stopped, she looked at her brother. "Isn't life," she stammered, "isn't life—" But what life was she couldn't explain. No matter. He quite understood.

"*Isn't* it, darling?" said Laurie.

—1922

# William Faulkner

1897–1962

As the sheer volume of the critical response to his work testifies, William Faulkner is one of America's most singular and difficult writers. One must learn how to read Faulkner in order to navigate the copious language, the kaleidoscopically shifting points of view, and the roiling stream-of-consciousness narration. Whereas many of his short stories are relatively conventional, novels like *The Sound and the Fury* (1929), *As I Lay Dying* (1930), and *Absalom, Absalom!* (1936) reject traditional narrative structures, withhold authorial commentary, and erode distinctions between past and present, truth and memory, and perception and reality.

Today Faulkner is recognized for his masterful ability to create "flesh-and-blood, living, suffering, anguishing human beings," but for much of his career he was regarded as a regional Southern writer of small importance. Though he would eventually receive the 1949 Nobel Prize in Literature, all his major novels were out of print just a few years before. In part this is because of their difficulty, but critics also objected to the "pathological delinquency" and "pageant of degeneracy" that they found in his work. But in Faulkner's view, the writer must suppress no tendency or tangent of human behaviour; it is not for him to judge, preach, or proselytize but only to show human beings "in the furious motion of being alive," to tell about "man in his constant struggle with his own heart, with the hearts of others, or with his environment."

"A Rose for Emily" (1930), Faulkner's best-known story, exemplifies his interest in the outer limits of human nature. Yet it is more than a tale of horror or a case study in abnormal psychology: like much of his fiction, it is also concerned with the grip of the myths and memories of a dead but unburied Southern past.

# A Rose for Emily

## I

When Miss Emily Grierson died, our whole town went to her funeral: the men through a sort of respectful affection for a fallen monument, the women mostly out of curiosity to see the inside of her house, which no one save an old manservant—a combined gardener and cook—had seen in at least ten years.

It was a big, squarish frame house that had once been white, decorated with cupolas and spires and scrolled balconies in the heavily lightsome style of the seventies, set on what had once been our most select street. But garages and cotton gins had encroached and obliterated even the august names of that neighbourhood; only Miss Emily's house was left, lifting its stubborn and coquettish decay above the cotton wagons and the gasoline pumps—an eyesore among eyesores. And now Miss Emily had gone to join the representatives of those august names where they lay in the cedar-bemused cemetery among the ranked and anonymous graves of Union and Confederate soldiers who fell at the battle of Jefferson.[1]

Alive, Miss Emily had been a tradition, a duty, and a care; a sort of hereditary obligation upon the town, dating from that day in 1894 when Colonel Sartoris, the mayor—he who fathered the edict that no Negro woman should appear on the streets without an apron—remitted her taxes, the dispensation dating from the death of her father on into perpetuity. Not that Miss Emily would have accepted charity. Colonel Sartoris invented an involved tale to the effect that Miss Emily's father had loaned money to the town, which the town, as a matter of business, preferred this way of repaying. Only a man of Colonel Sartoris' generation and thought could have invented it, and only a woman could have believed it.

When the next generation, with its more modern ideas, became mayors and aldermen, this arrangement created some little dissatisfaction. On the first of the year they mailed her a tax notice. February came, and there was no reply. They wrote her a formal letter, asking her to call at the sheriff's office at her convenience. A week later the mayor wrote her himself, offering to call or to send his car for her, and received in reply a note on paper of an archaic shape, in a thin, flowing calligraphy in faded ink, to the effect that she no longer went out at all. The tax notice was also enclosed, without comment.

They called a special meeting of the Board of Aldermen. A deputation waited upon her, knocked at the door through which no visitor had passed since she ceased giving china-painting lessons eight or ten years earlier. They were admitted by the old Negro into a dim hall from which a stairway mounted into still more shadow. It smelled of dust and disuse—a close, dank smell. The Negro led them into the parlour. It was furnished in heavy, leather-covered furniture. When the Negro opened the blinds of one window, a faint dust rose sluggishly about their thighs, spinning with slow motes in the single sun-ray. On a tarnished gilt easel before the fireplace stood a crayon portrait of Miss Emily's father.

They rose when she entered—a small, fat woman in black, with a thin gold chain descending to her waist and vanishing into her belt, leaning on an ebony cane with a tarnished gold head. Her skeleton was small and spare; perhaps that was why what would have been merely plumpness in another was obesity in her. She looked bloated, like a body long submerged in motionless water, and of that pallid hue. Her eyes, lost in the fatty ridges of her face, looked like

---

1   *Union and ... Jefferson* I.e., casualties of the American Civil War (1861–65).

two small pieces of coal pressed into a lump of dough as they moved from one face to another while the visitors stated their errand.

She did not ask them to sit. She just stood in the door and listened quietly until the spokesman came to a stumbling halt. Then they could hear the invisible watch ticking at the end of the gold chain.

Her voice was dry and cold. "I have no taxes in Jefferson. Colonel Sartoris explained it to me. Perhaps one of you can gain access to the city records and satisfy yourselves."

"But we have. We are the city authorities, Miss Emily. Didn't you get a notice from the sheriff, signed by him?"

"I received a paper, yes," Miss Emily said. "Perhaps he considers himself the sheriff.... I have no taxes in Jefferson."

"But there is nothing on the books to show that, you see. We must go by the—"

"See Colonel Sartoris. I have no taxes in Jefferson."

"But Miss Emily—"

"See Colonel Sartoris." (Colonel Sartoris had been dead almost ten years.) "I have no taxes in Jefferson. Tobe!" The Negro appeared. "Show these gentlemen out."

## II

So she vanquished them, horse and foot, just as she had vanquished their fathers thirty years before about the smell. That was two years after her father's death and a short time after her sweetheart—the one we believed would marry her—had deserted her. After her father's death she went out very little; after her sweetheart went away, people hardly saw her at all. A few of the ladies had the temerity to call, but were not received, and the only sign of life about the place was the Negro man—a young man then—going in and out with a market basket.

"Just as if a man—any man—could keep a kitchen properly," the ladies said; so they were not surprised when the smell developed. It was another link between the gross, teeming world and the high and mighty Griersons.

A neighbour, a woman, complained to the mayor, Judge Stevens, eighty years old.

"But what will you have me do about it, madam?" he said.

"Why, send her word to stop it," the woman said. "Isn't there a law?"

"I'm sure that won't be necessary," Judge Stevens said. "It's probably just a snake or a rat that nigger[1] of hers killed in the yard. I'll speak to him about it."

---

1   *nigger* This pejorative term remained in frequent use by many white Americans in the South until well into the 1960s.

The next day he received two more complaints, one from a man who came in diffident deprecation. "We really must do something about it, Judge. I'd be the last one in the world to bother Miss Emily, but we've got to do something." That night the Board of Aldermen met—three grey-beards and one younger man, a member of the rising generation.

"It's simple enough," he said. "Send her word to have her place cleaned up. Give her a certain time to do it in, and if she don't...."

"Dammit, sir," Judge Stevens said, "will you accuse a lady to her face of smelling bad?"

So the next night, after midnight, four men crossed Miss Emily's lawn and slunk about the house like burglars, sniffing along the base of the brickwork and at the cellar openings while one of them performed a regular sowing motion with his hand out of a sack slung from his shoulder. They broke open the cellar door and sprinkled lime there, and in all the outbuildings. As they recrossed the lawn, a window that had been dark was lighted and Miss Emily sat in it, the light behind her, and her upright torso motionless as that of an idol. They crept quietly across the lawn and into the shadow of the locusts that lined the street. After a week or two the smell went away.

That was when people had begun to feel really sorry for her. People in our town, remembering how old lady Wyatt, her great-aunt, had gone completely crazy at last, believed that the Griersons held themselves a little too high for what they really were. None of the young men were quite good enough for Miss Emily and such. We had long thought of them as a tableau; Miss Emily a slender figure in white in the background, her father a spraddled silhouette in the foreground, his back to her and clutching a horsewhip, the two of them framed by the backflung front door. So when she got to be thirty and was still single, we were not pleased exactly, but vindicated; even with insanity in the family she wouldn't have turned down all of her chances if they had really materialized.

When her father died, it got about that the house was all that was left to her; and in a way, people were glad. At last they could pity Miss Emily. Being left alone, and a pauper, she had become humanized. Now she too would know the old thrill and the old despair of a penny more or less.

The day after his death all the ladies prepared to call at the house and offer condolence and aid, as is our custom. Miss Emily met them at the door, dressed as usual and with no trace of grief on her face. She told them that her father was not dead. She did that for three days, with the ministers calling on her, and the doctors, trying to persuade her to let them dispose of the body. Just as they were about to resort to law and force, she broke down, and they buried her father quickly.

We did not say she was crazy then. We believed she had to do that. We remembered all the young men her father had driven away, and we knew that with nothing left, she would have to cling to that which had robbed her, as people will.

## III

She was sick for a long time. When we saw her again, her hair was cut short, making her look like a girl, with a vague resemblance to those angels in coloured church windows—sort of tragic and serene.

The town had just let the contracts for paving the sidewalks, and in the summer after her father's death they began to work. The construction company came with niggers and mules and machinery, and a foreman named Homer Barron, a Yankee[1]—a big, dark, ready man, with a big voice and eyes lighter than his face. The little boys would follow in groups to hear him cuss the niggers, and the niggers singing in time to the rise and fall of picks. Pretty soon he knew everybody in town. Whenever you heard a lot of laughing anywhere about the square, Homer Barron would be in the centre of the group. Presently we began to see him and Miss Emily on Sunday afternoons driving in the yellow-wheeled buggy and the matched team of bays from the livery stable.

At first we were glad that Miss Emily would have an interest, because the ladies all said, "Of course a Grierson would not think seriously of a Northerner, a day labourer." But there were still others, older people, who said that even grief could not cause a real lady to forget *noblesse oblige*[2]—without calling it *noblesse oblige*. They just said, "Poor Emily. Her kinsfolk should come to her." She had some kin in Alabama; but years ago her father had fallen out with them over the estate of old lady Wyatt, the crazy woman, and there was no communication between the two families. They had not even been represented at the funeral.

And as soon as the old people said, "Poor Emily," the whispering began. "Do you suppose it's really so?" they said to one another. "Of course it is. What else could...." This behind their hands; rustling of craned silk and satin behind jalousies[3] closed upon the sun of Sunday afternoon as the thin, swift clop-clop-clop of the matched team passed: "Poor Emily."

She carried her head high enough—even when we believed that she was fallen. It was as if she demanded more than ever the recognition of her dignity as the last Grierson; as if it had wanted that touch of earthiness to reaffirm her imperviousness. Like when she bought the rat poison, the arsenic. That was over a year after they had begun to say "Poor Emily," and while the two female cousins were visiting her.

---

1   *Yankee* Person from the Northern states.
2   *noblesse oblige* French: nobility obliges. In this case, the obligation of social élites to take an interest in those "below" them.
3   *jalousies* Shutters.

"I want some poison," she said to the druggist. She was over thirty then, still a slight woman, though thinner than usual, with cold, haughty black eyes in a face the flesh of which was strained across the temples and about the eyesockets as you imagine a lighthouse-keeper's face ought to look. "I want some poison," she said.

"Yes, Miss Emily. What kind? For rats and such? I'd recom—"

"I want the best you have. I don't care what kind."

The druggist named several. "They'll kill anything up to an elephant. But what you want is—"

"Arsenic," Miss Emily said. "Is that a good one?"

"Is ... arsenic? Yes, ma'am. But what you want—"

"I want arsenic."

The druggist looked down at her. She looked back at him, erect, her face like a strained flag. "Why, of course," the druggist said. "If that's what you want. But the law requires you to tell what you are going to use it for."

Miss Emily just stared at him, her head tilted back in order to look him eye for eye, until he looked away and went and got the arsenic and wrapped it up. The Negro delivery boy brought her the package; the druggist didn't come back. When she opened the package at home there was written on the box, under the skull and bones: "For rats."

IV

So the next day we all said, "She will kill herself"; and we said it would be the best thing. When she had first begun to be seen with Homer Barron, we had said, "She will marry him." Then we said, "She will persuade him yet," because Homer himself had remarked—he liked men, and it was known that he drank with the younger men in the Elk's Club—that he was not a marrying man. Later we said, "Poor Emily," behind the jalousies as they passed on Sunday afternoon in the glittering buggy, Miss Emily with her head high and Homer Barron with his hat cocked and a cigar in his teeth, reins and whip in a yellow glove.

Then some of the ladies began to say that it was a disgrace to the town and a bad example to the young people. The men did not want to interfere, but at last the ladies forced the Baptist minister—Miss Emily's people were Episcopal[1]—to call upon her. He would never divulge what happened during that interview, but he refused to go back again. The next Sunday they again drove about the streets, and the following day the minister's wife wrote to Miss Emily's relations in Alabama.

---

1   *Baptist ... Episcopal* In America at this time, aristocratic families were more likely to be Episcopalian and working-class families were more likely to be Baptist.

So she had blood-kin under her roof again and we sat back to watch developments. At first nothing happened. Then we were sure that they were to be married. We learned that Miss Emily had been to the jeweller's and ordered a man's toilet set in silver, with the letters H.B. on each piece. Two days later we learned that she had bought a complete outfit of men's clothing, including a nightshirt, and we said, "They are married." We were really glad. We were glad because the two female cousins were even more Grierson than Miss Emily had ever been.

So we were not surprised when Homer Barron—the streets had been finished some time since—was gone. We were a little disappointed that there was not a public blowing-off, but we believed that he had gone on to prepare for Miss Emily's coming, or to give her a chance to get rid of the cousins. (By that time it was a cabal,[1] and we were all Miss Emily's allies to help circumvent the cousins.) Sure enough, after another week they departed. And, as we had expected all along, within three days Homer Barron was back in town. A neighbour saw the Negro man admit him at the kitchen door at dusk one evening.

And that was the last we saw of Homer Barron. And of Miss Emily for some time. The Negro man went in and out with the market basket, but the front door remained closed. Now and then we would see her at a window for a moment, as the men did that night when they sprinkled the lime, but for almost six months she did not appear on the streets. Then we knew that this was to be expected too: as if that quality of her father which had thwarted her woman's life so many times had been too virulent and too furious to die.

When we next saw Miss Emily, she had grown fat and her hair was turning grey. During the next few years it grew greyer and greyer until it attained an even pepper-and-salt iron-grey, when it ceased turning. Up to the day of her death at seventy-four it was still that vigorous iron-grey, like the hair of an active man.

From that time on her front door remained closed, save for a period of six or seven years, when she was about forty, during which she gave lessons in china-painting. She fitted up a studio in one of the downstairs rooms, where the daughters and grand-daughters of Colonel Sartoris' contemporaries were sent to her with the same regularity and in the same spirit that they were sent on Sundays with a twenty-five cent piece for the collection plate. Meanwhile her taxes had been remitted.

Then the newer generation became the backbone and the spirit of the town, and the painting pupils grew up and fell away and did not send their children to her with boxes of colour and tedious brushes and pictures cut from

---

1    *cabal* Covert group of conspirators.

the ladies' magazines. The front door closed upon the last one and remained closed for good. When the town got free postal delivery Miss Emily alone refused to let them fasten the metal numbers above her door and attach a mailbox to it. She would not listen to them.

Daily, monthly, yearly we watched the Negro grow greyer and more stooped, going in and out with the market basket. Each December we sent her a tax notice, which would be returned by the post office a week later, unclaimed. Now and then we would see her in one of the downstairs windows—she had evidently shut up the top floor of the house—like the carven torso of an idol in a niche, looking or not looking at us, we could never tell which. Thus she passed from generation to generation—dear, inescapable, impervious, tranquil, and perverse.

And so she died. Fell ill in the house filled with dust and shadows, with only a doddering Negro man to wait on her. We did not even know she was sick; we had long since given up trying to get any information from the Negro. He talked to no one, probably not even to her, for his voice had grown harsh and rusty, as if from disuse.

She died in one of the downstairs rooms, in a heavy walnut bed with a curtain, her grey head propped on a pillow yellow and mouldy with age and lack of sunlight.

V

The Negro met the first of the ladies at the front door and let them in, with their hushed, sibilant voices and their quick, curious glances, and then he disappeared. He walked right through the house and out the back and was not seen again.

The two female cousins came at once. They held the funeral on the second day, with the town coming to look at Miss Emily beneath a mass of bought flowers, with the crayon face of her father musing profoundly above the bier and the ladies sibilant and macabre; and the very old men—some in their brushed Confederate uniforms—on the porch and the lawn, talking of Miss Emily as if she had been a contemporary of theirs, believing that they had danced with her and courted her perhaps, confusing time with its mathematical progression, as the old do, to whom all the past is not a diminishing road, but, instead, a huge meadow which no winter ever quite touches, divided from them now by the narrow bottleneck of the most recent decade of years.

Already we knew that there was one room in that region above stairs which no one had seen in forty years, and which would have to be forced. They waited until Miss Emily was decently in the ground before they opened it.

The violence of breaking down the door seemed to fill this room with pervading dust. A thin, acrid pall as of the tomb seemed to lie everywhere upon this room decked and furnished as for a bridal: upon the valance curtains of faded rose colour, upon the rose-shaded lights, upon the dressing table, upon the delicate array of crystal and the man's toilet things backed with tarnished silver, silver so tarnished that the monogram was obscured. Among them lay a collar and tie, as if they had just been removed, which, lifted, left upon the surface a pale crescent in the dust. Upon a chair hung the suit, carefully folded; beneath it the two mute shoes and the discarded socks.

The man himself lay in the bed.

For a long while we just stood there, looking down at the profound and fleshless grin. The body had apparently once lain in the attitude of an embrace, but now the long sleep that outlasts love, that conquers even the grimace of love, had cuckolded him. What was left of him, rotted beneath what was left of the nightshirt, had become inextricable from the bed in which he lay; and upon him and upon the pillow beside him lay that even coating of the patient and biding dust.

Then we noticed that in the second pillow was the indentation of a head. One of us lifted something from it, and leaning forward, that faint and invisible dust dry and acrid in the nostrils, we saw a long strand of iron-grey hair.

—1930

# Ernest Hemingway
## 1899–1961

Ernest Hemingway is considered one of the great American authors of the twentieth century. His influence can be seen in the objective style of writing he propagated, characterized by sparse sentences devoid of embellishment. Hemingway famously argues for his technique in *Death in the Afternoon* (1932): "If a writer of prose knows enough about what he is writing about he may omit things that he knows and the reader, if the writer is writing truly enough, will have a feeling of those things as strongly as though the writer had stated them. The dignity of movement of an iceberg is due to only one-eighth of it being above water." In 1952, Hemingway was awarded the Pulitzer Prize for his novel *The Old Man and the Sea*, the story of a Cuban fisherman's quest to reel in a giant marlin. In 1954, he was awarded the Nobel Prize in Literature for his "mastery of the art of narrative, most recently demonstrated in *The Old Man and the Sea*, and for the influence that he has exerted on contemporary style."

In 1918, Hemingway travelled to Italy as an ambulance driver for the American Red Cross. His injury and recuperation later that year removed him from service, but the experience inspired his 1929 novel, *A Farewell to Arms*. His first novel, *The Sun Also Rises* (1926), drew from his life as an expatriate in Paris in the 1920s. During the Spanish Civil War (1936–39), Hemingway raised money for the Republican cause and travelled throughout Spain as a journalist. This inspired his greatest commercial success, the 1939 novel *For Whom the Bell Tolls*, a semi-autobiographical story of a young American who fights fascism.

Hemingway's writing reflects his passion for pursuits such as bullfighting, fishing, and hunting, and often examines the cruel legacy of war. In presenting the Nobel Prize to Hemingway, Anders Osterling said: "It may be true that Hemingway's earlier writings display brutal, cynical, and callous sides which may be considered at variance with the Nobel Prize's requirement for a work of an ideal tendency. But on the other hand, he also possesses a heroic pathos which forms the basic element in his awareness of life, a manly love of danger and adventure with a natural admiration for every individual who fights the good fight in a world of reality overshadowed by violence and death."

Hemingway committed suicide in Idaho in 1961, after a period of serious depression.

# A Clean, Well-Lighted Place

It was very late and every one had left the café except an old man who sat in the shadow the leaves of the tree made against the electric light. In the day time the street was dusty, but at night the dew settled the dust and the old man liked to sit late because he was deaf and now at night it was quiet and he felt the difference. The two waiters inside the café knew that the old man was a little drunk, and while he was a good client they knew that if he became too drunk he would leave without paying, so they kept watch on him.

"Last week he tried to commit suicide," one waiter said.

"Why?"

"He was in despair."

"What about?"

"Nothing."

"How do you know it was nothing?"

"He has plenty of money."

They sat together at a table that was close against the wall near the door of the café and looked at the terrace where the tables were all empty except where the old man sat in the shadow of the leaves of the tree that moved slightly in the wind. A girl and a soldier went by in the street. The street light shone on the brass number on his collar. The girl wore no head covering and hurried beside him.

"The guard will pick him up," one waiter said.

"What does it matter if he gets what he's after?"

"He had better get off the street now. The guard will get him. They went by five minutes ago."

The old man sitting in the shadow rapped on his saucer with his glass. The younger waiter went over to him.

"What do you want?"

The old man looked at him. "Another brandy," he said.

"You'll be drunk," the waiter said. The old man looked at him. The waiter went away.

"He'll stay all night," he said to his colleague. "I'm sleepy now. I never get into bed before three o'clock. He should have killed himself last week."

The waiter took the brandy bottle and another saucer from the counter inside the café and marched out to the old man's table. He put down the saucer and poured the glass full of brandy.

"You should have killed yourself last week," he said to the deaf man. The old man motioned with his finger. "A little more," he said. The waiter poured on into the glass so that the brandy slopped over and ran down the stem into the top saucer of the pile. "Thank you," the old man said. The waiter took the bottle back inside the café. He sat down at the table with his colleague again.

"He's drunk now," he said.

"He's drunk every night."

"What did he want to kill himself for?"

"How should I know."

"How did he do it?"

"He hung himself with a rope."

"Who cut him down?"

"His niece."

"Why did they do it?"

"Fear for his soul."

"How much money has he got?"

"He's got plenty."

"He must be eighty years old."

"Anyway I should say he was eighty."

"I wish he would go home. I never get to bed before three o'clock. What kind of hour is that to go to bed?"

"He stays up because he likes it."

"He's lonely. I'm not lonely. I have a wife waiting in bed for me."

"He had a wife once too."

"A wife would be no good to him now."

"You can't tell. He might be better with a wife."

"His niece looks after him."

"I know. You said she cut him down."

"I wouldn't want to be that old. An old man is a nasty thing."

"Not always. This old man is clean. He drinks without spilling. Even now, drunk. Look at him."

"I don't want to look at him. I wish he would go home. He has no regard for those who must work."

The old man looked from his glass across the square, then over at the waiters.

"Another brandy," he said, pointing to his glass. The waiter who was in a hurry came over.

"Finished," he said, speaking with that omission of syntax stupid people employ when talking to drunken people or foreigners. "No more tonight. Close now."

"Another," said the old man.

"No. Finished." The waiter wiped the edge of the table with a towel and shook his head.

The old man stood up, slowly counted the saucers, took a leather coin purse from his pocket and paid for the drinks, leaving half a peseta tip.

The waiter watched him go down the street, a very old man walking unsteadily but with dignity.

"Why didn't you let him stay and drink?" the unhurried waiter asked. They were putting up the shutters. "It is not half-past two."

"I want to go home to bed."

"What is an hour?"

"More to me than to him."

"An hour is the same."

"You talk like an old man yourself. He can buy a bottle and drink at home."

"It's not the same."

"No, it is not," agreed the waiter with a wife. He did not wish to be unjust. He was only in a hurry.

"And you? You have no fear of going home before your usual hour?"

"Are you trying to insult me?"

"No, hombre,[1] only to make a joke."

"No," the waiter who was in a hurry said, rising from pulling down the metal shutters. "I have confidence. I am all confidence."

"You have youth, confidence, and a job," the older waiter said. "You have everything."

"And what do you lack?"

"Everything but work."

"You have everything I have."

"No. I have never had confidence and I am not young."

"Come on. Stop talking nonsense and lock up."

"I am of those who like to stay late at the café," the older waiter said. "With all those who do not want to go to bed. With all those who need a light for the night."

"I want to go home and into bed."

"We are of two different kinds," the older waiter said. He was now dressed to go home. "It is not only a question of youth and confidence although those things are very beautiful. Each night I am reluctant to close up because there may be some one who needs the café."

"Hombre, there are bodegas[2] open all night long."

"You do not understand. This is a clean and pleasant café. It is well lighted. The light is very good and also, now, there are shadows of the leaves."

---

1    *hombre* Spanish: man, dude.
2    *bodegas* Wine sellers, cheap drinking establishments.

"Good night," said the younger waiter.

"Good night," the other said. Turning off the electric light he continued the conversation with himself. It is the light of course but it is necessary that the place be clean and pleasant. You do not want music. Certainly you do not want music. Nor can you stand before a bar with dignity although that is all that is provided for these hours. What did he fear? It was not a fear or dread. It was a nothing that he knew too well. It was all a nothing and a man was nothing too. It was only that and light was all it needed and a certain cleanness and order. Some lived in it and never felt it but he knew it all was nada y pues nada[1] y nada y pues nada. Our nada who art in nada, nada be thy name thy kingdom nada thy will be nada in nada as it is in nada. Give us this nada our daily nada and nada us our nada as we nada our nadas and nada us not into nada but deliver us from nada; pues nada. Hail nothing full of nothing, nothing is with thee.[2] He smiled and stood before a bar with a shining steam pressure coffee machine.

"What's yours?" asked the barman.

"Nada."

"Otro loco más,"[3] said the barman and turned away.

"A little cup," said the waiter.

The barman poured it for him.

"The light is very bright and pleasant but the bar is unpolished," the waiter said.

The barman looked at him but did not answer. It was too late at night for conversation.

"You want another copita?"[4] the barman asked.

"No, thank you," said the waiter and went out. He disliked bars and bodegas. A clean, well-lighted café was a very different thing. Now, without thinking further, he would go home to his room. He would lie in the bed and finally, with daylight, he would go to sleep. After all, he said to himself, it is probably only insomnia. Many must have it.

—1933

---

1    *nada ... nada* Spanish: nothing and then nothing.
2    *Our nada ... with thee* Parodies the Lord's Prayer, which is included in the New Testament (see Matthew 6:9–13) and used in most Christian churches.
3    *Otro loco más* Spanish: One more madman.
4    *copita* Spanish: glass.

# Flannery O'Connor

## 1925–1964

Born in Savannah, Georgia, Mary Flannery O'Connor spent most of her life in the American South, where her novels and most of her short stories are set. Participating in the tradition of the "Southern Gothic," her writing blends humour and the grotesque, often incorporating bleak or violent events and physically deformed or morally twisted characters. O'Connor approached the "Southern Gothic" through the lens of her intensely deep Catholic faith; indeed, she writes that "the meaning of life is centered in our Redemption by Christ and what I see in the world I see in its relation to that."

After graduating from the Georgia State College for Women in 1945, O'Connor spent three years at the prestigious Writers' Workshop at the University of Iowa. She probably would have remained in the northern United States if she were not struck in 1950 by the first signs of lupus. Weakened by the disease and the debilitating cortisone treatments it required, she went to live with her mother in Milledgeville, Georgia, where she would remain for the rest of her life.

Although O'Connor was a deeply committed Catholic, her fiction is set in the Southern "Bible Belt" where Protestantism was predominant, and her characters are often Protestant fundamentalists who are both materially and spiritually poor. Her stories focus on terrible events befalling such characters, she said, in order to portray "the action of grace in territory held largely by the devil." She described her short story collection *A Good Man Is Hard to Find* (1955), which received the O. Henry first prize for short fiction, as a book of "stories about original sin."

In addition to *A Good Man Is Hard to Find*, O'Connor published two novels—*Wise Blood* (1952) and *The Violent Bear It Away* (1960)—before her early death in 1964 as a result of lupus. Her last short story collection, *Everything that Rises Must Converge*, was published posthumously the following year.

# A Good Man Is Hard to Find

The grandmother didn't want to go to Florida. She wanted to visit some of her connections in east Tennessee and she was seizing at every chance to change Bailey's mind. Bailey was the son she lived with, her only boy. He was sitting on the edge of his chair at the table, bent over the orange sports section of the *Journal*. "Now look here, Bailey," she said, "see here, read this," and she stood with one hand on her thin hip and the other rattling the newspaper at his bald head. "Here this fellow that calls himself The Misfit is aloose from the Federal Pen and headed toward Florida and you read here what it says he did to these people. Just you read it. I wouldn't take my children in any direction with a criminal like that aloose in it. I couldn't answer to my conscience if I did."

Bailey didn't look up from his reading so she wheeled around then and faced the children's mother, a young woman in slacks, whose face was as broad and innocent as a cabbage and was tied around with a green head-kerchief that had two points on the top like rabbit's ears. She was sitting on the sofa, feeding the baby his apricots out of a jar. "The children have been to Florida before," the old lady said. "You all ought to take them somewhere else for a change so they would see different parts of the world and be broad. They never have been to east Tennessee."

The children's mother didn't seem to hear her but the eight-year-old boy, John Wesley, a stocky child with glasses, said, "If you don't want to go to Florida, why dontcha stay at home?" He and the little girl, June Star, were reading the funny papers on the floor.

"She wouldn't stay at home to be queen for a day," June Star said without raising her yellow head.

"Yes and what would you do if this fellow, The Misfit, caught you?" the grandmother asked.

"I'd smack his face," John Wesley said.

"She wouldn't stay at home for a million bucks," June Star said. "Afraid she'd miss something. She has to go everywhere we go."

"All right, Miss," the grandmother said. "Just remember that the next time you want me to curl your hair."

June Star said her hair was naturally curly.

The next morning the grandmother was the first one in the car, ready to go. She had her big black valise that looked like the head of a hippopotamus in one corner, and underneath it she was hiding a basket with Pitty Sing, the cat, in it. She didn't intend for the cat to be left alone in the house for three days because he would miss her too much and she was afraid he might brush against one of the gas burners and accidentally asphyxiate himself. Her son, Bailey, didn't like to arrive at a motel with a cat.

She sat in the middle of the back seat with John Wesley and June Star on either side of her. Bailey and the children's mother and the baby sat in front and they left Atlanta at eight forty-five with the mileage on the car at 55890. The grandmother wrote this down because she thought it would be interesting to say how many miles they had been when they got back. It took them twenty minutes to reach the outskirts of the city.

The old lady settled herself comfortably, removing her white cotton gloves and putting them up with her purse on the shelf in front of the back window. The children's mother still had on slacks and still had her head tied up in a green kerchief, but the grandmother had on a navy blue straw sailor hat with a bunch of white violets on the brim and a navy blue dress with a small white dot in the print. Her collars and cuffs were white organdy trimmed with lace and at her neckline she had pinned a purple spray of cloth violets containing a sachet. In case of an accident, anyone seeing her dead on the highway would know at once that she was a lady.

She said she thought it was going to be a good day for driving, neither too hot nor too cold, and she cautioned Bailey that the speed limit was fifty-five miles an hour and that the patrolmen hid themselves behind billboards and small clumps of trees and sped out after you before you had a chance to slow down. She pointed out interesting details of the scenery: Stone Mountain; the blue granite that in some places came up to both sides of the highway; the brilliant red clay banks slightly streaked with purple; and the various crops that made rows of green lace-work on the ground. The trees were full of silver-white sunlight and the meanest of them sparkled. The children were reading comic magazines and their mother had gone back to sleep.

"Let's go through Georgia fast so we won't have to look at it much," John Wesley said.

"If I were a little boy," said the grandmother, "I wouldn't talk about my native state that way. Tennessee has the mountains and Georgia has the hills."

"Tennessee is just a hillbilly dumping ground," John Wesley said, "and Georgia is a lousy state too."

"You said it," June Star said.

"In my time," said the grandmother, folding her thin veined fingers, "children were more respectful of their native states and their parents and everything else. People did right then. Oh look at the cute little pickaninny!"[1] she said and pointed to a Negro child standing in the door of a shack. "Wouldn't that make a picture, now?" she asked and they all turned and looked at the little Negro out of the back window. He waved.

"He didn't have any britches on," June Star said.

"He probably didn't have any," the grandmother explained. "Little niggers[2] in the country don't have things like we do. If I could paint, I'd paint that picture," she said.

The children exchanged comic books.

The grandmother offered to hold the baby and the children's mother passed him over the front seat to her. She set him on her knee and bounced him and told him about the things they were passing. She rolled her eyes and screwed up her mouth and stuck her leathery thin face into his smooth bland

---

1    *pickaninny* Derogatory term for an African American child.

2    *niggers* This pejorative term remained in frequent use by many white Americans in the South until well into the 1960s.

one. Occasionally he gave her a faraway smile. They passed a large cotton field with five or six graves fenced in the middle of it, like a small island. "Look at the graveyard!" the grandmother said, pointing it out. "That was the old family burying ground. That belonged to the plantation."

"Where's the plantation?" John Wesley asked.

"Gone With the Wind," said the grandmother. "Ha. Ha."

When the children finished all the comic books they had brought, they opened the lunch and ate it. The grandmother ate a peanut butter sandwich and an olive and would not let the children throw the box and the paper napkins out the window. When there was nothing else to do they played a game by choosing a cloud and making the other two guess what shape it suggested. John Wesley took one the shape of a cow and June Star guessed a cow and John Wesley said, no, an automobile, and June Star said he didn't play fair, and they began to slap each other over the grandmother.

The grandmother said she would tell them a story if they would keep quiet. When she told a story, she rolled her eyes and waved her head and was very dramatic. She said once when she was a maiden lady she had been courted by a Mr. Edgar Atkins Teagarden from Jasper, Georgia. She said he was a very good-looking man and a gentleman and that he brought her a watermelon every Saturday afternoon with his initials cut in it, E.A.T. Well, one Saturday, she said, Mr. Teagarden brought the watermelon and there was nobody at home and he left it on the front porch and returned in his buggy to Jasper, but she never got the watermelon, she said, because a nigger boy ate it when he saw the initials, E.A.T.! This story tickled John Wesley's funny bone and he giggled and giggled but June Star didn't think it was any good. She said she wouldn't marry a man that just brought her a watermelon on Saturday. The grandmother said she would have done well to marry Mr. Teagarden because he was a gentleman and had bought Coca-Cola stock when it first came out and that he had died only a few years ago, a very wealthy man.

They stopped at The Tower for barbecued sandwiches. The Tower was a part stucco and part wood filling station and dance hall set in a clearing outside of Timothy. A fat man named Red Sammy Butts ran it and there were signs stuck here and there on the building and for miles up and down the highway saying, TRY RED SAMMY'S FAMOUS BARBECUE. NONE LIKE FAMOUS RED SAMMY'S! RED SAM! THE FAT BOY WITH THE HAPPY LAUGH. A VETERAN! RED SAMMY'S YOUR MAN!

Red Sammy was lying on the bare ground outside The Tower with his head under a truck while a grey monkey about a foot high, chained to a small chinaberry tree, chattered nearby. The monkey sprang back into the tree and got on the highest limb as soon as he saw the children jump out of the car and run toward him.

Inside, The Tower was a long dark room with a counter at one end and tables at the other and dancing space in the middle. They all sat down at a board table next to the nickelodeon and Red Sam's wife, a tall burnt-brown woman with hair and eyes lighter than her skin, came and took their order. The children's mother put a dime in the machine and played "The Tennessee Waltz," and the grandmother said that tune always made her want to dance. She asked Bailey if he would like to dance but he only glared at her. He didn't have a naturally sunny disposition like she did and trips made him nervous. The grandmother's brown eyes were very bright. She swayed her head from side to side and pretended she was dancing in her chair. June Star said play something she could tap to so the children's mother put in another dime and played a fast number and June Star stepped out onto the dance floor and did her tap routine.

"Ain't she cute?" Red Sam's wife said, leaning over the counter. "Would you like to come be my little girl?"

"No I certainly wouldn't," June Star said. "I wouldn't live in a broken-down place like this for a million bucks!" and she ran back to the table.

"Ain't she cute?" the woman repeated, stretching her mouth politely.

"Ain't you ashamed?" hissed the grandmother.

Red Sam came in and told his wife to quit lounging on the counter and hurry up with these people's order. His khaki trousers reached just to his hip bones and his stomach hung over them like a sack of meal swaying under his shirt. He came over and sat down at a table nearby and let out a combination sigh and yodel. "You can't win," he said. "You can't win," and he wiped his sweating red face off with a grey handkerchief. "These days you don't know who to trust," he said. "Ain't that the truth?"

"People are certainly not nice like they used to be," said the grandmother.

"Two fellers come in here last week," Red Sammy said, "driving a Chrysler. It was a old beat-up car but it was a good one and these boys looked all right to me. Said they worked at the mill and you know I let them fellers charge the gas they bought? Now why did I do that?"

"Because you're a good man!" the grandmother said at once.

"Yes'm, I suppose so," Red Sam said as if he were struck with this answer.

His wife brought the orders, carrying the five plates all at once without a tray, two in each hand and one balanced on her arm. "It isn't a soul in this green world of God's that you can trust," she said. "And I don't count nobody out of that, not nobody," she repeated, looking at Red Sammy.

"Did you read about that criminal, The Misfit, that's escaped?" asked the grandmother.

"I wouldn't be a bit surprised if he didn't attact this place right here," said the woman. "If he hears about it being here, I wouldn't be none surprised to see him. If he hears it's two cent in the cash register, I wouldn't be a tall surprised if he...."

"That'll do," Red Sam said. "Go bring these people their Co'-Colas," and the woman went off to get the rest of the order.

"A good man is hard to find," Red Sammy said. "Everything is getting terrible. I remember the day you could go off and leave your screen door unlatched. Not no more."

He and the grandmother discussed better times. The old lady said that in her opinion Europe was entirely to blame for the way things were now. She said the way Europe acted you would think we were made of money and Red Sam said it was no use talking about it, she was exactly right. The children ran outside into the white sunlight and looked at the monkey in the lacy chinaberry tree. He was busy catching fleas on himself and biting each one carefully between his teeth as if it were a delicacy.

They drove off again into the hot afternoon. The grandmother took cat naps and woke up every few minutes with her own snoring. Outside of Toombsboro she woke up and recalled an old plantation that she had visited in this neighbourhood once when she was a young lady. She said the house had six white columns across the front and that there was an avenue of oaks leading up to it and two little wooden trellis arbours on either side in front where you sat down with your suitor after a stroll in the garden. She recalled exactly which road to turn off to get to it. She knew that Bailey would not be willing to lose any time looking at an old house, but the more she talked about it, the more she wanted to see it once again and find out if the little twin arbours were still standing. "There was a secret panel in this house," she said craftily, not telling the truth but wishing that she were, "and the story went that all the family silver was hidden in it when Sherman[1] came through but it was never found ..."

"Hey!" John Wesley said. "Let's go see it! We'll find it! We'll poke all the woodwork and find it! Who lives there? Where do you turn off at? Hey Pop, can't we turn off there?"

"We never have seen a house with a secret panel!" June Star shrieked. "Let's go to the house with the secret panel! Hey, Pop, can't we go see the house with the secret panel!"

"It's not far from here, I know," the grandmother said. "It wouldn't take over twenty minutes."

Bailey was looking straight ahead. His jaw was as rigid as a horseshoe. "No," he said.

---

1    *Sherman* American Union commander William Tecumseh Sherman.

The children began to yell and scream that they wanted to see the house with the secret panel. John Wesley kicked the back of the front seat and June Star hung over her mother's shoulder and whined desperately into her ear that they never had any fun even on their vacation, that they could never do what THEY wanted to do. The baby began to scream and John Wesley kicked the back of the seat so hard that his father could feel the blows in his kidney.

"All right!" he shouted and drew the car to a stop at the side of the road. "Will you all shut up? Will you all just shut up for one second? If you don't shut up, we won't go anywhere."

"It would be very educational for them," the grandmother murmured.

"All right," Bailey said, "but get this: this is the only time we're going to stop for anything like this. This is the one and only time."

"The dirt road that you have to turn down is about a mile back," the grandmother directed. "I marked it when we passed."

"A dirt road," Bailey groaned.

After they had turned around and were headed toward the dirt road, the grandmother recalled other points about the house, the beautiful glass over the front doorway and the candle-lamp in the hall. John Wesley said that the secret panel was probably in the fireplace.

"You can't go inside this house," Bailey said. "You don't know who lives there."

"While you all talk to the people in front, I'll run around behind and get in a window," John Wesley suggested.

"We'll all stay in the car," his mother said.

They turned onto the dirt road and the car raced roughly along in a swirl of pink dust. The grandmother recalled the times when there were no paved roads and thirty miles was a day's journey. The dirt road was hilly and there were sudden washes in it and sharp curves on dangerous embankments. All at once they would be on a hill, looking down over the blue tops of trees for miles around, then the next minute, they would be in a red depression with the dust-coated trees looking down on them.

"This place had better turn up in a minute," Bailey said, "or I'm going to turn around."

The road looked as if no one had travelled on it in months.

"It's not much farther," the grandmother said and just as she said it, a horrible thought came to her. The thought was so embarrassing that she turned red in the face and her eyes dilated and her feet jumped up, upsetting her valise in the corner. The instant the valise moved, the newspaper top she had over the basket under it rose with a snarl and Pitty Sing, the cat, sprang onto Bailey's shoulder.

The children were thrown to the floor and their mother, clutching the baby, was thrown out the door onto the ground; the old lady was thrown into the front seat. The car turned over once and landed right-side-up in a gulch off the side of the road. Bailey remained in the driver's seat with the cat—grey-striped with a broad white face and an orange nose—clinging to his neck like a caterpillar.

As soon as the children saw they could move their arms and legs, they scrambled out of the car, shouting, "We've had an ACCIDENT!" The grandmother was curled up under the dashboard, hoping she was injured so that Bailey's wrath would not come down on her all at once. The horrible thought she had had before the accident was that the house she had remembered so vividly was not in Georgia but in Tennessee.

Bailey removed the cat from his neck with both hands and flung it out the window against the side of a pine tree. Then he got out of the car and started looking for the children's mother. She was sitting against the side of the red gutted ditch, holding the screaming baby, but she only had a cut down her face and a broken shoulder. "We've had an ACCIDENT!" the children screamed in a frenzy of delight.

"But nobody's killed," June Star said with disappointment as the grandmother limped out of the car, her hat still pinned to her head but the broken front brim standing up at a jaunty angle and the violet spray hanging off the side. They all sat down in the ditch, except the children, to recover from the shock. They were all shaking.

"Maybe a car will come along," said the children's mother hoarsely.

"I believe I have injured an organ," said the grandmother, pressing her side, but no one answered her. Bailey's teeth were clattering. He had on a yellow sport shirt with bright blue parrots designed in it and his face was as yellow as the shirt. The grandmother decided that she would not mention that the house was in Tennessee.

The road was about ten feet above and they could see only the tops of the trees on the other side of it. Behind the ditch they were sitting in there were more woods, tall and dark and deep. In a few minutes they saw a car some distance away on top of a hill, coming slowly as if the occupants were watching them. The grandmother stood up and waved both arms dramatically to attract their attention. The car continued to come on slowly, disappeared around a bend and appeared again, moving even slower, on top of the hill they had gone over. It was a big black battered hearse-like automobile. There were three men in it.

It came to a stop just over them and for some minutes, the driver looked down with a steady expressionless gaze to where they were sitting, and didn't speak. Then he turned his head and muttered something to the other two and they got out. One was a fat boy in black trousers and a red sweat shirt with a silver stallion embossed on the front of it. He moved around on the right side of them and stood staring, his mouth partly open in a kind of loose grin. The other had on khaki pants and a blue striped coat and a grey hat pulled down very low, hiding most of his face. He came around slowly on the left side. Neither spoke.

The driver got out of the car and stood by the side of it, looking down at them. He was an older man than the other two. His hair was just beginning to grey and he wore silver-rimmed spectacles that gave him a scholarly look. He had a long creased face and didn't have on any shirt or undershirt. He had on blue jeans that were too tight for him and was holding a black hat and a gun. The two boys also had guns.

"We've had an ACCIDENT!" the children screamed.

The grandmother had the peculiar feeling that the bespectacled man was someone she knew. His face was as familiar to her as if she had known him all her life but she could not recall who he was. He moved away from the car and began to come down the embankment, placing his feet carefully so that he wouldn't slip. He had on tan and white shoes and no socks, and his ankles were red and thin. "Good afternoon," he said. "I see you all had you a little spill."

"We turned over twice!" said the grandmother.

"Oncet," he corrected. "We seen it happen. Try their car and see will it run, Hiram," he said quietly to the boy with the grey hat.

"What you got that gun for?" John Wesley asked. "Whatcha gonna do with that gun?"

"Lady," the man said to the children's mother, "would you mind calling them children to sit down by you? Children make me nervous. I want all you all to sit down right together there where you're at."

"What are you telling US what to do for?" June Star asked.

Behind them the line of woods gaped like a dark open mouth. "Come here," said their mother.

"Look here now," Bailey began suddenly, "we're in a predicament! We're in...."

The grandmother shrieked. She scrambled to her feet and stood staring. "You're The Misfit!" she said. "I recognized you at once!"

"Yes'm," the man said, smiling slightly as if he were pleased in spite of himself to be known, "but it would have been better for all of you, lady, if you hadn't of reckernized me."

Bailey turned his head sharply and said something to his mother that shocked even the children. The old lady began to cry and The Misfit reddened.

"Lady," he said, "don't you get upset. Sometimes a man says things he don't mean. I don't reckon he meant to talk to you thataway."

"You wouldn't shoot a lady, would you?" the grandmother said and removed a clean handkerchief from her cuff and began to slap at her eyes with it.

The Misfit pointed the toe of his shoe into the ground and made a little hole and then covered it up again. "I would hate to have to," he said.

"Listen," the grandmother almost screamed, "I know you're a good man. You don't look a bit like you have common blood. I know you must come from nice people!"

"Yes mam," he said, "finest people in the world." When he smiled he showed a row of strong white teeth. "God never made a finer woman than my mother and my daddy's heart was pure gold," he said. The boy with the red sweat shirt had come around behind them and was standing with his gun at his hip. The Misfit squatted down on the ground. "Watch them children, Bobby Lee," he said. "You know they make me nervous." He looked at the six of them huddled together in front of him and he seemed to be embarrassed as if he couldn't think of anything to say. "Ain't a cloud in the sky," he remarked, looking up at it. "Don't see no sun but don't see no cloud neither."

"Yes, it's a beautiful day," said the grandmother. "Listen," she said, "you shouldn't call yourself The Misfit because I know you're a good man at heart. I can just look at you and tell."

"Hush!" Bailey yelled. "Hush! Everybody shut up and let me handle this!" He was squatting in the position of a runner about to sprint forward but he didn't move.

"I pre-chate that, lady," The Misfit said and drew a little circle in the ground with the butt of his gun.

"It'll take a half a hour to fix this here car," Hiram called, looking over the raised hood of it.

"Well, first you and Bobby Lee get him and that little boy to step over yonder with you," The Misfit said, pointing to Bailey and John Wesley. "The boys want to ast you something," he said to Bailey. "Would you mind stepping back in them woods there with them?"

"Listen," Bailey began, "we're in a terrible predicament! Nobody realizes what this is," and his voice cracked. His eyes were as blue and intense as the parrots in his shirt and he remained perfectly still.

The grandmother reached up to adjust her hat brim as if she were going to the woods with him but it came off in her hand. She stood staring at it and after a second she let it fall on the ground. Hiram pulled Bailey up by the arm as if he were assisting an old man. John Wesley caught hold of his father's hand and Bobby Lee followed. They went off toward the woods and just as they reached the dark edge, Bailey turned and supporting himself against a grey naked pine trunk, he shouted, "I'll be back in a minute, Mamma, wait on me!"

"Come back this instant!" his mother shrilled but they all disappeared into the woods.

"Bailey Boy!" the grandmother called in a tragic voice but she found she was looking at The Misfit squatting on the ground in front of her. "I just know you're a good man," she said desperately. "You're not a bit common!"

"Nome, I ain't a good man," The Misfit said after a second as if he had considered her statement carefully, "but I ain't the worst in the world neither. My daddy said I was a different breed of dog from my brothers and sisters. 'You know,' Daddy said, 'it's some that can live their whole life out without asking about it and it's others has to know why it is, and this boy is one of the latters. He's going to be into everything!'" He put on his black hat and looked up suddenly and then away deep into the woods as if he were embarrassed again. "I'm sorry I don't have on a shirt before you ladies," he said, hunching his shoulders slightly. "We buried our clothes that we had on when we escaped and we're just making do until we can get better. We borrowed these from some folks we met," he explained.

"That's perfectly all right," the grandmother said. "Maybe Bailey has an extra shirt in his suitcase."

"I'll look and see terrectly," The Misfit said.

"Where are they taking him?" the children's mother screamed.

"Daddy was a card himself," The Misfit said. "You couldn't put anything over on him. He never got in trouble with the Authorities though. Just had the knack of handling them."

"You could be honest too if you'd only try," said the grandmother. "Think how wonderful it would be to settle down and live a comfortable life and not have to think about somebody chasing you all the time."

The Misfit kept scratching in the ground with the butt of his gun as if he were thinking about it. "Yes'm, somebody is always after you," he murmured.

The grandmother noticed how thin his shoulder blades were just behind his hat because she was standing up looking down on him. "Do you ever pray?" she asked.

He shook his head. All she saw was the black hat wiggle between his shoulder blades. "Nome," he said.

There was a pistol shot from the woods, followed closely by another. Then silence. The old lady's head jerked around. She could hear the wind move through the tree tops like a long satisfied insuck of breath. "Bailey Boy!" she called.

"I was a gospel singer for a while," The Misfit said. "I been most everything. Been in the arm service, both land and sea, at home and abroad, been twict married, been an undertaker, been with the railroads, plowed Mother Earth, been in a tornado, seen a man burnt alive oncet," and he looked up at the children's mother and the little girl who were sitting close together, their faces white and their eyes glassy; "I even seen a woman flogged," he said.

"Pray, pray," the grandmother began, "pray, pray...."

"I never was a bad boy that I remember of," The Misfit said in an almost dreamy voice, "but somewheres along the line I done something wrong and got sent to the penitentiary. I was buried alive," and he looked up and held her attention to him by a steady stare.

"That's when you should have started to pray," she said. "What did you do to get sent to the penitentiary that first time?"

"Turn to the right, it was a wall," The Misfit said, looking up again at the cloudless sky. "Turn to the left, it was a wall. Look up it was a ceiling, look down it was a floor. I forget what I done, lady. I set there and set there, trying to remember what it was I done and I ain't recalled it to this day. Oncet in a while, I would think it was coming to me, but it never come."

"Maybe they put you in by mistake," the old lady said vaguely.

"Nome," he said. "It wasn't no mistake. They had the papers on me."

"You must have stolen something," she said.

The Misfit sneered slightly. "Nobody had nothing I wanted," he said. "It was a head-doctor at the penitentiary said what I had done was kill my daddy but I known that for a lie. My daddy died in nineteen ought nineteen of the epidemic flu and I never had a thing to do with it. He was buried in the Mount Hopewell Baptist churchyard and you can go there and see for yourself."

"If you would pray," the old lady said, "Jesus would help you."

"That's right," The Misfit said.

"Well then, why don't you pray?" she asked trembling with delight suddenly.

"I don't want no hep," he said. "I'm doing all right by myself."

Bobby Lee and Hiram came ambling back from the woods. Bobby Lee was dragging a yellow shirt with bright blue parrots in it.

"Thow me that shirt, Bobby Lee," The Misfit said. The shirt came flying at him and landed on his shoulder and he put it on. The grandmother couldn't name what the shirt reminded her of. "No, lady," The Misfit said while he was buttoning it up, "I found out the crime don't matter. You can do one thing or you can do another, kill a man or take a tire off his car, because sooner or later you're going to forget what it was you done and just be punished for it."

The children's mother had begun to make heaving noises as if she couldn't get her breath. "Lady," he asked, "would you and that little girl like to step off yonder with Bobby Lee and Hiram and join your husband?"

"Yes, thank you," the mother said faintly. Her left arm dangled helplessly and she was holding the baby, who had gone to sleep, in the other. "Hep that lady up, Hiram," The Misfit said as she struggled to climb out of the ditch, "and Bobby Lee, you hold onto that little girl's hand."

"I don't want to hold hands with him," June Star said. "He reminds me of a pig."

The fat boy blushed and laughed and caught her by the arm and pulled her into the woods after Hiram and her mother.

Alone with The Misfit, the grandmother found that she had lost her voice. There was not a cloud in the sky nor any sun. There was nothing around her but woods. She wanted to tell him that he must pray. She opened and closed her mouth several times before anything came out. Finally she found herself saying, "Jesus. Jesus," meaning, Jesus will help you, but the way she was saying it, it sounded as if she might be cursing.

"Yes'm," The Misfit said as if he agreed. "Jesus thown everything off balance. It was the same case with Him as with me except He hadn't committed any crime and they could prove I had committed one because they had the papers on me. Of course," he said, "they never shown me my papers. That's why I sign myself now. I said long ago, you get you a signature and sign everything you do and keep a copy of it. Then you'll know what you done and you can hold up the crime to the punishment and see do they match and in the end you'll have something to prove you ain't been treated right. I call myself The Misfit," he said, "because I can't make what all I done wrong fit what all I gone through in punishment."

There was a piercing scream from the woods, followed closely by a pistol report. "Does it seem right to you, lady, that one is punished a heap and another ain't punished at all?"

"Jesus!" the old lady cried. "You've got good blood! I know you wouldn't shoot a lady! I know you come from nice people! Pray! Jesus, you ought not to shoot a lady. I'll give you all the money I've got!"

"Lady," The Misfit said, looking beyond her far into the woods, "there never was a body that give the undertaker a tip."

There were two more pistol reports and the grandmother raised her head like a parched old turkey hen crying for water and called, "Bailey Boy, Bailey Boy!" as if her heart would break.

"Jesus was the only One that ever raised the dead," The Misfit continued, "and He shouldn't have done it. He thown everything off balance. If He did what He said, then it's nothing for you to do but thow away everything and follow Him, and if He didn't, then it's nothing for you to do but enjoy the few minutes you got left the best way you can—by killing somebody or burning down his house or doing some other meanness to him. No pleasure but meanness," he said and his voice had become almost a snarl.

"Maybe He didn't raise the dead," the old lady mumbled, not knowing what she was saying and feeling so dizzy that she sank down in the ditch with her legs twisted under her.

"I wasn't there so I can't say He didn't," The Misfit said. "I wisht I had of been there," he said, hitting the ground with his fist. "It ain't right I wasn't there because if I had of been there I would of known. Listen lady," he said in a high voice, "if I had of been there I would of known and I wouldn't be like I am now." His voice seemed about to crack and the grandmother's head cleared for an instant. She saw the man's face twisted close to her own as if he were going to cry and she murmured, "Why you're one of my babies. You're one of my own children!" She reached out and touched him on the shoulder. The Misfit sprang back as if a snake had bitten him and shot her three times through the chest. Then he put his gun down on the ground and took off his glasses and began to clean them.

Hiram and Bobby Lee returned from the woods and stood over the ditch, looking down at the grandmother who half sat and half lay in a puddle of blood with her legs crossed under her like a child's and her face smiling up at the cloudless sky.

Without his glasses, The Misfit's eyes were red-rimmed and pale and defenceless-looking. "Take her off and thow her where you thown the others," he said, picking up the cat that was rubbing itself against his leg.

"She was a talker, wasn't she?" Bobby Lee said, sliding down the ditch with a yodel.

"She would of been a good woman," The Misfit said, "if it had been somebody there to shoot her every minute of her life."

"Some fun!" Bobby Lee said.

"Shut up, Bobby Lee," The Misfit said. "It's no real pleasure in life."

—1953

# William Trevor

## 1928–2016

From George Moore and James Joyce to Elizabeth Bowen and Frank O'Connor, Ireland has produced a host of writers who have demonstrated a particular aptitude for the short story. Amongst these must surely be counted William Trevor, a prolific author known for minutely observed stories that peer into the loneliness and despair of ordinary people without venturing to intrude a moral perspective on their shortcomings.

A graduate of Trinity College, Dublin, Trevor worked as a schoolteacher, sculptor, and copywriter before wholly devoting himself to fiction after the success of his second novel, *The Old Boys* (1964). Because of its keenly satirical quality, reviewers compared Trevor's early work to that of English writers like Evelyn Waugh and Kingsley Amis. But Trevor's voice and style have more in common with the "scrupulous meanness" of Joyce's *Dubliners* and the Russian writer Anton Chekhov's bleak but humane portrayals of the incidental details of modest lives.

In his novels and short stories, Trevor typically withholds narrative commentary, cultivating an ironic detachment that is nevertheless compassionate in its refusal to condemn the failings of his characters. "I don't believe in the black and white," he has said of this unwillingness to impose judgment; "I believe in the grey shadows and the murkiness." Trevor's protagonists are frequently made to suffer the collapse of cherished illusions as they are confronted by the hollowness of the lies they tell themselves and each other.

Although Trevor's technique resembles mainstream realism, his fiction also manifests a modernist distrust of omniscience. His most characteristic stories, among them "Folie à Deux," rotate between multiple centres of consciousness, juxtaposing contrary points of view to reflect the difficulty of achieving meaningful connections with other human beings. But if these stories accept alienation as a condition of modern society, they also assert the importance of compassion as a means of overcoming it.

# Folie à Deux[1]

Aware of a presence close to him, Wilby glances up from the book he has just begun to read. The man standing there says nothing. He doesn't smile. A dishcloth hangs from where it's tucked into grubby apron-strings knotted at the front, and Wilby assumes that the man is an envoy sent from the kitchen to apologize for the delay in the cooking of the fish he has ordered.

---

1  *Folie à Deux* French: mental disorder shared by two closely associated individuals.

The place is modest, in rue Piques off rue de Sèvres:[1] Wilby didn't notice what it is called. A café as much as a brasserie,[2] it is poorly illuminated except for the bar, at which a couple are hunched over their glasses, conversing softly. One of the few tables belonging to the café is occupied by four elderly women playing cards and there are a few people at tables in the brasserie.

Still without communicating, the man who has come from the kitchen turns and goes away, leaving Wilby with the impression that he has been mistaken for someone else. He pours himself more wine and reads again. Wilby reads a lot, and drinks a lot.

He is a spare, sharp-faced man in his forties, clean-shaven, in a grey suit, with a striped blue-and-red tie almost but not quite striking a stylish note. He visits Paris once in a while to make the rounds of salerooms specializing in rare postage stamps, usually spinning out his time when he is there, since he can afford to. Three years ago he inherited his family's wine business in County Westmeath,[3] which he sold eighteen months later, planning to live on the proceeds while he indulged his interest in philately.[4] He occupies, alone now, the house he inherited at that time also, creeper-clad, just outside the Westmeath town where he was born. Marriage failed him there, or he it, and he doubts that he will make another attempt in that direction.

His food is brought to him by a small, old waiter, a more presentable figure than the man who came and went. He is attentive, addressing Wilby in conventional waiter's terms and supplying, when they are asked for, salt and pepper from another table. "*Voilà, monsieur*,"[5] he murmurs, his tone apologetic.

Wilby eats his fish, wondering what fish it is. He knew when he ordered it but has since forgotten, and the taste doesn't tell him much. The bread is the best part of his meal and he catches the waiter's attention to ask for more. His book is a paperback he has read before, *The Hand of Ethelberta*.[6]

He reads another page, orders more wine, finishes the *pommes frites*[7] but not the fish. He likes quiet places, and doesn't hurry. He orders coffee and— though not intending to—a calvados.[8] He drinks too much, he tells himself, and restrains the inclination to have another when the coffee comes. He reads again, indulging the pleasure of being in Paris, in a brasserie where Muzak[9]

---

1  *rue Piques … de Sèvres* Rue Piques is fictional; all the other streets named in the story are part of the Faubourg Saint-Germain, a district in Paris.
2  *brasserie* French: casual restaurant.
3  *Westmeath* County in Ireland.
4  *philately* Postage stamp collecting.
5  *Voilà, monsieur* French: Here you are, sir.
6  *The Hand of Ethelberta* 1876 novel by Thomas Hardy.
7  *pommes frites* French: fried potatoes.
8  *calvados* Apple brandy.
9  *Muzak* Mediocre recorded background music.

isn't playing, at a small corner table, engrossed in a story that's familiar yet has receded sufficiently to be blurred in places, like something good remembered. He never minds it when the food isn't up to much; wine matters more, and peace. He'll walk back to the Hôtel Merneuil;[1] with luck he'll be successful in the salerooms tomorrow.

He gestures for his bill, and pays. The old waiter has his overcoat ready for him at the door, and Wilby tips him a little for that. Outside, being late November, the night is chilly.

The man who came to look at him is there on the street, dressed as he was then. He stands still, not speaking. He might have come outside to have a cigarette, as waiters sometimes do. But there is no cigarette.

"*Bonsoir*,"[2] Wilby says.

"*Bonsoir*."

Saying that, quite suddenly the man is someone else. A resemblance flickers: the smooth black hair, the head like the rounded end of a bullet, the fringe that is not as once it was but is still a fringe, the dark eyes. There is a way of standing, without unease or agitation and yet awkward, hands lank, open.

"What is all this?" Even as he puts the question, Wilby's choice of words sounds absurd to him. "Anthony?" he says.

There is a movement, a hand's half gesture, meaningless, hardly a response. Then the man turns away, entering the brasserie by another door.

"Anthony," Wilby mutters again, but only to himself.

People have said that Anthony is dead.

• • •

The streets are emptier than they were, the bustle of the pavements gone. Obedient to pedestrian lights at rue de Babylone where there is fast-moving traffic again, Wilby waits with a woman in a pale waterproof coat, her legs slim beneath it, blonde hair brushed up. Not wanting to think about Anthony, he wonders if she's a tart, since she has that look, and for a moment sees her pale coat thrown down in some small room, the glow of an electric fire, money placed on a dressing-table: now and again when he travels he has a woman. But this one doesn't glance at him, and the red light changes to green.

It couldn't possibly have been Anthony, of course it couldn't. Even assuming that Anthony is alive, why would he be employed as a kitchen worker in Paris? "Yes, I'm afraid we fear the worst," his father said on the telephone, years ago now. "He sent a few belongings here, but that's a good while back. A note to you, unfinished, was caught up in the pages of a book. Nothing in it, really. Your name, no more."

---

1     *Hôtel Merneuil* The name is a play on the famous Hôtel Verneuil located in this neighbourhood.

2     *Bonsoir* French: Good evening.

In rue du Bac there is a window Wilby likes, with prints of the Revolution.[1] The display has hardly changed since he was here last: the death of Marie Antoinette, the Girondists on their way to the guillotine, the storming of the Bastille, Danton's death, Robespierre triumphant, Robespierre fallen from grace. Details aren't easy to make out in the dim street-light. Prints he hasn't seen before are indistinguishable at the back.

At a bar he has another calvados. He said himself when people asked him—a few had once—that he, too, imagined Anthony was dead. A disappearance so prolonged, with no reports of even a glimpse as the years advanced, did appear to confirm a conclusion that became less tentative, and in the end wasn't tentative at all.

In rue Montalembert a couple ask for directions to the Metro.[2] Wilby points it out, walking back a little way with them to do so, as grateful for this interruption as he was when the woman at the traffic crossing caught his interest.

"*Bonne nuit, monsieur.*"[3] In the hall of the Hôtel Merneuil the night porter holds open the lift doors. He closes them and the lift begins its smooth ascent. "The will to go on can fall away, you know," Anthony's father said on the telephone again, in touch to find out if there was anything to report.

• • •

Monsieur Jothy shakes his head over the pay packet that hasn't been picked up. It's on the windowsill above the sinks, where others have been ignored too. He writes a message on it and props it against an empty bottle.

At this late hour Monsieur Jothy has the kitchen to himself, a time for assessing what needs to be ordered, for satisfying himself that, in general, the kitchen is managing. He picks up Jean-André's note of what he particularly requires for tomorrow, and checks the shelves where the cleaning materials are kept. He has recently become suspicious of Jean-André, suspecting short-cuts. His risotto, once an attraction on the menu, is scarcely ever ordered now; and with reason in Monsieur Jothy's opinion, since it has lost the intensity of flavour that made it popular, and is often dry. But the kitchen at least is clean, and Monsieur Jothy, examining cutlery and plates, fails to find food clinging anywhere, or a rim left on a cup. Once he employed two dish-washers at the sinks, but now one does it on his own, and half the time forgets his wages. Anxious to keep him, Monsieur Jothy has wondered about finding somewhere for him to sleep on the premises instead of having the long journey to and from his room. But there isn't even a corner of a pantry, and when he asked

---

1   *the Revolution* I.e., the French Revolution (1789–99). The people and events depicted in the display are all from this period.
2   *Metro* Parisian subway system.
3   *Bonne nuit, monsieur* French: Good night, sir.

in the neighbourhood about accommodation near rue Piques he was also unsuccessful.

The dishcloths, washed and rinsed, are draped on the radiators and will be dry by the morning, the soup bowls are stacked; the glasses, in their rows, gleam on the side table. "*Très bon,*[1] *très bon,*" Monsieur Jothy murmurs before he turns the lights out and locks up.

• • •

Wilby does not sleep and cannot read, although he tries to.

"A marvel, isn't it?" Miss Davally said, the memory vivid, as if she'd said it yesterday. You wouldn't think apricots would so easily ripen in such a climate. Even on a wall lined with brick you wouldn't think it. She pointed at the branches sprawled out along their wires, and you could see the fruit in little clusters. "Delphiniums,"[2] she said, pointing again, and one after another named the flowers they passed on their way through the garden. "And this is Anthony," she said in the house.

The boy looked up from the playing cards he had spread out on the floor. "What's his name?" he asked, and Miss Davally said he knew because she had told him already. But even so she did so again. "Why's he called that?" Anthony asked. "Why're you called that?"

"It's my name."

"Shall we play in the garden?"

That first day, and every day afterwards, there were gingersnap biscuits in the middle of the morning. "Am I older than you?" Anthony asked. "Is six older?" He had a house, he said, in the bushes at the end of the garden, and they pretended there was a house. "Jericho he's called," Anthony said of the dog that followed them about, a black Labrador with an injured leg that hung limply, thirteen years old. "Miss Davally is an orphan," Anthony said. "That's why she lives with us. Do you know what an orphan is?"

In the yard the horses looked out over the half-doors of their stables; the hounds were in a smaller yard. Anthony's mother was never at lunch because her horse and the hounds were exercised then. But his father always was, each time wearing a different tweed jacket, his grey moustache clipped short, the olives he liked to see on the lunch table always there, the whiskey he took for his health. "Well, young chap, how are you?" he always asked.

On wet days they played marbles in the kitchen passages, the dog stretched out beside them. "You come to the sea in summer," Anthony said. "They told me." Every July: the long journey from Westmeath to the same holiday cottage on the cliffs above the bay that didn't have a name. It was Miss Davally

---

1    *Très bon*  French: Very good.
2    *Delphiniums*  Garden plants with blue flowers.

who had told Anthony all that, and in time—so that hospitality might be returned—she often drove Anthony there and back. An outing for her too, she used to say, and sometimes she brought a cake she'd made, being in the way of bringing a present when she went to people's houses. She liked it at the sea as much as Anthony did; she liked to turn the wheel of the bellows in the kitchen of the cottage and watch the sparks flying up; and Anthony liked the hard sand of the shore, and collecting flintstones, and netting shrimps. The dog prowled about the rocks, sniffing the seaweed, clawing at the sea-anemones. "Our house," Anthony called the cave they found when they crawled through an opening in the rocks, a cave no one knew was there.

• • •

Air from the window Wilby slightly opens at the top is refreshing and brings with it, for a moment, the chiming of two o'clock. His book is open, face downward to keep his place, his bedside light still on. But the dark is better, and he extinguishes it.

There was a blue vase in the recess of the staircase wall, nothing else there; and paperweights crowded the shallow landing shelves, all touching one another; forty-six, Anthony said. His mother played the piano in the drawing-room. "Hub," she said, holding out her hand and smiling. She wasn't much like someone who exercised foxhounds: slim and small and wearing scent, she was also beautiful. "Look!" Anthony said, pointing at the lady in the painting above the mantelpiece in the hall.

Miss Davally was a distant relative as well as being an orphan, and when she sat on the sands after her bathe[1] she often talked about her own childhood in the house where she'd been given a home: how a particularly unpleasant boy used to creep up on her and pull a cracker in her ear, how she hated her ribboned pigtails and persuaded a simple-minded maid to cut them off, how she taught the kitchen cat to dance and how people said they'd never seen the like.

Every lunchtime Anthony's father kept going a conversation about a world that was not yet known to his listeners. He spoke affectionately of the playboy pugilist Jack Doyle,[2] demonstrating the subtlety of his right punch and recalling the wonders of his hell-raising before poverty claimed him. He told of the exploits of an ingenious escapologist, Major Pat Reid.[3] He condemned the first Earl of Inchiquin[4] as the most disgraceful man ever to step out of Ireland.

---

1　*bathe* Swim.

2　*pugilist* Boxer; *Jack Doyle* Famous Irish boxer and wrestler.

3　*Major Pat Reid* British soldier famous for escaping a German prisoner-of-war camp during World War II.

4　*first Earl of Inchiquin* Murrough O'Brien (1614–74), a peer of Ireland reviled for his brutal behaviour toward the Irish Catholics on behalf of the English Protestants during the Irish Confederate War (1642–53).

Much other information was passed on at the lunch table: why aeroplanes flew, how clocks kept time, why spiders spun their webs and how they did it. Information was everything, Anthony's father maintained, and its lunchtime dissemination, with Miss Davally's reminiscences, nurtured curiosity: the unknown became a fascination. "What would happen if you didn't eat?" Anthony wondered; and there were attempts to see if it was possible to create a rainbow with a water hose when the sun was bright, and the discovery made that, in fact, it was. A jellyfish was scooped into a shrimp net to see if it would perish or survive when it was tipped out on to the sand. Miss Davally said to put it back, and warned that jellyfish could sting as terribly as wasps.

A friendship developed between Miss Davally and Wilby's mother—a formal association, first names not called upon, neither in conversation nor in the letters that came to be exchanged from one summer to the next. *Anthony is said to be clever*, Miss Davally's spidery handwriting told. And then, as if that perhaps required watering down, *Well, so they say*. It was reported also that when each July drew near Anthony began to count the days. *He values the friendship so!* Miss Davally commented. *How fortunate for two only children such a friendship is!*

Fortunate indeed it seemed to be. There was no quarrelling, no vying for authority, no competing. When, one summer, a yellow Lilo[1] was washed up, still inflated, it was taken to the cave that no one else knew about, neither claiming that it was his because he'd seen it first. "Someone lost that thing," Anthony said, but no one came looking for it. They didn't know what it was, only that it floated. They floated it themselves, the dog limping behind them when they carried it to the sea, his tail wagging madly, head cocked to one side. In the cave it became a bed for him, to clamber on to when he was tired.

The Lilo was another of the friendship's precious secrets, as the cave itself was. No other purpose was found for it, but its possession was enough to make it the highlight of that particular summer and on the last day of July it was again carried to the edge of the sea. "Now, now," the dog was calmed when he became excited. The waves that morning were hardly waves at all.

• • •

In the dark there is a pinprick glow of red somewhere on the television set. The air that comes into the room is colder and Wilby closes the window he has opened a crack, suppressing the murmur of a distant plane. Memory won't let him go now; he knows it won't and makes no effort to resist it.

Nothing was said when they watched the drowning of the dog. Old Jericho was clever, never at a loss when there was fun. Not moving, he was obedient, as he always was. He played his part, going with the Lilo when

---

1    *Lilo* Inflatable mattress.

it floated out, a deep black shadow, sharp against the garish yellow. They watched as they had watched the hosepipe rainbow gathering colour, as Miss Davally said she'd watched the shaky steps of the dancing cat. Far away already, the yellow of the Lilo became a blur on the water, was lost, was there again and lost again, and the barking began, and became a wail. Nothing was said then either. Nor when they clambered over the shingle and the rocks, and climbed up to the short-cut and passed through the gorse field. From the cliff they looked again, for the last time, far out to the horizon. The sea was undisturbed, glittering in the sunlight. "So what have you two been up to this morning?" Miss Davally asked. The next day, somewhere else, the dog was washed in.

Miss Davally blamed herself, for that was in her nature. But she could not be blamed. It was agreed that she could not be. Unaware of his limitations—more than a little blind, with only three active legs—old Jericho had had a way of going into the sea when he sensed a piece of driftwood bobbing about. Once too often he had done that. His grave was in the garden, a small slate plaque let into the turf, his name and dates.

They did not ever speak to one another about the drowning of the dog. They did not ever say they had not meant it to occur. There was no blame, no accusing. They had not called it a game, only said they wondered what would happen, what the dog would do. The silence had begun before they pushed the Lilo out.

Other summers brought other incidents, other experiences, but there was no such occurrence again. There were adjustments in the friendship, since passing time demanded that, and different games were played, and there were different conversations, and new discoveries.

Then, one winter, a letter from Miss Davally was less cheerful than her letters usually were. *Withdrawn*, she wrote, *and they are concerned*. What she declared, in detail after that, was confirmed when summer came: Anthony was different, and more different still in later summers, quieter, timid, seeming sometimes to be lost. It was a mystery when the dog's gravestone disappeared from the garden.

• • •

In the dark, the bright red dot of the television light still piercingly there, Wilby wonders, as so often he has, what influence there was when without incitement or persuasion, without words, they did what had been done. They were nine years old then, when secrets became deception.

It was snowing the evening he and Anthony met again, both of them waiting in the chapel cloisters for their names, as new boys, to be called out. It was not a surprise that Anthony was there, passing on from the school that years ago had declared him clever; nor was it by chance that they were to be together for what remained of their education. "Nice for Anthony to have someone he knows," his father said on the telephone, and confirmed that Anthony was still as he had become.

In the dim evening light the snow blew softly into the cloisters, and when the roll-call ended and a noisy dispersal began, the solitary figure remained, the same smooth black hair, a way of standing that hadn't changed. "How are you?" Wilby asked. His friend's smile, once so readily there, came as a shadow and then was lost in awkwardness.

Peculiar, Anthony was called at school, but wasn't bullied, as though it had been realized that bullying would yield no satisfaction. He lacked skill at games, avoided all pursuits that were not compulsory, displayed immediate evidence of his cleverness, science and mathematical subjects his forte. Religious boys attempted to befriend him, believing that to be a duty; kindly masters sought to draw him out. "Well, yes, I knew him," Wilby admitted, lamely explaining his association with someone who was so very much not like the friends he made now. "A long time ago," he nearly always added.

Passing by the windows of empty classrooms, he several times noticed Anthony, the only figure among the unoccupied desks. And often—on the drive that ended at the school gates, or often anywhere—there was the same lone figure in the distance. On the golf-course where senior boys were allowed to play, Anthony sometimes sat on a seat against a wall, watching the golfers as they approached, watching them as they walked on. He shied away when conversation threatened, creeping back into his shadowlands.

One day he wasn't there, his books left tidily in his desk, clothes hanging in his dormitory locker, his pyjamas under his pillow. He would be on his way home, since boys who kept themselves to themselves were often homesick. But he had not attempted to go home and was found still within the school grounds, having broken no rules except that he had ignored for a day the summoning of bells.

• • •

Dawn comes darkly, and Wilby sleeps. But his sleep is brief, his dreams forgotten when he wakes. The burden of guilt that came when in silence they clambered over the shingle and the rocks, when they passed through the gorse field, was muddled by bewilderment, a child's tormenting panic not yet constrained by suppression as later it would be. Long afterwards, when first he heard that Anthony was dead—and when he said it himself—the remnants of the shame guilt had become fell away.

He shaves and washes, dresses slowly. In the hall the reception clerks have just come on duty. They nod at him, wish him good-day. No call this morning for an umbrella, one says.

Outside it is not entirely day, or even day at all. The cleaning lorries[1] are on the streets, water pouring in the gutters, but there's no one about in rue du Bac, refuse sacks still waiting to be collected. A bar is open further on, men standing at the counter, disinclined for conversation with one another. A sleeping figure in a doorway has not been roused. What hovel, Wilby wonders as he passes, does a kitchen worker occupy?

In rue Piques the brasserie is shuttered, no lights showing anywhere. Cardboard boxes are stacked close to the glass of three upstairs windows, others are uncurtained; none suggests the domesticity of a dwelling. Le Père Jothy the place is called.

Wilby roams the nearby streets. A few more cafés are opening and in one coffee is brought to him. He sips it, breaking a croissant. There's no one else, except the barman.

He knows he should go away. He should take the train to Passy, to the salerooms he has planned to visit there; he should not ever return to rue Piques. He has lived easily with an aberration, then shaken it off: what happened was almost nothing.

Other men come in, a woman on her own, her face bruised on one side, no effort made to conceal the darkening weals. Her voice is low when she explains this injury to the barman, her fingers now and again touching it. Soundlessly, she weeps when she has taken her cognac to a table.

Oh, this is silly! his unspoken comment was when Miss Davally's letter came, its implications apparent only to him. For heaven's sake! he crossly muttered, the words kept to himself when he greeted Anthony in the cloisters, and again every time he caught sight of him on the golf-course. The old dog's life had been all but over. And Wilby remembers now—as harshly as he has in the night—the bitterness of his resentment when a friendship he delighted in was destroyed, when Anthony's world—the garden, the house, his mother, his father, Miss Davally—was no longer there.

"He has no use for us," his father said. "No use for anyone, we think."

• • •

Turning into rue Piques, Anthony notices at once the figure waiting outside the ribbon shop. It is November the twenty-fourth, the last Thursday of the month. This day won't come again.

"*Bonjour*,"[2] he says.

"How are you, Anthony?"

And Anthony says that Monday is the closed day. Not that Sunday isn't too. If someone waited outside the ribbon shop on a Monday or a Sunday it wouldn't be much good. Not that many people wait there.

---

1    *lorries* Trucks.
2    *Bonjour* French: Good day.

Wind blows a scrap of paper about, close to where they stand. In the window of the ribbon shop coils of ribbon are in all widths and colours, and there are swatches of trimming for other purposes, lace and velvet, and plain white edging, and a display of button cards.[1] Anthony often looks to see if there has been a change, but there never has been.

"How are you, Anthony?"

It is a fragment of a white paper bag that is blown about and Anthony identifies it from the remains of the red script that advertises the *boulangerie*[2] in rue Dupin. When it is blown closer to him he catches it under his shoe.

"People have wondered where you are, Anthony."

"I went away from Ireland."

Anthony bends and picks up the litter he has trapped. He says he has the ovens to do today. A Thursday, and he works in the morning.

"Miss Davally still writes, wondering if there is news of you."

Half past eight is his time on Thursdays. Anthony says that, and adds that there's never a complaint in the kitchen. One speck on the prong of a fork could lead to a complaint, a shred of fish skin could, a cabbage leaf. But there's never a complaint.

"People thought you were dead, Anthony."

• • •

Wilby says he sold the wineshop. He described it once, when they were children: the shelves of bottles, the different shapes, their contents red or white, pink if people wanted that. He tasted wine a few times, he remembers saying.

"Your father has died himself, Anthony. Your mother has. Miss Davally was left the house because there was no one else. She lives there now."

No response comes; Wilby has not expected one. He has become a philatelist, he says.

• • •

Anthony nods, waiting to cross the street. He knows his father died, his mother too. He has guessed Miss Davally inherited the house. The deaths were in the *Irish Times*, which he always read, cover to cover, all the years he was the night porter at the Cliff Castle Hotel in Dalkey.[3]

He doesn't mention the Cliff Castle Hotel. He doesn't say he misses the *Irish Times*, the familiar names, the political news, the photographs of places, the change there is in Ireland now. *Le Monde*[4] is more staid, more circumspect, more serious. Anthony doesn't say that either because he doubts that it's of interest to a visitor to Paris.

---

1    *button cards* Small packages of buttons for sale.
2    *boulangerie* French: bakery.
3    *Dalkey* Coastal village on the outskirts of Dublin.
4    *Le Monde* Major French newspaper.

A gap comes in the stream of cars that has begun to go by; but not trusting this opportunity, Anthony still waits. He is careful on the streets, even though he knows them well.

"I haven't died," he says.

• • •

Perfectly together, they shared an act that was too shameful to commit alone, taking a chance on a sunny morning in order to discover if an old dog's cleverness would see to his survival.

For a moment, while Anthony loses another opportunity to cross the street, Wilby gathers into sentences how he might attempt a denial that this was how it was, how best to put it differently. An accident, a misfortune beyond anticipation, the unexpected: with gentleness, for gentleness is due, he is about to plead. But Anthony crosses the street then, and opens with a key the side door of the brasserie. He makes no gesture of farewell, he does not look back.

• • •

Walking by the river on his way to the salerooms at Passy, Wilby wishes he'd said he was glad his friend was not dead. It is his only thought. The pleasure-boats slip by on the water beside him, hardly anyone on them. A child waves. Raised too late in response, Wilby's own hand drops to his side. The wind that blew the litter about in rue Piques has freshened. It snatches at the remaining leaves on the black-trunked trees that are an orderly line, following the river's course.

The salerooms are on the other bank, near the radio building and the apartment block that change the river's character. Several times he has visited this vast display in which the world's stamps are exhibited behind glass if they are notably valuable, on the tables, country by country, when they are not. That busy image has always excited Wilby's imagination and as he climbs the steps to the bridge he is near he attempts to anticipate it now, but does not entirely succeed.

It is not in punishment that the ovens are cleaned on another Thursday morning. It is not in expiation[1] that soon the first leavings of the day will be scraped from the lunchtime plates. There is no bothering with redemption. Looking down from the bridge at the sluggish flow of water, Wilby confidently asserts that. A morning murkiness, like dusk, has brought some lights on in the apartment block. Traffic crawls on distant streets.

For Anthony, the betrayal matters, the folly, the carelessness that would have been forgiven, the cruelty. It mattered in the silence—while they watched, while they clambered over the shingle and the rocks, while they passed through

---

1    *expiation* Atonement.

the gorse field. It matters now. The haunted sea is all the truth there is for Anthony, what he honours because it matters still.

The buyers move among the tables and Wilby knows that for him, in this safe, second-hand world of postage stamps, tranquillity will return. He knows where he is with all this; he knows what he's about, as he does in other aspects of his tidy life. And yet this morning he likes himself less than he likes his friend.

—2007

# Ursula K. Le Guin

## 1929–2018

Few writers have done more to elevate the standing of science fiction as a recognized literary genre than Ursula K. Le Guin. Together with fellow American authors Philip K. Dick and Samuel R. Delany, Le Guin was instrumental in the emergence of New Wave science fiction, a movement that distinguished itself from the genre's so-called Golden Age of the 1940s and 1950s by a greater attention to style, increasingly nuanced characterization, a mounting interest in experimental narrative, and a more forthright engagement with political and gender issues. Le Guin's finest works—amongst them the Hugo and Nebula Award-winning novels *The Left Hand of Darkness* (1969) and *The Dispossessed* (1974)—are remarkable not only for the fluent evenness of their prose and the conceptual seriousness of their subject matter but also for their political astuteness and the minutely observed social and cultural details of the worlds they imagine into being.

The daughter of a noted anthropologist and psychologist, Le Guin was educated at Radcliffe College and Columbia. Her early interest in cultural anthropology, Jungian psychology, and Taoist philosophy would eventually come to provide a unifying conceptual framework for her writing. In the tradition of J.R.R. Tolkien's world-building, many of Le Guin's novels and stories dramatize a conflict between vividly realized alien cultures that the protagonist—frequently a traveller—observes and participates in as a quasi anthropologist. Archetypal figures and settings such as psychologist Carl Jung believed to symbolize humanity's shared psychic heritage also figure prominently in her work, which often has a richly allegorical dimension. Taoism, a third key element in Le Guin's intellectual framework, is likewise central to many of her texts, particularly the doctrine of inaction, which urges passivity over aggression, and the principle of the relativity of opposites, which posits the interdependence of light and darkness, good and evil, and male and female.

More than a master storyteller, Le Guin did much to advance the place of science fiction as a literature of ideas. In affirming the importance of imagination to human experience, her work demonstrates that science fiction can reflect the world more faithfully than what conventionally passes for realism.

# The Ones Who Walk Away from Omelas

With a clamour of bells that set the swallows soaring, the Festival of Summer came to the city. Omelas, bright-towered by the sea. The rigging of the boats in harbour sparkled with flags. In the streets between houses with red roofs and painted walls, between old moss-grown gardens and under avenues of trees, past great parks and public buildings, processions moved. Some were decorous: old people in long stiff robes of mauve and grey, grave master work-men, quiet, merry women carrying their babies and chatting as they walked. In other streets the music beat faster, a shimmering of gong and tambourine, and the people went dancing, the procession was a dance. Children dodged in and out, their high calls rising like the swallows' crossing flights over the music and the singing. All the processions wound towards the north side of the city, where on the great water-meadow called the Green Fields boys and girls, naked in the bright air, with mud-stained feet and ankles and long, lithe arms, exercised their restive horses before the race. The horses wore no gear at all but a halter without bit. Their manes were braided with streamers of silver, gold, and green. They flared their nostrils and pranced and boasted to one another; they were vastly excited, the horse being the only animal who has adopted our ceremonies as his own. Far off to the north and west the mountains stood up half encircling Omelas on her bay. The air of morning was so clear that the snow still crowning the Eighteen Peaks burned with white-gold fire across the miles of sunlit air, under the dark blue of the sky. There was just enough wind to make the banners that marked the racecourse snap and flutter now and then. In the silence of the broad green meadows one could hear the music winding through the city streets, farther and nearer and ever approaching, a cheerful faint sweetness of the air that from time to time trembled and gathered together and broke out into the great joyous clanging of the bells.

Joyous! How is one to tell about joy? How describe the citizens of Omelas?

They were not simple folk, you see, though they were happy. But we do not say the words of cheer much any more. All smiles have become archaic.[1] Given a description such as this one tends to make certain assumptions. Given a description such as this one tends to look next for the King, mounted on a splendid stallion and surrounded by his noble knights, or perhaps in a golden litter borne by great-muscled slaves. But there was no king. They did not use swords, or keep slaves. They were not barbarians. I do not know the rules and laws of their society, but I suspect that they were singularly few.

---

1   *All smiles ... archaic* Reference to the "archaic smile," an expression found on the faces of many sculpted figures from Ancient Greece.

As they did without monarchy and slavery, so they also got on without the stock exchange, the advertisement, the secret police, and the bomb. Yet I repeat that these were not simple folk, not dulcet shepherds, noble savages, bland utopians. They were not less complex than us. The trouble is that we have a bad habit, encouraged by pedants and sophisticates, of considering happiness as something rather stupid. Only pain is intellectual, only evil interesting. This is the treason of the artist: a refusal to admit the banality of evil and the terrible boredom of pain. If you can't lick 'em, join 'em. If it hurts, repeat it. But to praise despair is to condemn delight, to embrace violence is to lose hold of everything else. We have almost lost hold; we can no longer describe a happy man, nor make any celebration of joy. How can I tell you about the people of Omelas? They were not naive and happy children—though their children were, in fact, happy. They were mature, intelligent, passionate adults whose lives were not wretched. O miracle! but I wish I could describe it better. I wish I could convince you. Omelas sounds in my words like a city in a fairy tale, long ago and far away, once upon a time. Perhaps it would be best if you imagined it as your own fancy bids, assuming it will rise to the occasion, for certainly I cannot suit you all. For instance, how about technology? I think that there would be no cars or helicopters in and above the streets; this follows from the fact that the people of Omelas are happy people. Happiness is based on a just discrimination of what is necessary, what is neither necessary nor destructive, and what is destructive. In the middle category, however—that of the unnecessary but undestructive, that of comfort, luxury, exuberance, etc.—they could perfectly well have central heating, subway trains, washing machines, and all kinds of marvellous devices not yet invented here, floating light-sources, fuelless power, a cure for the common cold. Or they could have none of that: it doesn't matter. As you like it. I incline to think that people from towns up and down the coast have been coming in to Omelas during the last days before the Festival on very fast little trains and double-decked trains and that the train station of Omelas is actually the handsomest building in town, though plainer than the magnificent Farmers' Market. But even granted trains, I fear that Omelas so far strikes some of you as goody-goody. Smiles, bells, parades, horses, bleh. If so, please add an orgy. If an orgy would help, don't hesitate. Let us not, however, have temples from which issue beautiful nude priests and priestesses already half in ecstasy and ready to copulate with any man or woman, lover or stranger, who desires union with the deep godhead of the blood, although that was my first idea. But really it would be better not to have any temples in Omelas—at least, not manned temples. Religion yes, clergy no. Surely the beautiful nudes can just wander about, offering themselves like divine soufflés to the hunger of the needy and the rapture of the flesh. Let them join the processions. Let tambourines be struck above the copulations, and the glory of desire be proclaimed upon the gongs, and (a not unimportant point) let the offspring of these delightful rituals be beloved and looked after by all. One thing I know there is none of in Omelas is guilt. But what else should there be? I thought at first there were no drugs, but that is puritanical. For those who like it, the faint insistent sweetness of *drooz* may perfume the ways of the city, *drooz* which first brings a great lightness and brilliance to the mind and limbs, and then after some hours a dreamy languor, and wonderful visions at last of the very arcana and inmost secrets of the Universe, as well as exciting the pleasure of sex beyond all belief; and it is not habit-forming. For more modest tastes I think there ought to be beer. What else, what else belongs in the joyous city? The sense of victory, surely, the celebration of courage. But as we did without clergy, let us do without soldiers. The joy built upon successful slaughter is not the right kind of joy; it will not do; it is fearful and it is trivial. A boundless and generous contentment, a magnanimous triumph felt not against some outer enemy but in communion with the finest and fairest in the souls of all men everywhere and the splendour of the world's summer: this is what swells the hearts of the people of Omelas, and the victory they celebrate is that of life. I really don't think many of them need to take *drooz*.

Most of the processions have reached the Green Fields by now. A marvellous smell of cooking goes forth from the red and blue tents of the provisioners. The faces of small children are amiably sticky; in the benign grey beard of a man a couple of crumbs of rich pastry are entangled. The youths and girls have mounted their horses and are beginning to group around the starting line of the course. An old woman, small, fat, and laughing, is passing out flowers from a basket, and tall young men wear her flowers in their shining hair. A child of nine or ten sits at the edge of the crowd, alone, playing on a wooden flute. People pause to listen, and they smile, but they do not speak to him, for he never ceases playing and never sees them, his dark eyes wholly rapt in the sweet, thin magic of the tune.

He finishes, and slowly lowers his hands holding the wooden flute.

As if that little private silence were the signal, all at once a trumpet sounds from the pavilion near the starting line: imperious, melancholy, piercing. The horses rear on their slender legs, and some of them neigh in answer. Soberfaced, the young riders stroke the horses' necks and soothe them, whispering, "Quiet, quiet, there my beauty, my hope...." They begin to form in rank along the starting line. The crowds along the racecourse are like a field of grass and flowers in the wind. The Festival of Summer has begun.

Do you believe? Do you accept the festival, the city, the joy? No? Then let me describe one more thing.

In a basement under one of the beautiful public buildings of Omelas, or perhaps in the cellar of one of its spacious private homes, there is a room. It has one locked door, and no window. A little light seeps in dustily between cracks in the boards, secondhand from a cobwebbed window somewhere across the cellar. In one corner of the little room a couple of mops, with stiff, clotted, foul-smelling heads, stand near a rusty bucket. The floor is dirt, a little damp to the touch, as cellar dirt usually is. The room is about three paces long and two wide: a mere broom closet or disused tool room. In the room a child is sitting. It could be a boy or a girl. It looks about six, but actually is nearly ten. It is feeble-minded. Perhaps it was born defective, or perhaps it has become imbecile through fear, malnutrition, and neglect. It picks its nose and occasionally fumbles vaguely with its toes or genitals, as it sits hunched in the corner farthest from the bucket and the two mops. It is afraid of the mops. It finds them horrible. It shuts its eyes, but it knows the mops are still standing there; and the door is locked; and nobody will come. The door is always locked; and nobody ever comes, except that sometimes—the child has no understanding of time or interval—sometimes the door rattles terribly and opens, and a person, or several people, are there. One of them may come in and kick the child to make it stand up. The others never come close, but peer in at it with frightened, disgusted eyes. The food bowl and the water jug are hastily filled, the door is locked, the eyes disappear. The people at the door never say anything, but the child, who has not always lived in the tool room, and can remember sunlight and its mother's voice, sometimes speaks. "I will be good," it says. "Please let me out. I will be good!" They never answer. The child used to scream for help at night, and cry a good deal, but now it only makes a kind of whining, "eh-haa, eh-haa," and it speaks less and less often. It is so thin there are no calves to its legs; its belly protrudes; it lives on a half-bowl of corn meal and grease a day. It is naked. Its buttocks and thighs are a mass of festered sores, as it sits in its own excrement continually.

They all know it is there, all the people of Omelas. Some of them have come to see it, others are content merely to know it is there. They all know that it has to be there. Some of them understand why, and some do not, but they all understand that their happiness, the beauty of their city, the tenderness of their friendships, the health of their children, the wisdom of their scholars, the skill of their makers, even the abundance of their harvest and the kindly weathers of their skies, depend wholly on this child's abominable misery.

This is usually explained to children when they are between eight and twelve, whenever they seem capable of understanding; and most of those who come to see the child are young people, though often enough an adult comes, or comes back, to see the child. No matter how well the matter has been explained to them, these young spectators are always shocked and sickened at the sight. They feel disgust, which they had thought themselves superior to. They feel anger, outrage, impotence, despite all the explanations. They would like to do something for the child. But there is nothing they can do. If the child were brought up into the sunlight out of that vile place, if it were cleaned and fed and comforted, that would be a good thing, indeed; but if it were done, in that day and hour all the prosperity and beauty and delight of Omelas would wither and be destroyed. Those are the terms. To exchange all the goodness and grace of every life in Omelas for that single, small improvement: to throw away the happiness of thousands for the chance of the happiness of one: that would be to let guilt within the walls indeed.

The terms are strict and absolute; there may not even be a kind word spoken to the child.

Often the young people go home in tears, or in a tearless rage, when they have seen the child and faced this terrible paradox. They may brood over it for weeks or years. But as time goes on they begin to realize that even if the child could be released, it would not get much good of its freedom: a little vague pleasure of warmth and food, no doubt, but little more. It is too degraded and imbecile to know any real joy. It has been afraid too long ever to be free of fear. Its habits are too uncouth for it to respond to humane treatment. Indeed, after so long it would probably be wretched without walls about it to protect it, and darkness for its eyes, and its own excrement to sit in. Their tears at the bitter injustice dry when they begin to perceive the terrible justice of reality and to accept it. Yet it is their tears and anger, the trying of their generosity and the acceptance of their helplessness, which are perhaps the true source of the splendour of their lives. Theirs is no vapid, irresponsible happiness. They know that they, like the child, are not free. They know compassion. It is the existence of the child, and their knowledge of its existence, that makes possible the nobility of their architecture, the poignancy of their music, the profundity of their science. It is because of the child that they are so gentle with children. They know that if the wretched one were not there snivelling in the dark, the other one, the flute-player, could make no joyful music as the young riders line up in their beauty for the race in the sunlight of the first morning of summer.

Now do you believe in them? Are they not more credible? But there is one more thing to tell, and this is quite incredible.

At times one of the adolescent girls or boys who go to see the child does not go home to weep or rage, does not, in fact, go home at all. Sometimes also a man or woman much older falls silent for a day or two, and then leaves home. These people go out into the street, and walk down the street alone. They keep walking, and walk straight out of the city of Omelas, through the beautiful gates. They keep walking across the farmlands of Omelas. Each one goes alone, youth or girl, man or woman. Night falls; the traveller must pass down village streets, between the houses with yellow-lit windows, and on out into the darkness of the fields. Each alone, they go west or north, towards the mountains. They go on. They leave Omelas, they walk ahead into the darkness, and they do not come back. The place they go towards is a place even less imaginable to most of us than the city of happiness. I cannot describe it at all. It is possible that it does not exist. But they seem to know where they are going, the ones who walk away from Omelas.

—1973

# Chinua Achebe

## 1930–2013

Chinua Achebe was born in Nigeria when the country was still a colonial territory of the British Empire. He established his place as an important figure in world literature with the publication of his first novel, *Things Fall Apart*, in 1958. It remains, perhaps, the work for which he is best known, but Achebe was a prolific and wide-ranging writer who steadily published novels, short stories, poetry, essays, and children's books until his death in 2013.

While still a student, Achebe read literary accounts of Africa written by Europeans, many of which he found "appalling." This experience taught him that more African voices should represent Africans; Achebe writes that he "decided that the story we had to tell could not be told by anyone else no matter how gifted or well intentioned." For Achebe, telling such stories accurately was of political as well as artistic importance because his writing was "concerned with universal human communication across racial and cultural boundaries as a means of fostering respect for all people" and, he believed, "such respect can only issue from understanding." This aim of understanding across racial and cultural boundaries is one of the reasons he chose to write in English.

As in the selection here, as well as in novels such as *No Longer at Ease* (1960) and *Arrow of God* (1964), Achebe's protagonists are often flawed individuals, recalling the characters of the classical tragedies. He resisted simple tales of good and evil, attempting instead to represent the complexity and uncertainty of the human experience.

# Dead Men's Path

Michael Obi's hopes were fulfilled much earlier than he had expected. He was appointed headmaster of Ndume Central School in January 1949. It had always been an unprogressive school, so the Mission authorities[1] decided to send a young and energetic man to run it. Obi accepted this responsibility with enthusiasm. He had many wonderful ideas and this was an opportunity to put them into practice. He had had sound secondary school education which designated him a "pivotal teacher" in the official records and set him apart from the other headmasters in the mission field. He was outspoken in his condemnation of the narrow views of these older and often less-educated ones.

---

1  *Mission authorities*  Many schools in African countries colonized by the British were run by Christian missionary organizations.

"We shall make a good job of it, shan't we?" he asked his young wife when they first heard the joyful news of his promotion.

"We shall do our best," she replied. "We shall have such beautiful gardens and everything will be just *modern* and delightful...." In their two years of married life she had become completely infected by his passion for "modern methods" and his denigration of "these old and superannuated people in the teaching field who would be better employed as traders in the Onitsha[1] market." She began to see herself already as the admired wife of the young headmaster, the queen of the school.

The wives of the other teachers would envy her position. She would set the fashion in everything.... Then, suddenly, it occurred to her that there might not be other wives. Wavering between hope and fear, she asked her husband, looking anxiously at him.

"All our colleagues are young and unmarried," he said with enthusiasm which for once she did not share. "Which is a good thing," he continued.

"Why?"

"Why? They will give all their time and energy to the school."

Nancy was downcast. For a few minutes she became skeptical about the new school; but it was only for a few minutes. Her little personal misfortune could not blind her to her husband's happy prospects. She looked at him as he sat folded up in a chair. He was stoop-shouldered and looked frail. But he sometimes surprised people with sudden bursts of physical energy. In his present posture, however, all his bodily strength seemed to have retired behind his deep-set eyes, giving them an extraordinary power of penetration. He was only twenty-six, but looked thirty or more. On the whole, he was not unhandsome.

"A penny for your thoughts, Mike," said Nancy after a while, imitating the woman's magazine she read.

"I was thinking what a grand opportunity we've got at last to show these people how a school should be run."

Ndume School was backward in every sense of the word. Mr. Obi put his whole life into the work, and his wife hers too. He had two aims. A high standard of teaching was insisted upon, and the school compound was to be turned into a place of beauty. Nancy's dream-gardens came to life with the coming of the rains, and blossomed. Beautiful hibiscus and allamanda hedges in brilliant red and yellow marked out the carefully tended school compound from the rank neighbourhood bushes.

---

1    *Onitsha* City in southeastern Nigeria; the Onitsha market is one of the largest in West Africa.

One evening as Obi was admiring his work he was scandalized to see an old woman from the village hobble right across the compound, through a marigold flower-bed and the hedges. On going up there he found faint signs of an almost disused path from the village across the school compound to the bush on the other side.

"It amazes me," said Obi to one of his teachers who had been three years in the school, "that you people allowed the villagers to make use of this footpath. It is simply incredible." He shook his head.

"The path," said the teacher apologetically, "appears to be very important to them. Although it is hardly used, it connects the village shrine with their place of burial."

"And what has that got to do with the school?" asked the headmaster.

"Well, I don't know," replied the other with a shrug of the shoulders. "But I remember there was a big row some time ago when we attempted to close it."

"That was some time ago. But it will not be used now," said Obi as he walked away. "What will the Government Education Officer think of this when he comes to inspect the school next week? The villagers might, for all I know, decide to use the schoolroom for a pagan ritual during the inspection."

Heavy sticks were planted closely across the path at the two places where it entered and left the school premises. These were further strengthened with barbed wire.

Three days later the village priest of *Ani*[1] called on the headmaster. He was an old man and walked with a slight stoop. He carried a stout walking-stick which he usually tapped on the floor, by way of emphasis, each time he made a new point in his argument.

"I have heard," he said after the usual exchange of cordialities, "that our ancestral footpath has recently been closed...."

"Yes," replied Mr. Obi. "We cannot allow people to make a highway of our school compound."

"Look here, my son," said the priest bringing down his walking-stick, "this path was here before you were born and before your father was born. The whole life of this village depends on it. Our dead relatives depart by it and our ancestors visit us by it. But most important, it is the path of children coming in to be born...."

Mr. Obi listened with a satisfied smile on his face.

"The whole purpose of our school," he said finally, "is to eradicate just such beliefs as that. Dead men do not require footpaths. The whole idea is just fantastic. Our duty is to teach your children to laugh at such ideas."

---

1    *Ani* Traditional belief system of the Igbo people of Nigeria, often called Odinani.

"What you say may be true," replied the priest, "but we follow the practices of our fathers. If you reopen the path we shall have nothing to quarrel about. What I always say is: let the hawk perch and let the eagle perch." He rose to go.

"I am sorry," said the young headmaster. "But the school compound cannot be a thoroughfare. It is against our regulations. I would suggest your constructing another path, skirting our premises. We can even get our boys to help in building it. I don't suppose the ancestors will find the little detour too burdensome."

"I have no more words to say," said the old priest, already outside.

Two days later a young woman in the village died in childbed. A diviner was immediately consulted and he prescribed heavy sacrifices to propitiate ancestors insulted by the fence.

Obi woke up next morning among the ruins of his work. The beautiful hedges were torn up not just near the path but right round the school, the flowers trampled to death and one of the school buildings pulled down ... That day, the white Supervisor came to inspect the school and wrote a nasty report on the state of the premises but more seriously about the "tribal-war situation developing between the school and the village, arising in part from the misguided zeal of the new headmaster."

—1953

# Alice Munro
b. 1931

Alice Munro is acclaimed as a writer with a keen eye for detail and a fine sense of emotional nuance. In 2009, when she received the Man Booker International Prize, the award panel commented that "she brings as much depth, wisdom, and precision to every story as most novelists bring to a lifetime of novels." On October 10, 2013 Munro was awarded the 2013 Nobel Prize in Literature.

Alice Laidlaw was born into a farming community in Wingham, Ontario. After graduating from high school, she won a partial scholarship to attend the University of Western Ontario. She completed two years towards a degree in English, but she was unable to continue her studies due to strained finances. In 1951, she married James Munro; they moved to Vancouver and then to Victoria, British Columbia, where the couple opened a bookstore. They eventually had three daughters; Munro has often commented that the genre of the short story is well-suited to a working mother whose time for writing is limited.

Munro's work began to receive wide attention with the 1971 publication of *The Lives of Girls and Women*, a collection of interlinked stories (described later by the author as "autobiographical in form but not in fact") that traces the development of Del Jordan as she grows up in the constricting atmosphere of the small town of Jubilee. Everyday concerns over money and class and love and sex are recurrent themes in Munro's stories. Sensational events do happen in her fiction, but, as Alison Lurie has observed, "they usually take place offstage"; the focus of a Munro story is typically on emotion, not on incident.

# Friend of My Youth

WITH THANKS TO R.J.T.

I used to dream about my mother, and though the details in the dream varied, the surprise in it was always the same. The dream stopped, I suppose because it was too transparent in its hopefulness, too easy in its forgiveness.

In the dream I would be the age I really was, living the life I was really living, and I would discover that my mother was still alive. (The fact is, she died when I was in my early twenties and she in her early fifties.) Sometimes I would find myself in our old kitchen, where my mother would be rolling out piecrust on the table, or washing the dishes in the battered cream-coloured dish-pan with the red rim. But other times I would run into her on the street, in places where I would never have expected to see her. She might be walking through a handsome hotel lobby, or lining up in an airport. She would be looking quite well—not exactly youthful, not entirely untouched by the paralyzing disease that held her in its grip for a decade or more before her death, but so much better than I remembered that I would be astonished. Oh, I just have this little tremor in my arm, she would say, and a little stiffness up this side of my face. It is a nuisance but I get around.

I recovered then what in waking life I had lost—my mother's liveliness of face and voice before her throat muscles stiffened and a woeful, impersonal mask fastened itself over her features. How could I have forgotten this, I would think in the dream—the casual humour she had, not ironic but merry, the lightness and impatience and confidence? I would say that I was sorry I hadn't been to see her in such a long time—meaning not that I felt guilty but that I was sorry I had kept a bugbear in my mind, instead of this reality—and the strangest, kindest thing of all to me was her matter-of-fact reply.

Oh, well, she said, better late than never. I was sure I'd see you someday.

When my mother was a young woman with a soft, mischievous face and shiny, opaque silk stockings on her plump legs (I have seen a photograph of her, with her pupils), she went to teach at a one-room school, called Grieves School, in the Ottawa Valley. The school was on a corner of the farm that belonged to the Grieves family—a very good farm for that country. Well-drained fields with none of the Precambrian rock[1] shouldering through the soil, a little willow-edged river running alongside, a sugar bush, log barns, and a large, unornamented house whose wooden walls had never been painted but had been left to weather. And when wood weathers in the Ottawa Valley, my mother said, I do not know why this is, but it never turns grey, it turns black. There must be something in the air, she said. She often spoke of the Ottawa Valley, which was her home—she had grown up about twenty miles away from Grieves School—in a dogmatic, mystified way, emphasizing things about it that distinguished it from any other place on earth. Houses turn black, maple syrup has a taste no maple syrup produced elsewhere can equal, bears amble within sight of farmhouses. Of course I was disappointed when I finally got to see this place. It was not a valley at all, if by that you mean a cleft between hills; it was a mixture of flat fields and low rocks and heavy bush and little lakes—a scrambled, disarranged sort of country with no easy harmony about it, not yielding readily to any description.

The log barns and unpainted house, common enough on poor farms, were not in the Grieveses' case a sign of poverty but of policy. They had the

---

1   *Precambrian rock*  I.e., the rock of the Canadian Shield, a plateau spanning a large portion of Eastern and Central Canada.

money but they did not spend it. That was what people told my mother. The Grieveses worked hard and they were far from ignorant, but they were very backward. They didn't have a car or electricity or a telephone or a tractor. Some people thought this was because they were Cameronians—they were the only people in the school district who were of that religion—but in fact their church (which they themselves always called the Reformed Presbyterian) did not forbid engines or electricity or any inventions of that sort, just card playing, dancing, movies, and, on Sundays, any activity at all that was not religious or unavoidable.

My mother could not say who the Cameronians were or why they were called that. Some freak religion from Scotland, she said from the perch of her obedient and lighthearted Anglicanism. The teacher always boarded with the Grieveses, and my mother was a little daunted at the thought of going to live in that black board house with its paralytic Sundays and coal-oil lamps and primitive notions. But she was engaged by that time, she wanted to work on her trousseau[1] instead of running around the country having a good time, and she figured she could get home one Sunday out of three. (On Sundays at the Grieveses' house, you could light a fire for heat but not for cooking, you could not even boil the kettle to make tea, and you were not supposed to write a letter or swat a fly. But it turned out that my mother was exempt from these rules. "No, no," said Flora Grieves, laughing at her. "That doesn't mean you. You must just go on as you're used to doing." And after a while my mother had made friends with Flora to such an extent that she wasn't even going home on the Sundays when she'd planned to.)

Flora and Ellie Grieves were the two sisters left of the family. Ellie was married, to a man called Robert Deal, who lived there and worked the farm but had not changed its name to Deal's in anyone's mind. By the way people spoke, my mother expected the Grieves sisters and Robert Deal to be middle-aged at least, but Ellie, the younger sister, was only about thirty, and Flora seven or eight years older. Robert Deal might be in between.

The house was divided in an unexpected way. The married couple didn't live with Flora. At the time of their marriage, she had given them the parlour and the dining room, the front bedrooms and staircase, the winter kitchen. There was no need to decide about the bathroom, because there wasn't one. Flora had the summer kitchen, with its open rafters and uncovered brick walls, the old pantry made into a narrow dining room and sitting room, and the two back bedrooms, one of which was my mother's. The teacher was housed with Flora, in the poorer part of the house. But my mother didn't mind. She

---

1    *trousseau* Collection of clothing and household items assembled by a bride in preparation for her wedding.

immediately preferred Flora, and Flora's cheerfulness, to the silence and sickroom atmosphere of the front rooms. In Flora's domain it was not even true
that all amusements were forbidden. She had a crokinole[1] board—she taught
my mother how to play.

The division had been made, of course, in the expectation that Robert
and Ellie would have a family, and that they would need the room. This hadn't
happened. They had been married for more than a dozen years and there had
not been a live child. Time and again Ellie had been pregnant, but two babies
had been stillborn, and the rest she had miscarried. During my mother's first
year, Ellie seemed to be staying in bed more and more of the time, and my
mother thought that she must be pregnant again, but there was no mention
of it. Such people would not mention it. You could not tell from the look of
Ellie, when she got up and walked around, because she showed a stretched
and ruined though slack-chested shape. She carried a sickbed odour, and she
fretted in a childish way about everything. Flora took care of her and did all the
work. She washed the clothes and tidied up the rooms and cooked the meals
served in both sides of the house, as well as helping Robert with the milking
and separating. She was up before daylight and never seemed to tire. During
the first spring my mother was there, a great housecleaning was embarked
upon, during which Flora climbed the ladders herself and carried down the
storm windows, washed and stacked them away, carried all the furniture out of
one room after another so that she could scrub the woodwork and varnish the
floors. She washed every dish and glass that was sitting in the cupboards supposedly clean already. She scalded every pot and spoon. Such need and energy
possessed her that she could hardly sleep—my mother would wake up to the
sound of stovepipes being taken down, or the broom, draped in a dish towel,
whacking at the smoky cobwebs. Through the washed uncurtained windows
came a torrent of unmerciful light. The cleanliness was devastating. My mother
slept now on sheets that had been bleached and starched and that gave her a
rash. Sick Ellie complained daily of the smell of varnish and cleansing powders.
Flora's hands were raw. But her disposition remained topnotch. Her kerchief
and apron and Robert's baggy overalls that she donned for the climbing jobs
gave her the air of a comedian—sportive, unpredictable.

My mother called her a whirling dervish.[2]

"You're a regular whirling dervish, Flora," she said, and Flora halted. She
wanted to know what was meant. My mother went ahead and explained,
though she was a little afraid lest piety should be offended. (Not piety ex-

---

1    *crokinole* Tabletop game played by flicking small disks toward a target at the centre of the
     board.
2    *whirling dervish* Islamic mystic whose spiritual practice includes an ecstatic, spinning
     dance; figuratively, "whirling dervish" refers to an extremely energetic person.

actly—you could not call it that. Religious strictness.) Of course it wasn't. There was not a trace of nastiness or smug vigilance in Flora's observance of her religion. She had no fear of heathens—she had always lived in the midst of them. She liked the idea of being a dervish, and went to tell her sister.

"Do you know what the teacher says I am?"

Flora and Ellie were both dark-haired, dark-eyed women, tall and narrow-shouldered and long-legged. Ellie was a wreck, of course, but Flora was still superbly straight and graceful. She could look like a queen, my mother said—even riding into town in that cart they had. For church they used a buggy or a cutter,[1] but when they went to town they often had to transport sacks of wool—they kept a few sheep—or of produce, to sell, and they had to bring provisions home. The trip of a few miles was not made often. Robert rode in front, to drive the horse—Flora could drive a horse perfectly well, but it must always be the man who drove. Flora would be standing behind holding on to the sacks. She rode to town and back standing up, keeping an easy balance, wearing her black hat. Almost ridiculous but not quite. A gypsy queen, my mother thought she looked like, with her black hair and her skin that always looked slightly tanned, and her lithe and bold serenity. Of course she lacked the gold bangles and the bright clothes. My mother envied her her slenderness, and her cheekbones.

Returning in the fall for her second year, my mother learned what was the matter with Ellie.

"My sister has a growth," Flora said. Nobody then spoke of cancer.

My mother had heard that before. People suspected it. My mother knew many people in the district by that time. She had made particular friends with a young woman who worked in the post office; this woman was going to be one of my mother's bridesmaids. The story of Flora and Ellie and Robert had been told—or all that people knew of it—in various versions. My mother did not feel that she was listening to gossip, because she was always on the alert for any disparaging remarks about Flora—she would not put up with that. But indeed nobody offered any. Everybody said that Flora had behaved like a saint. Even when she went to extremes, as in dividing up the house—that was like a saint.

Robert came to work at Grieveses' some months before the girls' father died. They knew him already, from church. (Oh, that church, my mother said, having attended it once, out of curiosity—that drear building miles on the other side of town, no organ or piano and plain glass in the windows and a doddery old minister with his hours-long sermon, a man hitting a tuning

---

1   *cutter* Sleigh.

fork for the singing.) Robert had come out from Scotland and was on his way west. He had stopped with relatives or people he knew, members of the scanty congregation. To earn some money, probably, he came to Grieveses'. Soon he and Flora were engaged. They could not go to dances or to card parties like other couples, but they went for long walks. The chaperone—unofficially— was Ellie. Ellie was then a wild tease, a long-haired, impudent, childish girl full of lolloping energy. She would run up hills and smite the mullein stalks with a stick, shouting and prancing and pretending to be a warrior on horseback. That, or the horse itself. This when she was fifteen, sixteen years old. Nobody but Flora could control her, and generally Flora just laughed at her, being too used to her to wonder if she was quite right in the head. They were wonderfully fond of each other. Ellie, with her long skinny body, her long pale face, was like a copy of Flora—the kind of copy you often see in families, in which because of some carelessness or exaggeration of features or colouring, the handsomeness of one person passes into the plainness—or almost plainness—of the other. But Ellie had no jealousy about this. She loved to comb out Flora's hair and pin it up. They had great times, washing each other's hair. Ellie would press her face into Flora's throat, like a colt nuzzling its mother. So when Robert laid claim to Flora, or Flora to him—nobody knew how it was—Ellie had to be included. She didn't show any spite toward Robert, but she pursued and waylaid them on their walks; she sprung on them out of the bushes or sneaked up behind them so softly that she could blow on their necks. People saw her do it. And they heard of her jokes. She had always been terrible for jokes and sometimes it had got her into trouble with her father, but Flora had protected her. Now she put thistles in Robert's bed. She set his place at the table with the knife and fork the wrong way around. She switched the milk pails to give him the old one with the hole in it. For Flora's sake, maybe, Robert humoured her.

The father had made Flora and Robert set the wedding day a year ahead, and after he died they did not move it any closer. Robert went on living in the house. Nobody knew how to speak to Flora about this being scandal- ous, or looking scandalous. Flora would just ask why. Instead of putting the wedding ahead, she put it back—from next spring to early fall, so that there should be a full year between it and her father's death. A year from wedding to funeral—that seemed proper to her. She trusted fully in Robert's patience and in her own purity.

So she might. But in the winter a commotion started. There was Ellie, vomiting, weeping, running off and hiding in the haymow, howling when they found her and pulled her out, jumping to the barn floor, running around in circles, rolling in the snow. Ellie was deranged. Flora had to call the doctor. She told him that her sister's periods had stopped—could the backup of blood be driving her wild? Robert had had to catch her and tie her up, and together he and Flora had put her to bed. She would not take food, just whipped her head from side to side, howling. It looked as if she would die speechless. But somehow the truth came out. Not from the doctor, who could not get close enough to examine her, with all her thrashing about. Probably, Robert confessed. Flora finally got wind of the truth, through all her high-mindedness. Now there had to be a wedding, though not the one that had been planned.

No cake, no new clothes, no wedding trip, no congratulations. Just a shameful hurry-up visit to the manse.[1] Some people, seeing the names in the paper, thought the editor must have got the sisters mixed up. They thought it must be Flora. A hurry-up wedding for Flora! But no—it was Flora who pressed Robert's suit—it must have been—and got Ellie out of bed and washed her and made her presentable. It would have been Flora who picked one geranium from the window plant and pinned it to her sister's dress. And Ellie hadn't torn it out. Ellie was meek now, no longer flailing or crying. She let Flora fix her up, she let herself be married, she was never wild from that day on.

Flora had the house divided. She herself helped Robert build the necessary partitions. The baby was carried full term—nobody even pretended that it was early—but it was born dead after a long, tearing labour. Perhaps Ellie had damaged it when she jumped from the barn beam and rolled in the snow and beat on herself. Even if she hadn't done that, people would have expected something to go wrong, with that child or maybe one that came later. God dealt out punishment for hurry-up marriages—not just Presbyterians but almost everybody else believed that. God rewarded lust with dead babies, idiots, harelips and withered limbs and clubfeet.

In this case the punishment continued. Ellie had one miscarriage after another, then another stillbirth and more miscarriages. She was constantly pregnant, and the pregnancies were full of vomiting fits that lasted for days, headaches, cramps, dizzy spells. The miscarriages were as agonizing as full-term births. Ellie could not do her own work. She walked around holding on to chairs. Her numb silence passed off, and she became a complainer. If anybody came to visit, she would talk about the peculiarities of her headaches or describe her latest fainting fit, or even—in front of men, in front of unmarried girls or children—go into bloody detail about what Flora called her "disappointments." When people changed the subject or dragged the children away, she turned sullen. She demanded new medicine, reviled the doctor, nagged Flora. She accused Flora of washing the dishes with a great clang and clatter, out of spite, of pulling her—Ellie's—hair when she combed it out, of stingily substituting water-and-molasses for her real medicine. No matter what she said, Flora soothed her. Everybody who came into the house had some story

---

1    *manse* Minister's house.

of that kind to tell. Flora said, "Where's my little girl, then? Where's my Ellie? This isn't my Ellie, this is some crosspatch[1] got in here in place of her!"

In the winter evenings after she came in from helping Robert with the barn chores, Flora would wash and change her clothes and go next door to read Ellie to sleep. My mother might invite herself along, taking whatever sewing she was doing, on some item of her trousseau. Ellie's bed was set up in the big dining room, where there was a gas lamp over the table. My mother sat on one side of the table, sewing, and Flora sat on the other side, reading aloud. Sometimes Ellie said, "I can't hear you." Or if Flora paused for a little rest Ellie said, "I'm not asleep yet."

What did Flora read? Stories about Scottish life—not classics. Stories about urchins and comic grandmothers. The only title my mother could remember was *Wee Macgregor*.[2] She could not follow the stories very well, or laugh when Flora laughed and Ellie gave a whimper, because so much was in Scots dialect or read with that thick accent. She was surprised that Flora could do it—it wasn't the way Flora ordinarily talked, at all.

(But wouldn't it be the way Robert talked? Perhaps that is why my mother never reports anything that Robert said, never has him contributing to the scene. He must have been there, he must have been sitting there in the room. They would only heat the main room of the house. I see him black-haired, heavy-shouldered, with the strength of a plow horse, and the same kind of sombre, shackled beauty.)

Then Flora would say, "That's all of that for tonight." She would pick up another book, an old book written by some preacher of their faith. There was in it such stuff as my mother had never heard. What stuff? She couldn't say. All the stuff that was in their monstrous old religion. That put Ellie to sleep, or made her pretend she was asleep, after a couple of pages.

All that configuration of the elect and the damned, my mother must have meant—all the arguments about the illusion and necessity of free will. Doom and slippery redemption. The torturing, defeating, but for some minds irresistible pileup of interlocking and contradictory notions. My mother could resist it. Her faith was easy, her spirits at that time robust. Ideas were not what she was curious about, ever.

But what sort of thing was that, she asked (silently), to read to a dying woman? This was the nearest she got to criticizing Flora.

The answer—that it was the only thing, if you believed it—never seemed to have occurred to her.

---

1    *crosspatch* Grump.
2    *Wee Macgregor* Comic short story collection by John Joy Bell (1902).

By spring a nurse had arrived. That was the way things were done then. People died at home, and a nurse came in to manage it.

The nurse's name was Audrey Atkinson. She was a stout woman with corsets as stiff as barrel hoops, marcelled[1] hair the colour of brass candlesticks, a mouth shaped by lipstick beyond its own stingy outlines. She drove a car into the yard—her own car, a dark-green coupé, shiny and smart. News of Audrey Atkinson and her car spread quickly. Questions were asked. Where did she get the money? Had some rich fool altered his will on her behalf? Had she exercised influence? Or simply helped herself to a stash of bills under the mattress? How was she to be trusted?

Hers was the first car ever to sit in the Grieveses' yard overnight.

Audrey Atkinson said that she had never been called out to tend a case in so primitive a house. It was beyond her, she said, how people could live in such a way.

"It's not that they're poor, even," she said to my mother. "It isn't, is it? That I could understand. Or it's not even their religion. So what is it? They do not care!"

She tried at first to cozy up to my mother, as if they would be natural allies in this benighted place. She spoke as if they were around the same age—both stylish, intelligent women who liked a good time and had modern ideas. She offered to teach my mother to drive the car. She offered her cigarettes. My mother was more tempted by the idea of learning to drive than she was by the cigarettes. But she said no, she would wait for her husband to teach her. Audrey Atkinson raised her pinkish-orange eyebrows at my mother behind Flora's back, and my mother was furious. She disliked the nurse far more than Flora did.

"I knew what she was like and Flora didn't," my mother said. She meant that she caught a whiff of a cheap life, maybe even of drinking establishments and unsavory men, of hard bargains, which Flora was too unworldly to notice.

Flora started into the great housecleaning again. She had the curtains spread out on stretchers, she beat the rugs on the line, she leapt up on the stepladder to attack the dust on the moulding. But she was impeded all the time by Nurse Atkinson's complaining.

"I wondered if we could have a little less of the running and clattering?" said Nurse Atkinson with offensive politeness. "I only ask for my patient's sake." She always spoke of Ellie as "my patient" and pretended that she was the only one to protect her and compel respect. But she was not so respectful of Ellie herself. "Allee-oop," she would say, dragging the poor creature up on her pillows. And she told Ellie she was not going to stand for fretting and whimpering. "You don't do yourself any good that way," she said. "And you

---

1    *marcelled* Artificially wavy.

certainly don't make me come any quicker. What you just as well might do is learn to control yourself." She exclaimed at Ellie's bedsores in a scolding way, as if they were a further disgrace of the house. She demanded lotions, ointments, expensive soap—most of them, no doubt, to protect her own skin, which she claimed suffered from the hard water. (How could it be hard, my mother asked her—sticking up for the household when nobody else would—how could it be hard when it came straight from the rain barrel?)

Nurse Atkinson wanted cream, too—she said that they should hold some back, not sell it all to the creamery. She wanted to make nourishing soups and puddings for her patient. She did make puddings, and jellies, from packaged mixes such as had never before entered this house. My mother was convinced that she ate them all herself.

Flora still read to Ellie, but now it was only short bits from the Bible. When she finished and stood up, Ellie tried to cling to her. Ellie wept, sometimes she made ridiculous complaints. She said there was a horned cow outside, trying to get into the room and kill her.

"They often get some kind of idea like that," Nurse Atkinson said.. "You mustn't give in to her or she won't let you go day or night. That's what they're like, they only think about themselves. Now, when I'm here alone with her, she behaves herself quite nice. I don't have any trouble at all. But after you been in here I have trouble all over again because she sees you and she gets upset. You don't want to make my job harder for me, do you? I mean, you brought me here to take charge, didn't you?"

"Ellie, now, Ellie dear, I must go," said Flora, and to the nurse she said, "I understand. I do understand that you have to be in charge and I admire you, I admire you for your work. In your work you have to have so much patience and kindness."

My mother wondered at this—was Flora really so blinded, or did she hope by this undeserved praise to exhort Nurse Atkinson to the patience and kindness that she didn't have? Nurse Atkinson was too thick-skinned and self-approving for any trick like that to work.

"It is a hard job, all right, and not many can do it," she said. "It's not like those nurses in the hospital, where they got everything laid out for them." She had no time for more conversation—she was trying to bring in "Make-Believe Ballroom"[1] on her battery radio.

My mother was busy with the final exams and the June exercises at the school. She was getting ready for her wedding in July. Friends came in cars and whisked her off to the dressmaker's, to parties, to choose the invitations

---

1    *"Make-Believe Ballroom"* Radio program (1930s–1950s) that broadcast recordings of popular music.

and order the cake. The lilacs came out, the evenings lengthened, the birds were back and nesting, my mother bloomed in everybody's attention, about to set out on the deliciously solemn adventure of marriage. Her dress was to be appliquéd with silk roses, her veil held by a cap of seed pearls. She belonged to the first generation of young women who saved their money and paid for their own weddings—far fancier than their parents could have afforded.

On her last evening, the friend from the post office came to drive her away, with her clothes and her books and the things she had made for her trousseau and the gifts her pupils and others had given her. There was great fuss and laughter about getting everything loaded into the car. Flora came out and helped. This getting married is even more of a nuisance than I thought, said Flora, laughing. She gave my mother a dresser scarf, which she had crocheted in secret. Nurse Atkinson could not be shut out of an important occasion—she presented a spray bottle of cologne. Flora stood on the slope at the side of the house to wave good-bye. She had been invited to the wedding, but of course she had said she could not come, she could not "go out" at such a time. The last my mother ever saw of her was this solitary, energetically waving figure in her housecleaning apron and bandanna, on the green slope by the black-walled house, in the evening light.

"Well, maybe now she'll get what she should've got the first time round," the friend from the post office said. "Maybe now they'll be able to get married. Is she too old to start a family? How old is she, anyway?"

My mother thought that this was a crude way of talking about Flora and replied that she didn't know. But she had to admit to herself that she had been thinking the very same thing.

When she was married and settled in her own home, three hundred miles away, my mother got a letter from Flora. Ellie was dead. She had died firm in her faith, Flora said, and grateful for her release. Nurse Atkinson was staying on for a little while, until it was time for her to go off to her next case. This was late in the summer.

News of what happened next did not come from Flora. When she wrote at Christmas, she seemed to take for granted that information would have gone ahead of her.

"You have in all probability heard," wrote Flora, "that Robert and Nurse Atkinson have been married. They are living on here, in Robert's part of the house. They are fixing it up to suit themselves. It is very impolite of me to call her Nurse Atkinson, as I see I have done. I ought to have called her Audrey."

Of course the post-office friend had written, and so had others. It was a great shock and scandal and a matter that excited the district—the wedding as secret and surprising as Robert's first one had been (though surely not for the same reason), Nurse Atkinson permanently installed in the community, Flora losing out for the second time. Nobody had been aware of any courtship, and they asked how the woman could have enticed him. Did she promise children, lying about her age?

The surprises were not to stop with the wedding. The bride got down to business immediately with the "fixing up" that Flora mentioned. In came the electricity and then the telephone. Now Nurse Atkinson—she would always be called Nurse Atkinson—was heard on the party line lambasting painters and paperhangers and delivery services. She was having everything done over. She was buying an electric stove and putting in a bathroom, and who knew where the money was coming from? Was it all hers, got in her deathbed dealings, in shady bequests? Was it Robert's, was he claiming his share? Ellie's share, left to him and Nurse Atkinson to enjoy themselves with, the shameless pair?

All these improvements took place on one side of the house only. Flora's side remained just as it was. No electric lights there, no fresh wallpaper or new venetian blinds. When the house was painted on the outside—cream with dark-green trim—Flora's side was left bare. This strange open statement was greeted at first with pity and disapproval, then with less sympathy, as a sign of Flora's stubbornness and eccentricity (she could have bought her own paint and made it look decent), and finally as a joke. People drove out of their way to see it.

There was always a dance given in the schoolhouse for a newly married couple. A cash collection—called "a purse of money"—was presented to them. Nurse Atkinson sent out word that she would not mind seeing this custom followed, even though it happened that the family she had married into was opposed to dancing. Some people thought it would be a disgrace to gratify her, a slap in the face to Flora. Others were too curious to hold back. They wanted to see how the newlyweds would behave. Would Robert dance? What sort of outfit would the bride show up in? They delayed a while, but finally the dance was held, and my mother got her report.

The bride wore the dress she had worn at her wedding, or so she said. But who would wear such a dress for a wedding at the manse? More than likely it was bought specially for her appearance at the dance. Pure-white satin with a sweetheart neckline, idiotically youthful. The groom was got up in a new dark-blue suit, and she had stuck a flower in his buttonhole. They were a sight. Her hair was freshly done to blind the eye with brassy reflections, and her face looked as if it would come off on a man's jacket, should she lay it against his shoulder in the dancing. Of course she did dance. She danced with every man present except the groom, who sat scrunched into one of the school desks along the wall. She danced with every man present—they all claimed they had to do it, it was the custom—and then she dragged Robert out to receive the money and to thank everybody for their best wishes. To the ladies in the cloakroom she even hinted that she was feeling unwell, for the usual newlywed reason. Nobody believed her, and indeed nothing ever came of this hope, if she really had it. Some of the women thought that she was lying to them out of malice, insulting them, making them out to be so credulous. But nobody challenged her, nobody was rude to her—maybe because it was plain that she could summon a rudeness of her own to knock anybody flat.

Flora was not present at the dance.

"My sister-in-law is not a dancer," said Nurse Atkinson. "She is stuck in the olden times." She invited them to laugh at Flora, whom she always called her sister-in-law, though she had no right to do so.

My mother wrote a letter to Flora after hearing about all these things. Being removed from the scene, and perhaps in a flurry of importance due to her own newly married state, she may have lost sight of the kind of person she was writing to. She offered sympathy and showed outrage, and said blunt disparaging things about the woman who had—as my mother saw it—dealt Flora such a blow. Back came a letter from Flora saying that she did not know where my mother had been getting her information, but that it seemed she had misunderstood, or listened to malicious people, or jumped to unjustified conclusions. What happened in Flora's family was nobody else's business, and certainly nobody needed to feel sorry for her or angry on her behalf. Flora said that she was happy and satisfied in her life, as she always had been, and she did not interfere with what others did or wanted, because such things did not concern her. She wished my mother all happiness in her marriage and hoped that she would soon be too busy with her own responsibilities to worry about the lives of people that she used to know.

This well-written letter cut my mother, as she said, to the quick. She and Flora stopped corresponding. My mother did become busy with her own life and finally a prisoner in it.

But she thought about Flora. In later years, when she sometimes talked about the things she might have been, or done, she would say, "If I could have been a writer—I do think I could have been; I could have been a writer—then I would have written the story of Flora's life. And do you know what I would have called it? 'The Maiden Lady.'"

*The Maiden Lady.* She said these words in a solemn and sentimental tone of voice that I had no use for. I knew, or thought I knew, exactly the value she found in them. The stateliness and mystery. The hint of derision turning to reverence. I was fifteen or sixteen years old by that time, and I believed that I could see into my mother's mind. I could see what she would do with Flora, what she had already done. She would make her into a noble figure, one who accepts defection, treachery, who forgives and stands aside, not once but twice. Never a moment of complaint. Flora goes about her cheerful labours, she cleans the house and shovels out the cow byre, she removes some bloody mess from her sister's bed, and when at last the future seems to open up for her—Ellie will die and Robert will beg forgiveness and Flora will silence him with the proud gift of herself—it is time for Audrey Atkinson to drive into the yard and shut Flora out again, more inexplicably and thoroughly the second time than the first. She must endure the painting of the house, the electric lights, all the prosperous activity next door. "Make-Believe Ballroom," "Amos 'n' Andy."[1] No more Scottish comedies or ancient sermons. She must see them drive off to the dance—her old lover and that coldhearted, stupid, by no means beautiful woman in the white satin wedding dress. She is mocked. (And of course she has made over the farm to Ellie and Robert, of course he has inherited it, and now everything belongs to Audrey Atkinson.) The wicked flourish. But it is all right. It is all right—the elect are veiled in patience and humility and lighted by a certainty that events cannot disturb.

That was what I believed my mother would make of things. In her own plight her notions had turned mystical, and there was sometimes a hush, a solemn thrill in her voice that grated on me, alerted me to what seemed a personal danger. I felt a great fog of platitudes and pieties lurking, an incontestable crippled-mother power, which could capture and choke me. There would be no end to it. I had to keep myself sharp-tongued and cynical, arguing and deflating. Eventually I gave up even that recognition and opposed her in silence.

This is a fancy way of saying that I was no comfort and poor company to her when she had almost nowhere else to turn.

I had my own ideas about Flora's story. I didn't think that I could have written a novel but that I would write one. I would take a different tack. I saw through my mother's story and put in what she left out. My Flora would be as black as hers was white. Rejoicing in the bad turns done to her and in her own forgiveness, spying on the shambles of her sister's life. A Presbyterian witch, reading out of her poisonous book. It takes a rival ruthlessness, the comparatively innocent brutality of the thick-skinned nurse, to drive her back, to flourish in her shade. But she is driven back; the power of sex and ordinary greed drive her back and shut her up in her own part of the house with the coal-oil lamps. She shrinks, she caves in, her bones harden and her joints thicken, and—oh, this is it, this is it, I see the bare beauty of the ending I will contrive!—she becomes crippled herself, with arthritis, hardly able to move. Now Audrey Atkinson comes into her full power—she demands the whole house. She wants those partitions knocked out that Robert put up with Flora's help when he married Ellie. She will provide Flora with a room, she will take

---

1   "Amos 'n' Andy" Comedy radio program (1928–58).

care of her. (Audrey Atkinson does not wish to be seen as a monster, and perhaps she really isn't one.) So one day Robert carries Flora—for the first and last time he carries her in his arms—to the room that his wife Audrey has prepared for her. And once Flora is settled in her well-lit, well-heated corner Audrey Atkinson undertakes to clean out the newly vacated rooms, Flora's rooms. She carries a heap of old books out into the yard. It's spring again, housecleaning time, the season when Flora herself performed such feats, and now the pale face of Flora appears behind the new net curtains. She has dragged herself from her corner, she sees the light-blue sky with its high skidding clouds over the watery fields, the contending crows, the flooded creeks, the reddening tree branches. She sees the smoke rise out of the incinerator in the yard, where her books are burning. Those smelly old books, as Audrey has called them. Words and pages, the ominous dark spines. The elect, the damned, the slim hopes, the mighty torments—up in smoke. There was the ending.

To me the really mysterious person in the story, as my mother told it, was Robert. He never has a word to say. He gets engaged to Flora. He is walking beside her along the river when Ellie leaps out at them. He finds Ellie's thistles in his bed. He does the carpentry made necessary by his and Ellie's marriage. He listens or does not listen while Flora reads. Finally he sits scrunched up in the school desk while his flashy bride dances by with all the men.

So much for his public acts and appearances. But he was the one who started everything, in secret. He *did it to* Ellie. He did it to that skinny wild girl at a time when he was engaged to her sister, and he did it to her again and again when she was nothing but a poor botched body, a failed childbearer, lying in bed.

He must have done it to Audrey Atkinson, too, but with less disastrous results.

Those words, *did it to*—the words my mother, no more than Flora, would never bring herself to speak—were simply exciting to me. I didn't feel any decent revulsion or reasonable indignation. I refused the warning. Not even the fate of Ellie could put me off. Not when I thought of that first encounter—the desperation of it, the ripping and striving. I used to sneak longing looks at men in those days. I admired their wrists and their necks and any bit of their chests a loose button let show, and even their ears and their feet in shoes. I expected nothing reasonable of them, only to be engulfed by their passion. I had similar thoughts about Robert.

What made Flora evil in my story was just what made her admirable in my mother's—her turning away from sex. I fought against everything my mother wanted to tell me on this subject; I despised even the drop in her voice, the gloomy caution, with which she approached it. My mother had grown up in a time and in a place where sex was a dark undertaking for women. She knew that you could die of it. So she honoured the decency, the prudery, the frigidity, that might protect you. And I grew up in horror of that very protection, the dainty tyranny that seemed to me to extend to all areas of life, to enforce tea parties and white gloves and all other sorts of tinkling inanities. I favoured bad words and a breakthrough, I teased myself with the thought of a man's recklessness and domination. The odd thing is that my mother's ideas were in line with some progressive notions of her times, and mine echoed the notions that were favoured in my time. This in spite of the fact that we both believed ourselves independent, and lived in backwaters that did not register such changes. It's as if tendencies that seem most deeply rooted in our minds, most private and singular, have come in as spores on the prevailing wind, looking for any likely place to land, any welcome.

Not long before she died, but when I was still at home, my mother got a letter from the real Flora. It came from that town near the farm, the town that Flora used to ride to, with Robert, in the cart, holding on to the sacks of wool or potatoes.

Flora wrote that she was no longer living on the farm.

"Robert and Audrey are still there," she wrote. "Robert has some trouble with his back but otherwise he is very well. Audrey has poor circulation and is often short of breath. The doctor says she must lose weight but none of the diets seem to work. The farm has been doing very well. They are out of sheep entirely and into dairy cattle. As you may have heard, the chief thing nowadays is to get your milk quota from the government and then you are set. The old stable is all fixed up with milking machines and the latest modern equipment, it is quite a marvel. When I go out there to visit I hardly know where I am."

She went on to say that she had been living in town for some years now, and that she had a job clerking in a store. She must have said what kind of a store this was, but I cannot now remember. She said nothing, of course, about what had led her to this decision—whether she had in fact been put off her own farm, or had sold out her share, apparently not to much advantage. She stressed the fact of her friendliness with Robert and Audrey. She said her health was good.

"I hear that you have not been so lucky in that way," she wrote. "I ran into Cleta Barnes who used to be Cleta Stapleton at the post office out at home, and she told me that there is some problem with your muscles and she said your speech is affected too. This is sad to hear but they can do such wonderful things nowadays so I am hoping that the doctors may be able to help you."

An unsettling letter, leaving so many things out. Nothing in it about God's will or His role in our afflictions. No mention of whether Flora still went to that church. I don't think my mother ever answered. Her fine legible handwriting, her schoolteacher's writing, had deteriorated, and she had difficulty holding a pen. She was always beginning letters and not finishing them. I would find them lying around the house. *My dearest Mary*, they began. *My darling Ruth, My dear little Joanne (though I realize you are not little anymore), My dear old friend Cleta, My lovely Margaret.* These women were friends from her teaching days, her Normal School days, and from high school. A few were former pupils. I have friends all over the country, she would say defiantly. I have dear, dear friends.

I remember seeing one letter that started out: *Friend of my Youth.* I don't know whom it was to. They were all friends of her youth. I don't recall one that began with *My dear and most admired Flora.* I would always look at them, try to read the salutation and the few sentences she had written, and because I could not bear to feel sadness I would feel an impatience with the flowery language, the direct appeal for love and pity. She would get more of that, I thought (more from myself, I meant), if she could manage to withdraw with dignity, instead of reaching out all the time to cast her stricken shadow.

I had lost interest in Flora by then. I was always thinking of stories, and by this time I probably had a new one on my mind.

But I have thought of her since. I have wondered what kind of a store. A hardware store or a five-and-ten, where she has to wear a coverall, or a drugstore, where she is uniformed like a nurse, or a Ladies' Wear, where she is expected to be genteelly fashionable? She might have had to learn about food blenders or chain saws, negligees, cosmetics, even condoms. She would have to work all day under electric lights, and operate a cash register. Would she get a permanent, paint her nails, put on lipstick? She must have found a place to live—a little apartment with a kitchenette, overlooking the main street, or a room in a boarding house. How could she go on being a Cameronian? How could she get to that out-of-the-way church unless she managed to buy a car and learned to drive it? And if she did that she might drive not only to church but to other places. She might go on holidays. She might rent a cottage on a lake for a week, learn to swim, visit a city. She might eat meals in a restaurant, possibly in a restaurant where drinks were served. She might make friends with women who were divorced.

She might meet a man. A friend's widowed brother, perhaps. A man who did not know that she was a Cameronian or what Cameronians were. Who knew nothing of her story. A man who had never heard about the partial painting of the house or the two betrayals, or that it took all her dignity and innocence to keep her from being a joke. He might want to take her dancing, and she would have to explain that she could not go. He would be surprised but not put off—all that Cameronian business might seem quaint to him, almost charming. So it would to everybody. She was brought up in some weird religion, people would say. She lived a long time out on some godforsaken farm. She is a little bit strange but really quite nice. Nice-looking, too. Especially since she went and got her hair done.

I might go into a store and find her.

No, no. She would be dead a long time now.

But suppose I had gone into a store—perhaps a department store. I see a place with the brisk atmosphere, the straightforward displays, the old-fashioned modern look of the fifties. Suppose a tall, handsome woman, nicely turned out, had come to wait on me, and I had known, somehow, in spite of the sprayed and puffed hair and the pink or coral lips and fingernails—I had known that this was Flora. I would have wanted to tell her that I knew, I knew her story, though we had never met. I imagine myself trying to tell her. (This is a dream now, I understand it as a dream.) I imagine her listening, with a pleasant composure. But she shakes her head. She smiles at me, and in her smile there is a degree of mockery, a faint, self-assured malice. Weariness, as well. She is not surprised that I am telling her this, but she is weary of it, of me and my idea of her, my information, my notion that I can know anything about her.

Of course it's my mother I'm thinking of, my mother as she was in those dreams, saying, It's nothing, just this little tremor; saying with such astonishing lighthearted forgiveness, Oh, I knew you'd come someday. My mother surprising me, and doing it almost indifferently. Her mask, her fate, and most of her affliction taken away. How relieved I was, and happy. But I now recall that I was disconcerted as well. I would have to say that I felt slightly cheated. Yes. Offended, tricked, cheated, by this welcome turnaround, this reprieve. My mother moving rather carelessly out of her old prison, showing options and powers I never dreamed she had, changes more than herself. She changes the bitter lump of love I have carried all this time into a phantom—something useless and uncalled for, like a phantom pregnancy.

The Cameronians, I have discovered, are or were an uncompromising remnant of the Covenanters—those Scots who in the seventeenth century bound themselves, with God, to resist prayer books, bishops, any taint of popery or interference by the King. Their name comes from Richard Cameron, an outlawed, or "field," preacher, soon cut down. The Cameronians—for a long time they have preferred to be called the Reformed Presbyterians—went into battle singing the seventy-fourth and the seventy-eighth Psalms. They hacked the haughty Bishop of St. Andrews to death on the highway and rode their horses over his body. One of their ministers, in a mood of firm rejoicing at his own hanging, excommunicated all the other preachers in the world.

—1990

# Alasdair Gray
b. 1934

Alasdair Gray is a novelist, poet, playwright, painter, and illustrator. He was born in 1934 to a working-class family in the suburb of Riddrie, in East Glasgow, Scotland. Gray claims that he began writing and sketching to stave off the doldrums of schoolboy life and to escape his perception of Glasgow as a dull and ordinary place. By his teens, Gray says, he realized that Glasgow "was as full of the materials of Heaven and Hell, of the possibilities of delight and horror, as anywhere else in the world or even the places you could invent." Gray has used Glasgow and Glasgow-like settings as the backdrop for much of his fiction, including *Lanark: A Life in Four Books* (1981)—a novel that he spent the better part of 30 years writing and the literary work for which he is best known.

Gray's parents were avid readers and kept many books in their home. As a child, Gray developed a particular fondness for authors who illustrated their own work, like Rudyard Kipling and William Blake. Gray was also captivated by the colourful and often imaginative artwork contained within volumes of the *Harmsworth Encyclopedia*. These early influences inspired Gray to enroll at the Glasgow School of Art and write fiction on the side. It was during his time as an art student that Gray began work on *Lanark* and wrote some of his finest short stories.

Critical response to Alasdair Gray's work is polarised. Upon reading *Lanark*, Anthony Burgess proclaimed Gray to be "the first major Scottish writer since Walter Scott" but retracted his praise after reading Gray's *1982, Janine* (1984), saying it displayed "the same large talent deployed to a somewhat juvenile end." Peter Levi offered even harsher criticism of *1982, Janine*, calling it "radio-active hogwash." Fellow Scottish author Irvine Welsh, however, is among a contingent of critics who believe that Gray is "one of the most gifted writers who have put pen to paper in the English language."

# The Star

A star had fallen beyond the horizon, in Canada perhaps. (He had an aunt in Canada.) The second was nearer, just beyond the iron works, so he was not surprised when the third fell into the backyard. A flash of gold light lit the walls of the enclosing tenements and he heard a low musical chord. The light turned deep red and went out, and he knew that somewhere below a star was cooling in the night air. Turning from the window he saw that no-one else had noticed. At the table his father, thoughtfully frowning, filled in a football coupon, his mother continued ironing under the pulley with its row of underwear. He said in a small voice, "A'm gawn out."

His mother said, "See you're no' long then."

He slipped through the lobby and onto the stairhead,[1] banging the door after him.

The stairs were cold and coldly lit at each landing by a weak electric bulb. He hurried down three flights to the black silent yard and began hunting backward and forward, combing with his fingers the lank grass round the base of the clothes-pole. He found it in the midden[2] on a decayed cabbage leaf. It was smooth and round, the size of a glass marble, and it shone with a light which made it seem to rest on a precious bit of green and yellow velvet. He picked it up. It was warm and filled his cupped palm with a ruby glow. He put it in his pocket and went back upstairs.

That night in bed he had a closer look. He slept with his brother who was not easily wakened. Wriggling carefully far down under the sheets, he opened his palm and gazed. The star shone white and blue, making the space around him like a cave in an iceberg. He brought it close to his eye. In its depth was the pattern of a snow-flake, the grandest thing he had ever seen. He looked through the flake's crystal lattice into an ocean of glittering blue-black waves under a sky full of huge galaxies. He heard a remote lulling sound like the sound in a sea-shell, and fell asleep with the star safely clenched in his hand.

He enjoyed it for nearly two weeks, gazing at it each night below the sheets, sometimes seeing the snow-flake, sometimes a flower, jewel, moon or land-scape. At first he kept it hidden during the day but soon took to carrying it

---

1   *stairhead* Landing above a staircase.
2   *midden* Household garbage heap.

about with him; the smooth rounded gentle warmth in his pocket gave comfort when he felt insulted or neglected.

At school one afternoon he decided to take a quick look. He was at the back of the classroom in a desk by himself. The teacher was among the boys at the front row and all heads were bowed over books. Quickly he brought out the star and looked. It contained an aloof eye with a cool green pupil which dimmed and trembled as if seen through water.

"What have you there, Cameron?"

He shuddered and shut his hand.

"Marbles are for the playground, not the classroom. You'd better give it to me."

"I cannae, sir."

"I don't tolerate disobedience, Cameron. Give me that thing."

The boy saw the teacher's face above him, the mouth opening and shutting under a clipped moustache. Suddenly he knew what to do and put the star in his mouth and swallowed. As the warmth sank toward his heart he felt relaxed and at ease. The teacher's face moved into the distance. Teacher, classroom, world receded like a rocket into a warm, easy blackness leaving behind a trail of glorious stars, and he was one of them.

—1951

# *Alistair MacLeod*

1936–2014

Alistair MacLeod was a Canadian short story writer and novelist. Born in North Battleford, Saskatchewan, to Nova Scotian parents, he was raised in Cape Breton, Nova Scotia, from the age of ten. MacLeod began publishing short stories in journals in the 1960s and 1970s, and attracted international recognition following the publication of "The Boat" in the *Massachusetts Review* in 1968. This story was republished in the annual volume of *Best American Short Stories* of 1969. His first collection, *The Lost Salt Gift of Blood*, was published to critical acclaim in 1976. His novel *No Great Mischief* (1999) made him the first Canadian to win the International IMPAC Dublin Literary Award in 2001.

Much of MacLeod's fiction depicts the psychological, physical, and emotional experience of the mining and fishing communities of Nova Scotia, set against the natural cycles of the seasons, of the sea, and of life and death. He often uses first-person present-tense narration, which lends immediacy to his subjects and themes and foregrounds the experience of memory. Joyce Carol Oates writes that the "single underlying motive" for the stories "is the urge to memorialize, the urge to sanctify." This elegiac tone is reminiscent of the Scottish and English traditions of oral literature, and the lyrical power of MacLeod's prose underscores this association, as does the natural ease of the storytelling.

MacLeod accepted a post at the University of Windsor in 1969, where he taught literature and creative writing. Each summer, he and his family returned to Inverness in Cape Breton, where he wrote his stories. He retired in 2000.

## As Birds Bring Forth the Sun

Once there was a family with a highland name who lived beside the sea. And the man had a dog of which he was very fond. She was large and grey, a sort of staghound from another time. And if she jumped up to lick his face, which she loved to do, her paws would jolt against his shoulders with such force that she would come close to knocking him down and he would be forced to take two or three backward steps before he could regain his balance. And he himself was not a small man, being slightly over six feet and perhaps one hundred and eighty pounds.

She had been left, when a pup, at the family's gate in a small handmade box and no one knew where she had come from or that she would eventually grow to such a size. Once, while still a small pup, she had been run over by the steel wheel of a horse-drawn cart which was hauling kelp from the shore to be used as fertilizer. It was in October and the rain had been falling for some weeks and the ground was soft. When the wheel of the cart passed over her, it sunk her body into the wet earth as well as crushing some of her ribs; and apparently the silhouette of her small crushed body was visible in the earth after the man lifted her to his chest while she yelped and screamed. He ran his fingers along her broken bones, ignoring the blood and urine which fell upon his shirt, trying to soothe her bulging eyes and her scrabbling front paws and her desperately licking tongue.

The more practical members of his family, who had seen run-over dogs before, suggested that her neck be broken by his strong hands or that he grasp her by the hind legs and swing her head against a rock, thus putting an end to her misery, but he would not do it.

Instead, he fashioned a small box and lined it with woollen remnants from a sheep's fleece and one of his old and frayed shirts. He placed her within the box and placed the box behind the stove and then he warmed some milk in a small saucepan and sweetened it with sugar. And he held open her small and trembling jaws with his left hand while spooning the sweetened milk with his right, ignoring the needle-like sharpness of her small teeth. She lay in the box most of the remaining fall and into the early winter, watching everything with her large brown eyes.

Although some members of the family complained about her presence and the odour from the box and the waste of time she involved, they gradually adjusted to her; and as the weeks passed by, it became evident that her ribs were knitting together in some form or other and that she was recovering with the resilience of the young. It also became evident that she would grow to a tremendous size, as she outgrew one box and then another and the grey hair began to feather from her huge front paws. In the spring she was outside almost all of the time and followed the man everywhere; and when she came inside during the following months, she had grown so large that she would no longer fit into her accustomed place behind the stove and was forced to lie beside it. She was never given a name but was referred to in Gaelic as *cù mòr glas*, the big grey dog.

By the time she came into her first heat, she had grown to a tremendous height, and although her signs and her odour attracted many panting and highly aroused suitors, none was big enough to mount her and the frenzy of their disappointment and the longing of her unfulfilment were more than the man could stand. He went, so the story goes, to a place where he knew there was a big dog. A dog not as big as she was, but still a big dog, and he brought him home with him. And at the proper time he took the *cù mòr glas* and the big dog down to the sea where he knew there was a hollow in the rock which appeared only at low tide. He took some sacking to provide footing for the male dog and he placed the *cù mòr glas* in the hollow of the rock and knelt beside her and steadied her with his left arm under her throat and helped position the male dog above her and guided his blood-engorged penis. He was a man used to working with the breeding of animals, with the guiding of rams and bulls and stallions and often with the funky smell of animal semen heavy on his large and gentle hands.

The winter that followed was a cold one and ice formed on the sea and frequent squalls and blizzards obliterated the offshore islands and caused the people to stay near their fires much of the time, mending clothes and nets and harness and waiting for the change in season. The *cù mòr glas* grew heavier and even more large until there was hardly room for her around the stove or even under the table. And then one morning, when it seemed that spring was about to break, she was gone.

The man and even his family, who had become more involved than they cared to admit, waited for her but she did not come. And as the frenzy of spring wore on, they busied themselves with readying their land and their fishing gear and all of the things that so desperately required their attention. And then they were into summer and fall and winter and another spring which saw the birth of the man and his wife's twelfth child. And then it was summer again.

That summer the man and two of his teenaged sons were pulling their herring nets about two miles offshore when the wind began to blow off the land and the water began to roughen. They became afraid that they could not make it safely back to shore, so they pulled in behind one of the offshore islands, knowing that they would be sheltered there and planning to outwait the storm. As the prow of their boat approached the gravelly shore they heard a sound above them, and looking up they saw the *cù mòr glas* silhouetted on the brow of the hill which was the small island's highest point.

"*M'eudal cù mòr glas*" shouted the man in his happiness—*m'eudal* meaning something like dear or darling; and as he shouted, he jumped over the side of his boat into the waist-deep water, struggling for footing on the rolling gravel as he waded eagerly and awkwardly towards her and the shore. At the same time, the *cù mòr glas* came hurtling down towards him in a shower of small rocks dislodged by her feet; and just as he was emerging from the water, she met him as she used to, rearing up on her hind legs and placing her huge front paws on his shoulders while extending her eager tongue.

The weight and speed of her momentum met him as he tried to hold his balance on the sloping angle and the water rolling gravel beneath his feet, and he staggered backwards and lost his footing and fell beneath her force. And in that instant again, as the story goes, there appeared over the brow of the hill six more huge grey dogs hurtling down towards the gravelled strand. They had never seen him before; and seeing him stretched prone beneath their mother, they misunderstood, like so many armies, the intention of their leader.

They fell upon him in a fury, slashing his face and tearing aside his lower jaw and ripping out his throat, crazed with blood-lust or duty or perhaps starvation. The *cù mòr glas* turned on them in her own savagery, slashing and snarling and, it seemed, crazed by their mistake; driving them bloodied and yelping before her, back over the brow of the hill where they vanished from sight but could still be heard screaming in the distance. It all took perhaps little more than a minute.

The man's two sons, who were still in the boat and had witnessed it all, ran sobbing through the salt water to where their mauled and mangled father lay; but there was little they could do other than hold his warm and bloodied hands for a few brief moments. Although his eyes "lived" for a small fraction of time, he could not speak to them because his face and throat had been torn away, and of course there was nothing they could do except to hold and be held tightly until that too slipped away and his eyes glazed over and they could no longer feel his hands holding theirs. The storm increased and they could not get home and so they were forced to spend the night huddled beside their father's body. They were afraid to try to carry the body to the rocking boat because he was so heavy and they were afraid that they might lose even what little of him remained and they were afraid also, huddled on the rocks, that the dogs might return. But they did not return at all and there was no sound from them, no sound at all, only the moaning of the wind and the washing of the water on the rocks.

In the morning they debated whether they should try to take his body with them or whether they should leave it and return in the company of older and wiser men. But they were afraid to leave it unattended and felt that the time needed to cover it with protective rocks would be better spent in trying to get across to their home shore. For a while they debated as to whether one should go in the boat and the other remain on the island, but each was afraid to be alone and so in the end they managed to drag and carry and almost float him towards the bobbing boat. They lay him face-down and covered him with what clothes there were and set off across the still-rolling sea. Those who waited on the shore missed the large presence of the man within the boat and some of them waded into the water and others rowed out in skiffs, attempting to hear the tearful messages called out across the rolling waves.

The *cù mòr glas* and her six young dogs were never seen again, or perhaps I should say they were never seen again in the same way. After some weeks, a group of men circled the island tentatively in their boats but they saw no sign. They went again and then again but found nothing. A year later, and grown much braver, they beached their boats and walked the island carefully, looking into the small sea caves and the hollows at the base of the wind-ripped trees, thinking perhaps that if they did not find the dogs, they might at least find their whitened bones; but again they discovered nothing.

The *cù mòr glas*, though, was supposed to be sighted here and there for a number of years. Seen on a hill in one region or silhouetted on a ridge in another or loping across the valleys or glens in the early morning or the shadowy evening. Always in the area of the half perceived. For a while she became rather like the Loch Ness Monster or the Sasquatch on a smaller scale. Seen but not recorded. Seen when there were no cameras. Seen but never taken.

The mystery of where she went became entangled with the mystery of whence she came. There was increased speculation about the handmade box in which she had been found and much theorizing as to the individual or individuals who might have left it. People went to look for the box but could not find it. It was felt she might have been part of a *buidseachd* or evil spell cast on the man by some mysterious enemy. But no one could go much farther than that. All of his caring for her was recounted over and over again and nobody missed any of the ironies.

What seemed literally known was that she had crossed the winter ice to have her pups and had been unable to get back. No one could remember ever seeing her swim; and in the early months at least, she could not have taken her young pups with her.

The large and gentle man with the smell of animal semen often heavy on his hands was my great-great-great-grandfather, and it may be argued that he died because he was too good at breeding animals or that he cared too much about their fulfillment and well-being. He was no longer there for his own child of the spring who, in turn, became my great-great-grandfather, and he was perhaps too much there in the memory of his older sons who saw him fall beneath the ambiguous force of the *cù mòr glas*. The youngest boy in the boat was haunted and tormented by the awfulness of what he had seen. He would wake at night screaming that he had seen the *cù mòr glas a'bhàis*, the big grey dog of death, and his screams filled the house and the ears and minds of the listeners, bringing home again and again the consequences of their loss. One morning, after a night in which he saw the *cù mòr glas a'bhàis* so vividly that his sheets were drenched with sweat, he walked to the high cliff which faced the island and there he cut his throat with a fish knife and fell into the sea.

The other brother lived to be forty, but, again so the story goes, he found himself in a Glasgow pub one night, perhaps looking for answers, deep and sodden with the whiskey which had become his anaesthetic. In the half darkness he saw a large, grey-haired man sitting by himself against the wall and mumbled something to him. Some say he saw the *cù mòr glas a'bhàis* or uttered the name. And perhaps the man heard the phrase through ears equally affected by drink and felt he was being called a dog or a son of a bitch or something of that nature. They rose to meet one another and struggled outside into the cobble-stoned passageway behind the pub where, most improbably, there were supposed to be six other large, grey-haired men who beat him to death on the cobblestones, smashing his bloodied head into the stone again and again before vanishing and leaving him to die with his face turned to the sky. The *cù mòr glas a'bhàis* had come again, said his family, as they tried to piece the tale together.

This is how the *cù mòr glas a'bhàis* came into our lives, and it is obvious that all of this happened a long, long time ago. Yet with succeeding generations it seemed the spectre had somehow come to stay and that it had become *ours*—not in the manner of an unwanted skeleton in the closet from a family's ancient past but more in the manner of something close to a genetic possibility. In the deaths of each generation, the grey dog was seen by some—by women who were to die in childbirth; by soldiers who went forth to the many wars but did not return; by those who went forth to feuds or dangerous love affairs; by those who answered mysterious midnight messages; by those who swerved on the highway to avoid the real or imagined grey dog and ended in masses of crumpled steel. And by one professional athlete who, in addition to his ritualized athletic superstitions, carried another fear or belief as well. Many of the man's descendants moved like careful hemophiliacs, fearing that they carried unwanted possibilities deep within them. And others, while they laughed, were like members of families in which there is a recurrence over the generations of repeated cancer or the diabetes which comes to those beyond middle age. The feeling of those who may say little to others but who may say often and quietly to themselves, "It has not happened to me," while adding always the cautionary "*yet.*"

I am thinking all of this now as the October rain falls on the city of Toronto and the pleasant, white-clad nurses pad confidently in and out of my father's room. He lies quietly amidst the whiteness, his head and shoulders elevated so that he is in that hospital position of being neither quite prone nor yet sitting. His hair is white upon his pillow and he breathes softly and sometimes unevenly, although it is difficult ever to be sure.

My five grey-haired brothers and I take turns beside his bedside, holding his heavy hands in ours and feeling their response, hoping ambiguously that he will speak to us, although we know that it may tire him. And trying to read his life and ours into his eyes when they are open. He has been with us for a long time, well into our middle age. Unlike those boys in that boat of so long ago, we did not see him taken from us in our youth. And unlike their youngest brother who, in turn, became our great-great-grandfather, we did not grow into a world in which there was no father's touch. We have been lucky to have this large and gentle man so deep into our lives.

No one in this hospital has mentioned the *cù mòr glas a'bhàis*. Yet as my mother said ten years ago, before slipping into her own death as quietly as a grownup child who leaves or enters her parents' house in the early hours, "It is hard to *not* know what you do know."

Even those who are most skeptical, like my oldest brother who has driven here from Montreal, betray themselves by their nervous actions. "I avoided the Greyhound bus stations in both Montreal and Toronto," he smiled upon his arrival, and then added, "Just in case."

He did not realize how ill our father was and has smiled little since then. I watch him turning the diamond ring upon his finger, knowing that he hopes he will not hear the Gaelic he knows too well. Not having the luxury, as he once said, of some who live in Montreal and are able to pretend they do not understand the "other" language. You cannot *not* know what you do know.

Sitting here, taking turns holding the hands of the man who gave us life, we are afraid for him and for ourselves. We are afraid of what he may see and we are afraid to hear the phrase born of the vision. We are aware that it may become confused with what the doctors call "the will to live" and we are aware that some beliefs are what others would dismiss as "garbage." We are aware that there are men who believe the earth is flat and that the birds bring forth the sun.

Bound here in our own peculiar mortality, we do not wish to see or see others see that which signifies life's demise. We do not want to hear the voice of our father, as did those other sons, calling down his own particular death upon him.

We would shut our eyes and plug our ears, even as we know such actions to be of no avail. Open still and fearful to the grey hair rising on our necks if and when we hear the scrabble of the paws and the scratching at the door.

—1985

# Raymond Carver
## 1938–1988

Born in Clatskanie, Oregon, to working-poor parents, Raymond Carver was raised in an abusive and unstable alcoholic home. By the age of 20, he was married with two children, working menial jobs, and drinking heavily. Struggling to pay the family's bills, he began writing poetry and short stories to earn extra money. Carver's experiences provided him with an intimate understanding of the hard-fought lives of America's struggling classes and he wrote about them with honesty and respect. "They're my people," said Carver. "I could never write down to them."

1977 marked the beginning of what Carver called his "second life." First, his collection of short stories *Will You Please Be Quiet, Please?* (1976) was nominated for a National Book Award; then he quit drinking and remained sober for the rest of his life. His subsequent collection *What We Talk about When We Talk about Love* (1981), which was an enormous success, moved critic Michael Wood to praise Carver's work for its "edges and silences" in which "a good deal of the unsayable gets said." Even greater success followed with the publication of *Cathedral* (1983), a collection that broke from the minimalism of Carver's previous work in favour of a new expansiveness.

Carver's next and final collection, *Where I'm Calling From* (1988), appeared only months before his death. A heavy smoker who once referred to himself as "a cigarette with a body attached to it," Carver succumbed to lung cancer at the age of 50. His grave lies in Port Angeles, Washington, and overlooks the Strait of Juan de Fuca.

# Cathedral

This blind man, an old friend of my wife's, he was on his way to spend the night. His wife had died. So he was visiting the dead wife's relatives in Connecticut. He called my wife from his in-laws'. Arrangements were made. He would come by train, a five-hour trip, and my wife would meet him at the station. She hadn't seen him since she worked for him one summer in Seattle ten years ago. But she and the blind man had kept in touch. They made tapes and mailed them back and forth. I wasn't enthusiastic about his visit. He was no one I knew. And his being blind bothered me. My idea of blindness came from the movies. In the movies, the blind moved slowly and never laughed. Sometimes they were led by seeing-eye dogs. A blind man in my house was not something I looked forward to.

That summer in Seattle she had needed a job. She didn't have any money. The man she was going to marry at the end of the summer was in officers' training school. He didn't have any money, either. But she was in love with the guy, and he was in love with her, etc. She'd seen something in the paper: HELP WANTED—*Reading to Blind Man*, and a telephone number. She phoned and went over, was hired on the spot. She'd worked with this blind man all summer. She read stuff to him, case studies, reports, that sort of thing. She helped him organize his little office in the county social-service department. They'd become good friends, my wife and the blind man. How do I know these things? She told me. And she told me something else. On her last day in the office, the blind man asked if he could touch her face. She agreed to this. She told me he touched his fingers to every part of her face, her nose—even her neck! She never forgot it. She even tried to write a poem about it. She was always trying to write a poem. She wrote a poem or two every year, usually after something really important had happened to her.

When we first started going out together, she showed me the poem. In the poem, she recalled his fingers and the way they had moved around over her face. In the poem, she talked about what she had felt at the time, about what went through her mind when the blind man touched her nose and lips. I can remember I didn't think much of the poem. Of course, I didn't tell her that. Maybe I just don't understand poetry. I admit it's not the first thing I reach for when I pick up something to read.

Anyway, this man who'd first enjoyed her favours, the officer-to-be, he'd been her childhood sweetheart. So okay. I'm saying that at the end of the summer she let the blind man run his hands over her face, said goodbye to him, married her childhood etc., who was now a commissioned officer, and she moved away from Seattle. But they'd kept in touch, she and the blind man. She made the first contact after a year or so. She called him up one night from an Air Force base in Alabama. She wanted to talk. They talked. He asked her to send him a tape and tell him about her life. She did this. She sent the tape. On the tape, she told the blind man about her husband and about their life together in the military. She told the blind man she loved her husband but she didn't like it where they lived and she didn't like it that he was a part of the military-industrial thing. She told the blind man she'd written a poem about what it was like to be an Air Force officer's wife. The poem wasn't finished yet. She was still writing it. The blind man made a tape. He sent her the tape. She made a tape. This went on for years. My wife's officer was posted to one base and then another. She sent tapes from Moody AFB, McGuire, McConnell, and finally Travis, near Sacramento, where one night she got to feeling lonely and cut off from people she kept losing in that moving-around life. She got to feeling she couldn't go it another step. She went in and swallowed all the pills and capsules in the medicine chest and washed them down with a bottle of gin. Then she got into a hot bath and passed out.

But instead of dying, she got sick. She threw up. Her officer—why should he have a name? he was the childhood sweetheart, and what more does he want?—came home from somewhere, found her, and called the ambulance. In time, she put it all on a tape and sent the tape to the blind man. Over the years, she put all kinds of stuff on tapes and sent the tapes off lickety-split. Next to writing a poem every year, I think it was her chief means of recreation. On one tape, she told the blind man she'd decided to live away from her officer for a time. On another tape, she told him about her divorce. She and I began going out, and of course she told her blind man about it. She told him everything, or so it seemed to me. Once she asked me if I'd like to hear the latest tape from the blind man. This was a year ago. I was on the tape, she said. So I said okay, I'd listen to it. I got us drinks and we settled down in the living room. We made ready to listen. First she inserted the tape into the player and adjusted a couple of dials. Then she pushed a lever. The tape squeaked and someone began to talk in this loud voice. She lowered the volume. After a few minutes of harmless chitchat, I heard my own name in the mouth of this stranger, this blind man I didn't even know! And then this: "From all you've said about him, I can only conclude—" But we were interrupted, a knock at the door, something, and we didn't ever get back to the tape. Maybe it was just as well. I'd heard all I wanted to.

Now this same blind man was coming to sleep in my house.

"Maybe I could take him bowling," I said to my wife. She was at the draining board doing scalloped potatoes. She put down the knife she was using and turned around.

"If you love me," she said, "you can do this for me. If you don't love me, okay. But if you had a friend, any friend, and the friend came to visit, I'd make him feel comfortable." She wiped her hands with the dish towel.

"I don't have any blind friends," I said.

"You don't have *any* friends," she said. "Period. Besides," she said, "god-damn it, his wife's just died! Don't you understand that? The man's lost his wife!"

I didn't answer. She'd told me a little about the blind man's wife. Her name was Beulah. Beulah! That's a name for a coloured woman.

"Was his wife a Negro?" I asked.

"Are you crazy?" my wife said. "Have you just flipped or something?" She picked up a potato. I saw it hit the floor, then roll under the stove. "What's wrong with you?" she said. "Are you drunk?"

"I'm just asking," I said.

Right then my wife filled me in with more detail than I cared to know. I made a drink and sat at the kitchen table to listen. Pieces of the story began to fall into place.

Beulah had gone to work for the blind man the summer after my wife had stopped working for him. Pretty soon Beulah and the blind man had themselves a church wedding. It was a little wedding—who'd want to go to such a wedding in the first place?—just the two of them, plus the minister and the minister's wife. But it was a church wedding just the same. It was what Beulah had wanted, he'd said. But even then Beulah must have been carrying the cancer in her glands. After they had been inseparable for eight years—my wife's word, *inseparable*—Beulah's health went into a rapid decline. She died in a Seattle hospital room, the blind man sitting beside the bed and holding on to her hand. They'd married, lived and worked together, slept together—had sex, sure—and then the blind man had to bury her. All this without his having ever seen what the goddamned woman looked like. It was beyond my understanding. Hearing this, I felt sorry for the blind man for a little bit. And then I found myself thinking what a pitiful life this woman must have led. Imagine a woman who could never see herself as she was seen in the eyes of her loved one. A woman who could go on day after day and never receive the smallest compliment from her beloved. A woman whose husband could never read the expression on her face, be it misery or something better. Someone who could wear makeup or not—what difference to him? She could, if she wanted, wear green eye-shadow around one eye, a straight pin in her nostril, yellow slacks and purple shoes, no matter. And then to slip off into death, the blind man's hand on her hand, his blind eyes streaming tears—I'm imagining now—her last thought maybe this: that he never even knew what she looked like, and she on an express to the grave. Robert was left with a small insurance policy and half of a twenty-peso Mexican coin. The other half of the coin went into the box with her. Pathetic.

So when the time rolled around, my wife went to the depot to pick him up. With nothing to do but wait—sure, I blamed him for that—I was having a drink and watching the TV when I heard the car pull into the drive. I got up from the sofa with my drink and went to the window to have a look.

I saw my wife laughing as she parked the car. I saw her get out of the car and shut the door. She was still wearing a smile. Just amazing. She went around to the other side to where the blind man was already starting to get out. This blind man, feature this, he was wearing a full beard! A beard on a blind man! Too much, I say. The blind man reached into the back seat and dragged out a suitcase. My wife took his arm, shut the car door, and, talking all the way, moved him down the drive and then up the steps to the front porch. I turned off the TV. I finished my drink, rinsed the glass, dried my hands. Then I went to the door.

My wife said, "I want you to meet Robert. Robert, this is my husband. I've told you all about him." She was beaming. She had this blind man by his coat sleeve.

The blind man let go of his suitcase and up came his hand.

I took it. He squeezed hard, held my hand, and then he let it go.

"I feel like we've already met," he boomed.

"Likewise," I said. I didn't know what else to say. Then I said, "Welcome. I've heard a lot about you." We began to move then, a little group, from the porch into the living room, my wife guiding him by the arm. The blind man was carrying his suitcase in his other hand. My wife said things like, "To your left here, Robert. That's right. Now watch it, there's a chair. That's it. Sit down right here. This is the sofa. We just bought this sofa two weeks ago."

I started to say something about the old sofa. I'd liked that old sofa. But I didn't say anything. Then I wanted to say something else, small-talk, about the scenic ride along the Hudson. How going *to* New York, you should sit on the right-hand side of the train, and coming *from* New York, the left-hand side.

"Did you have a good train ride?" I said. "Which side of the train did you sit on, by the way?"

"What a question, which side!" my wife said. "What's it matter which side?" she said.

"I just asked," I said.

"Right side," the blind man said. "I hadn't been on a train in nearly forty years. Not since I was a kid. With my folks. That's been a long time. I'd nearly forgotten the sensation. I have winter in my beard now," he said. "So I've been told, anyway. Do I look distinguished, my dear?" the blind man said to my wife.

"You look distinguished, Robert," she said. "Robert," she said. "Robert, it's just so good to see you."

My wife finally took her eyes off the blind man and looked at me. I had the feeling she didn't like what she saw. I shrugged.

I've never met, or personally known, anyone who was blind. This blind man was late forties, a heavy-set, balding man with stooped shoulders, as if he carried a great weight there. He wore brown slacks, brown shoes, a light-brown shirt, a tie, a sports coat. Spiffy. He also had this full beard. But he didn't use a cane and he didn't wear dark glasses. I'd always thought dark glasses were a must for the blind. Fact was, I wished he had a pair. At first glance, his eyes looked like anyone else's eyes. But if you looked close, there was something different about them. Too much white in the iris, for one thing, and the pupils seemed to move around in the sockets without his knowing it or being able to stop it. Creepy. As I stared at his face, I saw the left pupil turn in toward his nose while the other made an effort to keep in one place. But it was only an effort, for that eye was on the roam without his knowing it or wanting it to be.

I said, "Let me get you a drink. What's your pleasure? We have a little of everything. It's one of our pastimes."

"Bub, I'm a Scotch man myself," he said fast enough in this big voice.

"Right," I said. Bub! "Sure you are. I knew it."

He let his fingers touch his suitcase, which was sitting alongside the sofa. He was taking his bearings. I didn't blame him for that.

"I'll move that up to your room," my wife said.

"No, that's fine," the blind man said loudly. "It can go up when I go up."

"A little water with the Scotch?" I said.

"Very little," he said.

"I knew it," I said.

He said, "Just a tad. The Irish actor, Barry Fitzgerald? I'm like that fellow. When I drink water, Fitzgerald said, I drink water. When I drink whiskey, I drink whiskey." My wife laughed. The blind man brought his hand up under his beard. He lifted his beard slowly and let it drop.

I did the drinks, three big glasses of Scotch with a splash of water in each. Then we made ourselves comfortable and talked about Robert's travels. First the long flight from the West Coast to Connecticut, we covered that. Then from Connecticut up here by train. We had another drink concerning that leg of the trip.

I remembered having read somewhere that the blind didn't smoke because, as speculation had it, they couldn't see the smoke they exhaled. I thought I knew that much and that much only about blind people. But this blind man smoked his cigarette down to the nubbin and then lit another one. This blind man filled his ashtray and my wife emptied it.

When we sat down at the table for dinner, we had another drink. My wife heaped Robert's plate with cube steak, scalloped potatoes, green beans. I buttered him up two slices of bread. I said, "Here's bread and butter for you." I swallowed some of my drink. "Now let us pray," I said, and the blind man lowered his head. My wife looked at me, her mouth agape. "Pray the phone won't ring and the food doesn't get cold," I said.

We dug in. We ate everything there was to eat on the table. We ate like there was no tomorrow. We didn't talk. We ate. We scarfed. We grazed that table. We were into serious eating. The blind man had right away located his foods, he knew just where everything was on his plate. I watched with admiration as he used his knife and fork on the meat. He'd cut two pieces of meat, fork the meat into his mouth, and then go all out for the scalloped potatoes, the beans next, and then he'd tear off a hunk of buttered bread and eat that.

He'd follow this up with a big drink of milk. It didn't seem to bother him to use his fingers once in a while, either.

We finished everything, including half a strawberry pie. For a few moments, we sat as if stunned. Sweat beaded on our faces. Finally, we got up from the table and left the dirty plates. We didn't look back. We took ourselves into the living room and sank into our places again. Robert and my wife sat on the sofa. I took the big chair. We had us two or three more drinks while they talked about the major things that had come to pass for them in the past ten years. For the most part, I just listened. Now and then I joined in. I didn't want him to think I'd left the room, and I didn't want her to think I was feeling left out. They talked of things that had happened to them—to them!—these past ten years. I waited in vain to hear my name on my wife's sweet lips: "And then my dear husband came into my life"—something like that. But I heard nothing of the sort. More talk of Robert. Robert had done a little of everything, it seemed, a regular blind jack-of-all-trades. But most recently he and his wife had had an Amway[1] distributorship, from which, I gathered, they'd earned their living, such as it was. The blind man was also a ham radio operator. He talked in his loud voice about conversations he'd had with fellow operators in Guam, in the Philippines, in Alaska, and even in Tahiti. He said he'd have a lot of friends there if he ever wanted to go visit those places. From time to time, he'd turn his blind face toward me, put his hand under his beard, ask me something. How long had I been in my present position? (Three years.) Did I like my work? (I didn't.) Was I going to stay with it? (What were the options?) Finally, when I thought he was beginning to run down, I got up and turned on the TV.

My wife looked at me with irritation. She was heading toward a boil. Then she looked at the blind man and said, "Robert, do you have a TV?"

The blind man said, "My dear, I have two TVs. I have a colour set and a black-and-white thing, an old relic. It's funny, but if I turn the TV on, and I'm always turning it on, I turn on the colour set. It's funny, don't you think?"

I didn't know what to say to that. I had absolutely nothing to say to that. No opinion. So I watched the news program and tried to listen to what the announcer was saying.

"This is a colour TV," the blind man said. "Don't ask me how, but I can tell."

"We traded up a while ago." I said.

The blind man had another taste of his drink. He lifted his beard, sniffed it, and let it fall. He leaned forward on the sofa. He positioned his ashtray on the coffee table, then put the lighter to his cigarette. He leaned back on the sofa and crossed his legs at the ankles.

---

1    *Amway* Large pyramid sales company.

My wife covered her mouth, and then she yawned. She stretched. She said, "I think I'll go upstairs and put on my robe. I think I'll change into something else. Robert, you make yourself comfortable," she said.

"I'm comfortable," the blind man said.

"I want you to feel comfortable in this house," she said.

"I am comfortable," the blind man said.

After she'd left the room, he and I listened to the weather report and then to the sports roundup. By that time, she'd been gone so long I didn't know if she was going to come back. I thought she might have gone to bed. I wished she'd come back downstairs. I didn't want to be left alone with a blind man. I asked him if he wanted to smoke some dope with me. I said I'd just rolled a number. I hadn't, but I planned to do so in about two shakes.

"I'll try some with you," he said.

"Damn right," I said. "That's the stuff."

I got our drinks and sat down on the sofa with him. Then I rolled us two fat numbers. I lit one and passed it. I brought it to his fingers. He took it and inhaled.

"Hold it as long as you can," I said. I could tell he didn't know the first thing.

My wife came back downstairs wearing her pink robe and her pink slippers.

"What do I smell?" she said.

"We thought we'd have us some cannabis," I said.

My wife gave me a savage look. Then she looked at the blind man and said, "Robert, I didn't know you smoked."

He said, "I do now, my dear. There's a first time for everything. But I don't feel anything yet."

"This stuff is pretty mellow," I said. "This stuff is mild. It's dope you can reason with," I said. "It doesn't mess you up."

"Not much it doesn't, bub," he said, and laughed.

My wife sat on the sofa between the blind man and me. I passed her the number. She took it and toked and then passed it back to me. "Which way is this going?" she said. Then she said, "I shouldn't be smoking this. I can hardly keep my eyes open as it is. That dinner did me in. I shouldn't have eaten so much."

"It was the strawberry pie," the blind man said. "That's what did it," he said, and he laughed his big laugh. Then he shook his head.

"There's more strawberry pie," I said.

"Do you want some more, Robert?" my wife said.

"Maybe in a little while," he said.

We gave our attention to the TV. My wife yawned again. She said, "Your bed is made up when you feel like going to bed, Robert. I know you must have had a long day. When you're ready to go to bed, say so." She pulled his arm. "Robert?"

He came to and said, "I've had a real nice time. This beats tapes, doesn't it?"

I said, "Coming at you," and I put the number between his fingers. He inhaled, held the smoke, and then let it go. It was like he'd been doing it since he was nine years old.

"Thanks, bub," he said. "But I think this is all for me. I think I'm beginning to feel it," he said. He held the burning roach out for my wife.

"Same here," she said. "Ditto. Me, too." She took the roach and passed it to me. "I may just sit here for a while between you two guys with my eyes closed. But don't let me bother you, okay? Either one of you. If it bothers you, say so. Otherwise, I may just sit here with my eyes closed until you're ready to go to bed," she said. "Your bed's made up, Robert, when you're ready. It's right next to our room at the top of the stairs. We'll show you up when you're ready. You wake me up now, you guys, if I fall asleep." She said that and then she closed her eyes and went to sleep.

The news program ended. I got up and changed the channel. I sat back down on the sofa. I wished my wife hadn't pooped out. Her head lay across the back of the sofa, her mouth open. She'd turned so that her robe had slipped away from her legs, exposing a juicy thigh. I reached to draw her robe back over her, and it was then that I glanced at the blind man. What the hell! I flipped the robe open again.

"You say when you want some strawberry pie," I said.

"I will," he said.

I said, "Are you tired? Do you want me to take you up to your bed? Are you ready to hit the hay?"

"Not yet," he said. "No, I'll stay up with you, bub. If that's all right. I'll stay up until you're ready to turn in. We haven't had a chance to talk. Know what I mean? I feel like me and her monopolized the evening." He lifted his beard and he let it fall. He picked up his cigarettes and lighter.

"That's all right," I said. Then I said, "I'm glad for the company."

And I guess I was. Every night I smoked dope and stayed up as long as I could before I fell asleep. My wife and I hardly ever went to bed at the same time. When I did go to sleep, I had these dreams. Sometimes I'd wake up from one of them, my heart going crazy.

Something about the church and the Middle Ages was on the TV. Not your run-of-the-mill TV fare. I wanted to watch something else. I turned to the other channels. But there was nothing on them, either. So I turned back to the first channel and apologized.

"Bub, it's all right," the blind man said. "It's fine with me. Whatever you want to watch is okay. I'm always learning something. Learning never ends. It won't hurt me to learn something tonight. I got ears," he said.

We didn't say anything for a time. He was leaning forward with his head turned at me, his right ear aimed in the direction of the set. Very disconcerting. Now and then his eyelids dropped and then they snapped open again. Now and then he put his fingers into his beard and tugged, like he was thinking about something he was hearing on the television.

On the screen, a group of men wearing cowls was being set upon and tormented by men dressed in skeleton costumes and men dressed as devils. The men dressed as devils wore devil masks, horns, and long tails. This pageant was part of a procession. The Englishman who was narrating the thing said it took place in Spain once a year. I tried to explain to the blind man what was happening.

"Skeletons," he said. "I know about skeletons," he said and he nodded.

The TV showed this one cathedral. Then there was a long, slow look at another one. Finally, the picture switched to the famous one in Paris, with its flying buttresses and its spires reaching up to the clouds. The camera pulled away to show the whole of the cathedral rising above the skyline.

There were times when the Englishman who was telling the thing would shut up, would simply let the camera move around over the cathedrals. Or else the camera would tour the countryside, men in fields walking behind oxen. I waited as long as I could. Then I felt I had to say something. I said, "They're showing the outside of this cathedral now. Gargoyles. Little statues carved to look like monsters. Now I guess they're in Italy. Yeah, they're in Italy. There's paintings on the walls of this one church."

"Are those fresco paintings, bub?" he asked, and he sipped from his drink.

I reached for my glass. But it was empty. I tried to remember what I could remember. "You're asking me are those frescoes?" I said. "That's a good question. I don't know."

The camera moved to a cathedral outside Lisbon. The differences in the Portuguese cathedral compared with the French and Italian were not that great. But they were there. Mostly the interior stuff. Then something occurred to me, and I said, "Something has occurred to me. Do you have any idea what a cathedral is? What they look like, that is? Do you follow me? If somebody says cathedral to you, do you have any notion what they're talking about? Do you know the difference between that and a Baptist church, say?"

He let the smoke dribble from his mouth. "I know they took hundreds of workers fifty or a hundred years to build," he said. "I just heard the man say that, of course. I know generations of the same families worked on a cathedral. I heard him say that, too. The men who began their life's work on them, they never lived to see the completion of their work. In that wise, bub, they're no different from the rest of us, right?" He laughed. Then his eyelids drooped again. His head nodded. He seemed to be snoozing. Maybe he was imagining himself in Portugal. The TV was showing another cathedral now. This one was in Germany. The Englishman's voice droned on. "Cathedrals," the blind man said. He sat up and rolled his head back and forth. "If you want the truth, bub, that's about all I know. What I just said. What I heard him say. But maybe you could describe one to me? I wish you'd do it. I'd like that. If you want to know, I really don't have a good idea."

I stared hard at the shot of the cathedral on the TV. How could I even begin to describe it? But say my life depended on it. Say my life was being threatened by an insane guy who said I had to do it or else.

I stared some more at the cathedral before the picture flipped off into the countryside. There was no use. I turned to the blind man and said, "To begin with, they're very tall." I was looking around the room for clues. "They reach way up. Up and up. Toward the sky. They're so big, some of them, they have to have these supports. To help hold them up, so to speak. These supports are called buttresses. They remind me of viaducts, for some reason. But maybe you don't know viaducts, either? Sometimes the cathedrals have devils and such carved into the front. Sometimes lords and ladies. Don't ask me why this is," I said.

He was nodding. The whole upper part of his body seemed to be moving back and forth.

"I'm not doing so good, am I?" I said.

He stopped nodding and leaned forward on the edge of the sofa. As he listened to me, he was running his fingers through his beard. I wasn't getting through to him, I could see that. But he waited for me to go on just the same. He nodded, like he was trying to encourage me. I tried to think what else to say. "They're really big," I said. "They're massive. They're built of stone. Marble, too, sometimes. In those olden days, when they built cathedrals, men wanted to be close to God. In those olden days, God was an important part of everyone's life. You could tell this from their cathedral-building. I'm sorry," I said, "but it looks like that's the best I can do for you. I'm just no good at it."

"That's all right, bub," the blind man said. "Hey, listen, I hope you don't mind my asking you. Can I ask you something? Let me ask you a simple question, yes or no. I'm just curious and there's no offence. You're my host. But let me ask if you are in any way religious? You don't mind my asking?"

I shook my head. He couldn't see that, though. A wink is the same as a nod to a blind man. "I guess I don't believe in it. In anything. Sometimes it's hard. You know what I'm saying?"

"Sure, I do," he said.

"Right," I said.

The Englishman was still holding forth. My wife sighed in her sleep. She drew a long breath and went on with her sleeping.

"You'll have to forgive me," I said. "But I can't tell you what a cathedral looks like. It just isn't in me to do it. I can't do any more than I've done."

The blind man sat very still, his head down, as he listened to me.

I said, "The truth is, cathedrals don't mean anything special to me. Nothing. Cathedrals. They're something to look at on late-night TV. That's all they are."

It was then that the blind man cleared his throat. He brought something up. He took a handkerchief from his back pocket. Then he said, "I get it, bub. It's okay. It happens. Don't worry about it," he said. "Hey, listen to me. Will you do me a favour? I got an idea. Why don't you find us some heavy paper? And a pen. We'll do something. We'll draw one together. Get us a pen and some heavy paper. Go on, bub, get the stuff," he said.

So I went upstairs. My legs felt like they didn't have any strength in them. They felt like they did after I'd done some running. In my wife's room, I looked around. I found some ballpoints in a little basket on her table. And then I tried to think where to look for the kind of paper he was talking about.

Downstairs, in the kitchen, I found a shopping bag with onion skins at the bottom of the bag. I emptied the bag and shook it. I brought it into the living room and sat down with it near his legs. I moved some things, smoothed the wrinkles from the bag, spread it out on the coffee table.

The blind man got down from the sofa and sat next to me on the carpet.

He ran his fingers over the paper. He went up and down the sides of the paper. The edges, even the edges. He fingered the corners.

"All right," he said. "All right, let's do her."

He found my hand, the hand with the pen. He closed his hand over my hand. "Go ahead, bub, draw," he said. "Draw. You'll see. I'll follow along with you. It'll be okay. Just begin now like I'm telling you. You'll see. Draw," the blind man said.

So I began. First I drew a box that looked like a house. It could have been the house I lived in. Then I put a roof on it. At either end of the roof, I drew spires. Crazy.

"Swell," he said. "Terrific. You're doing fine," he said. "Never thought anything like this could happen in your lifetime, did you, bub? Well, it's a strange life, we all know that. Go on now. Keep it up."

I put in windows with arches. I drew flying buttresses. I hung great doors. I couldn't stop. The TV station went off the air. I put down the pen and closed and opened my fingers. The blind man felt around over the paper. He moved the tips of his fingers over the paper, all over what I had drawn, and he nodded.

"Doing fine," the blind man said.

I took up the pen again, and he found my hand. I kept at it. I'm no artist. But I kept drawing just the same.

My wife opened up her eyes and gazed at us. She sat up on the sofa, her robe hanging open. She said, "What are you doing? Tell me, I want to know."

I didn't answer her.

The blind man said, "We're drawing a cathedral. Me and him are working on it. Press hard," he said to me. "That's right. That's good," he said. "Sure. You got it, bub. I can tell. You didn't think you could. But you can, can't you? You're cooking with gas now. You know what I'm saying? We're going to really have us something here in a minute. How's the old arm?" he said. "Put some people in there now. What's a cathedral without people?"

My wife said, "What's going on? Robert, what are you doing? What's going on?"

"It's all right," he said to her. "Close your eyes now," the blind man said to me.

I did it. I closed them just like he said.

"Are they closed?" he said. "Don't fudge."

"They're closed," I said.

"Keep them that way," he said. He said, "Don't stop now. Draw."

So we kept on with it. His fingers rode my fingers as my hand went over the paper. It was like nothing else in my life up to now.

Then he said, "I think that's it. I think you got it," he said. "Take a look. What do you think?"

But I had my eyes closed. I thought I'd keep them that way for a little longer. I thought it was something I ought to do.

"Well?" he said. "Are you looking?"

My eyes were still closed. I was in my house. I knew that. But I didn't feel like I was inside anything.

"It's really something," I said.

—1983

# *Margaret Atwood*

b. 1939

Aptly described as "a nationalist who rankles nationalists, a feminist who rankles feminists," and "a political satirist who resists political solutions," Margaret Atwood is a writer who defies traditional categories. Her internationally renowned novels, short stories, and poems span and splice together a multitude of genres and have established her as a germinal figure in Canadian literature.

Atwood was born in Ottawa but spent much of her childhood in the Canadian bush. Educated at the University of Toronto and Radcliffe College, Atwood is a self-consciously Canadian writer, working in a tradition that she characterized in *Survival* (1972), her thematic survey of Canadian literature, as uniquely preoccupied with victimhood.

Although it was the stark, terse, eerily detached poetry in collections like *The Journals of Susanna Moodie* (1970) that made her reputation, Atwood's fiction is astonishing for its variety of tone, mingling seriousness, playful irony, sardonic humour, and even Gothic terror across a similarly diverse range of genres, from the dystopian "speculative fiction" of *The Handmaid's Tale* (1985) and *The Year of the Flood* (2009) to historical novels like *Alias Grace* (1996).

For Atwood, every art form is enclosed by a "set of brackets," conventions that check "the deviousness[,] inventiveness[,] audacity[,] and perversity of the creative spirit." In her work she aims to "expand the brackets," rewriting traditions to deliver the creative spirit from restraint. Though she has written a good deal of realist fiction, her fascination with storytelling has also led her to experiment widely with metafictional techniques, as in the at once open-ended and inexorable plots of "Happy Endings."

Of all the labels critics have applied to her, perhaps "trickster" suits Atwood best, for she is a master fabricator of great wit and imagination whose work refashions the rules to prove that, in the end, "art is what you can get away with."

# Happy Endings

*John and Mary meet.*
*What happens next?*
*If you want a happy ending, try A.*

A

John and Mary fall in love and get married. They both have worthwhile and remunerative jobs which they find stimulating and challenging. They buy a charming house. Real estate values go up. Eventually, when they can afford live-in help, they have two children, to whom they are devoted. The children turn out well. John and Mary have a stimulating and challenging sex life and worthwhile friends. They go on fun vacations together. They retire. They both have hobbies which they find stimulating and challenging. Eventually they die. This is the end of the story.

B

Mary falls in love with John but John doesn't fall in love with Mary. He merely uses her body for selfish pleasure and ego gratification of a tepid kind. He comes to her apartment twice a week and she cooks him dinner, you'll notice that he doesn't even consider her worth the price of a dinner out, and after he's eaten the dinner he fucks her and after that he falls asleep, while she does the dishes so he won't think she's untidy, having all those dirty dishes lying around, and puts on fresh lipstick so she'll look good when he wakes up, but when he wakes up he doesn't even notice, he puts on his socks and his shorts and his pants and his shirt and his tie and his shoes, the reverse order from the one in which he took them off. He doesn't take off Mary's clothes, she takes them off herself, she acts as if she's dying for it every time, not because she likes sex exactly, she doesn't, but she wants John to think she does because if they do it often enough surely he'll get used to her, he'll come to depend on her and they will get married, but John goes out the door with hardly so much as a goodnight and three days later he turns up at six o'clock and they do the whole thing over again.

Mary gets run-down. Crying is bad for your face, everyone knows that and so does Mary but she can't stop. People at work notice. Her friends tell her John is a rat, a pig, a dog, he isn't good enough for her, but she can't believe it. Inside John, she thinks, is another John, who is much nicer. This other John will emerge like a butterfly from a cocoon, a Jack from a box, a pit from a prune, if the first John is only squeezed enough.

One evening John complains about the food. He has never complained about the food before. Mary is hurt.

Her friends tell her they've seen him in a restaurant with another woman, whose name is Madge. It's not even Madge that finally gets to Mary: it's the restaurant. John has never taken Mary to a restaurant. Mary collects all the sleeping pills and aspirins she can find, and takes them and a half a bottle of sherry. You can see what kind of a woman she is by the fact that it's not even whiskey. She leaves a note for John. She hopes he'll discover her and get her to the hospital in time and repent and then they can get married, but this fails to happen and she dies.

John marries Madge and everything continues as in A.

## C

John, who is an older man, falls in love with Mary, and Mary, who is only twenty-two, feels sorry for him because he's worried about his hair falling out. She sleeps with him even though she's not in love with him. She met him at work. She's in love with someone called James, who is twenty-two also and not yet ready to settle down.

John on the contrary settled down long ago: this is what is bothering him. John has a steady, respectable job and is getting ahead in his field, but Mary isn't impressed by him, she's impressed by James, who has a motorcycle and a fabulous record collection. But James is often away on his motorcycle, being free. Freedom isn't the same for girls, so in the meantime Mary spends Thursday evenings with John. Thursdays are the only days John can get away.

John is married to a woman called Madge and they have two children, a charming house which they bought just before the real estate values went up, and hobbies which they find stimulating and challenging, when they have the time. John tells Mary how important she is to him, but of course he can't leave his wife because a commitment is a commitment. He goes on about this more than is necessary and Mary finds it boring, but older men can keep it up longer so on the whole she has a fairly good time.

One day James breezes in on his motorcycle with some top-grade California hybrid and James and Mary get higher than you'd believe possible and they climb into bed. Everything becomes very underwater, but along comes John, who has a key to Mary's apartment. He finds them stoned and entwined. He's hardly in any position to be jealous, considering Madge, but nevertheless he's overcome with despair. Finally he's middle-aged, in two years he'll be bald as an egg and he can't stand it. He purchases a handgun, saying he needs it for target practice—this is the thin part of the plot, but it can be dealt with later—and shoots the two of them and himself.

Madge, after a suitable period of mourning, marries an understanding man called Fred and everything continues as in A, but under different names.

## D

Fred and Madge have no problems. They get along exceptionally well and are good at working out any little difficulties that may arise. But their charming house is by the seashore and one day a giant tidal wave approaches. Real estate values go down. The rest of the story is about what caused the tidal wave and how they escape from it. They do, though thousands drown, but Fred and

Madge are virtuous and lucky. Finally on high ground they clasp each other, wet and dripping and grateful, and continue as in A.

E

Yes, but Fred has a bad heart. The rest of the story is about how kind they both are until Fred dies. Then Madge devotes herself to charity work until the end of A. If you like, it can be "Madge," "cancer," "guilty and confused," and "bird watching."

F

If you think this is all too bourgeois, make John a revolutionary and Mary a counterespionage agent and see how far that gets you. Remember, this is Canada. You'll still end up with A, though in between you may get a lustful brawling saga of passionate involvement; a chronicle of our times, sort of.

You'll have to face it, the endings are the same however you slice it. Don't be deluded by any other endings, they're all fake, either deliberately fake, with malicious intent to deceive, or just motivated by excessive optimism if not by downright sentimentality.
The only authentic ending is the one provided here:
*John and Mary die. John and Mary die. John and Mary die.*

So much for endings. Beginnings are always more fun. True connoisseurs, however, are known to favour the stretch in between, since it's the hardest to do anything with.
That's about all that can be said for plots, which anyway are just one thing after another, a what and a what and a what.

Now try How and Why.

—1983

# Ama Ata Aidoo
b. 1940

Born in a small village in Ghana, Ama Ata Aidoo is a prominent and accomplished author of plays, poetry, novels, and short stories, as well as an activist and academic. Her work often examines cultural and political conflicts between Africa and the West, directing particular attention to the everyday struggles of women in this postcolonial context. As Aidoo has explained, "in so many great literatures of the world, women are nearly always around to service the great male heroes. Since I am a woman it is natural that I not only write about women but with women in more central roles."

Known for her devotion to the cause of women's equality in Africa, Aidoo helped to found the Women's World Organization for Rights Development and Literature in 1994, and in 2000 she founded the Mbaasem Foundation, an NGO that "supports and promotes women's writing in Africa and across Ghana." Regarding the relationship between feminism and African politics, she argues that "every woman and every man should be a feminist—especially if they believe that Africans should take charge of our lands, its wealth, our lives and the burden of our own development. Because it is not possible to advocate independence for our continent without also believing that African women must have the best that the environment can offer."

Aidoo's writing is notable for combining influences from English-language written traditions with influences from West African oral traditions. In her fiction, the immediacy of her storytelling and her emphasis on dialogue combine to produce work that is, as she says, "written to be heard." Although she works in English, critics have remarked that her writing is sensitive to the rhythms and idioms of Ghanaian speech, as well as to the distinct voices of her individual characters.

In 1992, Aidoo was awarded the Commonwealth Writers' Prize for Best Book (Africa) for her novel *Changes* (1991). In addition to proving herself as a talented writer on the world stage, she has held positions at the University of Ghana, the University of Cape Coast, Stanford University, and Brown University.

# The Message

"Look here my sister, it should not be said but they say they opened her up."

"They opened her up?"

"Yes, opened her up."

"And the baby removed?"

"Yes, the baby removed."

"Yes, the baby removed."

"I say ..."

"They do not say, my sister."

"Have you heard it?"

"What?"

"This and this and that ..."

"A-a-ah! that is it ..."

"*Meewuo!*"[1]

"They don't say *meewuo* ..."

"And how is she?"

"Am I not here with you? Do I know the highway which leads to Cape Coast?"[2]

"Hmmm ..."

"And anyway how can she live? What is it like even giving birth with a stomach which is whole ... eh? ... I am asking you. And if you are always standing on the brink of death who go to war with a stomach that is whole, then how would she do whose stomach is open to the winds?"

"Oh, *poo*, pity ..."

"I say ..."

My little bundle, come. You and I are going to Cape Coast today.

I am taking one of her own cloths with me, just in case.[3] These people on the coast do not know how to do a thing and I am not going to have anybody mishandling my child's body. I hope they give it to me. Horrible things I have heard done to people's bodies. Cutting them up and using them for instructions. Whereas even murderers still have decent burials.

I see Mensima coming.... And there is Nkama too ... and Adwoa Meenu.... Now they are coming to ... "*poo* pity" me. Witches, witches, witches[4] ... they have picked mine up while theirs prosper around them, children, grandchildren and great-grandchildren—theirs shoot up like mushrooms.

---

1    *Meewuo*  Ewe: Dying.

2    *Cape Coast*  Port town in southern Ghana, the capital of its Central Region.

3    *just in case*  I.e., to use as a shroud if she is dead.

4    *Witches ... witches*  In Ghana, witchcraft is a common explanation for misfortune.

"Esi, we have heard of your misfortune ..."

"That our little lady's womb has been opened up ..."

"And her baby removed ..."

Thank you very much.

"Has she lived through it?"

I do not know.

"Esi, bring her here, back home whatever happens."

*Yoo*, thank you. If the government's people allow it, I shall bring her home.

"And have you got ready your things?"

Yes.... No.

I cannot even think well.

It feels so noisy in my head.... Oh my little child.... I am wasting time.... And so I am going ...

Yes, to Cape Coast.

No, I do not know anyone there now but do you think no one would show me the way to this big hospital ... if I asked around?

Hmmm ... it's me has ended up like this. I was thinking that everything was alright now.... *Yoo*. And thank you too. Shut the door for me when you are leaving. You may stay too long outside if you wait for me, so go home and be about your business. I will let you know when I bring her in.

"Maami Amfoa, where are you going?"

My daughter, I am going to Cape Coast.

"And what is our old mother going to do with such swift steps? Is it serious?"

My daughter, it is very serious.

"Mother, may God go with you."

*Yoo*, my daughter.

"Eno, and what calls at this hour of the day?"

They want me in Cape Coast.

"Does my friend want to go and see how much the city has changed since we went there to meet the new Wesleyan Chairman,[1] twenty years ago?"

My sister, do you think I have knees to go parading on the streets of Cape Coast?

"Is it heavy?"

Yes, very heavy indeed. They have opened up my grandchild at the hospital, *hi, hi, hi....*

"Eno *due, due, due* ... I did not know. May God go with you...."

---

1　*Wesleyan* Methodist. British Methodists began a missionary effort in Ghana in the nineteenth century, and the Church is now well-established there; *Wesleyan Chairman* Methodist church official responsible for a district.

Thank you. *Yaa.*

"O, the world!"

"It's her grandchild. The only daughter of her only son. Do you remember Kojo Amisa who went to sodja and fell in the great war, overseas?"

"Yes, it's his daughter...."

... O, *poo*, pity.

"Kobina, run to the street, tell Draba Anan to wait for Nana Amfoa."

"... Draba Anan, Draba, my mother says I must come and tell you to wait for Nana Amfoa."

"And where is she?"

"There she comes."

"Just look at how she hops like a bird ... does she think we are going to be here all day? And anyway we are full already ..."

O, you drivers!

"What have drivers done?"

"And do you think it shows respect when you speak in this way? It is only that things have not gone right; but she could, at least have been your mother...."

"But what have I said? I have not insulted her. I just think that only Youth must be permitted to see Cape Coast, the town of the Dear and Expensive...."

"And do you think she is going on a peaceful journey? The only daughter of her only son has been opened up and her baby removed from her womb."

O ... God.

O

O

O

*Poo*, pity.

"Me ... *poo*—pity, I am right about our modern wives I always say they are useless as compared with our mothers."

"You drivers!"

"Now what have your modern wives done?"

"Am I not right what I always say about them?"

"You go and watch them in the big towns. All so thin and dry as sticks— you can literally blow them away with your breath. No decent flesh anywhere. Wooden chairs groan when they meet with their hard exteriors."

"O you drivers...."

"But of course all drivers ..."

"What have I done? Don't all my male passengers agree with me? These modern girls.... Now here is one who cannot even have a baby in a decent way. But must have the baby removed from her stomach. *Tchiaa!*"

"What ..."

"Here is the old woman."

"Whose grandchild ...?"

"Yes."

"Nana, I hear you are coming to Cape Coast with us."

Yes my master.

"We nearly left you behind but we heard it was you and that it is a heavy journey you are making."

Yes my master ... thank you my master.

"Push up please ... push up. Won't you push up? Why do you all sit looking at me with such eyes as if I was a block of wood?"

"It is not that there is nowhere to push up to. Five fat women should go on that seat, but look at you!"

"And our own grandmother here is none too plump herself.... Nana, if they won't push, come to the front seat with me."

"... *Hei*, scholar, go to the back...."

"... And do not scowl on me. I know your sort too well. Something tells me you do not have any job at all. As for that suit you are wearing and looking so grand in, you hired or borrowed it...."

"Oh you drivers!"

Oh you drivers ...

The scholar who read this tengram thing, said it was made about three days ago. My lady's husband sent it.... Three days.... God—that is too long ago. Have they buried her ... where? Or did they cut her up.... I should not think about it ... or something will happen to me. Eleven or twelve ... Efua Panyin, Okuma, Kwame Gyasi and who else? But they should not have left me here. Sometimes ... ah, I hate this nausea. But it is this smell of petrol. Now I have remembered I never could travel in a lorry.[1] I always was so sick. But now I hope at least that will not happen. These young people will think it is because I am old and they will laugh. At least if I knew the child of my child was alive, it would have been good. And the little things she sent me.... Sometimes some people like Mensima and Nkansa make me feel as if I had been a barren woman instead of only one with whom infant-mortality pledged friendship ...

I will give her that set of earrings, bracelet and chain which Odwumfo Ata made for me. It is the most beautiful and the most expensive thing I have.... It does not hurt me to think that I am going to die very soon and have them and their children gloating over my things. After all what did they swallow my children for? It does not hurt me at all. If I had been someone else, I would have given them all away before I died. But it does not matter. They can share their own curse. Now, that is the end of me and my roots.... Eternal death has

---

1    *lorry* Truck.

worked like a warrior rat, with diabolical sense of duty, to gnaw my bottom. Everything is finished now. The vacant lot is swept and the scraps of old sugar-cane pulp, dry sticks and bunches of hair burnt ... how it reeks, the smoke!

"O, Nana do not weep ..."

"Is the old woman weeping?"

"If the only child of your only child died, won't you weep?"

"Why do you ask me? Did I know her grandchild is dead?"

"Where have you been, not in this lorry? Where were your ears when we were discussing it?"

"I do not go putting my mouth in other people's affairs ..."

"So what?"

"So go and die."

"*Hei, hei*, it is prohibited to quarrel in my lorry."

"Draba, here is me, sitting quiet and this lady of muscles and bones being cheeky to me."

"Look, I can beat you."

"Beat me ... beat me ... let's see."

"*Hei*, you are not civilized, eh?"

"Keep quiet and let us think, both of you, or I will put you down."

"Nana, do not weep. There is God above."

Thank you my master.

"But we are in Cape Coast already."

*Meewuo!* My God, hold me tight or something will happen to me.

My master, I will come down here.

"O Nana, I thought you said you were going to the hospital.... We are not there yet."

I am saying maybe I will get down here and ask my way around.

"Nana, you do not know these people, eh? They are very impudent here. They have no use for old age. So they do not respect it. Sit down, I will take you there."

Are you going there, my master?

"No, but I will take you there."

Ah, my master, your old mother thanks you. Do not shed a tear when you hear of my death ... my master, your old mother thanks you.

I hear there is somewhere where they keep corpses until their owners claim them ... if she has been buried, then I must find her husband ... Esi Amfoa, what did I come to do under this sky? I have buried all my children and now I am going to bury my only grandchild!

"Nana we are there."

Is this the hospital?

"Yes, Nana. What is your child's name?"

Esi Amfoa. Her father named her after me.

"Do you know her European name?"

No, my master.

"What shall we do?"

"... *Ei* lady, Lady Nurse, we are looking for somebody."

"You are looking for somebody and can you read? If you cannot, you must ask someone what the rules in the hospital are. You can only come and visit people at three o'clock."

Lady, please. She was my only grandchild ...

"Who? And anyway, it is none of our business."

"Nana, you must be patient ... and not cry ..."

"Old woman, why are you crying, it is not allowed here. No one must make any noise ..."

My lady, I am sorry but she was all I had.

"Who? Oh, are you the old woman who is looking for somebody?"

Yes.

"Who is he?"

She was my granddaughter—the only child of my only son.

"I mean, what was her name?"

Esi Amfoa.

"Esi Amfoa ... Esi Amfoa. I am sorry, we do not have anyone whom they call like that here."

Is that it?

"Nana, I told you they may know only her European name here."

My master, what shall we do then?

"What is she ill with?"

She came here to have a child ...

"... And they say, they opened her stomach and removed the baby."

"Oh ... oh, I see."

My Lord, hold me tight so that nothing will happen to me now.

"I see. It is the Caesarean[1] case."

"Nurse, you know her?"

And when I take her back, Anona Ebusuafo will say that I did not wait for them to come with me ...

"Yes. Are you her brother?"

"No. I am only the driver who brought the old woman."

"Did she bring all her clan?"

"No. She came alone."

---

1   *Caesarean* I.e., caesarean section, an operation in which a baby is delivered through an incision in the mother's abdomen.

"Strange thing for a villager to do."

I hope they have not cut her up already.

"Did she bring a whole bag full of cassava and plantain and kenkey?"[1]

"No. She has only her little bundle."

"Follow me. But you must not make any noise. This is not the hour for coming here ..."

My master, does she know her?

"Yes."

I hear it is very cold where they put them ...

• • •

It was feeding time for new babies. When old Esi Amfoa saw young Esi Amfoa, the latter was all neat and nice. White sheets and all. She did not see the beautiful stitches under the sheets. "This woman is a tough bundle," Dr. Gyamfi had declared after the identical twins had been removed, the last stitches had been threaded off and Mary Koomson, alias Esi Amfoa, had come to.

The old woman somersaulted into the room and lay groaning, not screaming, by the bed. For was not her last pot broken? So they lay them in state even in hospitals and not always cut them up for instruction?

The Nursing Sister was furious. Young Esi Amfoa spoke. And this time old Esi Amfoa wept loud and hard—wept all her tears.

Scrappy nurse-under-training, Jessy Treeson, second-generation-Cape-Coaster-her-grandmother-still-remembered-at-Egyaa[2] No. 7 said, "As for these villagers," and giggled.

Draba Anan looked hard at Jessy Treeson, looked hard at her, all of her: her starched uniform, apron and cap ... and then dismissed them all.... "Such a cassava stick ... but maybe I will break my toe if I kicked at her buttocks," he thought.

And by the bed the old woman was trying hard to rise and look at the only pot which had refused to get broken.

—1970

---

1    *cassava* Starchy root vegetable, a staple crop in Ghana; *plantain* Banana-like fruit, eaten cooked; *kenkey* Dumplings made of fermented white corn flour, a traditional Ghanaian dish.

2    *Egyaa* Town on the coast of Ghana.

# *Thomas King*
b. 1943

One of the first Native writers to gain a significant popular and critical following in Canada and the United States, Thomas King has explored Indigenous identities and experiences in a wide range of forms, genres, and mediums. Though often identified as a comic writer, King considers himself a satirist who uses comedy to deal with serious subjects—the exploitation of cultures, the loss of a way of life, the struggle for self-definition, and the question of authenticity—without descending into polemical denunciations. As King explains, "Tragedy is my topic. Comedy is my strategy."

In novels like *Green Grass, Running Water* (1993) and the stories collected in *A Short History of Indians in Canada* (2005), King often confronts head-on the traumatic legacy of colonization. His characters are not woebegone "solitary figures poised on the brink of extinction" but many-sided individuals bound by a nourishing sense of community. For King, the term *postcolonial* misleadingly implies that European contact was the primary generative impetus of Native literature. As he argues in "Godzilla vs. Post-Colonial" (1990), "the idea of post-colonial writing effectively cuts us off from our traditions, traditions that were in place before colonialism ever became a question, traditions which have come down to us through our cultures in spite of colonialism."

King takes up and carries forward many of these traditions, often fusing the conventions of oral storytelling with those of written narratives. Certain stories, including "A Short History of Indians in Canada," were written as oral performance pieces. In all his work, King aims not only to reclaim Native culture from reductive stereotypical representations but to reinforce "the notion that, in addition to the useable past that the concurrence of oral literature and traditional history provides us with, we also have an active present marked by cultural tenacity and a viable future."

## A Short History of Indians in Canada

Can't sleep, Bob Haynie tells the doorman at the King Eddie. Can't sleep, can't sleep.

First time in Toronto? says the doorman.

Yes, says Bob.

Businessman?

Yes.

Looking for some excitement?

Yes.

Bay Street,[1] sir, says the doorman.

Bob Haynie catches a cab to Bay Street at three in the morning. He loves the smell of concrete. He loves the look of city lights. He loves the sound of skyscrapers.

Bay Street.

Smack!

Bob looks up just in time to see a flock of Indians fly into the side of the building.

Smack! Smack!

Bob looks up just in time to get out of the way.

Whup!

An Indian hits the pavement in front of him.

Whup! Whup!

Two Indians hit the pavement behind him.

Holy Cow! shouts Bob, and he leaps out of the way of the falling Indians.

Whup! Whup! Whup!

Bob throws his hands over his head and dashes into the street. And is almost hit by a city truck.

Honk!

Two men jump out of the truck. Hi, I'm Bill. Hi, I'm Rudy.

Hi, I'm Bob.

Businessman? says Bill.

Yes.

First time in Toronto? says Rudy.

Yes.

Whup! Whup! Whup!

Look out! Bob shouts. There are Indians flying into the skyscrapers and falling on the sidewalk.

Whup!

Mohawk, says Bill.

Whup! Whup!

Couple of Cree over here, says Rudy.

Amazing, says Bob. How can you tell?

By the feathers, says Bill. We got a book.

It's our job, says Rudy.

Whup!

Bob looks around. What's this one? he says.

Holy! says Bill. Holy! says Rudy.

Check the book, says Bill. Just to be sure.

Flip, flip, flip.

---

1    *Bay Street*  Major street in Toronto's financial district.

Navajo!

Bill and Rudy put their arms around Bob. A Navajo! Don't normally see Navajos this far north. Don't normally see Navajos this far east.

Is she dead? says Bob.

Nope, says Bill. Just stunned.

Most of them are just stunned, says Rudy.

Some people never see this, says Bill. One of nature's mysteries. A natural phenomenon.

They're nomadic you know, says Rudy. And migratory.

Toronto's in the middle of the flyway, says Bill. The lights attract them.

Bob counts the bodies. Seventy-three. No. Seventy-four. What can I do to help?

Not much that anyone can do, says Bill. We tried turning off the lights in the buildings.

We tried broadcasting loud music from the roofs, says Rudy.

Rubber owls? asks Bob.

It's a real problem this time of the year, says Bill.

Whup! Whup! Whup!

Bill and Rudy pull green plastic bags out of their pockets and try to find the open ends.

The dead ones we bag, says Rudy.

The lives ones we tag, says Bill. Take them to the shelter. Nurse them back to health. Release them in the wild.

Amazing, says Bob.

A few wander off dazed and injured. If we don't find them right away, they don't stand a chance.

Amazing, says Bob.

You're one lucky guy, says Bill. In another couple of weeks, they'll be gone.

A family from Alberta came through last week and didn't even see an Ojibway, says Rudy.

Your first time in Toronto? says Bill.

It's a great town, says Bob. You're doing a great job.

Whup!

Don't worry, says Rudy. By the time the commuters show up, you'll never even know the Indians were here.

Bob catches a cab back to the King Eddie and shakes the doorman's hand. I saw the Indians, he says.

Thought you'd enjoy that, sir, says the doorman.

Thank you, says Bob. It was spectacular.

Not like the old days. The doorman sighs and looks up into the night. In the old days, when they came through, they would black out the entire sky.

—2005

# James Kelman
b. 1946

Widely esteemed as one of Scotland's most influential and innovative writers, James Kelman is also a literary iconoclast whose novels and short stories question the cultural standards by which they are often judged. Although his work has received and been shortlisted for many awards—including the Man Booker Prize, which he won amidst great controversy for his novel *How late it was, how late* (1994)—Kelman remains an outspoken critic of the literary establishment and what he considers its elitist, bourgeois values.

In his famous Booker Prize acceptance speech, the native Glaswegian defiantly declared: "My culture and my language have the right to exist, and no one has the authority to dismiss that right." Many critics have approached Kelman's fictional project as an affirmation of this right in the face of the dominant norms—linguistic, stylistic, narrative, even grammatical—of traditional British literature. For Kelman, who emerged as a writer at the height of the British class war in the 1970s, standard written English and other "genteel" formal conventions deny the validity of working-class culture, just as they misrepresent the reality of working-class experience.

Kelman rejects traditional realism; many of the stories collected in *Short Tales from the Night Shift* (1978) and *Not Not While the Giro* (1983) are highly compressed, essentially plotless, consisting of concrete statements of fact that allow the working-class subject matter to speak for itself without commentary from a perspective that pretends superiority. The influence of such writers as Franz Kafka and Ernest Hemingway on Kelman's work is evident in its preoccupation with themes of alienation, powerlessness, and thwarted masculinity.

# Acid

In this factory in the north of England acid was essential. It was contained in large vats. Gangways were laid above them. Before these gangways were made completely safe a young man fell into a vat feet first. His screams of agony were heard all over the department. Except for one old fellow the large body of men was so horrified that for a time not one of them could move. In an instant this old fellow who was also the young man's father had clambered up and along the gangway carrying a big pole. Sorry Hughie, he said. And then ducked the young man below the surface. Obviously the old fellow had had to do this because only the head and shoulders—in fact, that which had been seen above the acid was all that remained of the young man.

—1978

# *Octavia Butler*

1947–2006

Octavia Butler was an American author best known for psychologically realistic science fiction that examines racial, sexual, and environmental politics. A leading figure of the Afrofuturism movement, Butler addressed the history, present concerns, and possible futures of Black Americans through her fiction. A creator of complex speculative worlds, Butler was, in her own words, "a pessimist, a feminist always, a Black, a quiet egoist, a former Baptist, and an oil-and-water combination of ambition, laziness, insecurity, certainty, and drive."

Born in Pasadena, California, Butler was raised by her mother and grandmother. At the age of ten, she decided that writing was her vocation. After graduating from Pasadena Community College, Butler enrolled in a screenwriting workshop, where her talent was noticed by the established science-fiction writer Harlan Ellison, who would become her mentor. Butler's first novel, *Patternmaster* (1976), was well-received by critics, with Orson Scott Card describing the text as a "vibrant [study] of the ethics of power and submission." The novel became the first in a series employing concepts such as human selective breeding, genetic mutation, and social control though telepathy. As she worked on this series, Butler also published *Kindred* (1979), one of her most widely read novels, about a Black woman who is transported back in time to the era of slavery.

In the 1980s, as she published follow-ups to *Patternmaster* as well as other novels and short stories, Butler met with increasing critical and commercial success, winning two Hugo Awards and a Nebula Award. In the 1990s, she became the first science-fiction writer to receive a prestigious MacArthur "Genius Grant." Her last major works were the highly influential Earthseed books—*Parable of the Sower* (1993) and *Parable of the Talents* (1998)—in which she envisioned American society disintegrating as a result of extreme inequality and environmental degradation.

Through her penetrating engagement with racial, sexual, and social power structures, Butler challenged science fiction's domination by white men. "When I began writing science fiction ... I wasn't in any of this stuff I read," Butler once remarked in an interview with *The New York Times*. "I wrote myself in."

# Speech Sounds

There was trouble aboard the Washington Boulevard bus. Rye had expected trouble sooner or later in her journey. She had put off going until loneliness and hopelessness drove her out. She believed she might have one group of relatives left alive—a brother and his two children twenty miles away in Pasadena. That was a day's journey one-way, if she were lucky. The unexpected arrival of the bus as she left her Virginia Road home had seemed to be a piece of luck—until the trouble began.

Two young men were involved in a disagreement of some kind, or, more likely, a misunderstanding. They stood in the aisle, grunting and gesturing at each other, each in his own uncertain T stance as the bus lurched over the potholes. The driver seemed to be putting some effort into keeping them off balance. Still, their gestures stopped just short of contact—mock punches, hand games of intimidation to replace lost curses.

People watched the pair, then looked at one another and made small anxious sounds. Two children whimpered.

Rye sat a few feet behind the disputants and across from the back door. She watched the two carefully, knowing the fight would begin when someone's nerve broke or someone's hand slipped or someone came to the end of his limited ability to communicate. These things could happen anytime.

One of them happened as the bus hit an especially large pothole and one man, tall, thin, and sneering, was thrown into his shorter opponent.

Instantly, the shorter man drove his left fist into the disintegrating sneer. He hammered his larger opponent as though he neither had nor needed any weapon other than his left fist. He hit quickly enough, hard enough to batter his opponent down before the taller man could regain his balance or hit back even once.

People screamed or squawked in fear. Those nearby scrambled to get out of the way. Three more young men roared in excitement and gestured wildly. Then, somehow, a second dispute broke out between two of these three—probably because one inadvertently touched or hit the other.

As the second fight scattered frightened passengers, a woman shook the driver's shoulder and grunted as she gestured toward the fighting.

The driver grunted back through bared teeth. Frightened, the woman drew away.

Rye, knowing the methods of bus drivers, braced herself and held on to the crossbar of the seat in front of her. When the driver hit the brakes, she was ready and the combatants were not. They fell over seats and onto screaming passengers, creating even more confusion. At least one more fight started.

The instant the bus came to a full stop, Rye was on her feet, pushing the back door. At the second push, It opened and she jumped out, holding her pack in one arm. Several other passengers followed, but some stayed on the bus. Buses were rare and irregular now, people rode when they could, no matter what. There might not be another bus today—or tomorrow. People started walking, and if they saw a bus they flagged it down. People making intercity trips like Rye's from Los Angeles to Pasadena made plans to camp out, or risked seeking shelter with locals who might rob or murder them.

The bus did not move, but Rye moved away from it. She intended to wait until the trouble was over and get on again, but if there was shooting, she wanted the protection of a tree. Thus, she was near the curb when a battered blue Ford on the other side of the street made a U-turn and pulled up in front of the bus. Cars were rare these days—as rare as a severe shortage of fuel and of relatively unimpaired mechanics could make them. Cars that still ran were as likely to be used as weapons as they were to serve as transportation. Thus, when the driver of the Ford beckoned to Rye, she moved away warily. The driver got out—a big man, young, neatly bearded with dark, thick hair. He wore a long overcoat and a look of wariness that matched Rye's. She stood several feet from him, waiting to see what he would do. He looked at the bus, now rocking with the combat inside, then at the small cluster of passengers who had gotten off. Finally he looked at Rye again.

She returned his gaze, very much aware of the old forty-five automatic her jacket concealed. She watched his hands.

He pointed with his left hand toward the bus. The dark tinted windows prevented him from seeing what was happening inside.

His use of the left hand interested Rye more than his obvious question. Left-handed people tended to be less impaired, more reasonable and comprehending, less driven by frustration, confusion, and anger.

She imitated his gesture, pointing toward the bus with her own left hand, then punching the air with both fists.

The man took off his coat revealing a Los Angeles Police Department uniform complete with baton and service revolver.

Rye took another step back from him. There was no more LAPD, no more *any* large organization, governmental or private. There were neighbourhood patrols and armed individuals. That was all.

The man took something from his coat pocket, then threw the coat into the car. Then he gestured Rye back, back toward the rear of the bus. He had something made of plastic in his hand. Rye did not understand what he wanted until he went to the rear door of the bus and beckoned her to stand there. She obeyed mainly out of curiosity. Cop or not, maybe he could do something to stop the stupid fighting.

He walked around the front of the bus, to the street side where the driver's window was open. There, she thought she saw him throw something into the bus. She was still trying to peer through the tinted glass when people began stumbling out the rear door, choking and weeping. Gas.

Rye caught an old woman who would have fallen, lifted two little children down when they were in danger of being knocked down and trampled. She could see the bearded man helping people at the front door. She caught a thin old man shoved out by one of the combatants. Staggered by the old man's weight, she was barely able to get out of the way as the last of the young men pushed his way out. This one, bleeding from nose and mouth, stumbled into another, and they grappled blindly, still sobbing from the gas.

The bearded man helped the bus driver out through the front door, though the driver did not seem to appreciate his help. For a moment, Rye thought there would be another fight. The bearded man stepped back and watched the driver gesture threateningly, watched him shout in wordless anger.

The bearded man stood still, made no sound, refused to respond to clearly obscene gestures. The least impaired people tended to do this—stand back unless they were physically threatened and let those with less control scream and jump around. It was as though they felt it beneath them to be as touchy as the less comprehending. This was an attitude of superiority, and that was the way people like the bus driver perceived it. Such "superiority" was frequently punished by beatings, even by death. Rye had had close calls of her own. As a result, she never went unarmed. And in this world where the only likely common language was body language, being armed was often enough. She had rarely had to draw her gun or even display it.

The bearded man's revolver was on constant display. Apparently that was enough for the bus driver. The driver spat in disgust, glared at the bearded man for a moment longer, then strode back to his gas-filled bus. He stared at it for a moment, dearly wanting to get in, but the gas was still too strong. Of the windows, only his tiny driver's window actually opened. The front door was open, but the rear door would not stay open unless someone held it. Of course, the air conditioning had failed long ago. The bus would take some time to clear. It was the driver's property, his livelihood. He had pasted old magazine pictures of items he would accept as fare on its sides. Then he would use what he collected to feed his family or to trade. If his bus did not run, he did not eat. On the other hand, if the inside of his bus was torn apart by senseless fighting, he would not eat very well either. He was apparently unable to perceive this. All he could see was that it would be some time before he could use his bus again. He shook his fist at the bearded man and shouted. There seemed to be words in his shout, but Rye could not understand them. She did not know whether this was his fault or hers. She had heard so little coherent human speech for the past three years, she was no longer certain how well she recognized it, no longer certain of the degree of her own impairment.

The bearded man sighed. He glanced toward his car, then beckoned to Rye. He was ready to leave, but he wanted something from her first. No. No, he wanted her to leave with him. Risk getting into his car when, in spite of his uniform, law and order were nothing—not even words any longer.

She shook her head in a universally understood negative, but the man continued to beckon.

She waved him away. He was doing what the less impaired rarely did—drawing potentially negative attention to another of his kind. People from the bus had begun to look at her.

One of the men who had been fighting tapped another on the arm, then pointed from the bearded man to Rye, and finally held up the first two fingers of his right hand as though giving two-thirds of a Boy Scout salute. The gesture was very quick, its meaning obvious even at a distance. She had been grouped with the bearded man. Now what?

The man who had made the gesture started toward her.

She had no idea what he intended, but she stood her ground. The man was half a foot taller than she was and perhaps ten years younger. She did not imagine she could outrun him. Nor did she expect anyone to help her if she needed help. The people around her were all strangers.

She gestured once—a clear indication to the man to stop. She did not intend to repeat the gesture. Fortunately, the man obeyed. He gestured obscenely and several other men laughed. Loss of verbal language had spawned a whole new set of obscene gestures. The man, with stark simplicity, had accused her of sex with the bearded man and had suggested she accommodate the other men present—beginning with him.

Rye watched him wearily. People might very well stand by and watch if he tried to rape her. They would also stand and watch her shoot him. Would he push things that far?

He did not. After a series of obscene gestures that brought him no closer to her, he turned contemptuously and walked away.

And the bearded man still waited. He had removed his service revolver, holster and all. He beckoned again, both hands empty. No doubt his gun was in the car and within easy reach, but his taking it off impressed her. Maybe he was all right. Maybe he was just alone. She had been alone herself for three years. The illness had stripped her, killing her children one by one, killing her husband, her sister, her parents ...

The illness, if it was an illness, had cut even the living off from one another. As it swept over the country, people hardly had time to lay blame on the Soviets[1] (though they were falling silent along with the rest of the world), on a new virus, a new pollutant, radiation, divine retribution ... The illness was stroke-swift in the way it cut people down and strokelike in some of its effects.

---

1    *blame on the Soviets*  The second half of the twentieth century was characterized by political tensions between the United States and the Soviet Union, with continual threat of a nuclear war between the two nations. In 1991 the Soviet Union collapsed into Russia and other independent states.

But it was highly specific. Language was always lost or severely impaired. It was never regained. Often there was also paralysis, intellectual impairment, death.

Rye walked toward the bearded man, ignoring the whistling and applauding of two of the young men and their thumbs-up signs to the bearded man. If he had smiled at them or acknowledged them in any way, she would almost certainly have changed her mind. If she had let herself think of the possible deadly consequences of getting into a stranger's car, she would have changed her mind. Instead, she thought of the man who lived across the street from her. He rarely washed since his bout with the illness. And he had gotten into the habit of urinating wherever he happened to be. He had two women already—one tending each of his large gardens. They put up with him in exchange for his protection. He had made it clear that he wanted Rye to become his third woman.

She got into the car and the bearded man shut the door. She watched as he walked around to the driver's door—watched for his sake because his gun was on the seat beside her. And the bus driver and a pair of young men had come a few steps closer. They did nothing, though, until the bearded man was in the car. Then one of them threw a rock. Others followed his example, and as the car drove away, several rocks bounced off harmlessly.

When the bus was some distance behind them, Rye wiped sweat from her forehead and longed to relax. The bus would have taken her more than halfway to Pasadena. She would have had only ten miles to walk. She wondered how far she would have to walk now—and wondered if walking a long distance would be her only problem.

At Figueroa and Washington where the bus normally made a left turn, the bearded man stopped, looked at her, and indicated that she should choose a direction. When she directed him left and he actually turned left, she began to relax. If he was willing to go where she directed, perhaps he was safe.

As they passed blocks of burned, abandoned buildings, empty lots, and wrecked or stripped cars, he slipped a gold chain over his head and handed it to her. The pendant attached to it was a smooth, glassy, black rock. Obsidian. His name might be Rock or Peter[1] or Black, but she decided to think of him as Obsidian. Even her sometimes useless memory would retain a name like Obsidian.

She handed him her own name symbol—a pin in the shape of a large golden stalk of wheat. She had bought it long before the illness and the silence began. Now she wore it, thinking it was as close as she was likely to come to Rye. People like Obsidian who had not known her before probably thought

---

1    *Peter* The name Peter is derived from the Greek word for "stone."

of her as Wheat. Not that it mattered. She would never hear her name spoken again.

Obsidian handed her pin back to her. He caught her hand as she reached for it and rubbed his thumb over her calluses.

He stopped at First Street and asked which way again. Then, after turning right as she had indicated, he parked near the Music Center. There, he took a folded paper from the dashboard and unfolded it. Rye recognized it as a street map, though the writing on it meant nothing to her. He flattened the map, took her hand again, and put her index finger on one spot. He touched her, touched himself, pointed toward the floor. In effect, "We are here." She knew he wanted to know where she was going. She wanted to tell him, but she shook her head sadly. She had lost reading and writing. That was her most serious impairment and her most painful. She had taught history at UCLA. She had done freelance writing. Now she could not even read her own manuscripts. She had a houseful of books that she could neither read nor bring herself to use as fuel. And she had a memory that would not bring back to her much of what she had read before.

She stared at the map, trying to calculate. She had been born in Pasadena, had lived for fifteen years in Los Angeles. Now she was near L.A. Civic Center. She knew the relative positions of the two cities, knew streets, directions, even knew to stay away from freeways, which might be blocked by wrecked cars and destroyed overpasses. She ought to know how to point out Pasadena even though she could not recognize the word.

Hesitantly, she placed her hand over a pale orange patch in the upper right corner of the map. That should be right. Pasadena.

Obsidian lifted her hand and looked under it, then folded the map and put it back on the dashboard. He could read, she realized belatedly. He could probably write, too. Abruptly, she hated him—deep, bitter hatred. What did literacy mean to him—a grown man who played cops and robbers? But he was literate and she was not. She never would be. She felt sick to her stomach with hatred, frustration, and jealousy. And only a few inches from her hand was a loaded gun.

She held herself still, staring at him, almost seeing his blood. But her rage crested and ebbed and she did nothing.

Obsidian reached for her hand with hesitant familiarity. She looked at him. Her face had already revealed too much. No person still living in what was left of human society could fail to recognize that expression, that jealousy.

She closed her eyes wearily, drew a deep breath. She had experienced longing for the past, hatred of the present, growing hopelessness, purposelessness, but she had never experienced such a powerful urge to kill another person. She had left her home, finally, because she had come near to killing herself.

She had found no reason to stay alive. Perhaps that was why she had gotten into Obsidian's car. She had never before done such a thing.

He touched her mouth and made chatter motions with thumb and fingers. Could she speak?

She nodded and watched his milder envy come and go. Now both had admitted what it was not safe to admit, and there had been no violence. He tapped his mouth and forehead and shook his head. He did not speak or comprehend spoken language. The illness had played with them, taking away, she suspected, what each valued most.

She plucked at his sleeve, wondering why he had decided on his own to keep the LAPD alive with what he had left. He was sane enough otherwise. Why wasn't he at home raising corn, rabbits, and children? But she did not know how to ask. Then he put his hand on her thigh and she had another question to deal with.

She shook her head. Disease, pregnancy, helpless, solitary agony ... no.

He massaged her thigh gently and smiled in obvious disbelief.

No one had touched her for three years. She had not wanted anyone to touch her. What kind of world was this to chance bringing a child into even if the father were willing to stay and help raise it? It was too bad, though. Obsidian could not know how attractive he was to her—young, probably younger than she was, clean, asking for what he wanted rather than demanding it. But none of that mattered. What were a few moments of pleasure measured against a lifetime of consequences?

He pulled her closer to him and for a moment she let herself enjoy the closeness. He smelled good—male and good. She pulled away reluctantly.

He sighed, reached toward the glove compartment. She stiffened, not knowing what to expect, but all he took out was a small box. The writing on it meant nothing to her. She did not understand until he broke the seal, opened the box, and took out a condom. He looked at her, and she first looked away in surprise. Then she giggled. She could not remember when she had last giggled.

He grinned, gestured toward the backseat, and she laughed aloud. Even in her teens, she had disliked backseats of cars. But she looked around at the empty streets and ruined buildings, then she got out and into the backseat. He let her put the condom on him, then seemed surprised at her eagerness.

Sometime later, they sat together, covered by his coat, unwilling to become clothed near strangers again just yet. He made rock-the-baby gestures and looked questioningly at her.

She swallowed, shook her head. She did not know how to tell him her children were dead.

He took her hand and drew a cross in it with his index finger, then made his baby-rocking gesture again.

She nodded, held up three fingers, then turned away, trying to shut out a sudden flood of memories. She had told herself that the children growing up now were to be pitied. They would run through the downtown canyons with no real memory of what the buildings had been or even how they had come to be. Today's children gathered books as well as wood to be burned as fuel. They ran through the streets chasing one another and hooting like chimpanzees. They had no future. They were now all they would ever be.

He put his hand on her shoulder, and she turned suddenly, fumbling for his small box, then urging him to make love to her again. He could give her forgetfulness and pleasure. Until now, nothing had been able to do that. Until now, every day had brought her closer to the time when she would do what she had left home to avoid doing: putting her gun in her mouth and pulling the trigger.

She asked Obsidian if he would come home with her, stay with her.

He looked surprised and pleased once he understood. But he did not answer at once. Finally, he shook his head as she had feared he might. He was probably having too much fun playing cops and robbers and picking up women.

She dressed in silent disappointment, unable to feel any anger toward him. Perhaps he already had a wife and a home. That was likely. The illness had been harder on men than on women—had killed more men, had left male survivors more severely impaired. Men like Obsidian were rare. Women either settled for less or stayed alone. If they found an Obsidian, they did what they could to keep him. Rye suspected he had someone younger, prettier keeping him.

He touched her while she was strapping her gun on and asked with a complicated series of gestures whether it was loaded.

She nodded grimly.

He patted her arm.

She asked once more if he would come home with her, this time using a different series of gestures. He had seemed hesitant. Perhaps he could be courted.

He got out and into the front seat without responding.

She took her place in front again, watching him. Now he plucked at his uniform and looked at her. She thought she was being asked something but did not know what it was.

He took off his badge, tapped it with one finger, then tapped his chest. Of course.

She took the badge from his hand and pinned her wheat stalk to it. If playing cops and robbers was his only insanity, let him play. She would take him, uniform and all. It occurred to her that she might eventually lose him to someone he would meet as he had met her. But she would have him for a while.

He took the street map down again, tapped it, pointed vaguely northeast toward Pasadena, then looked at her.

She shrugged, tapped his shoulder, then her own, and held up her index and second fingers tight together, just to be sure.

He grasped the two fingers and nodded. He was with her.

She took the map from him and threw it onto the dashboard. She pointed back southwest—back toward home. Now he did not have to go to Pasadena. Now she could go on having a brother there and two nephews—three right-handed males. Now she did not have to find out for certain whether she was as alone as she feared. Now she was not alone.

Obsidian took Hill Street south, then Washington west, and she leaned back, wondering what it would be like to have someone again. With what she had scavenged, what she had preserved, and what she grew, there was easily enough food for them. There was certainly room enough in a four-bedroom house. He could move his possessions in. Best of all, the animal across the street would pull back and possibly not force her to kill him.

Obsidian had drawn her closer to him, and she had put her head on his shoulder when suddenly he braked hard, almost throwing her off the seat. Out of the corner of her eye, she saw that someone had run across the street in front of the car. One car on the street and someone had to run in front of it.

Straightening up, Rye saw that the runner was a woman, fleeing from an old frame house to a boarded-up storefront. She ran silently, but the man who followed her a moment later shouted what sounded like garbled words as he ran. He had something in his hand. Not a gun. A knife, perhaps.

The woman tried a door, found it locked, looked around desperately, finally snatched up a fragment of glass broken from the storefront window. With this she turned to face her pursuer. Rye thought she would be more likely to cut her own hand than to hurt anyone else with the glass.

Obsidian jumped from the car, shouting. It was the first time Rye had heard his voice—deep and hoarse from disuse. He made the same sound over and over the way some speechless people did, "Da, da, da!"

Rye got out of the car as Obsidian ran toward the couple. He had drawn his gun. Fearful, she drew her own and released the safety. She looked around to see who else might be attracted to the scene. She saw the man glance at Obsidian, then suddenly lunge at the woman. The woman jabbed his face with her glass, but he caught her arm and managed to stab her twice before Obsidian shot him.

The man doubled, then toppled, clutching his abdomen. Obsidian shouted, then gestured Rye over to help the woman.

Rye moved to the woman's side, remembering that she had little more than bandages and antiseptic in her pack. But the woman was beyond help. She had been stabbed with a long, slender boning knife.

She touched Obsidian to let him know the woman was dead. He had bent to check the wounded man who lay still and also seemed dead. But as Obsidian looked around to see what Rye wanted, the man opened his eyes. Face contorted, he seized Obsidian's just-holstered revolver and fired. The bullet caught Obsidian in the temple and he collapsed.

It happened just that simply, just that fast. An instant later, Rye shot the wounded man as he was turning the gun on her.

And Rye was alone—with three corpses.

She knelt beside Obsidian, dry-eyed, frowning, trying to understand why everything had suddenly changed. Obsidian was gone. He had died and left her—like everyone else.

Two very small children came out of the house from which the man and woman had run—a boy and girl perhaps three years old. Holding hands, they crossed the street toward Rye. They stared at her, then edged past her and went to the dead woman. The girl shook the woman's arm as though trying to wake her.

This was too much. Rye got up, feeling sick to her stomach with grief and anger. If the children began to cry, she thought she would vomit.

They were on their own, those two kids. They were old enough to scavenge. She did not need any more grief. She did not need a stranger's children who would grow up to be hairless chimps.

She went back to the car. She could drive home, at least. She remembered how to drive.

The thought that Obsidian should be buried occurred to her before she reached the car, and she did vomit.

She had found and lost the man so quickly. It was as though she had been snatched from comfort and security and given a sudden, inexplicable beating. Her head would not clear. She could not think.

Somehow, she made herself go back to him, look at him. She found herself on her knees beside him with no memory of having knelt. She stroked his face, his beard. One of the children made a noise and she looked at them, at the woman who was probably their mother. The children looked back at her, obviously frightened. Perhaps it was their fear that reached her finally.

She had been about to drive away and leave them. She had almost done it, almost left two toddlers to die. Surely there had been enough dying. She would have to take the children home with her. She would not be able to live with any other decision. She looked around for a place to bury three bodies. Or two. She wondered if the murderer were the children's father. Before the silence, the police had always said some of the most dangerous calls they went out on were domestic disturbance calls. Obsidian should have known that—not that the knowledge would have kept him in the car. It would not have held her back either. She could not have watched the woman murdered and done nothing.

She dragged Obsidian toward the car. She had nothing to dig with her, and no one to guard for her while she dug. Better to take the bodies with her and bury them next to her husband and her children. Obsidian would come home with her after all.

When she had gotten him onto the floor in the back, she returned for the woman. The little girl, thin, dirty, solemn, stood up and unknowingly gave Rye a gift. As Rye began to drag the woman by her arms, the little girl screamed, "No!"

Rye dropped the woman and stared at the girl.

"No!" the girl repeated. She came to stand beside the woman. "Go away!" she told Rye.

"Don't talk," the little boy said to her. There was no blurring or confusing of sounds. Both children had spoken and Rye had understood. The boy looked at the dead murderer and moved further from him. He took the girl's hand. "Be quiet," he whispered.

Fluent speech! Had the woman died because she could talk and had taught her children to talk? Had she been killed by a husband's festering anger or by a stranger's jealous rage?

And the children ... they must have been born after the silence. Had the disease run its course, then? Or were these children simply immune? Certainly they had had time to fall sick and silent. Rye's mind leaped ahead. What if children of three or fewer years were safe and able to learn language? What if all they needed were teachers? Teachers and protectors.

Rye glanced at the dead murderer. To her shame, she thought she could understand some of the passions that must have driven him, whomever he was. Anger, frustration, hopelessness, insane jealousy ... how many more of him were there—people willing to destroy what they could not have?

Obsidian had been the protector, had chosen that role for who knew what reason. Perhaps putting on an obsolete uniform and patrolling the empty streets had been what he did instead of putting a gun into his mouth. And now that there was something worth protecting, he was gone.

She had been a teacher. A good one. She had been a protector, too, though only of herself. She had kept herself alive when she had no reason to live. If the illness let these children alone, she could keep them alive.

Somehow she lifted the dead woman into her arms and placed her on the backseat of the car. The children began to cry, but she knelt on the broken pavement and whispered to them, fearful of frightening them with the harshness of her long unused voice.

"It's all right," she told them. "You're going with us, too. Come on." She lifted them both, one in each arm. They were so light. Had they been getting enough to eat?

The boy covered her mouth with his hand, but she moved her face away. "It's all right for me to talk," she told him. "As long as no one's around, it's all right." She put the boy down on the front seat of the car and he moved over without being told to, to make room for the girl. When they were both in the car, Rye leaned against the window, looking at them, seeing that they were less afraid now, that they watched her with at least as much curiosity as fear.

"I'm Valerie Rye," she said, savoring the words. "It's all right for you to talk to me."

—1983

# *Haruki Murakami*
## b. 1949

Though he was born in Kyoto to two professors of Japanese literature, Haruki Murakami didn't consider a career in writing until the age of 29. In the introduction to *Wind/Pinball*, the first English release of his two earliest novels, Murakami claims that he decided to become a writer, "for no reason and on no grounds whatsoever," during a baseball game in 1978. Over the following decades, Murakami has become probably the most widely read Japanese author outside Japan, as well as a literary celebrity in his native country—though his continual rejection of Japanese influences has rankled critics at home.

As a youth, Murakami immersed himself in Western culture, especially through jazz music and American crime novels. His first novel, *Hear the Wind Sing*, was written during evenings after work at the jazz café he ran in Tokyo with his wife. *Norwegian Wood* (1987), named after the Beatles song beloved by one of the novel's characters, was Murakami's first truly popular success. It is also, somewhat unusually for him, written in the realist style: most of Murakami's other novels possess a surreal element that contrasts with the almost blandly ordinary characters his narratives tend to follow, resulting in what Sam Anderson of *The New York Times* has described as "a strange broth of ennui and exoticism."

Since the 1970s Murakami has published more than a dozen novels, several collections of short stories, and some works of nonfiction. Increasingly, with novels such as *The Wind-Up Bird Chronicle* (1995), his writing has also touched on the dark and violent aspects of Japan's recent history, including its role in World War II, of which he is very critical. While John Wray of *The Paris Review* has described Murakami as the "voice of his generation" in Japan, Murakami's own literary influences range far beyond his home country, including Raymond Chandler, Franz Kafka, Fyodor Dostoevsky, and Leo Tolstoy. His work has been recognized by many awards including the World Fantasy Award and the prestigious Japanese Yomiuri Prize.

## On Seeing the 100% Perfect Girl One Beautiful April Morning[1]

One beautiful April morning, on a narrow side street in Tokyo's fashionable Harajuku neighbourhood, I walk past the 100% perfect girl.

Tell you the truth, she's not that good-looking. She doesn't stand out in any way. Her clothes are nothing special. The back of her hair is still bent out

---

1    *On Seeing ... Morning* Translated by Jay Rubin.

of shape from sleep. She isn't young, either—must be near thirty, not even close to a "girl," properly speaking. But still, I know from fifty yards away: She's the 100% perfect girl for me. The moment I see her, there's a rumbling in my chest, and my mouth is as dry as a desert.

Maybe you have your own particular favourite type of girl—one with slim ankles, say, or big eyes, or graceful fingers, or you're drawn for no good reason to girls who take their time with every meal. I have my own preferences, of course. Sometimes in a restaurant I'll catch myself staring at the girl at the table next to mine because I like the shape of her nose.

But no one can insist that his 100% perfect girl correspond to some pre-conceived type. Much as I like noses, I can't recall the shape of hers—or even if she had one. All I can remember for sure is that she was no great beauty. It's weird.

"Yesterday on the street I passed the 100% perfect girl," I tell someone.

"Yeah?" he says. "Good-looking?"

"Not really."

"Your favourite type, then?"

"I don't know. I can't seem to remember anything about her—the shape of her eyes or the size of her breasts."

"Strange."

"Yeah. Strange."

"So anyhow," he says, already bored, "what did you do? Talk to her? Follow her?"

"Nah. Just passed her on the street."

She's walking east to west, and I west to east. It's a really nice April morning.

Wish I could talk to her. Half an hour would be plenty: just ask her about herself, tell her about myself, and—what I'd really like to do—explain to her the complexities of fate that have led to our passing each other on a side street in Harajuku on a beautiful April morning in 1981. This was something sure to be crammed full of warm secrets, like an antique clock built when peace filled the world.

After talking, we'd have lunch somewhere, maybe see a Woody Allen[1] movie, stop by a hotel bar for cocktails. With any kind of luck, we might end up in bed.

Potentiality knocks on the door of my heart.

Now the distance between us has narrowed to fifteen yards.

How can I approach her? What should I say?

---

1   *Woody Allen* American film director (b. 1935).

"Good morning, miss. Do you think you could spare half an hour for a little conversation?"

Ridiculous. I'd sound like an insurance salesman.

"Pardon me, but would you happen to know if there is an all-night cleaners in the neighbourhood?"

No, this is just as ridiculous. I'm not carrying any laundry, for one thing. Who's going to buy a line like that?

Maybe the simple truth would do. "Good morning. You are the 100% perfect girl for me."

No, she wouldn't believe it. Or even if she did, she might not want to talk to me. Sorry, she could say, I might be the 100% perfect girl for you, but you're not the 100% perfect boy for me. It could happen. And if I found myself in that situation, I'd probably go to pieces. I'd never recover from the shock. I'm thirty-two, and that's what growing older is all about.

We pass in front of a flower shop. A small, warm air mass touches my skin. The asphalt is damp, and I catch the scent of roses. I can't bring myself to speak to her. She wears a white sweater, and in her right hand she holds a crisp white envelope lacking only a stamp. So: She's written somebody a letter, maybe spent the whole night writing, to judge from the sleepy look in her eyes. The envelope could contain every secret she's ever had.

I take a few more strides and turn: She's lost in the crowd.

Now, of course, I know exactly what I should have said to her. It would have been a long speech, though, far too long for me to have delivered it properly. The ideas I come up with are never very practical.

Oh, well. It would have started "Once upon a time" and ended "A sad story, don't you think?"

Once upon a time, there lived a boy and a girl. The boy was eighteen and the girl sixteen. He was not unusually handsome, and she was not especially beautiful. They were just an ordinary lonely boy and an ordinary lonely girl, like all the others. But they believed with their whole hearts that somewhere in the world there lived the 100% perfect boy and the 100% perfect girl for them. Yes, they believed in a miracle. And that miracle actually happened.

One day the two came upon each other on the corner of a street.

"This is amazing," he said. "I've been looking for you all my life. You may not believe this, but you're the 100% perfect girl for me."

"And you," she said to him, "are the 100% perfect boy for me, exactly as I'd pictured you in every detail. It's like a dream."

They sat on a park bench, held hands, and told each other their stories hour after hour. They were not lonely anymore. They had found and been found by their 100% perfect other. What a wonderful thing it is to find and be found by your 100% perfect other. It's a miracle, a cosmic miracle.

As they sat and talked, however, a tiny, tiny sliver of doubt took root in their hearts: Was it really all right for one's dreams to come true so easily?

And so, when there came a momentary lull in their conversation, the boy said to the girl, "Let's test ourselves—just once. If we really are each other's 100% perfect lovers, then sometime, somewhere, we will meet again without fail. And when that happens, and we know that we are the 100% perfect ones, we'll marry then and there. What do you think?"

"Yes," she said, "that is exactly what we should do."

And so they parted, she to the east, and he to the west.

The test they had agreed upon, however, was utterly unnecessary. They should never have undertaken it, because they really and truly were each other's 100% perfect lovers, and it was a miracle that they had ever met. But it was impossible for them to know this, young as they were. The cold, indifferent waves of fate proceeded to toss them unmercifully.

One winter, both the boy and the girl came down with the season's terrible influenza; and after drifting for weeks between life and death they lost all memory of their earlier years. When they awoke, their heads were as empty as the young D.H. Lawrence's piggy bank.[1]

They were two bright, determined young people, however, and through their unremitting efforts they were able to acquire once again the knowledge and feeling that qualified them to return as full-fledged members of society. Heaven be praised, they became truly upstanding citizens who knew how to transfer from one subway line to another, who were fully capable of sending a special-delivery letter at the post office. Indeed, they even experienced love again, sometimes as much as 75% or even 85% love.

Time passed with shocking swiftness, and soon the boy was thirty-two, the girl thirty.

One beautiful April morning, in search of a cup of coffee to start the day, the boy was walking from west to east, while the girl, intending to send a special-delivery letter, was walking from east to west, both along the same narrow street in the Harajuku neighbourhood of Tokyo. They passed each other in the very centre of the street. The faintest gleam of their lost memories glimmered for the briefest moment in their hearts. Each felt a rumbling in the chest. And they knew:

She is the 100% perfect girl for me.

He is the 100% perfect boy for me.

---

1   *as empty ... piggy bank* This reference has puzzled critics, but may simply refer to the childhood poverty of the novelist D.H. Lawrence (1885–1930).

But the glow of their memories was far too weak, and their thoughts no longer had the clarity of fourteen years earlier. Without a word, they passed each other, disappearing into the crowd. Forever.

A sad story, don't you think?

Yes, that's it, that is what I should have said to her.

—1993

# *Rohinton Mistry*
b. 1952

Rohinton Mistry is a Mumbai-born Canadian novelist and short story writer. In a review in *The New Yorker*, literary critic and fellow novelist John Updike wrote that he "harks back to the nineteenth-century novelists, for whom every detail, every urban alley, every character however lowly added a vital piece to the full social picture, and for whom every incident illustrated the eventually crushing weight of the world."

At 23, Mistry emigrated with his wife to Canada and settled in Toronto. He worked as a bank clerk but studied English literature at the University of Toronto, earning his BA in 1983. In 1987, he published *Tales from Firozsha Baag*, a collection of short stories set in both the writer's own minority Parsi community in Bombay (now Mumbai) and abroad. Each story deals with topics that would recur in Mistry's writing: community, identity, diaspora, poverty, dreams, and human conflict.

His first novel, *Such a Long Journey* (1991), set in Bombay during the Indian-Pakistan War of 1971, won the Governor General's Award and the Commonwealth Writers Prize. Mistry's second novel, *A Fine Balance* (1995), set in India during The Emergency imposed by Indira Gandhi, 1975–77, won a host of awards, including the Giller Prize. *Family Matters* (2002), set in mid-1990s Bombay, was another critical success, garnering the Kiriyama Pacific Rim Book Prize, a third straight Commonwealth Writers Prize, and a third straight appearance on the prestigious Man Booker Prize shortlist. In 2012, Mistry was awarded the Neustadt International Prize in recognition of his contributions to world literature.

# Squatter[1]

Whenever Nariman Hansotia returned in the evening from the Cawasji Framji Memorial Library in a good mood the signs were plainly evident.

First, he parked his 1932 Mercedes-Benz (he called it the apple of his eye) outside A Block, directly in front of his ground-floor veranda window, and beeped the horn three long times. It annoyed Rustomji who also had a ground-floor flat in A Block. Ever since he had defied Nariman in the matter of painting the exterior of the building, Rustomji was convinced that nothing

---

1   *Squatter* This story appeared in Mistry's *Tales from Firozsha Baag*, in which all of the short stories are linked to an apartment block in Mumbai, India. Most of the inhabitants of the block are Parsis, members of a Zoroastrian religious minority with Persian roots that has lived in India for the past thousand years.

the old coot did was untainted by the thought of vengeance and harassment, his retirement pastime.

But the beeping was merely Nariman's signal to let Hirabai inside know that though he was back he would not step indoors for a while. Then he raised the hood, whistling "Rose Marie,"[1] and leaned his tall frame over the engine. He checked the oil, wiped here and there with a rag, tightened the radiator cap, and lowered the hood. Finally, he polished the Mercedes star and let the whistling modulate into the march from *The Bridge on the River Kwai*.[2] The boys playing in the compound knew that Nariman was ready now to tell a story. They started to gather round.

"*Sahibji*, Nariman Uncle," someone said tentatively and Nariman nodded, careful not to lose his whistle, his bulbous nose flaring slightly. The pursed lips had temporarily raised and reshaped his Clark Gable[3] moustache. More boys walked up. One called out, "How about a story, Nariman Uncle?" at which point Nariman's eyes began to twinkle, and he imparted increased energy to the polishing. The cry was taken up by others, "Yes, yes, Nariman Uncle, a story!" He swung into a final verse of the march. Then the lips relinquished the whistle, the Clark Gable moustache descended. The rag was put away, and he began.

"You boys know the great cricketers: Contractor, Polly Umrigar, and recently, the young chap, Farokh Engineer.[4] Cricket *aficionados*, that's what you all are." Nariman liked to use new words, especially big ones, in the stories he told, believing it was his duty to expose young minds to as shimmering and varied a vocabulary as possible; if they could not spend their days at the Cawasji Framji Memorial Library then he, at least, could carry bits of the library out to them.

The boys nodded; the names of the cricketers were familiar.

"But does any one know about Savukshaw, the greatest of them all?" They shook their heads in unison.

"This, then, is the story about Savukshaw, how he saved the Indian team from a humiliating defeat when they were touring in England." Nariman sat on the steps of A Block. The few diehards who had continued with their games could not resist any longer when they saw the gathering circle, and ran up to

---

1    *"Rose Marie"* Popular theme song from a 1924 Broadway musical set in the Rocky Mountains of Canada, remade several times into Hollywood films.

2    *The Bridge ... Kwai* 1957 film about a group of Allied soldiers imprisoned in a Japanese prisoner-of-war camp in World War II.

3    *Clark Gable* American actor, most famous for his performance in the 1939 film *Gone with the Wind*.

4    *great cricketers ... Engineer* Cricket is a bat-and-ball sport popular in the United Kingdom and its past colonies, including India. The cricketers mentioned were all Parsi members of India's national team.

listen. They asked their neighbours in whispers what the story was about, and were told: Savukshaw the greatest cricketer. The whispering died down and Nariman began.

"The Indian team was to play the indomitable MCC as part of its tour of England. Contractor was our captain. Now the MCC being the strongest team they had to face, Contractor was almost certain of defeat. To add to Contractor's troubles, one of his star batsmen, Nadkarni, had caught influenza early in the tour, and would definitely not be well enough to play against the MCC. By the way, does anyone know what those letters stand for? You, Kersi, you wanted to be a cricketer once."

Kersi shook his head. None of the boys knew, even though they had heard the MCC mentioned in radio commentaries, because the full name was hardly ever used.

Then Jehangir Bulsara spoke up, or Bulsara Bookworm, as the boys called him. The name given by Pesi *paadmaroo*[1] had stuck even though it was now more than four years since Pesi had been sent away to boarding-school, and over two years since the death of Dr. Mody. Jehangir was still unliked by the boys in the Baag, though they had come to accept his aloofness and respect his knowledge and intellect. They were not surprised that he knew the answer to Nariman's question: "Marylebone Cricket Club."[2]

"Absolutely correct," said Nariman, and continued with the story. "The MCC won the toss and elected to bat. They scored four hundred and ninety-seven runs in the first inning before our spinners[3] could get them out. Early in the second day's play our team was dismissed for one hundred and nine runs, and the extra who had taken Nadkarni's place was injured by a vicious bumper[4] that opened a gash on his forehead." Nariman indicated the spot and the length of the gash on his furrowed brow. "Contractor's worst fears were coming true. The MCC waived their own second inning and gave the Indian team a follow-on,[5] wanting to inflict an inning's defeat. And this time he had to use the second extra. The second extra was a certain Savukshaw."

The younger boys listened attentively; some of them, like the two sons of the chartered accountant in B Block, had only recently been deemed old

---

1    *paadmaroo* Pesi is given this punning nickname in another story in *Tales from Firozsha Baag*; it is a reference to his pungent flatulence.

2    *Marylebone Cricket Club* Based in London, the MCC is the most famous cricket club in the world. The governing body of international cricket until 1993, the MCC holds the copyright to the sport's official laws.

3    *spinners* Cricket bowlers who use trickery to oust opposing batters, roughly equivalent to changeup pitchers in baseball.

4    *bumper* Ball pitched fast and bounced toward the batter's head.

5    *follow-on* Inning in which the team that has just batted is required to bat again because their score from the first inning is less than half the other team's.

enough by their parents to come out and play in the compound, and had not received any exposure to Nariman's stories. But the others like Jehangir, Kersi, and Viraf were familiar with Nariman's technique.

Once, Jehangir had overheard them discussing Nariman's stories, and he could not help expressing his opinion: that unpredictability was the brush he used to paint his tales with, and ambiguity the palette he mixed his colours in. The others looked at him with admiration. Then Viraf asked what exactly he meant by that. Jehangir said that Nariman sometimes told a funny incident in a very serious way, or expressed a significant matter in a light and playful manner. And these were only two rough divisions, in between were lots of subtle gradations of tone and texture. Which, then, was the funny story and which the serious? Their opinions were divided, but ultimately, said Jehangir, it was up to the listener to decide.

"So," continued Nariman, "Contractor first sent out his two regular open-ers, convinced that it was all hopeless. But after five wickets were lost[1] for just another thirty-eight runs, out came Savukshaw the extra. Nothing mattered any more."

The street lights outside the compound came on, illuminating the iron gate where the watchman stood. It was a load off the watchman's mind when Nariman told a story. It meant an early end to the hectic vigil during which he had to ensure that none of the children ran out on the main road, or tried to jump over the wall. For although keeping out riff-raff was his duty, keeping in the boys was as important if he wanted to retain the job.

"The first ball Savukshaw faced was wide outside the off stump.[2] He just lifted his bat and ignored it. But with what style! What panache! As if to say, come on, you blighters, play some polished cricket. The next ball was also wide, but not as much as the first. It missed the off stump narrowly. Again Savukshaw lifted his bat, boredom written all over him. Everyone was now watching closely. The bowler was annoyed by Savukshaw's arrogance, and the third delivery was a vicious fast pitch, right down on the middle stump.

"Savukshaw was ready, quick as lightning. No one even saw the stroke of his bat, but the ball went like a bullet towards the square leg.[3]

"Fielding at square leg was a giant of a fellow, about six feet seven, weigh-ing two hundred and fifty pounds, a veritable Brobdingnagian,[4] with arms like branches and hands like a pair of huge *sapaat*, the kind that Dr. Mody

---

1    *five … lost* I.e., five players were out.
2    *stump* One of the three standing wooden sticks that comprise a wicket. The batter stands in front of the wicket to protect it from the pitcher, who attempts to hit it; if the pitch knocks one of the stumps out of the ground, the player is out.
3    *square leg* Fielder positioned to the side of the batter.
4    *Brobdingnagian* Giant. See Jonathan Swift's *Gulliver's Travels* (1726).

used to wear, you remember what big feet Dr. Mody had." Jehangir was the only one who did; he nodded. "Just to see him standing there was scary. Not one ball had got past him, and he had taken some great catches. Savukshaw purposely aimed his shot right at him. But he was as quick as Savukshaw, and stuck out his huge *sapaat* of a hand to stop the ball. What do you think happened then, boys?"

The older boys knew what Nariman wanted to hear at this point. They asked, "What happened, Nariman Uncle, what happened?" Satisfied, Nariman continued.

"A howl is what happened. A howl from the giant fielder, a howl that rang through the entire stadium, that soared like the cry of a banshee[1] right up to the cheapest seats in the furthest, highest corners, a howl that echoed from the scoreboard and into the pavilion, into the kitchen, startling the chap inside who was preparing tea and scones for after the match, who spilled boiling water all over himself and was severely hurt. But not nearly as bad as the giant fielder at square leg. Never at any English stadium was a howl heard like that one, not in the whole history of cricket. And why do you think he was howling, boys?"

The chorus asked, "Why, Nariman Uncle, why?"

"Because of Savukshaw's bullet-like shot, of course. The hand he had reached out to stop it, he now held up for all to see, and *dhur-dhur, dhur-dhur* the blood was gushing like a fountain in an Italian piazza, like a burst water-main from the Vihar-Powai reservoir, dripping onto his shirt and his white pants, and sprinkling the green grass, and only because he was such a giant of a fellow could he suffer so much blood loss and not faint. But even he could not last forever; eventually, he felt dizzy, and was helped off the field. And where do you think the ball was, boys, that Savukshaw had smacked so hard?"

And the chorus rang out again on the now dark steps of A Block: "Where, Nariman Uncle, where?"

"Past the boundary line, of course. Lying near the fence. Rent asunder. Into two perfect leather hemispheres. All the stitches had ripped, and some of the insides had spilled out. So the umpires sent for a new one, and the game resumed. Now none of the fielders dared to touch any ball that Savukshaw hit. Every shot went to the boundary, all the way for four runs. Single-handedly, Savukshaw wiped out the deficit, and had it not been for loss of time due to rain, he would have taken the Indian team to a thumping victory against the MCC. As it was, the match ended in a draw."

Nariman was pleased with the awed faces of the youngest ones around him. Kersi and Viraf were grinning away and whispering something. From

---

1    *banshee* Fairy woman in Irish folklore whose wail foretells death.

one of the flats the smell of frying fish swam out to explore the night air, and tickled Nariman's nostrils. He sniffed appreciatively, aware that it was in his good wife Hirabai's pan that the frying was taking place. This morning, he had seen the pomfret[1] she had purchased at the door, waiting to be cleaned, its mouth open and eyes wide, like the eyes of some of these youngsters. It was time to wind up the story.

"The MCC will not forget the number of new balls they had to produce that day because of Savukshaw's deadly strokes. Their annual ball budget was thrown badly out of balance. Any other bat would have cracked under the strain, but Savukshaw's was seasoned with a special combination of oils, a secret formula given to him by a *sadhu*[2] who had seen him one day playing cricket when he was a small boy. But Savukshaw used to say his real secret was practice, lots of practice, that was the advice he gave to any young lad who wanted to play cricket."

The story was now clearly finished, but none of the boys showed any sign of dispersing. "Tell us about more matches that Savukshaw played in," they said.

"More nothing. This was his greatest match. Anyway, he did not play cricket for long because soon after the match against the MCC he became a champion bicyclist, the fastest human on two wheels. And later, a pole-vaulter—when he glided over on his pole, so graceful, it was like watching a bird in flight. But he gave that up, too, and became a hunter, the mightiest hunter ever known, absolutely fearless, and so skilful, with a gun he could have, from the third floor of A Block, shaved the whisker of a cat in the backyard of C Block."

"Tell us about that," they said, "about Savukshaw the hunter!"

The fat ayah,[3] Jaakaylee, arrived to take the chartered accountant's two children home. But they refused to go without hearing about Savukshaw the hunter. When she scolded them and things became a little hysterical, some other boys tried to resurrect the ghost she had once seen: "Ayah *bhoot*![4] Ayah *bhoot*!" Nariman raised a finger in warning—that subject was still taboo in Firozsha Baag; none of the adults was in a hurry to relive the wild and rampageous days that Pesi *paadmaroo* had ushered in, once upon a time, with the *bhoot* games.

Jaakaylee sat down, unwilling to return without the children, and whispered to Nariman to make it short. The smell of frying fish which had tickled Nariman's nostrils ventured into and awakened his stomach. But the story of Savukshaw the hunter was one he had wanted to tell for a long time.

---

1     *pomfret* Fish common in southern Asia.
2     *sadhu* Gujarati: monk.
3     *ayah* Nanny.
4     *bhoot* Gujarati: ghost.

"Savukshaw always went hunting alone, he preferred it that way. There are many incidents in the life of Savukshaw the hunter, but the one I am telling you about involves a terrifying situation. Terrifying for us, of course; Savukshaw was never terrified of anything. What happened was, one night he set up camp, started a fire and warmed up his bowl of chicken-*dhansaak*."

The frying fish had precipitated famishment upon Nariman, and the subject of chicken-*dhansaak* suited him well. His own mouth watering, he elaborated: "Mrs. Savukshaw was as famous for her *dhansaak* as Mr. was for hunting. She used to put in tamarind and brinjal, coriander and cumin, cloves and cinnamon, and dozens of other spices no one knows about. Women used to come from miles around to stand outside her window while she cooked it, to enjoy the fragrance and try to penetrate her secret, hoping to identify the ingredients as the aroma floated out, layer by layer, growing more complex and delicious. But always, the delectable fragrance enveloped the women and they just surrendered to the ecstasy, forgetting what they had come for. Mrs. Savukshaw's secret was safe."

Jaakaylee motioned to Nariman to hurry up, it was past the children's dinner-time. He continued: "The aroma of savoury spices soon filled the night air in the jungle, and when the *dhansaak* was piping hot he started to eat, his rifle beside him. But as soon as he lifted the first morsel to his lips, a tiger's eyes flashed in the bushes! Not twelve feet from him! He emerged licking his chops! What do you think happened then, boys?"

"What, what, Nariman Uncle?"

Before he could tell them, the door of his flat opened. Hirabai put her head out and said, "*Chaalo ni*,[1] Nariman, it's time. Then if it gets cold you won't like it."

That decided the matter. To let Hirabai's fried fish, crisp on the outside, yet tender and juicy inside, marinated in turmeric and cayenne—to let that get cold would be something that *Khoedaiji*[2] above would not easily forgive. "Sorry boys, have to go. Next time about Savukshaw and the tiger."

There were some groans of disappointment. They hoped Nariman's good spirits would extend into the morrow when he returned from the Memorial Library, or the story would get cold.

But a whole week elapsed before Nariman again parked the apple of his eye outside his ground-floor flat and beeped the horn three times. When he had raised the hood, checked the oil, polished the star and swung into the "Colonel Bogie March,"[3] the boys began drifting towards A Block.

---

1   *Chaalo ni* Gujarati: Come along now.
2   *Khoedaiji* Gujarati: God.
3   *"Colonel Bogie March"* Marching song of the imprisoned soldiers in *Bridge on the River Kwai*.

Some of them recalled the incomplete story of Savukshaw and the tiger, but they knew better than to remind him. It was never wise to prompt Nariman until he had dropped the first hint himself, or things would turn out badly.

Nariman inspected the faces: the two who stood at the back, always looking superior and wise, were missing. So was the quiet Bulsara boy, the intelligent one. "Call Kersi, Viraf, and Jehangir," he said. "I want them to listen to today's story."

Jehangir was sitting alone on the stone steps of C Block. The others were chatting by the compound gate with the watchman. Someone went to fetch them.

"Sorry to disturb your conference, boys, and your meditation, Jehangir," Nariman said facetiously, "but I thought you would like to hear this story. Especially since some of you are planning to go abroad."

This was not strictly accurate, but Kersi and Viraf did talk a lot about America and Canada. Kersi had started writing to universities there since his final high-school year, and had also sent letters of inquiry to the Canadian High Commission in New Delhi and to the US Consulate at Breach Candy. But so far he had not made any progress. He and Viraf replied with as much sarcasm as their unripe years allowed, "Oh yes, next week, just have to pack our bags."

"Riiiight," drawled Nariman. Although he spoke perfect English, this was the one word with which he allowed himself to take liberties, indulging in a broadness of vowel more American than anything else. "But before we go on with today's story, what did you learn about Savukshaw, from last week's story?"

"That he was a very talented man," said someone.

"What else?"

"He was also a very lucky man, to have so many talents," said Viraf.

"Yes, but what else?"

There was silence for a few moments. Then Jehangir said, timidly: "He was a man searching for happiness, by trying all kinds of different things."

"Exactly! And he never found it. He kept looking for new experiences, and though he was very successful at everything he attempted, it did not bring him happiness. Remember this, success alone does not bring happiness. Nor does failure have to bring unhappiness. Keep it in mind when you listen to today's story."

A chant started somewhere in the back: "We-want-a-story! We-want-a-story!"

"Riiiight," said Nariman. "Now, everyone remembers Vera and Dolly, daughters of Najamai from C Block." There were whistles and hoots; Viraf nudged Kersi with his elbow, who was smiling wistfully. Nariman held up his hand: "Now now, boys, behave yourselves. Those two girls went abroad for studies many years ago, and never came back. They settled there happily.

"And like them, a fellow called Sarosh also went abroad, to Toronto, but did not find happiness there. This story is about him. You probably don't know him, he does not live in Firozsha Baag, though he is related to someone who does."

"Who? Who?"

"Curiosity killed the cat," said Nariman, running a finger over each branch of his moustache, "and what's important is the tale. So let us continue. This Sarosh began calling himself Sid after living in Toronto for a few months, but in our story he will be Sarosh and nothing but Sarosh, for that is his proper Parsi name. Besides, that was his own stipulation when he entrusted me with the sad but instructive chronicle of his recent life." Nariman polished his glasses with his handkerchief, put them on again, and began.

"At the point where our story commences, Sarosh had been living in Toronto for ten years. We find him depressed and miserable, perched on top of the toilet, crouching on his haunches, feet planted firmly for balance upon the white plastic oval of the toilet seat.

"Daily for a decade had Sarosh suffered this position. Morning after morning, he had no choice but to climb up and simulate the squat of our Indian latrines. If he sat down, no amount of exertion could produce success.

"At first, this inability was not more than mildly incommodious. As time went by, however, the frustrated attempts caused him grave anxiety. And when the failure stretched unbroken over ten years, it began to torment and haunt all his waking hours."

Some of the boys struggled hard to keep straight faces. They suspected that Nariman was not telling just a funny story, because if he intended them to laugh there was always some unmistakable way to let them know. Only the thought of displeasing Nariman and prematurely terminating the story kept their paroxysms of mirth from bursting forth unchecked.

Nariman continued: "You see, ten years was the time Sarosh had set himself to achieve complete adaptation to the new country. But how could he claim adaptation with any honesty if the acceptable catharsis[1] continually failed to favour him? Obtaining his new citizenship had not helped either. He remained dependent on the old way, and this unalterable fact, strengthened afresh every morning of his life in the new country, suffocated him.

"The ten-year time limit was more an accident than anything else. But it hung over him with the awesome presence and sharpness of a guillotine.

---

1   *catharsis* Purgation; usually refers to emotional release, but can also refer to defecation.

Careless words, boys, careless words in a moment of lightheartedness, as is so often the case with us all, had led to it.

"Ten years before, Sarosh had returned triumphantly to Bombay after fulfilling the immigration requirements of the Canadian High Commission in New Delhi. News of his imminent departure spread amongst relatives and friends. A farewell party was organized. In fact, it was given by his relatives in Firozsha Baag. Most of you will be too young to remember it, but it was a very loud party, went on till late in the night. Very lengthy and heated arguments took place, which is not the thing to do at a party. It started like this: Sarosh was told by some what a smart decision he had made, that his whole life would change for the better; others said he was making a mistake, emigration was all wrong, but if he wanted to be unhappy that was his business, they wished him well.

"By and by, after substantial amounts of Scotch and soda and rum and Coke had disappeared, a fierce debate started between the two groups. To this day Sarosh does not know what made him raise his glass and announce: 'My dear family, my dear friends, if I do not become completely Canadian in exactly ten years from the time I land there, then I will come back. I promise. So please, no more arguments. Enjoy the party.' His words were greeted with cheers and shouts of hear! hear! They told him never to fear embarrassment; there was no shame if he decided to return to the country of his birth.

"But shortly, his poor worried mother pulled him aside. She led him to the back room and withdrew her worn and aged prayer book from her purse, saying, 'I want you to place your hand upon the *Avesta*[1] and swear that you will keep that promise.'

"He told her not to be silly, that it was just a joke. But she insisted. '*Kassum khà*[2]—on the *Avesta*. One last thing for your mother. Who knows when you will see me again?' and her voice grew tremulous as it always did when she turned deeply emotional. Sarosh complied, and the prayer book was returned to her purse.

"His mother continued: 'It is better to live in want among your family and your friends, who love you and care for you, than to be unhappy surrounded by vacuum cleaners and dishwashers and big shiny motor cars.' She hugged him. Then they joined the celebration in progress.

"And Sarosh's careless words spoken at the party gradually forged themselves into a commitment as much to himself as to his mother and the others. It stayed with him all his years in the new land, reminding him every morning

---

1    *Avesta*  Sacred text of Zoroastrianism.
2    *Kassum khà*  Gujarati: Swear.

of what must happen at the end of the tenth, as it reminded him now while he descended from his perch."

Jehangir wished the titters and chortles around him would settle down, he found them annoying. When Nariman structured his sentences so carefully and chose his words with extreme care as he was doing now, Jehangir found it most pleasurable to listen. Sometimes, he remembered certain words Nariman had used, or combinations of words, and repeated them to himself, enjoying again the beauty of their sounds when he went for his walks to the Hanging Gardens[1] or was sitting alone on the stone steps of C Block. Mumbling to himself did nothing to mitigate the isolation which the other boys in the Baag had dropped around him like a heavy cloak, but he had grown used to all that by now.

Nariman continued: "In his own apartment Sarosh squatted barefoot. Elsewhere, if he had to go with his shoes on, he would carefully cover the seat with toilet paper before climbing up. He learnt to do this after the first time, when his shoes had left telltale footprints on the seat. He had had to clean it with a wet paper towel. Luckily, no one had seen him.

"But there was not much he could keep secret about his ways. The world of washrooms is private and at the same time very public. The absence of his feet below the stall door, the smell of faeces, the rustle of paper, glimpses caught through the narrow crack between stall door and jamb—all these added up to only one thing: a foreign presence in the stall, not doing things in the conventional way. And if the one outside could receive the fetor of Sarosh's business wafting through the door, poor unhappy Sarosh too could detect something malodorous in the air: the presence of xenophobia and hostility."

What a feast, thought Jehangir, what a feast of words! This would be the finest story Nariman had ever told, he just knew it.

"But Sarosh did not give up trying. Each morning he seated himself to push and grunt, grunt and push, squirming and writhing unavailingly on the white plastic oval. Exhausted, he then hopped up, expert at balancing now, and completed the movement quite effortlessly.

"The long morning hours in the washroom created new difficulties. He was late going to work on several occasions, and one such day, the supervisor called him in: 'Here's your time-sheet for this month. You've been late eleven times. What's the problem?'"

Here, Nariman stopped because his neighbour Rustomji's door creaked open. Rustomji peered out, scowling and muttered, "*Saala*[2] loafers, sitting all

---

1    *Hanging Gardens* Terraced gardens in Bombay (Mumbai) featuring hedges sculpted into animal shapes.

2    *Saala* Hindi swear word.

evening outside people's houses, making a nuisance, and being encouraged by grownups at that."

He stood there a moment longer, fingering the greying chest hair that was easily accessible through his *sudra*, then went inside. The boys immediately took up a soft and low chant: "Rustomji-the-curmudgeon! Rustomji-the-curmudgeon!"

Nariman held up his hand disapprovingly. But secretly, he was pleased that the name was still popular, the name he had given Rustomji when the latter had refused to pay his share for painting the building. "Quiet, quiet!" said he. "Do you want me to continue or not?"

"Yes, yes!" The chanting died away, and Nariman resumed the story.

"So Sarosh was told by his supervisor that he was coming late to work too often. What could poor Sarosh say?"

"What, Nariman Uncle?" rose the refrain.

"Nothing, of course. The supervisor, noting his silence, continued: 'If it keeps up, the consequences could be serious as far as your career is concerned.'

"Sarosh decided to speak. He said embarrassedly, 'It's a different kind of problem. I ... I don't know how to explain ... it's an immigration-related problem.'

"Now this supervisor must have had experience with other immigrants, because right away he told Sarosh, 'No problem. Just contact your Immigrant Aid Society. They should be able to help you. Every ethnic group has one: Vietnamese, Chinese—I'm certain that one exists for Indians. If you need time off to go there, no problem. That can be arranged, no problem. As long as you do something about your lateness, there's no problem.' That's the way they talk over there, nothing is ever a problem.

"So Sarosh thanked him and went to his desk. For the umpteenth time he bitterly rued his oversight. Could fate have plotted it, concealing the western toilet behind a shroud of anxieties which had appeared out of nowhere to beset him just before he left India? After all, he had readied himself meticulously for the new life. Even for the great, merciless Canadian cold he had heard so much about. How could he have overlooked preparation for the western toilet with its matutinal[1] demands unless fate had conspired? In Bombay, you know that offices of foreign businesses offer both options in their bathrooms. So do all hotels with three stars or more. By practising in familiar surroundings, Sarosh was convinced he could have mastered a seated evacuation before departure.

"But perhaps there was something in what the supervisor said. Sarosh found a telephone number for the Indian Immigrant Aid Society and made

---

1    *matutinal* Early-morning.

an appointment. That afternoon, he met Mrs. Maha-Lepate[1] at the Society's office."

Kersi and Viraf looked at each other and smiled. Nariman Uncle had a nerve, there was more *lepate* in his own stories than anywhere else.

"Mrs. Maha-Lepate was very understanding, and made Sarosh feel at ease despite the very personal nature of his problem. She said, 'Yes, we get many referrals. There was a man here last month who couldn't eat Wonder Bread—it made him throw up.'

"By the way, boys, Wonder Bread is a Canadian bread which all happy families eat to be happy in the same way; the unhappy families are unhappy in their own fashion[2] by eating other brands." Jehangir was the only one who understood, and murmured, "Tolstoy," at Nariman's little joke. Nariman noticed it, pleased. He continued.

"Mrs. Maha-Lepate told Sarosh about that case: 'Our immigrant specialist, Dr. No-Ilaaz, recommended that the patient eat cake instead.[3] He explained that Wonder Bread caused vomiting because the digestive system was used to Indian bread only, made with Indian flour in the village he came from. However, since his system was unfamiliar with cake, Canadian or otherwise, it did not react but was digested as a newfound food. In this way he got used to Canadian flour first in cake form. Just yesterday we received a report from Dr. No-Ilaaz. The patient successfully ate his first slice of whole-wheat Wonder Bread with no ill effects. The ultimate goal is pure white Wonder Bread.'

"Like a polite Parsi boy, Sarosh said, 'That's very interesting.' The garrulous Mrs. Maha-Lepate was about to continue, and he tried to interject: 'But I—' but Mrs. Maha-Lepate was too quick for him: 'Oh, there are so many interesting cases I could tell you about. Like the woman from Sri Lanka—referred to us because they don't have their own Society—who could not drink the water here. Dr. No-Ilaaz said it was due to the different mineral content. So he started her on Coca-Cola and then began diluting it with water, bit by bit. Six weeks later she took her first sip of unadulterated Canadian water and managed to keep it down.'

"Sarosh could not halt Mrs. Maha-Lepate as she launched from one case history into another: 'Right now, Dr. No-Ilaaz is working on a very unusual case. Involves a whole Pakistani family. Ever since immigrating to Canada,

1    *Maha-Lepate* Hindi: Great Yarn-Teller.
2    *the unhappy ... own fashion* See the opening sentence of Leo Tolstoy's classic Russian novel *Anna Karenina* (1873–77): "Happy families are all alike; every unhappy family is unhappy in its own way."
3    *No-Ilaaz* Hindi: No-Cure; *eat cake instead* Reference to a quotation attributed to Marie Antoinette (1755–93), Queen of France. When told that the peasants had no bread to eat, she supposedly declared, "let them eat cake."

none of them can swallow. They choke on their own saliva, and have to spit constantly. But we are confident that Dr. No-Ilaaz will find a remedy. He has never been stumped by any immigrant problems. Besides, we have an information network with other third-world Immigrant Aid Societies. We all seem to share a history of similar maladies, and regularly compare notes. Some of us thought these problems were linked to retention of original citizenship. But this was a false lead.'

"Sarosh, out of his own experience, vigorously nodded agreement. By now he was truly fascinated by Mrs. Maha-Lepate's wealth of information. Reluctantly, he interrupted: 'But will Dr. No-Ilaaz be able to solve my problem?'

"'I have every confidence that he will,' replied Mrs. Maha-Lepate in great earnest. 'And if he has no remedy for you right away, he will be delighted to start working on one. He loves to take up new projects.'"

Nariman halted to blow his nose, and a clear shrill voice travelled the night air of the Firozsha Baag compound from C Block to where the boys had collected around Nariman in A Block: "Jehangoo! O Jehangoo! Eight o'clock! Upstairs now!"

Jehangir stared at his feet in embarrassment. Nariman looked at his watch and said, "Yes, it's eight." But Jehangir did not move, so he continued.

"Mrs. Maha-Lepate was able to arrange an appointment while Sarosh waited, and he went directly to the doctor's office. What he had heard so far sounded quite promising. Then he cautioned himself not to get overly optimistic, that was the worst mistake he could make. But along the way to the doctor's, he could not help thinking what a lovely city Toronto was. It was the same way he had felt when he first saw it ten years ago, before all the joy had dissolved in the acid of his anxieties."

Once again that shrill voice travelled through the clear night: "*Arré* Jehangoo! *Muà*, do I have to come down and drag you upstairs!"

Jehangir's mortification was now complete. Nariman made it easy for him, though: "The first part of the story is over. Second part continues tomorrow. Same time, same place." The boys were surprised, Nariman did not make such commitments. But never before had he told such a long story. They began drifting back to their homes.

As Jehangir strode hurriedly to C Block, falsettos and piercing shrieks followed him in the darkness: "*Arré* Jehangoo! *Muà*, Jehangoo! Bulsara Bookworm! Eight o'clock Jehangoo!" Shaking his head, Nariman went indoors to Hirabai.

Next evening the story punctually resumed when Nariman took his place on the topmost step of A Block: "You remember that we left Sarosh on his way to see the Immigrant Aid Society's doctor. Well, Dr. No-Ilaaz listened patiently to Sarosh's concerns, then said, 'As a matter of fact, there is a remedy which is so new even the IAS does not know about it. Not even that Mrs. Maha-Lepate who knows it all,' he added drolly, twirling his stethoscope like a stunted lasso. He slipped it on around his neck before continuing: 'It involves a minor operation which was developed with financial assistance from the Multicultural Department. A small device, *Crappus Non Interruptus*, or CNI as we call it, is implanted in the bowel. The device is controlled by an external handheld transmitter similar to the ones used for automatic garage door-openers—you may have seen them in hardware stores."

Nariman noticed that most of the boys wore puzzled looks and realized he had to make some things clearer. "The Multicultural Department is a Canadian invention. It is supposed to ensure that ethnic cultures are able to flourish, so that Canadian society will consist of a mosaic of cultures—that's their favourite word, mosaic—instead of one uniform mix, like the American melting pot. If you ask me, mosaic and melting pot are both nonsense, and ethnic is a polite way of saying bloody foreigner. But anyway, you understand Multicultural Department? Good. So Sarosh nodded, and Dr. No-Ilaaz went on: 'You can encode the hand-held transmitter with a personal ten-digit code. Then all you do is position yourself on the toilet seat and activate your transmitter. Just like a garage door, your bowel will open without pushing or grunting.'"

There was some snickering in the audience, and Nariman raised his eyebrows, whereupon they covered up their mouths with their hands. "The doctor asked Sarosh if he had any questions. Sarosh thought for a moment, then asked if it required any maintenance.

"Dr. No-Ilaaz replied: 'CNI is semi-permanent and operates on solar energy. Which means you would have to make it a point to get some sun periodically, or it would cease and lead to constipation. However, you don't have to strip for a tan. Exposing ten percent of your skin surface once a week during summer will let the device store sufficient energy for year-round operation.'

"Sarosh's next question was: 'Is there any hope that someday the bowels can work on their own, without operating the device?' at which Dr. No-Ilaaz grimly shook his head: 'I'm afraid not. You must think very, very carefully before making a decision. Once CNI is implanted, you can never pass a motion in the natural way—neither sitting nor squatting.'

"He stopped to allow Sarosh time to think it over, then continued: 'And you must understand what that means. You will never be able to live a normal life again. You will be permanently different from your family and friends because of this basic internal modification. In fact, in this country or that, it will set you apart from your fellow countrymen. So you must consider the whole thing most carefully.'

"Dr. No-Ilaaz paused, toyed with his stethoscope, shuffled some papers on his desk, then resumed: 'There are other dangers you should know about.

Just as a garage door can be accidentally opened by a neighbour's transmitter on the same frequency, CNI can also be activated by someone with similar apparatus.' To ease the tension he attempted a quick laugh and said, 'Very embarrassing, eh, if it happened at the wrong place and time. Mind you, the risk is not so great at present, because the chances of finding yourself within a fifty-foot radius of another transmitter on the same frequency are infinitesimal. But what about the future? What if CNI becomes very popular? Sufficient permutations may not be available for transmitter frequencies and you could be sharing the code with others. Then the risk of accidents becomes greater.'"

Something landed with a loud thud in the yard behind A Block, making Nariman startle. Immediately, a yowling and screeching and caterwauling went up from the stray cats there, and the *kuchrawalli's*[1] dog started barking. Some of the boys went around the side of A Block to peer over the fence into the backyard. But the commotion soon died down of its own accord. The boys returned and, once again, Nariman's voice was the only sound to be heard.

"By now, Sarosh was on the verge of deciding against the operation. Dr. No-Ilaaz observed this and was pleased. He took pride in being able to dissuade his patients from following the very remedies which he first so painstakingly described. True to his name, Dr. No-Ilaaz believed no remedy is the best remedy, rather than prescribing this-mycin and that-mycin for every little ailment. So he continued: 'And what about our sons and daughters? And the quality of their lives? We still don't know about the long-term effects of CNI. Some researchers speculate that it could generate a genetic deficiency, that the offspring of a CNI parent would also require CNI. On the other hand, they could be perfectly healthy toilet seat-users, without any congenital defects. We just don't know at this stage.'

"Sarosh rose from his chair: 'Thank you very much for your time, Dr. No-Ilaaz. But I don't think I want to take such a drastic step. As you suggest, I will think it over carefully.'

"'Good, good,' said Dr. No-Ilaaz, 'I was hoping you would say that. There is one more thing. The operation is extremely expensive, and is not covered by the province's Health Insurance Plan. Many immigrant groups are lobbying to obtain coverage for special immigration-related health problems. If they succeed, then good for you.'

"Sarosh left Dr. No-Ilaaz's office with his mind made up. Time was running out. There had been a time when it was perfectly natural to squat. Now it seemed a grotesquely aberrant thing to do. Wherever he went he was reminded of the ignominy of his way. If he could not be westernized in all respects, he was nothing but a failure in this land—a failure not just in the washrooms

---

1    *kuchrawalli* Garbage collector.

of the nation but everywhere. He knew what he must do if he was to be true to himself and to the decade-old commitment. So what do you think Sarosh did next?"

"What, Nariman Uncle?"

"He went to the travel agent specializing in tickets to India. He bought a fully refundable ticket to Bombay for the day when he would complete exactly ten immigrant years—if he succeeded even once before that day dawned, he would cancel the booking.

"The travel agent asked sympathetically, 'Trouble at home?' His name was Mr. Rawaana, and he was from Bombay too.

"'No,' said Sarosh, 'trouble in Toronto.'

"'That's a shame,' said Mr. Rawaana. 'I don't want to poke my nose into your business, but in my line of work I meet so many people who are going back to their homeland because of their problems here. Sometimes I forget I'm a travel agent, that my interest is to convince them to travel. Instead, I tell them: don't give up, God is great, stay and try again. It's bad for my profits but gives me a different, a spiritual kind of satisfaction when I succeed. And I succeed about half the time. Which means,' he added with a wry laugh, 'I could double my profits if I minded my own business.'

"After the lengthy sessions with Mrs. Maha-Lepate and Dr. No-Ilaaz, Sarosh felt he had listened to enough advice and kind words. Much as he disliked doing it, he had to hurt Mr. Rawaana's feelings and leave his predicament undiscussed: 'I'm sorry, but I'm in a hurry. Will you be able to look after the booking?'

"'Well, okay,' said Mr. Rawaana, a trifle crestfallen; he did not relish the travel business as much as he did counselling immigrants. 'Hope you solve your problem. I will be happy to refund your fare, believe me.'

"Sarosh hurried home. With only four weeks to departure, every spare minute, every possible method had to be concentrated on a final attempt at adaptation.

"He tried laxatives, crunching down the tablets with a prayer that these would assist the sitting position. Changing brands did not help, and neither did various types of suppositories. He spent long stretches on the toilet seat each morning. The supervisor continued to reprimand him for tardiness. To make matters worse, Sarosh left his desk every time he felt the slightest urge, hoping: maybe this time.

"The working hours expended in the washroom were noted with unflagging vigilance by the supervisor. More counselling sessions followed. Sarosh refused to extinguish his last hope, and the supervisor punctiliously recorded 'No Improvement' in his daily log. Finally, Sarosh was fired. It would soon have been time to resign in any case, and he could not care less.

"Now whole days went by seated on the toilet, and he stubbornly refused to relieve himself the other way. The doorbell would ring only to be ignored. The telephone went unanswered. Sometimes, he would awake suddenly in the dark hours before dawn and rush to the washroom like a madman."

Without warning, Rustomji flung open his door and stormed: "Ridiculous nonsense this is becoming! Two days in a row, whole Firozsha Baag gathers here! This is not Chaupatty beach,[1] this is not a squatters' colony, this is a building, people want to live here in peace and quiet!" Then just as suddenly, he stamped inside and slammed the door. Right on cue, Nariman continued, before the boys could say anything.

"Time for meals was the only time Sarosh allowed himself off the seat. Even in his desperation he remembered that if he did not eat well, he was doomed—the downward pressure on his gut was essential if there was to be any chance of success.

"But the ineluctable day of departure dawned, with grey skies and the scent of rain, while success remained out of sight. At the airport Sarosh checked in and went to the dreary lounge. Out of sheer habit he started towards the washroom. Then he realized the hopelessness of it and returned to the cold, clammy plastic of the lounge seats. Airport seats are the same almost anywhere in the world.

"The boarding announcement was made, and Sarosh was the first to step onto the plane. The skies were darker now. Out of the window he saw a flash of lightning fork through the clouds. For some reason, everything he'd learned years ago in St. Xavier's about sheet lightning and forked lightning went through his mind. He wished it would change to sheet, there was something sinister and unpropitious about forked lightning."

Kersi, absorbedly listening, began cracking his knuckles quite unconsciously. His childhood habit still persisted. Jehangir frowned at the disturbance, and Viraf nudged Kersi to stop it.

"Sarosh fastened his seat-belt and attempted to turn his thoughts towards the long journey home: to the questions he would be expected to answer, the sympathy and criticism that would be thrust upon him. But what remained uppermost in his mind was the present moment—him in the plane, dark skies lowering, lightning on the horizon—irrevocably spelling out: defeat.

"But wait. Something else was happening now. A tiny rumble. Inside him. Or was it his imagination? Was it really thunder outside which, in his present disoriented state, he was internalizing? No, there it was again. He had to go.

"He reached the washroom, and almost immediately the sign flashed to 'Please return to seat and fasten seat-belts.' Sarosh debated whether to squat

---

1    *Chaupatty beach* Public beach in Bombay (Mumbai).

and finish the business quickly, abandoning the perfunctory seated attempt. But the plane started to move and that decided him; it would be difficult now to balance while squatting.

"He pushed. The plane continued to move. He pushed again, trembling with the effort. The seat-belt sign flashed quicker and brighter now. The plane moved faster and faster. And Sarosh pushed hard, harder than he had ever pushed before, harder than in all his ten years of trying in the new land. And the memories of Bombay, the immigration interview in New Delhi, the farewell party, his mother's tattered prayer book, all these, of their own accord, emerged from beyond the region of the ten years to push with him and give him newfound strength."

Nariman paused and cleared his throat. Dusk was falling, and the frequency of B.E.S.T. buses plying the main road outside Firozsha Baag had dropped. Bats began to fly madly from one end of the compound to the other, silent shadows engaged in endless laps over the buildings.

"With a thunderous clap the rain started to fall. Sarosh felt a splash under him. Could it really be? He glanced down to make certain. Yes, it was. He had succeeded!

"But was it already too late? The plane waited at its assigned position on the runway, jet engines at full thrust. Rain was falling in torrents and takeoff could be delayed. Perhaps even now they would allow him to cancel his flight, to disembark. He lurched out of the constricting cubicle.

"A stewardess hurried towards him: 'Excuse me, sir, but you must return to your seat immediately and fasten your belt.'

"'You don't understand!' Sarosh shouted excitedly. 'I must get off the plane! Everything is all right. I don't have to go anymore ...'

"'That's impossible, sir!' said the stewardess, aghast. 'No one can leave now. Takeoff procedures are in progress!' The wild look in his sleepless eyes, and the dark rings around them scared her. She beckoned for help.

"Sarosh continued to argue, and a steward and the chief stewardess hurried over: 'What seems to be the problem, sir? You *must* resume your seat. We are authorized, if necessary, to forcibly restrain you, sir.'

"The plane began to move again, and suddenly Sarosh felt all the urgency leaving him. His feverish mind, the product of nightmarish days and tortuous nights, was filled again with the calm which had fled a decade ago, and he spoke softly now: 'That ... that will not be necessary ... it's okay, I understand.' He readily returned to his seat.

"As the aircraft sped down the runway, Sarosh's first reaction was one of joy. The process of adaptation was complete. But later, he could not help wondering if success came before or after the ten-year limit had expired. And since he had already passed through the customs and security check, was he really an immigrant in every sense of the word at the moment of achievement?

"But such questions were merely academic. Or were they? He could not decide. If he returned, what would it be like? Ten years ago, the immigration officer who had stamped his passport had said, 'Welcome to Canada.' It was one of Sarosh's dearest memories, and thinking of it, he fell asleep.

"The plane was flying above the rainclouds. Sunshine streamed into the cabin. A few raindrops were still clinging miraculously to the windows, reminders of what was happening below. They sparkled as the sunlight caught them."

Some of the boys made as if to leave, thinking the story was finally over. Clearly, they had not found this one as interesting as the others Nariman had told. What dolts, thought Jehangir, they cannot recognize a masterpiece when they hear one. Nariman motioned with his hand for silence.

"But our story does not end there. There was a welcome-home party for Sarosh a few days after he arrived in Bombay. It was not in Firozsha Baag this time because his relatives in the Baag had a serious sickness in the house. But I was invited to it anyway. Sarosh's family and friends were considerate enough to wait till the jet lag had worked its way out of his system. They wanted him to really enjoy this one.

"Drinks began to flow freely again in his honour: Scotch and soda, rum and Coke, brandy. Sarosh noticed that during his absence all the brand names had changed—the labels were different and unfamiliar. Even for the mixes. Instead of Coke there was Thums-Up, and he remembered reading in the papers about Coca-Cola being kicked out by the Indian Government for refusing to reveal their secret formula.

"People slapped him on the back and shook his hand vigorously, over and over, right through the evening. They said: 'Telling the truth, you made the right decision, look how happy your mother is to live to see this day'; or they asked: 'Well, bossy, what changed your mind?' Sarosh smiled and nodded his way through it all, passing around Canadian currency at the insistence of some of the curious ones who, egged on by his mother, also pestered him to display his Canadian passport and citizenship card. She had been badgering him since his arrival to tell her the real reason: '*Saachoo kahé*,[1] what brought you back?' and was hoping that tonight, among his friends, he might raise his glass and reveal something. But she remained disappointed.

"Weeks went by and Sarosh found himself desperately searching for his old place in the pattern of life he had vacated ten years ago. Friends who had organized the welcome-home party gradually disappeared. He went walking

---

1   *Saachoo kahé* Gujarati: Tell the truth.

in the evenings along Marine Drive, by the sea-wall, where the old crowd used to congregate. But the people who sat on the parapet while waves crashed behind their backs were strangers. The tetrapods[1] were still there, staunchly protecting the reclaimed land from the fury of the sea. He had watched as a kid when cranes had lowered these cement and concrete hulks of respectable grey into the water. They were grimy black now, and from their angularities rose the distinct stench of human excrement. The old pattern was never found by Sarosh; he searched in vain. Patterns of life are selfish and unforgiving.

"Then one day, as I was driving past Marine Drive, I saw someone sitting alone. He looked familiar, so I stopped. For a moment I did not recognize Sarosh, so forlorn and woebegone was his countenance. I parked the apple of my eye and went to him, saying, 'Hullo, Sid, what are you doing here on your lonesome?' And he said, 'No, no! No more Sid, please, that name reminds me of all my troubles.' Then, on the parapet at Marine Drive, he told me his unhappy and wretched tale, with the waves battering away at the tetrapods, and around us the hawkers screaming about coconut-water and sugar-cane juice and *paan*.[2]

"When he finished, he said that he had related to me the whole sad saga because he knew how I told stories to boys in the Baag, and he wanted me to tell this one, especially to those who were planning to go abroad. 'Tell them,' said Sarosh, 'that the world can be a bewildering place, and dreams and ambitions are often paths to the most pernicious of traps.' As he spoke, I could see that Sarosh was somewhere far away, perhaps in New Delhi at his immigration interview, seeing himself as he was then, with what he thought was a life of hope and promise stretching endlessly before him. Poor Sarosh. Then he was back beside me on the parapet.

"'I pray you, in your stories,' said Sarosh, his old sense of humour returning as he deepened his voice for his favourite *Othello* lines"—and here, Nariman produced a basso profundo of his own—"'when you shall these unlucky deeds relate, speak of me as I am; nothing extenuate, nor set down aught in malice: tell them that in Toronto once there lived a Parsi boy as best as he could. Set you down this; and say, besides, that for some it was good and for some it was bad, but for me life in the land of milk and honey was just a pain in the posterior.'"[3]

And now, Nariman allowed his low-pitched rumbles to turn into chuckles. The boys broke into cheers and loud applause and cries of "Encore!"

---

1    *tetrapods* Four-pointed concrete shapes placed on the shoreline to prevent erosion.
2    *paan* Preparation of betel leaves, a natural stimulant.
3    *"I pray you ... the posterior"* Parody of Othello's last words in Shakespeare's *Othello*.

and "More!" Finally, Nariman had to silence them by pointing warningly at Rustomji-the-curmudgeon's door.

While Kersi and Viraf were joking and wondering what to make of it all, Jehangir edged forward and told Nariman this was the best story he had ever told. Nariman patted his shoulder and smiled. Jehangir left, wondering if Nariman would have been as popular if Dr. Mody was still alive. Probably, since the two were liked for different reasons: Dr. Mody used to be constantly jovial, whereas Nariman had his periodic story-telling urges.

Now the group of boys who had really enjoyed the Savukshaw story during the previous week spoke up. Capitalizing on Nariman's extraordinarily good mood, they began clamouring for more Savukshaw: "Nariman Uncle, tell the one about Savukshaw the hunter, the one you had started that day."

"What hunter? I don't know which one you mean." He refused to be reminded of it, and got up to leave. But there was a loud protest, and the boys started chanting, "We-want-Savukshaw! We-want-Savukshaw!"

Nariman looked fearfully towards Rustomji's door and held up his hands placatingly: "All right, all right! Next time it will be Savukshaw again. Savukshaw the artist. The story of Parsi Picasso."[1]

—1987

---

1    *Parsi Picasso*  Pun on the name of Spanish artist Pablo Picasso (1881–1973).

# *Kazuo Ishiguro*

b. 1954

Kazuo Ishiguro was born in Nagasaki, Japan. He and his family moved to England in 1960, when his father accepted a two-year research post at the National Institute of Oceanography. The family considered their life in England a temporary situation. Ishiguro has said that his parents "didn't have the mentality of immigrants because they always thought they would go home at some stage." The confluence of Ishiguro's memory of Japan—"a few hazy images"—his family's continued observance of Japanese culture in the home, and his growth to maturity in England informs his work, which often speaks of regret, unresolved emotion, and a yearning to recapture the past.

Before the age of 35, Ishiguro wrote three novels that established his credentials as a serious author: *A Pale View of Hills* (1982), which was awarded the Winifred Holtby Memorial Prize; *An Artist of the Floating World* (1986), which was awarded the Whitbread Book of the Year award and was shortlisted for the Man Booker Prize for Fiction; and *The Remains of the Day* (1989), which was awarded the Man Booker Prize for Fiction and was made into a full-length feature film. Ishiguro won the 2017 Nobel Prize in Literature.

Ishiguro's fourth novel, *The Unconsoled* (1995), revealed a change in his artistic direction, previously mischaracterized, he believes, as realist. The novel received mixed reviews and baffled many readers, including the critic James Wood, who said that it "invented its own category of badness." Nevertheless, *The Unconsoled* won the Cheltenham Prize, which is awarded yearly to a book of considerable merit that is overlooked by critics. Since *The Unconsoled*, Ishiguro has continued to produce works that challenge and interrogate the novel's conventions, including *Never Let Me Go* (2005), the second of his novels to be made into a feature film. He has also written two original screenplays, *The Saddest Music in the World* (2003) and *The White Countess* (2005).

# A Family Supper

Fugu is a fish caught off the Pacific shores of Japan. The fish has held a special significance for me ever since my mother died through eating one. The poison resides in the sexual glands of the fish, inside two fragile bags. When preparing the fish, these bags must be removed with caution, for any clumsiness will result in the poison leaking into the veins. Regrettably, it is not easy to tell whether or not this operation has been carried out successfully. The proof is, as it were, in the eating.

Fugu poisoning is hideously painful and almost always fatal. If the fish has been eaten during the evening, the victim is usually overtaken by pain during his sleep. He rolls about in agony for a few hours and is dead by morning. The fish became extremely popular in Japan after the war. Until stricter regulations were imposed, it was all the rage to perform the hazardous gutting operation in one's own kitchen, then to invite neighbours and friends round for the feast.

At the time of my mother's death, I was living in California. My relationship with my parents had become somewhat strained around that period, and consequently I did not learn of the circumstances surrounding her death until I returned to Tokyo two years later. Apparently, my mother had always refused to eat fugu, but on this particular occasion she had made an exception, having been invited by an old schoolfriend whom she was anxious not to offend. It was my father who supplied me with the details as we drove from the airport to his house in the Kamakura district. When we finally arrived, it was nearing the end of a sunny autumn day.

"Did you eat on the plane?" my father asked. We were sitting on the tatami[1] floor of his tea-room.

"They gave me a light snack."

"You must be hungry. We'll eat as soon as Kikuko arrives."

My father was a formidable-looking man with a large stony jaw and furious black eyebrows. I think now in retrospect that he much resembled Chou En-lai,[2] although he would not have cherished such a comparison, being particularly proud of the pure samurai blood that ran in the family. His general presence was not one which encouraged relaxed conversation; neither were things helped much by his odd way of stating each remark as if it were the concluding one. In fact, as I sat opposite him that afternoon, a boyhood memory came back to me of the time he had struck me several times around the head for "chattering like an old woman." Inevitably, our conversation since my arrival at the airport had been punctuated by long pauses.

"I'm sorry to hear about the firm," I said when neither of us had spoken for some time. He nodded gravely.

"In fact the story didn't end there," he said. "After the firm's collapse, Watanabe killed himself. He didn't wish to live with the disgrace."

"I see."

"We were partners for seventeen years. A man of principle and honour. I respected him very much."

"Will you go into business again?" I asked.

---

1    *tatami* Straw mat traditionally used as floor covering in Japanese homes.
2    *Chou En-lai* Chinese communist politician (1898–1976).

"I am—in retirement. I'm too old to involve myself in new ventures now. Business these days has become so different. Dealing with foreigners. Doing things their way. I don't understand how we've come to this. Neither did Watanabe." He sighed. "A fine man. A man of principle."

The tea-room looked out over the garden. From where I sat I could make out the ancient well which as a child I had believed haunted. It was just visible now through the thick foliage. The sun had sunk low and much of the garden had fallen into shadow.

"I'm glad in any case that you've decided to come back," my father said. "More than a short visit, I hope."

"I'm not sure what my plans will be."

"I for one am prepared to forget the past. Your mother too was always ready to welcome you back—upset as she was by your behaviour."

"I appreciate your sympathy. As I say, I'm not sure what my plans are."

"I've come to believe now that there were no evil intentions in your mind," my father continued. "You were swayed by certain—influences. Like so many others."

"Perhaps we should forget it, as you suggest."

"As you will. More tea?"

Just then a girl's voice came echoing through the house.

"At last." My father rose to his feet. "Kikuko has arrived."

Despite our difference in years, my sister and I had always been close. Seeing me again seemed to make her excessively excited and for a while she did nothing but giggle nervously. But she calmed down somewhat when my father started to question her about Osaka and her university. She answered him with short formal replies. She in turn asked me a few questions, but she seemed inhibited by the fear that her questions might lead to awkward topics. After a while, the conversation had become even sparser than prior to Kikuko's arrival. Then my father stood up, saying: "I must attend to the supper. Please excuse me for being burdened down by such matters. Kikuko will look after you."

My sister relaxed quite visibly once he had left the room. Within a few minutes, she was chatting freely about her friends in Osaka and about her classes at university. Then quite suddenly she decided we should walk in the garden and went striding out onto the veranda. We put on some straw sandals that had been left along the veranda rail and stepped out into the garden. The daylight had almost gone.

"I've been dying for a smoke for the last half-hour," she said, lighting a cigarette.

"Then why didn't you smoke?"

She made a furtive gesture back towards the house, then grinned mischievously.

"Oh I see," I said.

"Guess what? I've got a boyfriend now."

"Oh yes?"

"Except I'm wondering what to do. I haven't made up my mind yet."

"Quite understandable."

"You see, he's making plans to go to America. He wants me to go with him as soon as I finish studying."

"I see. And you want to go to America?"

"If we go, we're going to hitch-hike." Kikuko waved a thumb in front of my face. "People say it's dangerous, but I've done it in Osaka and it's fine."

"I see. So what is it you're unsure about?"

We were following a narrow path that wound through the shrubs and finished by the old well. As we walked, Kikuko persisted in taking unnecessarily theatrical puffs on her cigarette.

"Well. I've got lots of friends now in Osaka. I like it there. I'm not sure I want to leave them all behind just yet. And Suichi—I like him, but I'm not sure I want to spend so much time with him. Do you understand?"

"Oh perfectly."

She grinned again, then skipped on ahead of me until she had reached the well. "Do you remember," she said, as I came walking up to her, "how you used to say this well was haunted?"

"Yes, I remember."

We both peered over the side.

"Mother always told me it was the old woman from the vegetable store you'd seen that night," she said. "But I never believed her and never came out here alone."

"Mother used to tell me that too. She even told me once the old woman had confessed to being the ghost. Apparently she'd been taking a short cut through our garden. I imagine she had some trouble clambering over these walls."

Kikuko gave a giggle. She then turned her back to the well, casting her gaze about the garden.

"Mother never really blamed you, you know," she said, in a new voice. I remained silent. "She always used to say to me how it was their fault, hers and Father's, for not bringing you up correctly. She used to tell me how much more careful they'd been with me, and that's why I was so good." She looked up and the mischievous grin had returned to her face. "Poor Mother," she said.

"Yes. Poor Mother."

"Are you going back to California?"

"I don't know. I'll have to see."

"What happened to—to her? To Vicki?"

"That's all finished with," I said. "There's nothing much left for me now in California."

"Do you think I ought to go there?"

"Why not? I don't know. You'll probably like it." I glanced towards the house. "Perhaps we'd better go in soon. Father might need a hand with the supper."

But my sister was once more peering down into the well. "I can't see any ghosts," she said. Her voice echoed a little.

"Is Father very upset about his firm collapsing?"

"Don't know. You can never tell with Father." Then suddenly she straightened up and turned to me. "Did he tell you about old Watanabe? What he did?"

"I heard he committed suicide."

"Well, that wasn't all. He took his whole family with him. His wife and his two little girls."

"Oh yes?"

"Those two beautiful little girls. He turned on the gas while they were all asleep. Then he cut his stomach with a meat knife."

"Yes, Father was just telling me how Watanabe was a man of principle."

"Sick." My sister turned back to the well.

"Careful. You'll fall right in."

"I can't see any ghost," she said. "You were lying to me all that time."

"But I never said it lived down the well."

"Where is it, then?"

We both looked around at the trees and shrubs. The light in the garden had grown very dim. Eventually I pointed to a small clearing some ten yards away.

"Just there I saw it. Just there."

We stared at the spot.

"What did it look like?"

"I couldn't see very well. It was dark."

"But you must have seen something."

"It was an old woman. She was just standing there, watching me."

We kept staring at the spot as if mesmerized.

"She was wearing a white kimono," I said. "Some of her hair had come undone. It was blowing around a little."

Kikuko pushed her elbow against my arm. "Oh be quiet. You're trying to frighten me all over again." She trod on the remains of her cigarette, then for a brief moment stood regarding it with a perplexed expression. She kicked some pine needles over it, then once more displayed her grin. "Let's see if supper's ready," she said.

We found my father in the kitchen. He gave us a quick glance, then carried on with what he was doing.

"Father's become quite a chef since he's had to manage on his own," Kikuko said with a laugh. He turned and looked at my sister coldly.

"Hardly a skill I'm proud of," he said. "Kikuko, come here and help."

For some moments my sister did not move. Then she stepped forward and took an apron hanging from a drawer.

"Just these vegetables need cooking now," he said to her. "The rest just needs watching." Then he looked up and regarded me strangely for some seconds. "I expect you want to look around the house," he said eventually. He put down the chopsticks he had been holding. "It's a long time since you've seen it."

As we left the kitchen I glanced back towards Kikuko, but her back was turned.

"She's a good girl," my father said quietly.

I followed my father from room to room. I had forgotten how large the house was. A panel would slide open and another room would appear. But the rooms were all startlingly empty. In one of the rooms the lights did not come on, and we stared at the stark walls and tatami in the pale light that came from the windows.

"This house is too large for a man to live in alone," my father said. "I don't have much use for most of these rooms now."

But eventually my father opened the door to a room packed full of books and papers. There were flowers in vases and pictures on the walls. Then I noticed something on a low table in the corner of the room. I came nearer and saw it was a plastic model of a battleship, the kind constructed by children. It had been placed on some newspaper; scattered around it were assorted pieces of grey plastic.

My father gave a laugh. He came up to the table and picked up the model.

"Since the firm folded," he said, "I have a little more time on my hands." He laughed again, rather strangely. For a moment his face looked almost gentle. "A little more time."

"That seems odd," I said. "You were always so busy."

"Too busy perhaps." He looked at me with a small smile. "Perhaps I should have been a more attentive father."

I laughed. He went on contemplating his battleship. Then he looked up. "I hadn't meant to tell you this, but perhaps it's best that I do. It's my belief that your mother's death was no accident. She had many worries. And some disappointments."

We both gazed at the plastic battleship.

"Surely," I said eventually, "my mother didn't expect me to live here forever."

"Obviously you don't see. You don't see how it is for some parents. Not only must they lose their children, they must lose them to things they don't understand." He spun the battleship in his fingers. "These little gunboats here could have been better glued, don't you think?"

"Perhaps. I think it looks fine."

"During the war I spent some time on a ship rather like this. But my ambition was always the air force. I figured it like this. If your ship was struck by the enemy, all you could do was struggle in the water hoping for a lifeline. But in an aeroplane—well—there was always the final weapon." He put the model back onto the table. "I don't suppose you believe in war."

"Not particularly."

He cast an eye around the room. "Supper should be ready by now," he said. "You must be hungry."

Supper was waiting in a dimly lit room next to the kitchen. The only source of light was a big lantern that hung over the table, casting the rest of the room into shadow. We bowed to each other before starting the meal.

There was little conversation. When I made some polite comment about the food, Kikuko giggled a little. Her earlier nervousness seemed to have returned to her. My father did not speak for several minutes. Finally he said:

"It must feel strange for you, being back in Japan."

"Yes, it is a little strange."

"Already, perhaps, you regret leaving America."

"A little. Not so much. I didn't leave behind much. Just some empty rooms."

"I see."

I glanced across the table. My father's face looked stony and forbidding in the half-light. We ate on in silence.

Then my eye caught something at the back of the room. At first I continued eating, then my hands became still. The others noticed and looked at me. I went on gazing into the darkness past my father's shoulder.

"Who is that? In that photograph there?"

"Which photograph?" My father turned slightly, trying to follow my gaze.

"The lowest one. The old woman in the white kimono."

My father put down his chopsticks. He looked first at the photograph, then at me.

"Your mother." His voice had become very hard. "Can't you recognize your own mother?"

"My mother. You see, it's dark. I can't see it very well."

No one spoke for a few seconds, then Kikuko rose to her feet. She took the photograph down from the wall, came back to the table and gave it to me.

"She looks a lot older," I said.

"It was taken shortly before her death," said my father.

"It was the dark. I couldn't see very well."

I looked up and noticed my father holding out a hand. I gave him the photograph. He looked at it intently, then held it towards Kikuko. Obediently, my sister rose to her feet once more and returned the picture to the wall.

There was a large pot left unopened at the centre of the table. When Kikuko had seated herself again, my father reached forward and lifted the lid. A cloud of steam rose up and curled towards the lantern. He pushed the pot a little towards me.

"You must be hungry," he said. One side of his face had fallen into shadow.

"Thank you." I reached forward with my chopsticks. The steam was almost scalding. "What is it?"

"Fish."

"It smells very good."

In amidst soup were strips of fish that had curled almost into balls. I picked one out and brought it to my bowl.

"Help yourself. There's plenty."

"Thank you." I took a little more, then pushed the pot towards my father. I watched him take several pieces to his bowl. Then we both watched as Kikuko served herself.

My father bowed slightly. "You must be hungry," he said again. He took some fish to his mouth and started to eat. Then I too chose a piece and put it in my mouth. It felt soft, quite fleshy against my tongue.

"Very good," I said. "What is it?"

"Just fish."

"It's very good."

The three of us ate on in silence. Several minutes went by.

"Some more?"

"Is there enough?"

"There's plenty for all of us." My father lifted the lid and once more steam rose up. We all reached forward and helped ourselves.

"Here," I said to my father, "you have this last piece."

"Thank you."

When we had finished the meal, my father stretched out his arms and yawned with an air of satisfaction. "Kikuko," he said. "Prepare a pot of tea, please."

My sister looked at him, then left the room without comment. My father stood up.

"Let's retire to the other room. It's rather warm in here."

I got to my feet and followed him into the tea-room. The large sliding windows had been left open, bringing in a breeze from the garden. For a while we sat in silence.

"Father," I said, finally.

"Yes?"

"Kikuko tells me Watanabe-San took his whole family with him."

My father lowered his eyes and nodded. For some moments he seemed deep in thought. "Watanabe was very devoted to his work," he said at last. "The collapse of the firm was a great blow to him. I fear it must have weakened his judgment."

"You think what he did—it was a mistake?"

"Why, of course. Do you see it otherwise?"

"No, no. Of course not."

"There are other things besides work."

"Yes."

We fell silent again. The sound of locusts came in from the garden. I looked out into the darkness. The well was no longer visible.

"What do you think you will do now?" my father asked. "Will you stay in Japan for a while?"

"To be honest, I hadn't thought that far ahead."

"If you wish to stay here, I mean here in this house, you would be very welcome. That is, if you don't mind living with an old man."

"Thank you. I'll have to think about it."

I gazed out once more into the darkness.

"But of course," said my father, "this house is so dreary now. You'll no doubt return to America before long."

"Perhaps. I don't know yet."

"No doubt you will."

For some time my father seemed to be studying the back of his hands. Then he looked up and sighed.

"Kikuko is due to complete her studies next spring," he said. "Perhaps she will want to come home then. She's a good girl."

"Perhaps she will."

"Things will improve then."

"Yes, I'm sure they will."

We fell silent once more, waiting for Kikuko to bring the tea.

—1982

# *Ali Smith*

b. 1962

Praised by critics as a "deliciously quirky postmodern" writer and a "master of stylistic daring," Ali Smith is a British author and a Fellow of the Royal Society of Literature. Smith divides her attention between the genres of short fiction and the novel, with her novels in particular receiving critical acclaim. Her second novel, *Hotel World* (2001), and her third, *The Accidental* (2005), were each shortlisted for both the Orange Prize for Fiction and the Man Booker Prize for Fiction.

Smith was born in Scotland to working-class parents. She came to writing fiction in a roundabout way, and her first short story collection, *Free Love and Other Stories* (1995), was not published until she was in her early thirties. Smith's stories are often centred around the lives of women, but Amanda Thursfield, writing for the British Council's Arts Group, catalogues a wide range of interests: "The themes she chooses to write about are ambitious: love, particularly that between women, death, loss, guilt, grief, illness, time and the chasms of misunderstanding between the generations where affection can become lost in impatience and incomprehension."

Smith's writing is frequently playful and usually in some way experimental, and she is noted for the tight construction and precise language of her work. She considers short stories a challenging genre for readers "because they are hard. They are closer to poetry in their demands. The easiest thing in the world is to read a blockbuster—you can skip and skim in a way that is impossible if every word counts." This tension between the formal qualities of the short story and the novel provides one of the key elements in the work included here.

# True Short Story

There were two men in the café at the table next to mine. One was younger, one was older. They could have been father and son, but there was none of that practised diffidence, none of the cloudy anger that there almost always is between fathers and sons. Maybe they were the result of a parental divorce, the father keen to be a father now that his son was properly into his adulthood, the son keen to be a man in front of his father now that his father was opposite him for at least the length of time of a cup of coffee. No. More likely the older man was the kind of family friend who provides a fathership on summer weekends for the small boy of a divorce-family; a man who knows his responsibility, and now look, the boy had grown up, the man was an older man, and there was this unsaid understanding between them, etc.

I stopped making them up. It felt a bit wrong to. Instead, I listened to what they were saying. They were talking about literature, which happens to be interesting to me, though it wouldn't interest a lot of people. The younger man was talking about the difference between the novel and the short story. The novel, he was saying, was a flabby old whore.

A flabby old whore! the older man said looking delighted.

She was serviceable, roomy, warm and familiar, the younger was saying, but really a bit used up, really a bit too slack and loose.

Slack and loose! the older said laughing.

Whereas the short story, by comparison, was a nimble goddess, a slim nymph.[1] Because so few people had mastered the short story she was still in very good shape.

Very good shape! The older man was smiling from ear to ear at this. He was presumably old enough to remember years in his life, and not so long ago, when it would have been at least a bit dodgy to talk like this. I idly wondered how many of the books in my house were fuckable and how good they'd be in bed. Then I sighed, and got my mobile out and phoned my friend, with whom I usually go to this café on Friday mornings.

She knows quite a lot about the short story. She's spent a lot of her life reading them, writing about them, teaching them, even on occasion writing them. She's read more short stories than most people know (or care) exist. I suppose you could call it a lifelong act of love, though she's not very old, was that morning still in her late thirties. A life-so-far act of love. But already she knew more about the short story and about the people all over the world who write and have written short stories than anyone I've ever met.

She was in hospital, on this particular Friday a couple of years ago now, because a course of chemotherapy had destroyed every single one of her tiny white blood cells and after it had she'd picked up an infection in a wisdom tooth.

I waited for the automaton voice of the hospital phone system to tell me all about itself, then to recite robotically back to me the number I'd just called, then to mispronounce my friend's name, which is Kasia, then to tell me exactly how much it was charging me to listen to it tell me all this, and then to tell me how much it would cost to speak to my friend per minute. Then it connected me.

Hi, I said. It's me.

Are you on your mobile? she said. Don't, Ali, it's expensive on this system. I'll call you back.

---

[1]　*nymph* Sexually desirable young woman; also, in mythology, a beautiful nature spirit.

No worries, I said. It's just a quickie. Listen. Is the short story a goddess and a nymph and is the novel an old whore?

Is what what? she said.

An old whore, kind of Dickensian[1] one, maybe, I said. Like that prostitute who first teaches David Niven[2] how to have sex in that book.

David Niven? she said.

You know, I said. The prostitute he goes to in The Moon's a Balloon when he's about fourteen, and she's really sweet and she initiates him and he loses his virginity, and he's still wearing his socks, or maybe that's the prostitute who's still wearing the socks, I can't remember, anyway, she's really sweet to him and then he goes back to see her in later life when she's an old whore and he's an internationally famous movie star, and he brings her a lot of presents because he's such a nice man and never forgets a kindness. And is the short story more like Princess Diana?[3]

The short story like Princess Diana, she said. Right.

I sensed the two men, who were getting ready to leave the café, looking at me curiously. I held up my phone.

I'm just asking my friend what she thinks about your nymph thesis, I said.

Both men looked slightly startled. Then both men left the café without looking back.

I told her about the conversation I'd just overheard.

I was thinking of Diana because she's a bit nymphy, I suppose, I said. I can't think of a goddess who's like a nymph. All the goddesses that come into my head are, like, Kali, or Sheela-Na-Gig.[4] Or Aphrodite,[5] she was pretty tough. All that deer-slaying. Didn't she slay deer?

Why is the short story like a nymph, Kasia said. Sounds like a dirty joke. Ha.

Okay, I said. Come on then. Why is the short story like a nymph?

I'll think about it, she said. It'll give me something to do in here.

---

1    *Dickensian* Relating to the style or works of Charles Dickens (1812–70), a popular English novelist known for his depictions of harsh social conditions.

2    *David Niven* British actor and novelist, author of *The Moon's a Balloon: Reminiscences* (1971), an account of his early life.

3    *Princess Diana* Diana Frances Spencer (1961–97), former wife of Charles, Prince of Wales. Her charitable efforts and popular public persona attracted immense media coverage.

4    *Kali* Hindu goddess linked with death and violent sexuality. She slays demons and often wears a necklace of skulls; *Sheela-Na-Gig* Irish term for medieval carvings of exaggerated female figures, usually displaying grotesque sexuality. It has been suggested that these figures are linked to a Celtic goddess.

5    *Aphrodite* Ancient Greek goddess of love. In Ovid's *Metamorphoses* (c. 8 CE), she hunts deer with her mortal lover, but refuses to hunt more dangerous animals.

Kasia and I have been friends now for just over twenty years, which doesn't feel at all long, though it sounds quite long. "Long" and "short" are relative. What was long was every single day she was spending in hospital; today was her tenth long day in one of the cancer wards, being injected with a cocktail of antibiotics and waiting for her temperature to come down and her white cell count to go up. When those two tiny personal adjustments happened in the world, then she'd be allowed to go home. Also, there was a lot of sadness round her in the ward. After ten long days the heaviness of that sadness, which might sound bearably small if you're not a person who has to think about it or is being forced by circumstance to address it, but is close to epic if you are, was considerable.

She phoned me back later that afternoon and left a message on the answerphone. I could hear the clanking hospital and the voices of other people in the ward in the recorded air around her voice.

*Okay. Listen to this. It depends what you mean by "nymph." So, depending. A short story is like a nymph because satyrs[1] want to sleep with it all the time. A short story is like a nymph because both like to live on mountains and in groves and by springs and rivers and in valleys and cool grottoes. A short story is like a nymph because it likes to accompany Artemis[2] on her travels. Not very funny yet, I know, but I'm working on it.*

I heard the phone being hung up. Message received at three forty-three, my answerphone's robot voice said. I called her back and went through the exact echo of the morning's call to the system. She answered and before I could even say hello she said:

Listen! Listen! A short story is like a nymphomaniac because both like to sleep around—or get into lots of anthologies—but neither accepts money for the pleasure.

I laughed out loud.

Unlike the bawdy old whore, the novel, ha ha, she said. And when I was speaking to my father at lunchtime he told me you can fish for trout with a nymph. They're a kind of fishing fly. He says there are people who carry magnifying glasses around with them all the time in case they get the chance to look at real nymphs,[3] so as to be able to copy them even more exactly in the fishing flies they make.

I tell you, I said. The world is full of astounding things.

I know, she said. What do you reckon to the anthology joke?

---

1   *satyrs* Mythological creatures who are part human, part animal. Satyrs are frequently depicted behaving lecherously toward nymphs.

2   *Artemis* Ancient Greek goddess of virginity and the hunt, who lives in the wilderness with an entourage of maidens.

3   *nymphs* Larvae of some insects, such as dragonflies.

Six out of ten, I said.

Rubbish then, she said. Okay. I'll try and think of something better.

Maybe there's mileage in the nymphs-at-your-flies thing, I said.

Ha ha, she said. But I'll have to leave the nymph thing this afternoon and get back on the Herceptin trail.

God, I said.

I'm exhausted, she said. We're drafting letters.

When is an anti-cancer drug not an anti-cancer drug? I said.

When people can't afford it, she said. Ha ha.

Lots of love, I said.

You too, she said. Cup of tea?

I'll make us one, I said. Speak soon.

I heard the phone go dead. I put my phone down and went through and switched the kettle on. I watched it reach the boil and the steam come out of the spout. I filled two cups with boiling water and dropped the teabags in. I drank my tea watching the steam rise off the other cup.

This is what Kasia meant by "Herceptin trail."

Herceptin is a drug that's been being used in breast cancer treatment for a while now. Doctors had, at the point in time that Kasia and I were having the conversations in this story, very recently discovered that it really helps some women—those who over-produce the HER2 protein—in the early stages of the disease. When given to a receptive case it can cut the risk of the cancer returning by 50 per cent. Doctors all over the world were excited about it because it amounted to a paradigm shift in breast cancer treatment.

I had never heard of any of this till Kasia told me, and she had never heard of any of it until a small truth, less than two centimetres in size, which a doctor found in April that year in one of her breasts, had meant a paradigm shift in everyday life. It was now August. In May her doctor had told her about how good Herceptin is, and how she'd definitely be able to have it at the end of her chemotherapy on the NHS.[1] Then at the end of July her doctor was visited by a member of the PCT, which stands for the words Primary, Care and Trust, and is concerned with NHS funding. The PCT member instructed my friend's doctor not to tell any more of the women affected in the hospital's catchment area about the wonders of Herceptin until a group called NICE[2] had approved its cost-effectiveness. At the time, they thought this might take about nine months or maybe a year (by which time it would be too late for my friend and many other women). Though Kasia knew that if she wanted to buy Herceptin

---

1    *NHS* National Health Service, a mainly publicly funded system of state-provided medical services in the UK.

2    *NICE* National Institute for Health and Clinical Excellence.

on BUPA,[1] right then, for roughly twenty-seven thousand pounds, she could. This kind of thing will be happening to an urgently needed drug right now, somewhere near you.

"Primary." "Care." "Trust." "Nice."

Here's a short story that most people already think they know about a nymph. (It also happens to be one of the earliest manifestations in literature of what we now call anorexia.)

Echo was an Oread, which is a kind of mountain nymph. She was well known among the nymphs and shepherds not just for her glorious garrulousness but for her ability to save her nymph friends from the wrath of the goddess Juno.[2] For instance, her friends would be lying about on the hillside in the sun and Juno would come round the corner, about to catch them slacking, and Echo, who had a talent for knowing when Juno was about to turn up, would leap to her feet and head the goddess off by running up to her and distracting her with stories and talk, talk and stories, until all the slacker nymphs were up and working like they'd never been slacking at all.

When Juno worked out what Echo was doing she was a bit annoyed. She pointed at her with her curse-finger and threw off the first suitable curse that came into her head.

From now on, she said, you will be able only to repeat out loud the words you've heard others say just a moment before. Won't you?

Won't you, Echo said.

Her eyes grew large. Her mouth fell open.

That's you sorted, Juno said.

You sordid, Echo said.

Right. I'm off back to the hunt, Juno said.

The cunt, Echo said.

Actually, I'm making up that small rebellion. There is actually no rebelliousness for Echo in Ovid's[3] original version of the story. It seems that after she's robbed of being able to talk on her own terms, and of being able to watch her friends' backs for them, there's nothing left for her—in terms of story—but to fall in love with a boy so in love with himself that he spends all his days bent over a pool of his own desire and eventually pines to near-death (then transforms, instead of dying, from a boy into a little white flower).[4]

---

1    *BUPA* British United Provident Association, a private healthcare and health insurance company.

2    *garrulousness* Talkativeness; *Juno* Roman goddess of marriage, queen of the Gods, and wife of Jupiter.

3    *Ovid* Echo's story appears in Ovid's *Metamorphoses*.

4    *a boy ... flower* The "boy" is Narcissus, whose story is also told in Ovid's *Metamorphoses*.

Echo pined too. Her weight dropped off her. She became fashionably skinny, then she became nothing but bones, then all that was left of her was a whiny, piny voice which floated bodilessly about, saying over and over exactly the same things that everybody else was saying.

Here, by contrast, is the story of the moment I met my friend Kasia, more than twenty years ago.

I was a postgraduate student at Cambridge and I had lost my voice. I don't mean I'd lost it because I had a cold or a throat infection, I mean that two years of a system of hierarchies so entrenched that girls and women were still a bit of a novelty to it had somehow knocked what voice I had out of me.

So I was sitting at the back of a room not even really listening properly any more, and I heard a voice. It was from somewhere up ahead of me. It was a girl's voice and it was directly asking the person giving the seminar and the chair of the seminar a question about the American writer Carson McCullers.[1]

Because it seems to me that McCullers is obviously very relevant at all levels in this discussion, the voice said.

The person and the chair of the meeting both looked a bit shocked that anyone had said anything out loud. The chair cleared his throat.

I found myself leaning forward. I hadn't heard anyone speak like this, with such an open and carefree display of knowledge and forthrightness, for a couple of years. More: earlier that day I had been talking with an undergraduate student who had been unable to find anyone in the whole of Cambridge University English Department to supervise her dissertation on McCullers. It seemed nobody eligible to teach had read her.

Anyway, I venture to say you'll find McCullers not at all of the same stature, the person giving the paper on Literature After Henry James[2] said.

Well, the thing is, I disagree, the voice said.

I laughed out loud. It was a noise never heard in such a room; heads turned to see who was making such an unlikely noise. The new girl carried on politely asking questions which no one answered. She mentioned, I remember, how McCullers had been fond of a maxim: nothing human is alien to me.

At the end of the seminar I ran after that girl. I stopped her in the street. It was winter. She was wearing a red coat.

She told me her name. I heard myself tell her mine.

---

1   *Carson McCullers* American author (1917–67) known for her stories of the American South.

2   *Henry James* American novelist and critic (1843–1916) whose work is a common focus of scholarly interest.

Franz Kafka[1] says that the short story is a cage in search of a bird. (Kafka's been dead for more than eighty years, but I can still say Kafka says. That's just one of the ways art deals with our mortality.)

Tzvetan Todorov[2] says that the thing about a short story is that it's so short it doesn't allow us the time to forget that it's only literature and not actually life.

Nadine Gordimer[3] says short stories are absolutely about the present moment, like the brief flash of a number of fireflies here and there in the dark.

Elizabeth Bowen[4] says the short story has the advantage over the novel of a special kind of concentration, and that it creates narrative every time absolutely on its own terms.

Eudora Welty[5] says that short stories often problematize their own best interests and that this is what makes them interesting.

Henry James says that the short story, being so condensed, can give a particularized perspective on both complexity and continuity.

Jorge Luis Borges[6] says that short stories can be the perfect form for novelists too lazy to write anything longer than fifteen pages.

Ernest Hemingway[7] says that short stories are made by their own change and movement, and that even when a story seems static and you can't make out any movement in it at all it is probably changing and moving regardless, just unseen by you.

William Carlos Williams[8] says that the short story, which acts like the flare of a match struck in the dark, is the only real form for describing the briefness, the brokenness and the simultaneous wholeness of people's lives.

Walter Benjamin[9] says that short stories are stronger than the real, lived moment, because they can go on releasing the real, lived moment after the real, lived moment is dead.

Cynthia Ozick[10] says that the difference between a short story and a novel is that the novel is a book whose journey, if it's a good working novel, actually alters a reader, whereas a short story is more like the talismanic gift given to the protagonist of a fairy tale—something complete, powerful, whose power

---

1    *Franz Kafka*  Influential German-language author (1883–1924) best known for his novella *Metamorphosis* (1915).
2    *Tzvetan Todorov*  Franco-Bulgarian literary and cultural theorist (1939–2017).
3    *Nadine Gordimer*  Nobel Prize-winning South African novelist and short story writer (1923–2014).
4    *Elizabeth Bowen*  British novelist and short story writer (1889–1973).
5    *Eudora Welty*  American short story writer and novelist (1909–2001).
6    *Jorge Luis Borges*  Argentine writer (1899–1986) best known for his fantastic short stories.
7    *Ernest Hemingway*  Influential American novelist and short story writer (1899–1961).
8    *William Carlos Williams*  American modernist poet and prose author (1883–1963).
9    *Walter Benjamin*  German literary and social theorist (1892–1940).
10   *Cynthia Ozick*  American novelist, essayist, and short story writer (b. 1928).

may not yet be understood, which can be held in the hands or tucked into the pocket and taken through the forest on the dark journey.

Grace Paley[1] says that she chose to write only short stories in her life because art is too long and life is too short, and that short stories are, by nature, about life, and that life itself is always found in dialogue and argument.

Alice Munro[2] says that every short story is at least two short stories.

There were two men in the café at the table next to mine. One was younger, one was older. We sat in the same café for only a brief amount of time but we disagreed long enough for me to know there was a story in it.

This story was written in discussion with my friend Kasia, and in celebration of her (and all) tireless articulacy—one of the reasons, in this instance, that a lot more people were able to have that particular drug when they needed it.

So when is the short story like a nymph?

When the echo of it answers back.

—2008

---

1    *Grace Paley* American activist, poet, and short story writer (1922–2007).
2    *Alice Munro* Canadian short story writer (b. 1931).

# *Sherman Alexie*
b. 1966

Critical assessments of the novels, poems, and short stories of Sherman Alexie frequently begin with a summary statement of his Native American origins and upbringing. In some ways this is fitting: Alexie is a member of the Spokane and Coeur d'Alene tribes, and much of his early work—notably *The Lone Ranger and Tonto Fistfight in Heaven* (1993) and *Reservation Blues* (1995)—unflinchingly confronts the systemic poverty, hopelessness, and alcoholism that marked his own childhood experience of rural reservation life. But Alexie is uncomfortable with the label *Native American writer*, especially the presumption that he is a representative spokesman for "Indian country."

Drawing heavily on irony and satire, Alexie delights in upending stereotypical assumptions about traditional Native "storytelling." His work is strewn with references to mainstream American culture, and, in his more recent fiction, including the story "Flight Patterns" from the collection *Ten Little Indians* (2009), he tends to be less interested in representing a separate and distinct tribal reality than with the urban experience of life beyond the reservation. As he puts it: "I try to write about everyday Indians, the kind of Indian I am, who is just as influenced by *The Brady Bunch* as I am by my tribal traditions, who spends as much time going to the movies as I do going to ceremonies."

Alexie's writing, though preoccupied with trauma, prejudice, and alienation, also enacts and celebrates the redemptive power of humour and imagination to transmute anger into a vital creative force and sow the strength necessary to survive hardship. In his work as in his life, the concept of survival remains uppermost: "Indians fight their way to the end," he writes, "holding onto the last good thing, because our whole lives have to do with survival." Far from succumbing to a sense of what one critic has called "doomed Indianness," many of Alexie's characters are defiant survivors.

# Flight Patterns

At 5:05 A.M., Patsy Cline[1] fell loudly to pieces on William's clock radio. He hit the snooze button, silencing lonesome Patsy, and dozed for fifteen more minutes before Donna Fargo[2] bragged about being the happiest girl in the

---

1    *Patsy Cline* American country singer known for sad love ballads such as "I Fall to Pieces" (1961).

2    *Donna Fargo* Stage name of Yvonne Vaughan, American country singer-songwriter best known for her song "The Happiest Girl in the Whole USA" (1972).

whole USA. William wondered what had ever happened to Donna Fargo, whose birth name was the infinitely more interesting Yvonne Vaughn, and wondered *why* he knew Donna Fargo's birth name. Ah, he was the bemused and slightly embarrassed owner of a twenty-first-century American mind. His intellect was a big comfy couch stuffed with sacred and profane trivia. He knew the names of all nine of Elizabeth Taylor's[1] husbands and could quote from memory the entire Declaration of Independence. William knew Donna Fargo's birth name because he *wanted* to know her birth name. He wanted to know all of the great big and tiny little American details. He didn't want to choose between Ernie Hemingway and the Spokane tribal elders, between Mia Hamm and Crazy Horse, between *The Heart Is a Lonely Hunter* and Chief Dan George.[2] William wanted all of it. Hunger was his crime. As for dear Miss Fargo, William figured she probably played the Indian casino circuit along with the Righteous Brothers, Smokey Robinson, Eddie Money, Pat Benatar, RATT, REO Speedwagon, and dozens of other formerly famous rock- and country-music stars. Many of the Indian casino acts were bad, and most of the rest were pure nostalgic entertainment, but a small number made beautiful and timeless music. William knew the genius Merle Haggard[3] played thirty or forty Indian casinos every year, so long live Haggard and long live tribal economic sovereignty. Who cares about fishing and hunting rights? Who cares about uranium mines and nuclear-waste-dump sites[4] on sacred land? Who cares about the recovery of tribal languages? Give me Freddy Fender[5] singing "Before the Next Teardrop Falls" in English and Spanish to 206 Spokane Indians, William thought, and I will be a happy man.

But William wasn't happy this morning. He'd slept poorly—he always slept poorly—and wondered again if his insomnia was a physical or a mental condition. His doctor had offered him sleeping-pill prescriptions, but William declined for philosophical reasons. He was an Indian who didn't smoke or drink or eat processed sugar. He lifted weights three days a week, ran every day,

---

1   *Elizabeth Taylor* Hollywood movie star (1932–2011) who had a long and prestigious acting career as well as a dramatic romantic life.

2   *Ernie Hemingway* Ernest Hemingway (1899–1961), influential white American author; *Spokane* Native North American people primarily located in Washington; *Mia Hamm* Record-breaking white American soccer player (b. 1972); *Crazy Horse* Famous Sioux war chief and activist (c. 1842–77); *The Heart Is a Lonely Hunter* Acclaimed 1940 novel by white Southern American writer Carson McCullers; *Chief Dan George* Salish chief, author, and film and television actor (1899–1981).

3   *Merle Haggard* Influential country singer and songwriter (1937–2016).

4   *uranium mines ... dump sites* An open-pit uranium mine on the Spokane Reservation closed in 1981; some of the pits were filled in with radioactive waste from the mine.

5   *Freddy Fender* Mexican-American country musician known for bilingual hits such as "Before the Next Teardrop Falls" (1975).

and competed in four triathlons a year. A two-mile swim, a 150-mile bike ride, and a full marathon. A triathlon was a religious quest. If Saint Francis[1] were still around, he'd be a triathlete. Another exaggeration! Theological hyperbole! Rabid self-justification! Diagnostically speaking, William was an obsessive-compulsive workaholic who was afraid of pills. So he suffered sleepless nights and constant daytime fatigue.

This morning, awake and not awake, William turned down the radio, changing Yvonne Vaughn's celebratory anthem into whispered blues, and rolled off the couch onto his hands and knees. His back and legs were sore because he'd slept on the living room couch so the alarm wouldn't disturb his wife and daughter upstairs. Still on his hands and knees, William stretched his spine, using the twelve basic exercises he'd learned from Dr. Adams, that master practitioner of white middle-class chiropractic voodoo. This was all part of William's regular morning ceremony. Other people find God in ornate ritual, but William called out to Geronimo, Jesus Christ, Saint Therese, Buddha, Allah, Billie Holiday, Simon Ortiz, Abe Lincoln, Bessie Smith, Howard Hughes, Leslie Marmon Silko, Joan of Arc and Joan of Collins, John Woo, Wilma Mankiller, and Karl and Groucho Marx[2] while he pumped out fifty push-ups and fifty abdominal crunches. William wasn't particularly religious; he was generally religious. Finished with his morning calisthenics, William showered in the basement, suffering the water that was always too cold down there, and threaded his long black hair into two tight braids—the indigenous businessman's tonsorial[3] special—and dressed in his best travel suit, a navy three-button pinstripe he'd ordered online. He'd worried about the fit, but his tailor was a magician and had only mildly chastised William for such an impulsive purchase. After knotting his blue paisley tie, purchased in person and on sale, William walked upstairs in bare feet and kissed his wife, Marie, good-bye.

---

1    *Saint Francis* Francis of Assisi (c. 1181–1226), mystic and founder of the Franciscan monastic order.

2    *Geronimo* Apache resistance leader (c. 1829–1909); *Saint Therese* Thérèse of Liseux, a devout French nun (1873–97); *Billie Holiday* African American jazz singer (1915–59); *Simon Ortiz* Pueblo poet and prose writer (b. 1941); *Bessie Smith* African American blues singer (1898–1937); *Howard Hughes* White American billionaire (1905–76) who invested in film and aviation; *Leslie Marmon Silko* Laguna-Mexican-Anglo writer (b. 1948); *Joan of Collins* Nickname for English actor and writer Joan Collins (b. 1933); *John Woo* Chinese action filmmaker (b. 1946) who works in Hong Kong and Hollywood; *Wilma Mankiller* Wilma Pearl Mankiller (1945–2010), the first female Cherokee chief; *Karl and Groucho Marx* Karl Marx, German theorist best known for co-authoring *The Communist Manifesto* (1848), and Groucho Marx (1895–1977), member of the American comedy group "The Marx Brothers."

3    *tonsorial* Of hairdressing.

"Cancel your flight," she said. "And come back to bed."

"You're supposed to be asleep," he said.

She was a small and dark woman who seemed to be smaller and darker at that time of the morning. Her long black hair had once again defeated its braids, but she didn't care. She sometimes went two or three days without brushing it. William was obsessive about his mane, tying and retying his ponytail, knotting and reknotting his braids, experimenting with this shampoo and that conditioner. He greased down his cowlicks (inherited from a cowlicked father and grandfather) with shiny pomade, but Marie's hair was always unkempt, wild, and renegade. William's hair hung around the fort, but Marie's rode on the war path! She constantly pulled stray strands out of her mouth. William loved her for it. During sex, they spent as much time readjusting her hair as they did readjusting positions. Such were the erotic dangers of loving a Spokane Indian woman.

"Take off your clothes and get in bed," Marie pleaded now.

"I can't do that," William said. "They're counting on me."

"Oh, the plane will be filled with salesmen. Let some other salesman sell what you're selling."

"Your breath stinks."

"So do my feet, my pits, and my butt, but you still love me. Come back to bed, and I'll make it worth your while."

William kissed Marie, reached beneath her pajama top, and squeezed her breasts. He thought about reaching inside her pajama bottoms. She wrapped her arms and legs around him and tried to wrestle him into bed. Oh, God, he wanted to climb into bed and make love. He wanted to fornicate, to sex, to breed, to screw, to make the beast with two backs. *Oh, sweetheart, be my little synonym*! He wanted her to be both subject and object. Perhaps it was wrong (and unavoidable) to objectify female strangers, but shouldn't every husband seek to objectify his wife at least once a day? William loved and respected his wife, and delighted in her intelligence, humour, and kindness, but he also loved to watch her lovely ass when she walked, and stare down the front of her loose shirts when she leaned over, and grab her breasts at wildly inappropriate times—during dinner parties and piano recitals and uncontrolled intersections, for instance. He constantly made passes at her, not necessarily expecting to be successful, but to remind her he still desired her and was excited by the thought of her. She was his passive and active.

"Come on," she said. "If you stay home, I'll make you Scooby."

He laughed at the inside joke, created one night while he tried to give her sexual directions and was so aroused that he sounded exactly like Scooby-Doo.

"Stay home, stay home, stay home," she chanted and wrapped herself tighter around him. He was supporting all of her weight, holding her two feet off the bed.

"I'm not strong enough to do this," he said.

"Baby, baby, I'll make you strong," she sang, and it sounded like she was writing a Top 40 hit in the Brill Building,[1] circa 1962. How could he leave a woman who sang like that? He hated to leave, but he loved his work. He was a man, and men needed to work. More sexism! More masculine tunnel vision! More need for gender-sensitivity workshops! He pulled away from her, dropping her back onto the bed, and stepped away.

"Willy Loman," she said, "you must pay attention to me."[2]

"I love you," he said, but she'd already fallen back to sleep—a narcoleptic gift William envied—and he wondered if she would dream about a man who never left her, about some unemployed agoraphobic Indian warrior who liked to cook and wash dishes.

William tiptoed into his daughter's bedroom, expecting to hear her light snore, but she was awake and sitting up in bed, and looked so magical and androgynous with her huge brown eyes and crew-cut hair. She'd wanted to completely shave her head: *I don't want long hair, I don't want short hair, I don't want hair at all, and I don't want to be a girl or a boy, I want to be a yellow and orange leaf some little kid picks up and pastes in his scrapbook.*

"Daddy," she said.

"Grace," he said. "You should be asleep. You have school today."

"I know," she said. "But I wanted to see you before you left."

"Okay," said William as he kissed her forehead, nose, and chin. "You've seen me. Now go back to sleep. I love you and I'm going to miss you."

She fiercely hugged him.

"Oh," he said. "You're such a lovely, lovely girl."

Preternaturally serious, she took his face in her eyes and studied his eyes. Morally examined by a kindergartner!

"Daddy," she said. "Go be silly for those people far away."

She cried as William left her room. Already quite sure he was only an adequate husband, he wondered, as he often did, if he was a bad father. During these mornings, he felt generic and violent, like some caveman leaving the fire to hunt animals in the cold and dark. Maybe his hands were smooth and clean, but they felt bloody.

---

1   *Brill Building* New York music industry songwriting headquarters where staff writers composed pop hits in the 1950s and 1960s.

2   *Willy Loman* Title character of Arthur Miller's *Death of a Salesman* (1949); *you must ... to me* In *Death of a Salesman*, Willy Loman's wife says that "attention must be paid" to him.

Downstairs, he put on his socks and shoes and overcoat and listened for his daughter's crying, but she was quiet, having inherited her mother's gift for instant sleep. She had probably fallen back into one of her odd little dreams. While he was gone, she often drew pictures of those dreams, colouring the sky green and the grass blue—everything backward and wrong—and had once sketched a man in a suit crashing an airplane into the bright yellow sun. Ah, the rage, fear, and loneliness of a five-year-old, simple and true! She'd been especially afraid since September 11 of the previous year and constantly quizzed William about what he would do if terrorists hijacked his plane.

"I'd tell them I was your father," he'd said to her before he left for his last business trip. "And they'd stop being bad."

"You're lying," she'd said. "I'm not supposed to listen to liars. If you lie to me, I can't love you."

He couldn't argue with her logic. Maybe she was the most logical person on the planet. Maybe she should be illegally elected president of the United States.

William understood her fear of flying and of his flight. He was afraid of flying, too, but not of terrorists. After the horrible violence of September 11, he figured hijacking was no longer a useful weapon in the terrorist arsenal. These days, a terrorist armed with a box cutter would be torn to pieces by all of the coach-class passengers and fed to the first-class upgrades. However, no matter how much he tried to laugh his fear away, William always scanned the airports and airplanes for little brown guys who reeked of fundamentalism. That meant William was equally afraid of Osama bin Laden and Jerry Falwell[1] wearing the last vestiges of a summer tan. William himself was a little brown guy, so the other travellers were always sniffing around him, but he smelled only of Dove soap, Mennen deodorant, and sarcasm. Still, he understood why people were afraid of him, a brown-skinned man with dark hair and eyes. If Norwegian terrorists had exploded the World Trade Center, then blue-eyed blondes would be viewed with more suspicion. Or so he hoped.

Locking the front door behind him, William stepped away from his house, carried his garment bag and briefcase onto the front porch, and waited for his taxi to arrive. It was a cold and foggy October morning. William could smell the saltwater of Elliott Bay and the freshwater of Lake Washington. Surrounded by grey water and grey fog and grey skies and grey mountains and a grey sun, he'd lived with his family in Seattle for three years and loved it. He couldn't imagine living anywhere else, with any other wife or child, in any other time.

---

1    *Jerry Falwell* White American minister, televangelist, and leader in fundamentalist Christian politics (1932–2007).

William was tired and happy and romantic and exaggerating the size of his familial devotion so he could justify his departure, so he could survive his departure. He did sometimes think about other women and other possible lives with them. He wondered how his life would have been different if he'd married a white woman and fathered half-white children who grew up to complain and brag about their biracial identities: *Oh, the only box they have for me is Other! I'm not going to check any box! I'm not the Other! I am Tiger Woods!*[1] But William most often fantasized about being single and free to travel as often as he wished—maybe two million miles a year—and how much he'd enjoy the benefits of being a platinum frequent flier. Maybe he'd have one-night stands with a long series of travelling saleswomen, all of them thousands of miles away from husbands and children who kept looking up "feminism" in the dictionary. William knew that was yet another sexist thought. In this capital-istic and democratic culture, talented women should also enjoy the freedom to emotionally and physically abandon their families. After all, talented and educated men have been doing it for generations. Let freedom ring!

Marie had left her job as a corporate accountant to be a full-time mother to Grace. William loved his wife for making the decision, and he tried to do his share of the housework, but he suspected he was an old-fashioned bastard who wanted his wife to stay at home and wait, wait, wait for him.

Marie was always waiting for William to call, to come home, to leave messages saying he was getting on the plane, getting off the plane, checking in to the hotel, going to sleep, waking up, heading for the meeting, catching an earlier or later flight home. He spent one third of his life trying to sleep in uncomfortable beds and one third of his life trying to stay awake in airports. He travelled with thousands of other capitalistic foot soldiers, mostly men but increasing numbers of women, and stayed in the same Ramadas, Holiday Inns, and Radissons. He ate the same room-service meals and ran the same exercise-room treadmills and watched the same pay-per-view porn and stared out the windows at the same strange and lonely cityscapes. Sure, he was an en-rolled member of the Spokane Indian tribe, but he was also a fully recognized member of the notebook-computer tribe and the security-checkpoint tribe and the rental-car tribe and the hotel-shuttle-bus tribe and the cell-phone-roaming-charge tribe.

William travelled so often, the Seattle-based flight attendants knew him by first name.

At five minutes to six, the Orange Top taxi pulled into the driveway. The driver, a short and thin black man, stepped out of the cab and waved. William

---

1    *Tiger Woods*  American professional golfer (b. 1975) whose ancestry is African American, Thai, Chinese, Dutch, and Native American.

rushed down the stairs and across the pavement. He wanted to get away from the house before he changed his mind about leaving.

"Is that everything, sir?" asked the taxi driver, his accent a colonial cocktail of American English, formal British, and French sibilants added to a base of what must have been North African.

"Yes, it is, sir," said William, self-consciously trying to erase any class differences between them. In Spain the previous summer, an elderly porter had cursed at William when he insisted on carrying his own bags into the hotel. "Perhaps there is something wrong with the caste system, sir," the hotel concierge had explained to William. "But all of us, we want to do our jobs, and we want to do them well."

William didn't want to insult anybody; he wanted the world to be a fair and decent place. At least that was what he wanted to want. More than anything, he wanted to stay home with his fair and decent family. He supposed he wanted the world to be fairer and more decent to his family. We are special, he thought, though he suspected they were just one more family on this block of neighbours, in this city of neighbours, in this country of neighbours, in a world of neighbours. He looked back at his house, at the windows behind which slept his beloved wife and daughter. When he travelled, he had nightmares about strangers breaking into the house and killing and raping Marie and Grace. In other nightmares, he arrived home in time to save his family by beating the intruders and chasing them away. During longer business trips, William's nightmares became more violent as the days and nights passed. If he was gone over a week, he dreamed about mutilating the rapists and eating them alive while his wife and daughter cheered for him.

"Let me take your bags, sir," said the taxi driver.

"What?" asked William, momentarily confused.

"Your bags, sir."

William handed him the briefcase but held on to the heavier garment bag. A stupid compromise, thought William, but it's too late to change it now. God, I'm supposed to be some electric aboriginal warrior, but I'm really a wimpy liberal pacifist. *Dear Lord, how much longer should I mourn the death of Jerry Garcia?*[1]

The taxi driver tried to take the garment bag from William.

"I've got this one," said William, then added, "I've got it, sir."

The taxi driver hesitated, shrugged, opened the trunk, and set the briefcase inside. William laid the garment bag next to his briefcase. The taxi driver shut the trunk and walked around to open William's door.

---

1   *Jerry Garcia* American singer and guitarist (1942–95) best known for his leadership of The Grateful Dead, a band associated with the hippie movement.

"No, sir," said William as he awkwardly stepped in front of the taxi driver, opened the door, and took a seat. "I've got it."

"I'm sorry, sir," said the taxi driver and hurried around to the driver's seat. This strange American was making him uncomfortable, and he wanted to get behind the wheel and drive. Driving comforted him.

"To the airport, sir?" asked the taxi driver as he started the meter.

"Yes," said William. "United Airlines."

"Very good, sir."

In silence, they drove along Martin Luther King Jr. Way, the bisector of an African American neighbourhood that was rapidly gentrifying. William and his family were Native American gentry! They were the very first Indian family to ever move into a neighbourhood and bring up the property values! That was one of William's favourite jokes, self-deprecating and politely racist. White folks could laugh at a joke like that and not feel guilty. But how guilty could white people feel in Seattle? Seattle might be the only city in the country where white people lived comfortably on a street named after Martin Luther King, Jr.

No matter where he lived, William always felt uncomfortable, so he enjoyed other people's discomfort. These days, in the airports, he loved to watch white people enduring random security checks. It was a perverse thrill, to be sure, but William couldn't help himself. He knew those white folks wanted to scream and rage: *Do I look like a terrorist?* And he knew the security officers, most often low-paid brown folks, wanted to scream back: *Define terror you Anglo bastard!* William figured he'd been pulled over for pat-down searches about 75 percent of the time. Random, my ass! But that was okay! William might have wanted to irritate other people, but he didn't want to scare them. He wanted his fellow travellers to know exactly who and what he was: *I am a Native American and therefore have ten thousand more reasons to terrorize the US than any of those Taliban[1] jerk-offs, but I have chosen instead to become a civic American citizen, so all of you white folks should be celebrating my kindness and moral decency and awesome ability to forgive!* Maybe William should have worn beaded vests when he travelled. Maybe he should have brought a hand drum and sang "Way, ya, way, ya, hey." Maybe he should have thrown casino chips into the crowd.

The taxi driver turned west on Cherry, drove twenty blocks into downtown, took the entrance ramp onto I-5, and headed south for the airport. The freeway was moderately busy for that time of morning.

"Where are you going, sir?" asked the taxi driver.

---

1   *Taliban* Islamic fundamentalist organization linked to al-Qaeda, the terrorist group responsible for the 11 September 2001 attacks on the World Trade Center and other American targets.

"I've got business in Chicago," William said. He didn't really want to talk. He needed to meditate in silence. He needed to put his fear of flying inside an imaginary safe deposit box and lock it away. We all have our ceremonies, thought William, our personal narratives. He'd always needed to meditate in the taxi on the way to the airport. Immediately upon arrival at the departure gate, he'd listen to a tape he'd made of rock stars who died in plane crashes. Buddy Holly, Otis Redding, Stevie Ray, "Oh Donna," "Chantilly Lace," "(Sittin' on) The Dock of the Bay." William figured God would never kill a man who listened to such a morbid collection of music. Too easy a target, and plus, God could never justify killing a planeful of innocents to punish one minor sinner.

"What do you do, sir?" asked the taxi driver.

"You know, I'm not sure," said William and laughed. It was true. He worked for a think tank and sold ideas about how to improve other ideas. Two years ago, his company had made a few hundred thousand dollars by designing and selling the idea of a better shopping cart. The CGI prototype was amazing. It looked like a mobile walk-in closet. But it had yet to be manufactured and probably never would be.

"You wear a good suit," said the taxi driver, not sure why William was laughing. "You must be a businessman, no? You must make lots of money."

"I do okay."

"Your house is big and beautiful."

"Yes, I suppose it is."

"You are a family man, yes?"

"I have a wife and daughter."

"Are they beautiful?"

William was pleasantly surprised to be asked such a question. "Yes," he said. "Their names are Marie and Grace. They're very beautiful. I love them very much."

"You must miss them when you travel."

"I miss them so much I go crazy," said William. "I start thinking I'm going to disappear, you know, just vanish, if I'm not home. Sometimes I worry their love is the only thing that makes me human, you know? I think if they stopped loving me, I might burn up, spontaneously combust, and turn into little pieces of oxygen and hydrogen and carbon. Do you know what I'm saying?"

"Yes sir, I understand love can be so large."

William wondered why he was being honest and poetic with a taxi driver. There is emotional safety in anonymity, he thought.

"I have a wife and three sons," said the driver. "But they live in Ethiopia with my mother and father. I have not seen any of them for many years."

For the first time, William looked closely at the driver. He was clear-eyed and handsome, strong of shoulder and arm, maybe fifty years old, maybe older. A thick scar ran from his right ear down his neck and beneath his collar. A black man with a violent history; William thought and immediately reprimanded himself for racially profiling the driver: *Excuse me, sir, but I pulled you over because your scar doesn't belong in this neighbourhood.*

"I still think of my children as children," the driver said. "But they are men now. Taller and stronger than me. They are older now than I was when I last saw them."

William did the math and wondered how this driver could function with such fatherly pain. "I bet you can't wait to go home and see them again," he said, following the official handbook of the frightened American male: *When confronted with the mysterious you can defend yourself by speaking in obvious generalities.*

"I cannot go home," said the taxi driver, "and I fear I will never see them again."

William didn't want to be having this conversation. He wondered if his silence would silence the taxi driver. But it was too late for that.

"What are you?" the driver asked.

"What do you mean?"

"I mean, you are not white, your skin, it is dark like mine."

"Not as dark as yours."

"No," said the driver and laughed. "Not so dark, but too dark to be white. What are you? Are you Jewish?"

Because they were so often Muslim, taxi drivers all over the world had often asked William if he was Jewish. William was always being confused for something else. He was ambiguously ethnic, living somewhere in the darker section of the Great American Crayola Box, but he was more beige than brown, more mauve than sienna.

"Why do you want to know if I'm Jewish?" William asked.

"Oh, I'm sorry, sir, if I offended you. I am not anti-Semitic. I love all of my brothers and sisters. Jews, Catholics, Buddhists, even the atheists, I love them all. Like you Americans sing, 'Joy to the world and Jeremiah Bullfrog!'"[1]

The taxi driver laughed again, and William laughed with him.

"I'm Indian," William said.

"From India?"

"No, not jewel-on-the-forehead Indian," said William. "I'm a bows-and-arrows Indian."

"Oh, you mean ten little, nine little, eight little Indians?"

"Yeah, sort of," said William. "I'm that kind of Indian, but much smarter. I'm a Spokane Indian. We're salmon people."

---

1   *Joy to ... Bullfrog* Garbled reference to the popular rock song "Joy to the World" (1971).

"In England, they call you Red Indians."

"You've been to England?"

"Yes, I studied physics at Oxford."

"Wow," said William, wondering if this man was a liar.

"You are surprised by this, I imagine. Perhaps you think I'm a liar?"

William covered his mouth with one hand. He smiled this way when he was embarrassed.

"Aha, you do think I'm lying. You ask yourself questions about me. How could a physicist drive a taxi? Well, in the United States, I am a cabdriver, but in Ethiopia, I was a jet-fighter pilot."

By coincidence or magic, or as a coincidence that could wilfully be interpreted as magic, they drove past Boeing Field at that exact moment.

"Ah, you see," said the taxi driver, "I can fly any of those planes. The prop planes, the jet planes, even the very large passenger planes. I can also fly the experimental ones that don't fly. But I could make them fly because I am the best pilot in the world. Do you believe me?"

"I don't know," said William, very doubtful of this man but fascinated as well. If he was a liar, then he was a magnificent liar.

On both sides of the freeway, blue-collared men and women drove trucks and forklifts, unloaded trains, trucks, and ships, built computers, televisions, and airplanes. Seattle was a city of industry, of hard work, of calluses on the palms of hands. So many men and women working so hard. William worried that his job—his selling of the purely theoretical—wasn't a real job at all. He didn't build anything. He couldn't walk into department and grocery stores and buy what he'd created, manufactured, and shipped. William's life was measured by imaginary numbers: the binary code of computer languages, the amount of money in his bank accounts, the interest rate on his mortgage, and the rise and fall of the stock market. He invested much of his money in socially responsible funds. Imagine that! Imagine choosing to trust your money with companies that supposedly made their millions through ethical means. Imagine the breathtaking privilege of such a choice. All right, so maybe this was an old story for white men. For most of American history, who else but a white man could endure the existential crisis of economic success? But this story was original and aboriginal for William. For thousands of years, Spokane Indians had lived subsistence lives, using every last part of the salmon and deer because they'd die without every last part, but William only ordered salmon from menus and saw deer on television. Maybe he romanticized the primal—for thousands of years, Indians also died of ear infections—but William wanted his comfortable and safe life to contain more *wilderness*.

"Sir, forgive me for saying this," the taxi driver said, "but you do not look like the Red Indians I have seen before."

"I know," William said. "People usually think I'm a longhaired Mexican."

"What do you say to them when they think such a thing?"

"*No habla español. Indio de Norteamericanos.*"[1]

"People think I'm black American. They always want to hip-hop rap to me. 'Are you East Coast or West Coast?' they ask me, and I tell them I am Ivory Coast."[2]

"How have things been since September eleventh?"

"Ah, a good question, sir. It's been interesting. Because people think I'm black, they don't see me as a terrorist, only as a crackhead addict on welfare. So I am a victim of only one misguided idea about who I am."

"We're all trapped by other people's ideas, aren't we?"

"I suppose that is true, sir. How has it been for you?"

"It's all backward," William said. "A few days after it happened, I was walking out of my gym downtown, and this big phallic pickup pulled up in front of me in the crosswalk. Yeah, this big truck with big phallic tires and a big phallic flagpole and a big phallic flag flying, and the big phallic symbol inside leaned out of his window and yelled at me, 'Go back to your own country!'"

"Oh, that is sad and funny," the taxi driver said.

"Yeah," William said. "And it wasn't so much a hate crime as it was a crime of irony, right? And I was laughing so hard, the truck was halfway down the block before I could get breath enough to yell back, 'You first!'"

William and the taxi driver laughed and laughed together. Two dark men laughing at dark jokes.

"I had to fly on the first day you could fly," William said. "And I was flying into Baltimore, you know, and D.C. and Baltimore are pretty much the same damn town, so it was like flying into Ground Zero, you know?"

"It must have been terrifying."

"It was, it was. I was sitting in the plane here in Seattle, getting ready to take off, and I started looking around for suspicious brown guys. I was scared of little brown guys. So was everybody else. We were all afraid of the same things. I started looking around for big white guys because I figured they'd be undercover cops, right?"

"Imagine wanting to be surrounded by white cops!"

"Exactly! I didn't want to see some pacifist, vegan, whole-wheat, free-range, organic, progressive, grey-ponytail, communist, liberal, draft-dodging, NPR[3]-listening wimp! What are they going to do if somebody tries to hijack the plane? Throw a Birkenstock at him? Offer him some pot?"

---

1    *No habla ... Norteamericanos* Spanish: Don't speak Spanish. North American Indian.

2    *Ivory Coast* Country in West Africa.

3    *NPR* American public radio network.

"Marijuana might actually stop the violence everywhere in the world," the taxi driver said.

"You're right," William said. "But on that plane, I was hoping for about twenty-five NRA-loving, gun-nut, serial-killing, psychopathic, Ollie North, Norman Schwarzkopf, right-wing, Agent Orange,[1] post-traumatic-stress-disorder, CIA, FBI, automatic-weapon, smart-bomb, laser-sighting bastards!"

"You wouldn't want to invite them for dinner," the taxi driver said. "But you want them to protect your children, am I correct?"

"Yes, but it doesn't make sense. None of it makes sense. It's all contradictions."

"The contradictions are the story, yes?"

"Yes."

"I have a story about contradictions," said the taxi driver. "Because you are a Red Indian, I think you will understand my pain."

"*Su-num-twee*," said William.

"What is that? What did you say?"

"*Su-num-twee*. It's Spokane. My language."

"What does it mean?"

"Listen to me."

"Ah, yes, that's good. *Su-num-twee, su-num-twee*. So, what is your name?"

"William."

The taxi driver sat high and straight in his seat, like he was going to say something important. "William, my name is Fekadu. I am Oromo[2] and Muslim, and I come from Addis Ababa in Ethiopia, and I want you to *su-num-twee*."

There was nothing more important than a person's name and the names of his clan, tribe, city, religion, and country. By the social rules of his tribe, William should have reciprocated and officially identified himself. He should have been polite and generous. He was expected to live by so many rules, he sometimes felt like he was living inside an indigenous version of an Edith Wharton[3] novel.

1    *NRA* National Rifle Association, an American organization opposing laws that restrict gun ownership; *Ollie North* American military official Oliver North (b. 1943), a member of the National Security Council who was tried for illegally providing military aid to anticommunist fighters in Nicaragua; *Norman Schwarzkopf* American general who secured a quick victory as commander in the 1991 Gulf War; *Agent Orange* Extremely toxic chemical weapon used by the American military during the Vietnam War (1954–75).

2    *Oromo* Member of the Oromo people, an ethnic group in Ethiopia and Somalia.

3    *Edith Wharton* American Pulitzer Prize-winning author (1862–1937) whose most famous novels satirize the social conventions of high society.

"Mr. William," asked Fekadu, "do you want to hear my story? Do you want to *su-num-twee*?"

"Yes, I do, sure, yes, please," said William. He was lying. He was twenty minutes away from the airport and so close to departure.

"I was not born into an important family," said Fekadu. "But my father worked for an important family. And this important family worked for the family of Emperor Haile Selassie.[1] He was a great and good and kind and terrible man, and he loved his country and killed many of his people. Have you heard of him?"

"No, I'm sorry, I haven't."

"He was magical. Ruled our country for forty-three years. Imagine that! We Ethiopians are strong. White people have never conquered us. We won every war we fought against white people. For all of our history, our emperors have been strong, and Selassie was the strongest. There has never been a man capable of such love and destruction."

"You fought against him?"

Fekadu breathed in so deeply that William recognized it as a religious moment, as the first act of a ceremony, and with the second act, an exhalation, the ceremony truly began.

"No," Fekadu said. "I was a smart child. A genius. A prodigy. It was Selassie who sent me to Oxford. And there I studied physics and learned the math and art of flight. I came back home and flew jets for Selassie's army."

"Did you fly in wars?" William asked.

"Ask me what you really want to ask me, William. You want to know if I was a killer, no?"

William had a vision of his wife and daughter huddling terrified in their Seattle basement while military jets screamed overhead. It happened every August when the US Navy Blue Angels came to entertain the masses with their aerial acrobatics.

"Do you want to know if I was a killer?" asked Fekadu. "Ask me if I was a killer."

William wanted to know the terrible answer without asking the terrible question.

"Will you not ask me what I am?" asked Fekadu.

"I can't."

"I dropped bombs on my own people."

---

1    *Haile Selassie* Emperor of Ethiopia, an internationally respected authoritarian leader who encouraged his country to modernize. He lost popular support toward the end of his reign and was deposed by military coup in 1974.

In the sky above them, William counted four, five, six jets flying in holding patterns while awaiting permission to land.

"For three years, I killed my own people," said Fekadu. "And then, on the third of June in 1974, I could not do it anymore. I kissed my wife and sons good-bye that morning, and I kissed my mother and father, and I lied to them and told them I would be back that evening. They had no idea where I was going. But I went to the base, got into my plane, and flew away."

"You defected?" William asked. How could a man steal a fighter plane? Was that possible? And if possible, how much courage would it take to commit such a crime? William was quite sure he could never be that courageous.

"Yes, I defected," said Fekadu. "I flew my plane to France and was almost shot down when I violated their airspace, but they let me land, and they arrested me, and soon enough, they gave me asylum. I came to Seattle five years ago, and I think I will live here the rest of my days."

Fekadu took the next exit. They were two minutes away from the airport. William was surprised to discover that he didn't want this journey to end so soon. He wondered if he should invite Fekadu for coffee and a sandwich, for a slice of pie, for brotherhood. William wanted to hear more of this man's stories and learn from them, whether they were true or not. Perhaps it didn't matter if any one man's stories were true. Fekadu's autobiography might have been completely fabricated, but William was convinced that somewhere in the world, somewhere in Africa or the United States, a man, a jet pilot, wanted to fly away from the war he was supposed to fight. There must be hundreds, maybe thousands, of such men, and how many were courageous enough to fly away? If Fekadu wasn't describing his own true pain and loneliness, then he might have been accidentally describing the pain of a real and lonely man.

"What about your family?" asked William, because he didn't know what else to ask and because he was thinking of his wife and daughter. "Weren't they in danger? Wouldn't Selassie want to hurt them?"

"I could only pray Selassie would leave them be. He had always been good to me, but he saw me as impulsive, so I hoped he would know my family had nothing to do with my flight. I was a coward for staying and a coward for leaving. But none of it mattered, because Selassie was overthrown a few weeks after I defected."

"A coup?"

"Yes, the Derg[1] deposed him, and they slaughtered all of their enemies and their enemies' families. They suffocated Selassie with a pillow the next year. And now I could never return to Ethiopia because Selassie's people would

---

1  *Derg* Military group that ruled Ethiopia as a socialist state from 1974 until it was defeated by popular uprising in 1991.

always want to kill me for my betrayal and the Derg would always want to kill me for being Selassie's soldier. Every night and day, I worry that any of them might harm my family. I want to go there and defend them. I want to bring them here. They can sleep on my floor! But even now, after democracy has almost come to Ethiopia,[1] I cannot go back. There is too much history and pain, and I am too afraid."

"How long has it been since you've talked to your family?"

"We write letters to each other, and sometimes we receive them. They sent me photos once, but they never arrived for me to see. And for two days, I waited by the telephone because they were going to call, but it never rang."

Fekadu pulled the taxi to a slow stop at the airport curb. "We are here, sir," he said. "United Airlines."

William didn't know how this ceremony was supposed to end. He felt small and powerless against the collected history. "What am I supposed to do now?" he asked.

"Sir, you must pay me thirty-eight dollars for this ride," said Fekadu and laughed. "Plus a very good tip."

"How much is good?"

"You see, sometimes I send cash to my family. I wrap it up and try to hide it inside the envelope. I know it gets stolen, but I hope some of it gets through to my family. I hope they buy themselves gifts from me. I hope."

"You pray for this?"

"Yes, William, I pray for this. And I pray for your safety on your trip, and I pray for the safety of your wife and daughter while you are gone."

"Pop the trunk, I'll get my own bags," said William as he gave sixty dollars to Fekadu, exited the taxi, took his luggage out of the trunk, and slammed it shut. Then William walked over to the passenger-side window, leaned in, and studied Fekadu's face and the terrible scar on his neck.

"Where did you get that?" William asked.

Fekadu ran a finger along the old wound. "Ah," he said. "You must think I got this flying in a war. But no, I got this in a taxicab wreck. William, I am a much better jet pilot than a car driver."

Fekadu laughed loudly and joyously. William wondered how this poor man could be capable of such happiness, however temporary it was.

"Your stories," said William. "I want to believe you."

"Then believe me," said Fekadu.

Unsure, afraid, William stepped back.

"Good-bye, William American," Fekadu said and drove away.

---

1   *democracy ... Ethiopia* Ethiopia had its first multi-party elections in 1995.

Standing at curbside, William couldn't breathe well. He wondered if he was dying. Of course he was dying, a flawed mortal dying day by day, but he felt like he might fall over from a heart attack or stroke right there on the sidewalk. He left his bags and ran inside the terminal. Let a luggage porter think his bags were dangerous! Let a security guard x-ray the bags and find mysterious shapes! Let a bomb-squad cowboy explode the bags as precaution! Let an airport manager shut down the airport and search every possible traveller! Let the FAA[1] president order every airplane to land! Let the American skies be empty of everything with wings! Let the birds stop flying! Let the very air go still and cold! William didn't care. He ran through the terminal, searching for an available pay phone, a landline, something true and connected to the ground, and he finally found one and dropped two quarters into the slot and dialed his home number, and it rang and rang and rang and rang, and William worried that his wife and daughter were harmed, were lying dead on the floor, but then Marie answered.

"Hello, William," she said.

"I'm here," he said.

—2003

---

1    *FAA* Federal Aviation Administration.

# Jhumpa Lahiri
b. 1967

Many of the characters in the finely crafted stories of Jhumpa Lahiri—who was born in England to Indian immigrants and raised in the United States—are from different continents and cultures but are at home in none. Those who leave their native land become strangers, forced to rely on their children to help them navigate the language and customs of their vastly changed environments. The sons and daughters are likewise outsiders, fluent in both the ancestral and the adopted ways but more observers than participants, destined to remain at a distance from the world they inhabit by virtue of being its interpreters. As Lahiri has observed, "Almost all my characters are translators insofar as they must make sense of the foreign to survive." This foreignness is by no means strictly cultural, just as the idea of home is not simply geographic: Lahiri's men and women are often as estranged from one another as they are from their surroundings.

Since the appearance of her first collection of short stories, the Pulitzer Prize-winning *Interpreter of Maladies* (1999), critics have approached Lahiri as a postcolonial voice of the South Asian diaspora in the tradition of writers like Salman Rushdie and V.S. Naipaul. Yet Lahiri resists the simplistic notion that, as a prominent author of Bengali descent, she represents and speaks for a particular group. Informed by her early life as a newcomer to upper middle-class New England, much of her work illuminates the immigrant experience, but Lahiri is interested above all in the experience of being human.

## Interpreter of Maladies

At the tea stall Mr. and Mrs. Das bickered about who should take Tina to the toilet. Eventually Mrs. Das relented when Mr. Das pointed out that he had given the girl her bath the night before. In the rearview mirror Mr. Kapasi watched as Mrs. Das emerged slowly from his bulky white Ambassador, dragging her shaved, largely bare legs across the back seat. She did not hold the little girl's hand as they walked to the rest room.

They were on their way to see the Sun Temple at Konarak.[1] It was a dry, bright Saturday, the mid-July heat tempered by a steady ocean breeze, ideal weather for sightseeing. Ordinarily Mr. Kapasi would not have stopped so soon along the way, but less than five minutes after he'd picked up the family that

---

1   *Sun Temple at Konarak* Famous Hindu temple (c. 1241) representing the chariot of the sun god Surya. Its location, Konarak, is a town in Orissa, a coastal state in northeastern India.

morning in front of Hotel Sandy Villa, the little girl had complained. The first thing Mr. Kapasi had noticed when he saw Mr. and Mrs. Das, standing with their children under the portico of the hotel, was that they were very young, perhaps not even thirty. In addition to Tina they had two boys, Ronny and Bobby, who appeared very close in age and had teeth covered in a network of flashing silver wires. The family looked Indian but dressed as foreigners did, the children in stiff, brightly coloured clothing and caps with translucent visors. Mr. Kapasi was accustomed to foreign tourists; he was assigned to them regularly because he could speak English. Yesterday he had driven an elderly couple from Scotland, both with spotted faces and fluffy white hair so thin it exposed their sunburnt scalps. In comparison, the tanned, youthful faces of Mr. and Mrs. Das were all the more striking. When he'd introduced himself, Mr. Kapasi had pressed his palms together in greeting, but Mr. Das squeezed hands like an American so that Mr. Kapasi felt it in his elbow. Mrs. Das, for her part, had flexed one side of her mouth, smiling dutifully at Mr. Kapasi, without displaying any interest in him.

As they waited at the tea stall, Ronny, who looked like the older of the two boys, clambered suddenly out of the back seat, intrigued by a goat tied to a stake in the ground.

"Don't touch it," Mr. Das said. He glanced up from his paperback tour book, which said "INDIA" in yellow letters and looked as if it had been published abroad. His voice, somehow tentative and a little shrill, sounded as though it had not yet settled into maturity.

"I want to give it a piece of gum," the boy called back as he trotted ahead.

Mr. Das stepped out of the car and stretched his legs by squatting briefly to the ground. A clean-shaven man, he looked exactly like a magnified version of Ronny. He had a sapphire blue visor, and was dressed in shorts, sneakers, and a T-shirt. The camera slung around his neck, with an impressive telephoto lens and numerous buttons and markings, was the only complicated thing he wore. He frowned, watching as Ronny rushed toward the goat, but appeared to have no intention of intervening. "Bobby, make sure that your brother doesn't do anything stupid."

"I don't feel like it," Bobby said, not moving. He was sitting in the front seat beside Mr. Kapasi, studying a picture of the elephant god taped to the glove compartment.

"No need to worry," Mr. Kapasi said. "They are quite tame." Mr. Kapasi was forty-six years old, with receding hair that had gone completely silver but his butterscotch complexion and his unlined brow, which he treated in spare moments to dabs of lotus-oil balm, made it easy to imagine what he must have looked like at an earlier age. He wore grey trousers and a matching jacket-style shirt, tapered at the waist, with short sleeves and a large pointed collar, made of a thin but durable synthetic material. He had specified both the cut and the fabric to his tailor—it was his preferred uniform for giving tours because it did not get crushed during his long hours behind the wheel. Through the windshield he watched as Ronny circled around the goat, touched it quickly on its side, then trotted back to the car.

"You left India as a child?" Mr. Kapasi asked when Mr. Das had settled once again into the passenger seat.

"Oh, Mina and I were both born in America," Mr. Das announced with an air of sudden confidence. "Born and raised. Our parents live here now, in Assansol.[1] They retired. We visit them every couple years." He turned to watch as the little girl ran toward the car, the wide purple bows of her sundress flopping on her narrow brown shoulders. She was holding to her chest a doll with yellow hair that looked as if it had been chopped, as a punitive measure, with a pair of dull scissors. "This is Tina's first trip to India, isn't it, Tina?"

"I don't have to go to the bathroom anymore," Tina announced.

"Where's Mina?" Mr. Das asked.

Mr. Kapasi found it strange that Mr. Das should refer to his wife by her first name when speaking to the little girl. Tina pointed to where Mrs. Das was purchasing something from one of the shirtless men who worked at the tea stall. Mr. Kapasi heard one of the shirtless men sing a phrase from a popular Hindi love song as Mrs. Das walked back to the car, but she did not appear to understand the words of the song, for she did not express irritation, or embarrassment, or react in any other way to the man's declarations.

He observed her. She wore a red-and-white-checkered skirt that stopped above her knees, slip-on shoes with a square wooden heel, and a close-fitting blouse styled like a man's undershirt. The blouse was decorated at chest-level with a calico appliqué in the shape of a strawberry. She was a short woman, with small hands like paws, her frosty pink fingernails painted to match her lips, and was slightly plump in her figure. Her hair, shorn only a little longer than her husband's, was parted far to one side. She was wearing large dark brown sunglasses with a pinkish tint to them, and carried a big straw bag, almost as big as her torso, shaped like a bowl, with a water bottle poking out of it. She walked slowly, carrying some puffed rice tossed with peanuts and chili peppers in a large packet made from newspapers. Mr. Kapasi turned to Mr. Das.

"Where in America do you live?"

"New Brunswick, New Jersey."

"Next to New York?"

"Exactly. I teach middle school there."

---

1   *Assansol* City in West Bengal, the state north of Orissa.

"What subject?"

"Science. In fact, every year I take my students on a trip to the Museum of Natural History in New York City. In a way we have a lot in common, you could say, you and I. How long have you been a tour guide, Mr. Kapasi?"

"Five years."

Mrs. Das reached the car. "How long's the trip?" she asked, shutting the door.

"About two and a half hours," Mr. Kapasi replied.

At this Mrs. Das gave an impatient sigh, as if she had been travelling her whole life without pause. She fanned herself with a folded Bombay film magazine written in English.

"I thought that the Sun Temple is only eighteen miles north of Puri,"[1] Mr. Das said, tapping on the tour book.

"The roads to Konarak are poor. Actually it is a distance of fifty-two miles," Mr. Kapasi explained.

Mr. Das nodded, readjusting the camera strap where it had begun to chafe the back of his neck.

Before starting the ignition, Mr. Kapasi reached back to make sure the cranklike locks on the inside of each of the back doors were secured. As soon as the car began to move the little girl began to play with the lock on her side, clicking it with some effort forward and backward, but Mrs. Das said nothing to stop her. She sat a bit slouched at one end of the back seat, not offering her puffed rice to anyone. Ronny and Tina sat on either side of her, both snapping bright green gum.

"Look," Bobby said as the car began to gather speed. He pointed with his finger to the tall trees that lined the road. "Look."

"Monkeys!" Ronny shrieked. "Wow!"

They were seated in groups along the branches, with shining black faces, silver bodies, horizontal eyebrows, and crested heads. Their long grey tails dangled like a series of ropes among the leaves. A few scratched themselves with black leathery hands, or swung their feet, staring as the car passed.

"We call them the hanuman," Mr. Kapasi said. "They are quite common in the area."

As soon as he spoke, one of the monkeys leaped into the middle of the road, causing Mr. Kapasi to brake suddenly. Another bounced onto the hood of the car, then sprang away. Mr. Kapasi beeped his horn. The children began to get excited, sucking in their breath and covering their faces partly with their hands. They had never seen monkeys outside of a zoo, Mr. Das explained. He asked Mr. Kapasi to stop the car so that he could take a picture.

---

1    *Puri*  Major city in Orissa.

While Mr. Das adjusted his telephoto lens, Mrs. Das reached into her straw bag and pulled out a bottle of colourless nail polish, which she proceeded to stroke on the tip of her index finger.

The little girl stuck out a hand. "Mine too. Mommy, do mine too."

"Leave me alone," Mrs. Das said, blowing on her nail and turning her body slightly. "You're making me mess up."

The little girl occupied herself by buttoning and unbuttoning a pinafore on the doll's plastic body.

"All set," Mr. Das said, replacing the lens cap.

The car rattled considerably as it raced along the dusty road, causing them all to pop up from their seats every now and then, but Mrs. Das continued to polish her nails. Mr. Kapasi eased up on the accelerator, hoping to produce a smoother ride. When he reached for the gearshift the boy in front accommodated him by swinging his hairless knees out of the way. Mr. Kapasi noted that this boy was slightly paler than the other children. "Daddy, why is the driver sitting on the wrong side in this car, too?" the boy asked.

"They all do that here, dummy," Ronny said.

"Don't call your brother a dummy," Mr. Das said. He turned to Mr. Kapasi. "In America, you know ... it confuses them."

"Oh yes, I am well aware," Mr. Kapasi said. As delicately as he could, he shifted gears again, accelerating as they approached a hill in the road. "I see it on *Dallas*,[1] the steering wheels are on the left-hand side."

"What's *Dallas*?" Tina asked, banging her now naked doll on the seat behind Mr. Kapasi.

"It went off the air," Mr. Das explained. "It's a television show."

They were all like siblings, Mr. Kapasi thought as they passed a row of date trees. Mr. and Mrs. Das behaved like an older brother and sister, not parents. It seemed that they were in charge of the children only for the day; it was hard to believe they were regularly responsible for anything other than themselves. Mr. Das tapped on his lens cap, and his tour book, dragging his thumbnail occasionally across the pages so that they made a scraping sound. Mrs. Das continued to polish her nails. She had still not removed her sunglasses. Every now and then Tina renewed her plea that she wanted her nails done, too, and so at one point Mrs. Das flicked a drop of polish on the little girl's finger before depositing the bottle back inside her straw bag.

"Isn't this an air-conditioned car?" she asked, still blowing on her hand. The window on Tina's side was broken and could not be rolled down.

"Quit complaining," Mr. Das said. "It isn't so hot."

---

1   *Dallas* Popular American soap opera (1978–91) set in Dallas, Texas.

"I told you to get a car with air-conditioning," Mrs. Das continued. "Why do you do this, Raj, just to save a few stupid rupees. What are you saving us, fifty cents?"

Their accents sounded just like the ones Mr. Kapasi heard on American television programs, though not like the ones on *Dallas*.

"Doesn't it get tiresome, Mr. Kapasi, showing people the same thing every day?" Mr. Das asked, rolling down his own window all the way. "Hey do you mind stopping the car. I just want to get a shot of this guy."

Mr. Kapasi pulled over to the side of the road as Mr. Das took a picture of a barefoot man, his head wrapped in a dirty turban, seated on top of a cart of grain sacks pulled by a pair of bullocks.[1] Both the man and the bullocks were emaciated. In the back seat Mrs. Das gazed out another window, at the sky, where nearly transparent clouds passed quickly in front of one another.

"I look forward to it, actually," Mr. Kapasi said as they continued on their way. "The Sun Temple is one of my favourite places. In that way it is a reward for me. I give tours on Fridays and Saturdays only. I have another job during the week."

"Oh? Where?" Mr. Das asked.

"I work in a doctor's office."

"You're a doctor?"

"I am not a doctor. I work with one. As an interpreter."

"What does a doctor need an interpreter for?"

"He has a number of Gujarati[2] patients. My father was Gujarati, but many people do not speak Gujarati in this area, including the doctor. And so the doctor asked me to work in his office, interpreting what the patients say."

"Interesting. I've never heard of anything like that," Mr. Das said.

Mr. Kapasi shrugged. "It is a job like any other."

"But so romantic," Mrs. Das said dreamily breaking her extended silence. She lifted her pinkish brown sunglasses and arranged them on top of her head like a tiara. For the first time, her eyes met Mr. Kapasi's in the rearview mirror: pale, a bit small, their gaze fixed but drowsy.

Mr. Das craned to look at her. "What's so romantic about it?"

"I don't know. Something." She shrugged, knitting her brows together for an instant. "Would you like a piece of gum, Mr. Kapasi?" she asked brightly. She reached into her straw bag and handed him a small square wrapped in green-and-white-striped paper. As soon as Mr. Kapasi put the gum in his mouth a thick sweet liquid burst onto his tongue.

"Tell us more about your job, Mr. Kapasi," Mrs. Das said.

---

1    *bullocks* Young bulls.
2    *Gujarati* Member of the Gujarati ethnic group, located primarily in western India.

"What would you like to know, madame?"

"I don't know," again she shrugged, munching on some puffed rice and licking the mustard oil from the corners of her mouth. "Tell us a typical situation." She settled back in her seat, her head tilted in a patch of sun, and closed her eyes. "I want to picture what happens."

"Very well. The other day a man came in with a pain in his throat."

"Did he smoke cigarettes?"

"No. It was very curious. He complained that he felt as if there were long pieces of straw stuck in his throat. When I told the doctor he was able to prescribe the proper medication."

"That's so neat."

"Yes," Mr. Kapasi agreed after some hesitation.

"So these patients are totally dependent on you," Mrs. Das said. She spoke slowly as if she were thinking aloud. "In a way more dependent on you than the doctor."

"How do you mean? How could it be?"

"Well, for example, you could tell the doctor that the pain felt like a burning, not straw. The patient would never know what you had told the doctor, and the doctor wouldn't know that you had told the wrong thing. It's a big responsibility."

"Yes, a big responsibility you have there, Mr. Kapasi," Mr. Das agreed.

Mr. Kapasi had never thought of his job in such complimentary terms. To him it was a thankless occupation. He found nothing noble in interpreting people's maladies, assiduously translating the symptoms of so many swollen bones, countless cramps of bellies and bowels, spots on people's palms that changed colour, shape, or size. The doctor, nearly half his age, had an affinity for bell-bottom trousers and made humourless jokes about the Congress party.[1] Together they worked in a stale little infirmary where Mr. Kapasi's smartly tailored clothes clung to him in the heat, in spite of the blackened blades of a ceiling fan churning over their heads.

The job was a sign of his failings. In his youth he'd been a devoted scholar of foreign languages, the owner of an impressive collection of dictionaries. He had dreamed of being an interpreter for diplomats and dignitaries, resolving conflicts between people and nations, settling disputes of which he alone could understand both sides. He was a self-educated man. In a series of notebooks, in the evenings before his parents settled his marriage, he had listed the common etymologies of words, and at one point in his life he was confident that he could converse, if given the opportunity, in English, French, Russian, Portu-

---

1   *Congress party* One of India's major political parties; after India's independence in 1947, it dominated the government for most of the rest of the century.

guese, and Italian, not to mention Hindi, Bengali, Oriya, and Gujarati. Now only a handful of European phrases remained in his memory, scattered words for things like saucers and chairs. English was the only non-Indian language he spoke fluently anymore. Mr. Kapasi knew it was not a remarkable talent. Sometimes he feared that his children knew better English than he did, just from watching television. Still, it came in handy for the tours.

He had taken the job as an interpreter after his first son, at the age of seven, contracted typhoid—that was how he had first made the acquaintance of the doctor. At the time Mr. Kapasi had been teaching English in a grammar school, and he bartered his skills as an interpreter to pay the increasingly exorbitant medical bills. In the end the boy had died one evening in his mother's arms, his limbs burning with fever, but then there was the funeral to pay for, and the other children who were born soon enough, and the newer, bigger house, and the good schools and tutors, and the fine shoes and the television, and the countless other ways he tried to console his wife and to keep her from crying in her sleep, and so when the doctor offered to pay him twice as much as he earned at the grammar school, he accepted. Mr. Kapasi knew that his wife had little regard for his career as an interpreter. He knew it reminded her of the son she'd lost, and that she resented the other lives he helped, in his own small way, to save. If ever she referred to his position, she used the phrase "doctor's assistant," as if the process of interpretation were equal to taking someone's temperature, or changing a bedpan. She never asked him about the patients who came to the doctor's office, or said that his job was a big responsibility.

For this reason it flattered Mr. Kapasi that Mrs. Das was so intrigued by his job. Unlike his wife, she had reminded him of its intellectual challenges. She had also used the word "romantic." She did not behave in a romantic way toward her husband, and yet she had used the word to describe him. He wondered if Mr. and Mrs. Das were a bad match, just as he and his wife were. Perhaps they too, had little in common apart from three children and a decade of their lives. The signs he recognized from his own marriage were there—the bickering, the indifference, the protracted silences. Her sudden interest in him, an interest she did not express in either her husband or her children, was mildly intoxicating. When Mr. Kapasi thought once again about how she had said "romantic," the feeling of intoxication grew.

He began to check his reflection in the rearview mirror as he drove, feeling grateful that he had chosen the grey suit that morning and not the brown one, which tended to sag a little in the knees. From time to time he glanced through the mirror at Mrs. Das. In addition to glancing at her face he glanced at the strawberry between her breasts, and the golden brown hollow in her throat. He decided to tell Mrs. Das about another patient, and another: the young woman who had complained of a sensation of raindrops in her spine, the gentleman whose birthmark had begun to sprout hairs. Mrs. Das listened attentively, stroking her hair with a small plastic brush that resembled an oval bed of nails, asking more questions, for yet another example. The children were quiet, intent on spotting more monkeys in the trees, and Mr. Das was absorbed by his tour book, so it seemed like a private conversation between Mr. Kapasi and Mrs. Das. In this manner the next half hour passed, and when they stopped for lunch at a roadside restaurant that sold fritters and omelette sandwiches, usually something Mr. Kapasi looked forward to on his tours so that he could sit in peace and enjoy some hot tea, he was disappointed. As the Das family settled together under a magenta umbrella fringed with white and orange tassels, and placed their orders with one of the waiters who marched about in tricornered caps, Mr. Kapasi reluctantly headed toward a neighbouring table.

"Mr. Kapasi, wait. There's room here," Mrs. Das called out. She gathered Tina onto her lap, insisting that he accompany them. And so, together, they had bottled mango juice and sandwiches and plates of onions and potatoes deep-fried in graham-flour batter. After finishing two omelette sandwiches Mr. Das took more pictures of the group as they ate.

"How much longer?" he asked Mr. Kapasi as he paused to load a new roll of film in the camera.

"About half an hour more."

By now the children had gotten up from the table to look at more monkeys perched in a nearby tree, so there was a considerable space between Mrs. Das and Mr. Kapasi. Mr. Das placed the camera to his face and squeezed one eye shut, his tongue exposed at one corner of his mouth. "This looks funny. Mina, you need to lean in closer to Mr. Kapasi."

She did. He could smell a scent on her skin, like a mixture of whiskey and rosewater. He worried suddenly that she could smell his perspiration, which he knew had collected beneath the synthetic material of his shirt. He polished off his mango juice in one gulp and smoothed his silver hair with his hands. A bit of the juice dripped onto his chin. He wondered if Mrs. Das had noticed.

She had not. "What's your address, Mr. Kapasi?" she inquired, fishing for something inside her straw bag.

"You would like my address?"

"So we can send you copies," she said. "Of the pictures." She handed him a scrap of paper which she had hastily ripped from a page of her film magazine. The blank portion was limited, for the narrow strip was crowded by lines of text and a tiny picture of a hero and heroine embracing under a eucalyptus tree.

The paper curled as Mr. Kapasi wrote his address in clear, careful letters. She would write to him, asking about his days interpreting at the doctor's office, and he would respond eloquently choosing only the most entertaining anecdotes, ones that would make her laugh out loud as she read them in her house in New Jersey. In time she would reveal the disappointment of her marriage, and he his. In this way their friendship would grow, and flourish. He would possess a picture of the two of them, eating fried onions under a magenta umbrella, which he would keep, he decided, safely tucked between the pages of his Russian grammar. As his mind raced, Mr. Kapasi experienced a mild and pleasant shock. It was similar to a feeling he used to experience long ago when, after months of translating with the aid of a dictionary he would finally read a passage from a French novel, or an Italian sonnet, and understand the words, one after another, unencumbered by his own efforts. In those moments Mr. Kapasi used to believe that all was right with the world, that all struggles were rewarded, that all of life's mistakes made sense in the end. The promise that he would hear from Mrs. Das now filled him with the same belief.

When he finished writing his address Mr. Kapasi handed her the paper, but as soon as he did so he worried that he had either misspelled his name, or accidentally reversed the numbers of his postal code. He dreaded the possibility of a lost letter, the photograph never reaching him, hovering somewhere in Orissa, close but ultimately unattainable. He thought of asking for the slip of paper again, just to make sure he had written his address accurately but Mrs. Das had already dropped it into the jumble of her bag.

They reached Konarak at two-thirty. The temple, made of sandstone, was a massive pyramid-like structure in the shape of a chariot. It was dedicated to the great master of life, the sun, which struck three sides of the edifice as it made its journey each day across the sky. Twenty-four giant wheels were carved on the north and south sides of the plinth. The whole thing was drawn by a team of seven horses, speeding as if through the heavens. As they approached, Mr. Kapasi explained that the temple had been built between A.D. 1243 and 1255, with the efforts of twelve hundred artisans, by the great ruler of the Ganga dynasty, King Narasimhadeva the First, to commemorate his victory against the Muslim army.

"It says the temple occupies about a hundred and seventy acres of land," Mr. Das said, reading from his book.

"It's like a desert," Ronny said, his eyes wandering across the sand that stretched on all sides beyond the temple.

"The Chandrabhaga River once flowed one mile north of here. It is dry now," Mr. Kapasi said, turning off the engine.

They got out and walked toward the temple, posing first for pictures by the pair of lions that flanked the steps. Mr. Kapasi led them next to one of the wheels of the chariot, higher than any human being, nine feet in diameter.

"'The wheels are supposed to symbolize the wheel of life,'" Mr. Das read. "'They depict the cycle of creation, preservation, and achievement of realization.' Cool." He turned the page of his book. "'Each wheel is divided into eight thick and thin spokes, dividing the day into eight equal parts. The rims are carved with designs of birds and animals, whereas the medallions in the spokes are carved with women in luxurious poses, largely erotic in nature.'"

What he referred to were the countless friezes of entwined naked bodies, making love in various positions, women clinging to the necks of men, their knees wrapped eternally around their lovers' thighs. In addition to these were assorted scenes from daily life, of hunting and trading, of deer being killed with bows and arrows and marching warriors holding swords in their hands.

It was no longer possible to enter the temple, for it had filled with rubble years ago, but they admired the exterior, as did all the tourists Mr. Kapasi brought there, slowly strolling along each of its sides. Mr. Das trailed behind, taking pictures. The children ran ahead, pointing to figures of naked people, intrigued in particular by the Nagamithunas, the half-human, half-serpentine couples who were said, Mr. Kapasi told them, to live in the deepest waters of the sea. Mr. Kapasi was pleased that they liked the temple, pleased especially that it appealed to Mrs. Das. She stopped every three or four paces, staring silently at the carved lovers, and the processions of elephants, and the topless female musicians beating on two-sided drums.

Though Mr. Kapasi had been to the temple countless times, it occurred to him, as he, too, gazed at the topless women, that he had never seen his own wife fully naked. Even when they had made love she kept the panels of her blouse hooked together, the string of her petticoat knotted around her waist. He had never admired the backs of his wife's legs the way he now admired those of Mrs. Das, walking as if for his benefit alone. He had, of course, seen plenty of bare limbs before, belonging to the American and European ladies who took his tours. But Mrs. Das was different. Unlike the other women, who had an interest only in the temple, and kept their noses buried in a guidebook, or their eyes behind the lens of a camera, Mrs. Das had taken an interest in him.

Mr. Kapasi was anxious to be alone with her, to continue their private conversation, yet he felt nervous to walk at her side. She was lost behind her sunglasses, ignoring her husband's requests that she pose for another picture, walking past her children as if they were strangers. Worried that he might disturb her, Mr. Kapasi walked ahead, to admire, as he always did, the three life-sized bronze avatars of Surya, the sun god, each emerging from its own niche on the temple facade to greet the sun at dawn, noon, and evening. They wore elaborate headdresses, their languid, elongated eyes closed, their bare chests draped with carved chains and amulets. Hibiscus petals, offerings from previous visitors, were strewn at their grey-green feet. The last statue, on the northern wall of the temple, was Mr. Kapasi's favourite. This Surya had a tired expression, weary after a hard day of work, sitting astride a horse with folded legs. Even his horse's eyes were drowsy. Around his body were smaller sculptures of women in pairs, their hips thrust to one side.

"Who's that?" Mrs. Das asked. He was startled to see that she was standing beside him.

"He is the Astachala-Surya," Mr. Kapasi said. "The setting sun."

"So in a couple of hours the sun will set right here?" She slipped a foot out of one of her square-heeled shoes, rubbed her toes on the back of her other leg.

"That is correct."

She raised her sunglasses for a moment, then put them back on again. "Neat."

Mr. Kapasi was not certain exactly what the word suggested, but he had a feeling it was a favourable response. He hoped that Mrs. Das had understood Surya's beauty, his power. Perhaps they would discuss it further in their letters. He would explain things to her, things about India, and she would explain things to him about America. In its own way this correspondence would fulfill his dream, of serving as an interpreter between nations. He looked at her straw bag, delighted that his address lay nestled among its contents. When he pictured her so many thousands of miles away he plummeted, so much so that he had an overwhelming urge to wrap his arms around her, to freeze with her, even for an instant, in an embrace witnessed by his favourite Surya. But Mrs. Das had already started walking.

"When do you return to America?" he asked, trying to sound placid.

"In ten days."

He calculated: A week to settle in, a week to develop the pictures, a few days to compose her letter, two weeks to get to India by air. According to his schedule, allowing room for delays, he would hear from Mrs. Das in approximately six weeks' time.

The family was silent as Mr. Kapasi drove them back, a little past four-thirty, to Hotel Sandy Villa. The children had bought miniature granite versions of the chariot's wheels at a souvenir stand, and they turned them round in their hands. Mr. Das continued to read his book. Mrs. Das untangled Tina's hair with her brush and divided it into two little ponytails.

Mr. Kapasi was beginning to dread the thought of dropping them off. He was not prepared to begin his six-week wait to hear from Mrs. Das. As he stole glances at her in the rearview mirror, wrapping elastic bands around Tina's hair, he wondered how he might make the tour last a little longer. Ordinarily he sped back to Puri using a shortcut, eager to return home, scrub his feet and hands with sandalwood soap, and enjoy the evening newspaper and a cup of tea that his wife would serve him in silence. The thought of that silence, something to which he'd long been resigned, now oppressed him. It was then that he suggested visiting the hills at Udayagiri and Khandagiri, where a number of monastic dwellings were hewn out of the ground, facing one another across a defile.[1] It was some miles away but well worth seeing, Mr. Kapasi told them.

"Oh yeah, there's something mentioned about it in this book," Mr. Das said. "Built by a Jain[2] king or something."

"Shall we go then?" Mr. Kapasi asked. He paused at a turn in the road. "It's to the left."

Mr. Das turned to look at Mrs. Das. Both of them shrugged.

"Left, left," the children chanted.

Mr. Kapasi turned the wheel, almost delirious with relief. He did not know what he would do or say to Mrs. Das once they arrived at the hills. Perhaps he would tell her what a pleasing smile she had. Perhaps he would compliment her strawberry shirt, which he found irresistibly becoming. Perhaps, when Mr. Das was busy taking a picture, he would take her hand.

He did not have to worry. When they got to the hills, divided by a steep path thick with trees, Mrs. Das refused to get out of the car. All along the path, dozens of monkeys were seated on stones, as well as on the branches of the trees. Their hind legs were stretched out in front and raised to shoulder level, their arms resting on their knees.

"My legs are tired," she said, sinking low in her seat. "I'll stay here."

"Why did you have to wear those stupid shoes?" Mr. Das said. "You won't be in the pictures."

"Pretend I'm there."

"But we could use one of these pictures for our Christmas card this year. We didn't get one of all five of us at the Sun Temple. Mr. Kapasi could take it."

"I'm not coming. Anyway, those monkeys give me the creeps."

"But they're harmless," Mr. Das said. He turned to Mr. Kapasi. "Aren't they?"

"They are more hungry than dangerous," Mr. Kapasi said. "Do not provoke them with food, and they will not bother you."

Mr. Das headed up the defile with the children, the boys at his side, the little girl on his shoulders. Mr. Kapasi watched as they crossed paths with a Japanese man and woman, the only other tourists there, who paused for a final photograph, then stepped into a nearby car and drove away. As the car disap-

---

1   *defile* Narrow gorge.

2   *Jain* Adherent of Jainism, an Indian religion related to Hinduism and notable for asceticism, belief in the transmigration of souls, and advocating the avoidance of harm to all living creatures.

peared out of view some of the monkeys called out, emitting soft whooping sounds, and then walked on their flat black hands and feet up the path. At one point a group of them formed a little ring around Mr. Das and the children. Tina screamed in delight. Ronny ran in circles around his father. Bobby bent down and picked up a fat stick on the ground. When he extended it, one of the monkeys approached him and snatched it, then briefly beat the ground.

"I'll join them," Mr. Kapasi said, unlocking the door on his side. "There is much to explain about the caves."

"No. Stay a minute," Mrs. Das said. She got out of the back seat and slipped in beside Mr. Kapasi. "Raj has his dumb book anyway." Together, through the windshield, Mrs. Das and Mr. Kapasi watched as Bobby and the monkey passed the stick back and forth between them.

"A brave little boy," Mr. Kapasi commented.

"It's not so surprising," Mrs. Das said.

"No?"

"He's not his."

"I beg your pardon?"

"Raj's. He's not Raj's son."

Mr. Kapasi felt a prickle on his skin. He reached into his shirt pocket for the small tin of lotus-oil balm he carried with him at all times, and applied it to three spots on his forehead. He knew that Mrs. Das was watching him, but he did not turn to face her. Instead he watched as the figures of Mr. Das and the children grew smaller, climbing up the steep path, pausing every now and then for a picture, surrounded by a growing number of monkeys.

"Are you surprised?" The way she put it made him choose his words with care.

"It's not the type of thing one assumes," Mr. Kapasi replied slowly. He put the tin of lotus-oil balm back in his pocket.

"No, of course not. And no one knows, of course. No one at all. I've kept it a secret for eight whole years." She looked at Mr. Kapasi, tilting her chin as if to gain a fresh perspective. "But now I've told you."

Mr. Kapasi nodded. He felt suddenly parched, and his forehead was warm and slightly numb from the balm. He considered asking Mrs. Das for a sip of water, then decided against it.

"We met when we were very young," she said. She reached into her straw bag in search of something, then pulled out a packet of puffed rice. "Want some?"

"No, thank you."

She put a fistful in her mouth, sank into the seat a little, and looked away from Mr. Kapasi, out the window on her side of the car. "We married when we were still in college. We were in high school when he proposed. We went to the same college, of course. Back then we couldn't stand the thought of being separated, not for a day, not for a minute. Our parents were best friends who lived in the same town. My entire life I saw him every weekend, either at our house or theirs. We were sent upstairs to play together while our parents joked about our marriage. Imagine! They never caught us at anything, though in a way I think it was all more or less a setup. The things we did those Friday and Saturday nights, while our parents sat downstairs drinking tea ... I could tell you stories, Mr. Kapasi."

As a result of spending all her time in college with Raj, she continued, she did not make many close friends. There was no one to confide in about him at the end of a difficult day or to share a passing thought or a worry. Her parents now lived on the other side of the world, but she had never been very close to them, anyway. After marrying so young she was overwhelmed by it all, having a child so quickly and nursing, and warming up bottles of milk and testing their temperature against her wrist while Raj was at work, dressed in sweaters and corduroy pants, teaching his students about rocks and dinosaurs. Raj never looked cross or harried, or plump as she had become after the first baby.

Always tired, she declined invitations from her one or two college girlfriends, to have lunch or shop in Manhattan. Eventually the friends stopped calling her, so that she was left at home all day with the baby, surrounded by toys that made her trip when she walked or wince when she sat, always cross and tired. Only occasionally did they go out after Ronny was born, and even more rarely did they entertain. Raj didn't mind; he looked forward to coming home from teaching and watching television and bouncing Ronny on his knee. She had been outraged when Raj told her that a Punjabi[1] friend, someone whom she had once met but did not remember, would be staying with them for a week for some job interviews in the New Brunswick area.

Bobby was conceived in the afternoon, on a sofa littered with rubber teething toys, after the friend learned that a London pharmaceutical company had hired him, while Ronny cried to be freed from his playpen. She made no protest when the friend touched the small of her back as she was about to make a pot of coffee, then pulled her against his crisp navy suit. He made love to her swiftly in silence, with an expertise she had never known, without the meaningful expressions and smiles Raj always insisted on afterward. The next day Raj drove the friend to JFK. He was married now, to a Punjabi girl, and they lived in London still, and every year they exchanged Christmas cards with Raj and Mina, each couple tucking photos of their families into the envelopes. He did not know that he was Bobby's father. He never would.

---

1   *Punjabi* From the Punjab region in northwestern India.

"I beg your pardon, Mrs. Das, but why have you told me this information?" Mr. Kapasi asked when she had finally finished speaking, and had turned to face him once again.

"For God's sake, stop calling me Mrs. Das. I'm twenty-eight. You probably have children my age."

"Not quite." It disturbed Mr. Kapasi to learn that she thought of him as a parent. The feeling he had had toward her, that had made him check his reflection in the rearview mirror as they drove, evaporated a little.

"I told you because of your talents." She put the packet of puffed rice back into her bag without folding over the top.

"I don't understand," Mr. Kapasi said.

"Don't you see? For eight years I haven't been able to express this to anybody, not to friends, certainly not to Raj. He doesn't even suspect it. He thinks I'm still in love with him. Well, don't you have anything to say?"

"About what?"

"About what I've just told you. About my secret, and about how terrible it makes me feel. I feel terrible looking at my children, and at Raj, always terrible. I have terrible urges, Mr. Kapasi, to throw things away. One day I had the urge to throw everything I own out the window, the television, the children, everything. Don't you think it's unhealthy?"

He was silent.

"Mr. Kapasi, don't you have anything to say? I thought that was your job."

"My job is to give tours, Mrs. Das."

"Not that. Your other job. As an interpreter."

"But we do not face a language barrier. What need is there for an interpreter?"

"That's not what I mean. I would never have told you otherwise. Don't you realize what it means for me to tell you?"

"What does it mean?"

"It means that I'm tired of feeling so terrible all the time. Eight years, Mr. Kapasi, I've been in pain eight years. I was hoping you could help me feel better, say the right thing. Suggest some kind of remedy."

He looked at her, in her red plaid skirt and strawberry T-shirt, a woman not yet thirty, who loved neither her husband nor her children, who had already fallen out of love with life. Her confession depressed him, depressed him all the more when he thought of Mr. Das at the top of the path, Tina clinging to his shoulders, taking pictures of ancient monastic cells cut into the hills to show his students in America, unsuspecting and unaware that one of his sons was not his own. Mr. Kapasi felt insulted that Mrs. Das should ask him to interpret her common, trivial little secret. She did not resemble the patients in the doctor's office, those who came glassy-eyed and desperate, unable to sleep or breathe or urinate with ease, unable, above all, to give words to their pains. Still, Mr. Kapasi believed it was his duty to assist Mrs. Das. Perhaps he ought to tell her to confess the truth to Mr. Das. He would explain that honesty was the best policy. Honesty surely would help her feel better, as she'd put it. Perhaps he would offer to preside over the discussion, as a mediator. He decided to begin with the most obvious question, to get to the heart of the matter, and so he asked, "Is it really pain you feel, Mrs. Das, or is it guilt?"

She turned to him and glared, mustard oil thick on her frosty pink lips. She opened her mouth to say something, but as she glared at Mr. Kapasi some certain knowledge seemed to pass before her eyes, and she stopped. It crushed him; he knew at that moment that he was not even important enough to be properly insulted. She opened the car door and began walking up the path, wobbling a little on her square wooden heels, reaching into her straw bag to eat handfuls of puffed rice. It fell through her fingers, leaving a zigzagging trail, causing a monkey to leap down from a tree and devour the little white grains. In search of more, the monkey began to follow Mrs. Das. Others joined him, so that she was soon being followed by about half a dozen of them, their velvety tails dragging behind.

Mr. Kapasi stepped out of the car. He wanted to holler, to alert her in some way but he worried that if she knew they were behind her, she would grow nervous. Perhaps she would lose her balance. Perhaps they would pull at her bag or her hair. He began to jog up the path, taking a fallen branch in his hand to scare away the monkeys. Mrs. Das continued walking, oblivious, trailing grains of puffed rice. Near the top of the incline, before a group of cells fronted by a row of squat stone pillars, Mr. Das was kneeling on the ground, focusing the lens of his camera. The children stood under the arcade, now hiding, now emerging from view.

"Wait for me," Mrs. Das called out. "I'm coming."

Tina jumped up and down. "Here comes Mommy!"

"Great," Mr. Das said without looking up. "Just in time. We'll get Mr. Kapasi to take a picture of the five of us."

Mr. Kapasi quickened his pace, waving his branch so that the monkeys scampered away distracted, in another direction.

"Where's Bobby?" Mrs. Das asked when she stopped.

Mr. Das looked up from the camera. "I don't know. Ronny, where's Bobby?"

Ronny shrugged. "I thought he was right here."

"Where is he?" Mrs. Das repeated sharply. "What's wrong with all of you?"

They began calling his name, wandering up and down the path a bit. Because they were calling, they did not initially hear the boy's screams. When they found him, a little farther down the path under a tree, he was surrounded by a group of monkeys, over a dozen of them, pulling at his T-shirt with their long black fingers. The puffed rice Mrs. Das had spilled was scattered at his feet, raked over by the monkeys' hands. The boy was silent, his body frozen, swift tears running down his startled face. His bare legs were dusty and red with welts from where one of the monkeys struck him repeatedly with the stick he had given to it earlier.

"Daddy, the monkey's hurting Bobby," Tina said.

Mr. Das wiped his palms on the front of his shorts. In his nervousness he accidentally pressed the shutter on his camera; the whirring noise of the advancing film excited the monkeys, and the one with the stick began to beat Bobby more intently. "What are we supposed to do? What if they start attacking?"

"Mr. Kapasi," Mrs. Das shrieked, noticing him standing to one side. "Do something, for God's sake, do something!"

Mr. Kapasi took his branch and shooed them away hissing at the ones that remained, stomping his feet to scare them. The animals retreated slowly, with a measured gait, obedient but unintimidated. Mr. Kapasi gathered Bobby in his arms and brought him back to where his parents and siblings were standing. As he carried him he was tempted to whisper a secret into the boy's ear. But Bobby was stunned, and shivering with fright, his legs bleeding slightly where the stick had broken the skin. When Mr. Kapasi delivered him to his parents, Mr. Das brushed some dirt off the boy's T-shirt and put the visor on him the right way. Mrs. Das reached into her straw bag to find a bandage which she taped over the cut on his knee. Ronny offered his brother a fresh piece of gum. "He's fine. Just a little scared, right, Bobby?" Mr. Das said, patting the top of his head.

"God, let's get out of here," Mrs. Das said. She folded her arms across the strawberry on her chest. "This place gives me the creeps."

"Yeah. Back to the hotel, definitely," Mr. Das agreed.

"Poor Bobby," Mrs. Das said. "Come here a second. Let Mommy fix your hair." Again she reached into her straw bag, this time for her hairbrush, and began to run it around the edges of the translucent visor. When she whipped out the hairbrush, the slip of paper with Mr. Kapasi's address on it fluttered away in the wind. No one but Mr. Kapasi noticed. He watched as it rose, carried higher and higher by the breeze, into the trees where the monkeys now sat, solemnly observing the scene below. Mr. Kapasi observed it too, knowing that this was the picture of the Das family he would preserve forever in his mind.

—1998

# *Eden Robinson*
b. 1968

Eden Robinson, the author of some of the most startling and macabre fiction in contemporary Canadian literature, counts among her major influences Edgar Allan Poe, Stephen King, and filmmaker David Cronenberg. In many of her best-known stories, notably those in her first collection, *Traplines* (1996), extremes of physical and psychological violence are not disruptions of a peaceful norm but rather part of everyday, less to be wondered at than endured as a matter of course.

Much, though not all, of Robinson's work engages with the lives of First Nations people today, and Robinson herself was born to a Heiltsuk mother and a Haisla father on a reserve in northern British Columbia. However, Robinson, like so many writers, is suspicious of labels, including the label of "Native writer." As she has observed: "Once you've been put in the box of being a native writer, then it's hard to get out."

It is difficult to fashion any sort of box to hold Robinson's fiction: it is dark, disturbing, traversed by characters she describes as "flamboyant psychopaths," and yet full of humour. While Robinson gained much acclaim for *Traplines*, her first novel, *Monkey Beach* (2000), became a national bestseller and was nominated for both the Scotiabank Giller Prize and the Governor General's Award. A story that follows the journey of a young Haisla woman as she seeks to unravel the mystery of her missing brother, it is both stylistically bold and intensely readable. Robinson's latest novel is *Son of a Trickster* (2017), which was shortlisted for the Scotiabank Giller Prize.

# Terminal Avenue

His brother once held a peeled orange slice up against the sun. When the light shone through it, the slice became a brilliant amber: the setting sun is this colour, ripe orange. The uniforms of the five advancing Peace Officers are robin's egg blue, but the slanting light catches their visors and sets their faces aflame.

&

In his memory, the water of the Douglas Channel[1] is a hard blue, baked to a glassy translucence by the August sun. The mountains in the distance form a crown; *Gabiswa*, the mountain in the centre, is the same shade of blue as his lover's veins.

She raises her arms to sweep her hair from her face. Her breasts lift. In the cool morning air, her nipples harden to knobby raspberries. Her eyes are widening in indignation: he once saw that shade of blue in a dragonfly's wing, but this is another thing he will keep secret.

∞

Say nothing, his mother said, without moving her lips, careful not to attract attention. They waited in their car in silence after that. His father and mother were in the front seat, stiff.

Blood plastered his father's hair to his skull; blood leaked down his father's blank face. In the flashing lights of the patrol car, the blood looked black and moved like honey.

∞

A rocket has entered the event horizon[2] of a black hole. To an observer who is watching this from a safe distance, the rocket trapped here, in the black hole's inescapable halo of gravity, will appear to stop.

To an astronaut in the rocket, however, gravity is a rack that stretches his body like taffy, thinner and thinner, until there is nothing left but x-rays.

∞

In full body-armour, the five Peace Officers are sexless and anonymous. With their visors down, they look like old-fashioned astronauts. The landscape they move across is the rapid transit line, the Surreycentral Skytrain station, but if they remove their body-armour, it may as well be the moon.

The Peace Officers begin to match strides until they move like a machine. This is an intimidation tactic that works, is working on him even though he knows what it is. He finds himself frozen. He can't move, even as they roll towards him, a train on invisible tracks.

∞

---

1    *Douglas Channel* Inlet on the coast of northern British Columbia. At the end of the inlet is Kitamaat Village, the site of a Haisla First Nations community.

2    *event horizon* Boundary at the edge of a black hole where the force of gravity becomes so strong that no light can escape.

Once, when his brother dared him, he jumped off the high diving tower. He wasn't really scared until he stepped away from the platform. In that moment, he realized he couldn't change his mind.

You stupid shit, his brother said when he surfaced.

In his dreams, everything is the same, except there is no water in the swimming pool and he crashes into the concrete like a dropped pumpkin.

ဆ

He thinks of his brother, who is so perfect he wasn't born, but chiselled from stone. There is nothing he can do against that brown Apollo's face, nothing he can say that will justify his inaction. Kevin would know what to do, with doom coming towards him in formation.

But Kevin is dead. He walked through their mother's door one day, wearing the robin's egg blue uniform of the great enemy, and his mother struck him down. She summoned the ghost of their father and put him in the room, sat him beside her, bloody and stunned. Against this Kevin said, I can stop it, Mom. I have the power to change things now.

She turned away, then the family turned away. Kevin looked at him, pleading, before he left her house and never came back, disappeared. Wil closed his eyes, a dark, secret joy welling in him, to watch his brother fall: Kevin never made the little mistakes in his life, never so much as sprouted a pimple. He made up for it though by doing the unforgivable.

Wil wonders if his brother knows what is happening. If, in fact, he isn't one of the Peace Officers, filled himself with secret joy.

ဆ

His lover will wait for him tonight. Ironically, she will be wearing a complete Peace Officer's uniform, bought at great expense on the black market, and very, very illegal. She will wait at the door of her club, Terminal Avenue, and she will frisk clients that she knows will enjoy it. She will have the playroom ready, with its great wooden beams stuck through with hook and cages, with its expensive equipment built for the exclusive purpose of causing pain. On a steel cart, her toys will be spread out as neatly as surgical instruments.

When he walks through the door, she likes to have her bouncers, also dressed as Peace Officers, hurl him against the wall. They let him struggle before they handcuff him. Their uniforms are slippery as rubber. He can't get a grip on them. The uniforms are padded with the latest in wonderfabric so no matter how hard he punches them, he can't hurt them. They will drag him into the back and strip-search him in front of clients who pay for the privilege of watching. He stands under a spotlight that shines an impersonal cone of light from the ceiling. The rest of the room is darkened. He can see reflections of glasses, red-eyed cigarettes, the glint of ice clinking against glass, shadows shifting. He can hear zippers coming undone, low moans; he can smell the cum when he's beaten into passivity.

Once, he wanted to cut his hair, but she wouldn't let him, said she'd never speak to him again if he did. She likes it when the bouncers grab him by his hair and drag him to the exploratory table in the centre of the room. She says she likes the way it veils his face when he's kneeling.

In the playroom though, she changes. He can't hurt her the way she wants him to; she is tiring of him. He whips her half-heartedly until she tells the bouncer to do it properly.

A man walked in one day, in a robin's egg blue uniform, and Wil froze. When he could breathe again, when he could think, he found her watching him, thoughtful.

She borrowed the man's uniform and lay on the table, her face blank and smooth and round as a basketball under the visor. He put a painstick against the left nipple. It darkened and bruised. Her screams were muffled by the helmet. Her bouncers whispered things to her as they pinned her to the table, and he hurt her. When she begged him to stop, he moved the painstick to her right nipple.

He kept going until he was shaking so hard he had to stop.

That's enough for tonight, she said, breathless, wrapping her arms around him, telling the bouncers to leave when he started to cry. My poor virgin. It's not pain so much as it is a cleansing.

Is it, he asked her, one of those whiteguilt things?

She laughed, kissed him. Rocked him and forgave him, on the evening he discovered that it wasn't just easy to do terrible things to another person: it could give pleasure. It could give power.

She said she'd kill him if he told anyone what happened in the playroom. She has a reputation and is vaguely ashamed of her secret weakness. He wouldn't tell, not ever. He is addicted to her pain.

To distinguish it from real uniforms, hers has an inverted black triangle[1] on the left side, just over her heart: asocialism, she says with a laugh, and he doesn't get it. She won't explain it, her blue eyes black with desire as her pupils widened suddenly like a cat's.

The uniforms advancing on him, however, are clean and pure and real.

&

---

1   *inverted black triangle*  Badge given to Nazi concentration camp inmates to mark them as "asocial"—a broad category that included prostitutes, lesbians, and homeless people.

Wil wanted to be an astronaut. He bought the books, he watched the movies and he dreamed. He did well in Physics, Math, and Sciences, and his mother bragged, He's got my brains.

He was so dedicated, he would test himself, just like the astronauts on TV. He locked himself in his closet once with nothing but a bag of potato chips and a bottle of pop. He wanted to see if he could spend time in a small space, alone and deprived. It was July and they had no air conditioning. He fainted in the heat, dreamed that he was floating over the Earth on his way to Mars, weightless.

Kevin found him, dragged him from the closet, and laughed at him.

You stupid shit, he said. Don't you know anything?

When his father slid off the hood leaving a snail's trail of blood, Kevin ran out of the car.

Stop it! Kevin screamed, his face contorted in the headlight's beam. Shadows loomed over him, but he was undaunted. Stop it!

Kevin threw himself on their dad and saved his life.

Wil stayed with their father in the hospital, never left his side. He was there when the Peace Officers came and took their father's statement. When they closed the door in his face and he heard his father screaming. The nurses took him away and he let them. Wil watched his father withdraw into himself after that, never quite healing.

He knew the names of all the constellations, the distances of the stars, the equations that would launch a ship to reach them. He knew how to stay alive in any conditions, except when someone didn't want to stay alive.

No one was surprised when his father shot himself.

At the funeral potlatch, his mother split his father's ceremonial regalia between Wil and Kevin. She gave Kevin his father's frontlet.[1] He placed it immediately on his head and danced. The room became still, the family shocked at his lack of tact. When Kevin stopped dancing, she gave Wil his father's button blanket.[2] The dark wool held his smell. Wil knew then that he would never be an astronaut. He didn't have a backup dream and drifted through school, coasting on a reputation of Brain he'd stopped trying to earn.

Kevin, on the other hand, ran away and joined the Mohawk Warriors.[3] He was at Oka[4] on August 16 when the bombs rained down and the last Canadian reserve was Adjusted.

---

1   *frontlet* Headdress worn on the forehead, used in Haisla regalia.
2   *button blanket* Ceremonial wool blanket decorated with abalone buttons.
3   *Mohawk Warriors* Native activist group.
4   *Oka* Quebec town and site of the 1990 Oka Crisis, a Mohawk protest over disputed land that developed into a violent conflict with government military and police forces. The government used guns and tear gas, but did not bomb the activists.

Wil expected him to come back broken. He was ready with patience, with forgiveness. Kevin came back a Peace Officer.

Why? his aunts, his uncles, cousins, and friends asked.

How could you? his mother asked.

Wil said nothing. When his brother looked up, Wil knew the truth, even if Kevin didn't. There were things that adjusted to rapid change—pigeons, dogs, rats, cockroaches. Then there were things that didn't—panda bears, whales, flamingos, Atlantic cod, salmon, owls.

Kevin would survive the Adjustment. Kevin had found a way to come through it and be better for it. He instinctively felt the changes coming and adapted. I, on the other hand, he thought, am going the way of the dodo bird.

∞

There are rumours in the neighbourhood. No one from the Vancouver Urban Reserve #2 can get into Terminal Avenue. They don't have the money or the connections. Whispers follow him, anyway, but no one will ask him to his face. He suspects that his mother suspects. He has been careful, but he sees the questions in her eyes when he leaves for work. Someday she'll ask him what he really does and he'll lie to her.

To allay suspicion, he smuggles cigarettes and sweetgrass[1] from the downtown core to Surreycentral. This is useful, makes him friends, adds a kick to his evening train ride. He finds that he needs these kicks. Has a morbid fear of becoming dead like his father, talking and breathing and eating, but frightened into vacancy, a living blankness.

His identity card that gets him to the downtown core says *Occupation: Waiter*. He pins it to his jacket so that no one will mistake him for a terrorist and shoot him.

He is not really alive until he steps past the industrial black doors of his lover's club. Until that moment, he is living inside his head, lost in memories. He knows that he is a novelty item, a real living Indian: that is why his prices are so inflated. He knows there will come a time when he is yesterday's condom.

He walks past the club's façade, the elegant dining rooms filled with the glittering people who watch the screens or dance across the dimly-lit ballroom-sized floor. He descends the stairs where his lover waits for him with her games and her toys, where they do things that aren't sanctioned by the Purity laws, where he gets hurt and gives hurt.

---

1   *sweetgrass* Marijuana; also refers to a herb used in First Nations spiritual ceremonies.

He is greeted by his high priestess. He enters her temple of discipline and submits. When the pain becomes too much, he hallucinates. There is no preparing for that moment when reality shifts and he is free.

∞

They have formed a circle around him. Another standard intimidation tactic. The Peace Officer facing him is waiting for him to talk. He stares up at it. This will be different from the club. He is about to become an example.

*Wilson Wilson?* the Officer says. The voice sounds male but is altered by computers so it won't be recognizable.

He smiles. The name is one of his mother's little jokes, a little defiance. He has hated her for it all his life, but now he doesn't mind. He is in a forgiving mood. *Yes, that's me.*

In the silence that stretches, Wil realizes that he always believed this moment would come. That he has been preparing himself for it. The smiling-faced lies from the TV haven't fooled him, or anyone else. After the Uprisings, it was only a matter of time before someone decided to solve the Indian problem once and for all.

The Peace Officer raises his club and brings it down.

∞

His father held a potlatch before they left Kitamaat, before they came to Vancouver to earn a living, after the aluminum smelter closed.

They had to hold it in secret, so they hired three large seiners[1] for the family and rode to Monkey Beach. They left in their old beat-up speedboat, early in the morning, when the Douglas Channel was calm and flat, before the winds blew in from the ocean, turning the water choppy. The seine boats fell far behind them, heavy with people. Kevin begged and begged to steer and his father laughingly gave in.

Wil knelt on the bow and held his arms open, wishing he could take off his lifejacket. In four hours they will land on Monkey Beach and will set up for the potlatch where they will dance and sing and say goodbye. His father will cook salmon around fires, roasted the old-fashioned way: split down the centre and splayed open like butterflies, thin sticks of cedar woven through the skin to hold the fish open, the sticks planted in the sand; as the flesh darkens, the juice runs down and hisses on the fire. The smell will permeate the beach. Camouflage nets will be set up all over the beach so they won't be spotted by planes. Family will lounge under them as if they were beach umbrellas. The

---

1    *seiners* Fishing boats.

more daring of the family will dash into the water, which is still glacier-cold and shocking.

This will happen when they land in four hours, but Wil chooses to re-member the boat ride with his mother resting in his father's arm when Wil comes back from the bow and sits beside them. She is wearing a blue scarf and black sunglasses and red lipstick. She can't stop smiling even though they are going to leave home soon. She looks like a movie star. His father has his hair slicked back, and it makes him look like an otter. He kisses her, and she kisses him back.

Kevin is so excited that he raises one arm and makes the Mohawk salute they see on TV all the time. He loses control of the boat, and they swerve violently. His father cuffs Kevin and takes the wheel.

The sun rises as they pass Costi Island, and the water sparkles and shifts. The sky hardens into a deep summer blue.

The wind and the noise of the engine prevent them from talking. His father begins to sing. Wil doesn't understand the words, couldn't pronounce them if he tried. He can see that his father is happy. Maybe he's drunk on the excitement of the day, on the way that his wife touches him, tenderly. He gives Wil the wheel.

His father puts on his button blanket, rests it solemnly on his shoulders. He balances on the boat with the ease of someone who's spent all his life on the water. He does a twirl, when he reaches the bow of the speedboat and the but-ton blanket opens, a navy lotus. The abalone buttons sparkle when they catch the light. She's laughing as he poses. He dances, suddenly inspired, exuberant.

Later he will understand what his father is doing, the rules he is breaking, the risks he is taking, and the price he will pay on a deserted road, when the siren goes off and the lights flash and they are pulled over.

At the time, though, Wil is white-knuckled, afraid to move the boat in a wrong way and toss his father overboard. He is also embarrassed, wishing his father were more reserved. Wishing he was being normal instead of dancing, a whirling shadow against the sun, blocking his view of the Channel.

This is the moment he chooses to be in, the place he goes to when the club flattens him to the Surreycentral tiles. He holds himself there, in the boat with his brother, his father, his mother. The sun on the water makes pale northern lights flicker against everyone's faces, and the smell of the water is clean and salty, and the boat's spray is cool against his skin.

—1996

# *Emma Donoghue*
b. 1969

In her novels, plays, short stories, and nonfiction, Emma Donoghue investigates contemporary and historical gender roles and what she has described as the "fluidity and unpredictability of human sexuality." Influenced by writers such as Jeanette Winterson and Margaret Atwood, much of Donoghue's work is constructed around female characters who find themselves "drifting into attraction rather than discovering a crystal-clear sense of identity." While Donoghue identifies herself as a feminist, she sees herself as a writer first, arguing that "Writers should never be trusted as the political 'voices of the community' because our loyalties are generally to literature."

The daughter of a renowned literary scholar, Donoghue is also an accomplished critic in her own right. After graduating from University College Dublin with a degree in English and French literature, she left her native Ireland to pursue a doctorate at Cambridge and has since published a number of highly regarded critical studies, including *Passions between Women: British Lesbian Culture 1668–1801* (1993) and *Inseparable: Desire between Women in Literature* (2010).

Donoghue has demonstrated a particular talent for fiction based on true events, and meticulously researched novels such as *Slammerkin* (2000), the story of an eighteenth-century prostitute involved in a brutal murder, and *Room* (2010), which recounts the forced confinement of a mother and child from the child's point of view, have won her a large international popular and critical following.

# Seven Pictures Not Taken

1: Rhubarb

Climbing up the slope behind your house, returning from the river you've been showing me before your fortieth birthday party begins, digging our feet into the unashamed grassy breast of what you call your back yard (though the word yard to me means a hard paved thing), our eyes meet momentarily (by that I mean for a moment, you would mean in a moment's time). Neither of us is English, and our Englishes will always be a word or two apart. Our bodies talk better than our minds, even that first day, when our eyes are spread wide by sunlight.

I like the look of the few downy whiskers on your chin. We are standing beside the hugely overgrown rhubarb bush, some sticks as tall as us, gone black with age, others still new and pink. We both call it a rhubarb bush, good to know we can agree on something.

Though I have only just met you, I want to give you something, to make you remember me. It all begins with vanity, not generosity.

Later you will tell me that you remembered me making rhubarb crumble for your guests. But if you had not met me again, I am sure you would have forgotten my face in a week, my rhubarb crumble in another. It is only in retrospect that strangers seem instantly memorable. I know I would have remembered you, but mostly because my eyes tend to look for pictures to remember. Maybe I invented you, summoned you up as a holiday vision.

All I know is that for a week after your party I had scalding dreams of lying down together on that particular spot, that curve of sundried grass behind your house. The vertical hold becomes a horizontal flow. So by the time you actually laid hands on me, I had drawn out the whole story already.

2: River

This picture is about light on wet skin. I am watching you but the picture is of both of us. Women troop down to the water in the late afternoon; the midges hover, aroused by our heat. I pull black silk up and over my head, step through satin mud and slide in. Under the meniscus[1] I lose my shyness. I watch you as I tread water, kicking off the years. I am a newborn baby in the slip of hills.

How we met was a web of chance rivers, meandering across three continents. If A had not bumped into B in the hottest country she'd ever been in, after (or was it before?) meeting you on the west coast, then driving south with you this summer she would never have introduced you to B's ex-lover C, who happened to bring me (who had made friends with B and C half a world away) to your birthday party. It scares me that if any one of us had stepped out of any one of those streams, I would never have met you, would never even have known there was a you to meet, but I suppose I have to lie back in the current of coincidence, trusting that it has been shaped for us just as the river has been carved through the mountains to reach your house so that I can bathe in it, treading water, looking up at you. Afterwards, as we all dry ourselves on the bank, you tell me that you only own this bit of river to midstream, which must confuse it.

3: Room

The next picture is taken in the dark. No dark is ever entire, of course, there is always enough light to begin to find out shapes. We are practically strangers,

---

1    *meniscus* Here, surface of the water.

at this time of sharing a bed in our mutual friend's mother's house. You could always sleep in the other room, but as I have mentioned to you in passing, the bed there is very hard; we are in agreement that it would not be good for your bad back. This is true but also a barefaced lie. In the dark you ask me if I want to cuddle up, and I do.

In this picture, I am lying awake, marvelling at your strange weight against me, much too aware of you to move. I can't catch a breath; my arm is numb; my arthritic hip is screaming to shift position. I inch it backwards. I do not want to disturb you in case you'll twist away, with the selfishness of the half-awake. I want you to keep resting deeply, coiled around me. I decide to find out how little breath I can manage on, how long my muscles will obey me. I am glad to offer you my discomfort, even if you will never know it.

This room is so dark, fifty miles from a city; no way could a picture of this be taken with an ordinary camera. For all I know this is the only night I will ever spend in your arms.

4: Forest

We are twenty years past wasting time.

The ferns are sharp under the purple cloak I have spread for us, Walter Raleigh style.[1] Their dry fingers idly scratch our hips. Sounds of brass and woodwind leak through the woods from the concert we are missing. Sun slithers through the lattice of maples to lie across your back. My lips, drawn across your shoulder bone, find invisible fur. Desire has twitched and bitten and marked us all day as the brazen mosquitoes do now, here on the forest floor where we are lying.

Seen from high above in the canopy of leaves, we must be pale as mushrooms that have pushed up overnight. Two women, two dark heads, two dark triangles, a maze of limbs arranged by the geometry of pleasure. We press close, my hipbone wedded to your thighs, my breast quilting your ribs, to leave as little body exposed to the insects as we can.

It is hot and uncomfortable and exactly where I want to be. At certain moments what your body is doing to mine wipes away all awareness of the insect bites, the concert, the time, the other women in our pasts and futures, the other days in our lives, all other sights there are to be seen.

---

1    *purple cloak ... Raleigh style* Sir Walter Ralegh (1554–1618), a prominent courtier to Queen Elizabeth I, is said to have thrown his cloak over a puddle so that the Queen could cross without wetting her shoes.

## 5: Body

It is what you call fall, in this picture, and I persist in calling autumn, even though I'm back on your territory again. The patches on your back yard where my ecstatic hands ripped out grass in the summer are covered with leaves now.

We are sitting on your sofa looking through your photo albums in chronological order. You find it hard to believe that I am truly interested enough to turn every page. But I want the whole picture, the full hand of decades. I interrogate you through baby snaps, family crises, teenage hairstyles. I pause on one of you in the first week of your uniform, grinning with an innocent gun; it chills me. You remark that you're glad they kicked you out for being a pervert; you're finally glad. You repeat for me a line from a folk song:

> *I will not use my body as a weapon of war*
> *That's not what any body's for.*

I look at the photograph to memorize it. I wonder what this body in the albums, that has come through so many changes in front of my browsing eyes, is for. I'm going too fast. I regret, absurdly, that I was not here to see you grow up. I am having to learn it all in a weekend with the leaves dancing by the window, mocking me with their message of phoenix fire. We have so little time, the most careful picture is a snapshot.

## 6: Real

The last day of that five-day weekend, I say: I don't want to get in the way of your real life.

Life doesn't get any more real than this, you tell me.

I am momentarily content. But neither of us is sure whether any of this is happening. It seems too good to be actual. Too sure, too easy and unmixed, as bliss goes, to be anything other than some kind of trip.

Down by the river you take out your camera. We sit on rocks and lean over the water, taking turns to pose, laughing at the absurdity of our ambition to capture the moment.

But wouldn't it be worse if photos were better than the real thing? Sometimes I shut a book of fabulous pictures, and my own life seems like a puny little after-image. Better this feeling of overflow. Thank god for times like these when I remember: there is too much life to fit into art.

You take a final photo anyway, with a timer, to prove it happened, that we were in this frame together, that there was no space for light between our faces.

I almost expect the pictures to come out blank. But when you airmail them to me they are full of colour. I look at this middle-aged couple embracing against the sun-polished rocks. Already they are not us. Already they are figures in a collage. Already we are not the same.

7: Frame

In this last of the pictures I never took, it is New Year and I am standing at your window again, looking out at the mountains under their shirt of snow. I make a diamond frame with my hands to shape the picture: dark verticals of trees, angles of snow, some silver birch trees to complicate the contrast. The river is frozen black except for some swirls of white near the bank. It is a beautiful picture, but it is flattening into two dimensions already.

Having flown here for green summer and orange leaves and white snow, and not much wanting to see the mud season, I get the feeling that I am not going to be back. And it turns my stomach to watch myself framing this away, folding it over, when it is still good, before anything has actually happened to put an end to it.

I know I'm speeding, way over the limit, slapping down each image as soon as I catch it, dashing on to the next. Why the hell can't I live in the present, like my friends keep telling me to? They say youth is the hasty time, but I've been in the biggest hurry ever since I entered my forties. I have this craving to see everything I've got left.

The snow fills up the window in this picture, kindly and indifferent.

Maybe this thing needs to be over before I can see it. Maybe in my twisted way I am ending it now so that I can understand and represent it, so the story has an ending to match its beginning. Maybe (what bullshit, what cowardly bullshit), maybe this turning of my back is a version of love.

—1996

# Lynn Coady
b. 1970

Canadian novelist and journalist Lynn Coady's work has been praised for its honesty and its "shrewd examination of the underexplored byways of human psychology." "I'm trying to get at something a little transcendent between humans," she said in an interview with the *National Post*. "But at the same time, there's all that baggage: What's beautiful about humans is what's balanced by what's kind of ugly and petty and depressing."

Born in Port Hawkesbury, Nova Scotia, Coady began making up stories at a young age. She began to write in earnest when, as a young adult, she briefly worked for her hometown's social services and investigated cases of abused or neglected children. "[I]t was kind of like a Flannery O'Connor story," Coady explains, and she found the resemblance inspiring: "I wrote about a family of little girls, the kind of family that social services would be concerned about." Though Coady left Nova Scotia at 18 to attend Carleton University, she is still considered an important Atlantic Canadian writer; she edited the collection *Victory Meat: New Fiction from Atlantic Canada* in 2003.

In 1996, Coady earned an MFA in creative writing from the University of British Columbia. Her work has received much critical recognition: her first book, *Strange Heaven* (1998), was shortlisted for the Governor-General's Award; her third novel, *The Antagonist* (2011), about a hockey enforcer learning to define himself, was nominated for the Giller Prize; and two years later, Coady won the Giller for *Hellgoing* (2013), a collection whose titular story is included here. A regular contributor to *The Globe and Mail* (often writing on relationships), Coady has also published work in *Chatelaine* and *This Magazine*, and she is the founding editor of the literary magazine *Eighteen Bridges*.

# Hellgoing

Once she got back Theresa told her friends about how her father said she was overweight not even an hour into the visit. Just—boom, *you're fat*, he lays this on her. "Not, you know," said Theresa, "you look well, or you look healthy or, you know, maybe: however you might look, it's good to see you." Her friends held their faces and smiled in pain, the same way her brother had when he was sitting across the kitchen table from her with their father hunched and slurping tea between them.

Her brother had been her enemy once. Even though it was just the two of them, and only a year's difference in their age, they had never been the kind of siblings who were each other's greatest ally and defender. They weren't really each other's greatest enemy either—just petty rivals, but the rivalry was immediate and ongoing. The longer Theresa had been away as an adult, however, the nicer and better-adjusted Ricky seemed to get.

She had expected the worst when he decided to move in with their father after their mother's death and Ricky's divorce. She had expected the two men, who were so alike already, to simply merge into one horrific masculine amalgam. And end up one of those bachelor pairs of fathers and sons that she knew so well from back home, finishing each other's sentences, eating the same thing every day—cereal, cheddar, toast, bologna with ketchup—pissing in the kitchen sink because the bathroom was too far away, wiping their hands on the arms of their chairs after finishing up a meal of cereal and cheese. Served on a TV tray. A TV tray never folded and put away, never scrubbed free of solidified ketchup puddles, never not stationed in front of the chair.

But Ricky got better instead of worse—he'd refused to merge into the two-headed, tea-slurping father-thing that haunted Theresa. Maybe it had haunted Ricky too, that bogeyman—perhaps he'd steeled himself against it. He had taken to wearing ironed, button-front shirts, for example, clean ones, even around the house, instead of T-shirts and sweats. He didn't wear a ball cap anymore, which was astounding because Theresa had never seen him out of one since seventh grade—he'd spent adolescent eternities in front of the hallway mirror attempting to get the curve of the brim just right.

Theresa arrived in their childhood home to find things neat, dust-free and zero TV trays in sight. Their father was expected to come to the table when his tea was ready—he didn't get it brought to him, like their mother would have done. "I'm not here to wait on ya, buddy," Ricky would call into the living room. "Get your arse to the table." He somehow had made it a new ritual from what it was when their mother was alive—something tougher, less domestic. Just a couple of dudes drinking tea. As if coming to the table was now a minor challenge thrown down from son to father, like their dad would be sort of a pussy if he didn't rise to the occasion. She wanted to applaud at that first sight of the old man heaving himself to his feet without so much as an irritated grunt. She wanted to take her brother aside and congratulate him on it.

She told a potted version of all this to her girlfriends as they sat around drinking vodka gimlets—they were on a gimlet kick—in Dana's living room. To set them up for the climax of the story, the big outrage: *Put on a few pounds, didn't ya?* She used the pissing in the sink line to make them smile, but also to ensure they had a solid sense of where Theresa and her father stood. Ruth's father, by way of contrast, was a provincial supreme court justice, long divorced, and he and Ruth went on cruises together to a different part of the world every year, where they had pictures taken of themselves holding hands.

Theresa had packed off her girls to their dad's house and flown home for the Thanksgiving long weekend. It was a long way to come for three days, but Ricky called her and asked her.

"Jeez, Ricky," she'd said on the phone, "I'd love to, but we're into mid-terms now. I'd planned on spending the whole time marking."

"With Mom gone," Ricky interrupted—it didn't feel like an interruption so much as an ambush, a bludgeoning. He silenced her by breaking the rules of their brother-sister interactions as she'd understood them up to this point. Theresa had been busy making her breezy, half-assed excuse and out of no-where Ricky hits her with the grotesque reality of *with Mom gone*.

"With Mom gone," said Ricky, "I feel like we all have to make an extra effort here."

For years, she and Ricky were not in touch. They weren't estranged, it just never occurred to them to call each other. They sent Christmas cards, some Christmases. It took Ricky forever to get the hang of email, but once he was on email, they emailed. Ricky "wasn't much for typing," though. So they didn't email very often. Point being, Theresa knew what Ricky was saying in evoking their lack of mother—he was acknowledging that they had for years depended on their mother to give a shit on everybody else's behalf. Their mother giving a shit was the only thing that kept the family together. It was their mother who, at Christmas, made sure everyone had a present for everyone else. It was their mother who always passed the phone to Ricky when Theresa called on Christmas Eve. Their mother gave Theresa Ricky's news throughout the year (the divorce, the knee operation) and gave Ricky Theresa's (the divorce, tenure).

"The women of our mothers' generation," Theresa said to her friends. "That's what they do, right? That's their job—to give a shit so the rest of us don't have to bother—"

Jenn was sprawled on the loveseat shaking her head tightly as she spat an olive pit into her palm. "I get so mad, I get so mad," she interrupted. "My mom hauling out the address book every year and writing Christmas cards to everyone she's ever met in her life. I mean it takes her *days*. Then she carries them all over to Dad's chair for him to sign. It just—it infuriates me! Like he's had to put any effort into it whatsoever. Gavin—he doesn't get why it pisses me off so much when I'm sending a present to his mom or someone. He al-ways goes, Hey, can we go in on that together? And I'm like, No, we fucking can't! I went *shopping* for your *mother*. I put actual *thought* into it. It took me an *afternoon* of my own *free time*! And I bought her a *card* and I *wrapped* the present and I'm going to drop it off at the *post office*. Do you know why you didn't do any of that? Because it's a pain in the ass! It's *effort*! But now you wanna get in on it? No! Go and get your mother a present *yourself* if you want to send her a present."

Everybody laughed. Jenn was playing up her anger for effect, because who among them hadn't tried to get in on someone else's present, piggybacking on another, better person's kindness? Her friends were being angry in solidarity with Theresa, dredging up their own slights and outrages and laying them neatly down like place settings—napkins, knives and forks.

"So what happens when women stop giving a shit?" asked Ruth then, trying to turn things into a seminar all of a sudden. You could always hear the 'y' when Ruth said "women"—*womyn*. Just like she wrote it. They all loved Ruth, but she never "punched the clock," as Dana liked to say. Her students all adored her, because she was like them—what her friends referred to, in private, as a "true believer."

Theresa spoke next in order to shut Ruth down—to avoid the classroom discussion her question was meant to provoke and get back to her story. "The real question is," she said, "what happens when they all die off, our mothers?"

It was not the nicest way to get things back on track. Everyone else's mother but Theresa's was still alive, so every brow but her own was pinched in existential dread. But at least the attention was back on Theresa. This was her particular gift, she knew, after years of running seminars and sitting on panels. She knew how to manipulate the attention of others—to get it where she needed it to be. She knew how to be ruthless when she had to and she knew this was a trait she had inherited.

"What happens, I guess," said Theresa, "sometimes at least, is that people, sons, step up, the way Ricky has."

Ricky saw what a motherless future might hold and, by God, he took the helm. Yes, he moved in with a parent, but at least he didn't wear a ball cap anymore. (He must have looked in the mirror one day and thought: This is ridiculous. The hair is gone and everyone knows it.) And he hired a housekeeper to come in once a week—a masterstroke. And the housekeeper, she laundered the flowered armchair covers Theresa's mother had sewn years ago precisely in response to her husband's habit of wiping his food-smeared hands on the arms of the chair. It all meant that clean, orderly adulthood continued apace on Ricky's watch, with or without a mother on hand. Theresa had been fully braced for everything in her childhood home, including the dregs of her family (because what was her mother if not the best of their family, the cream, and what were Ricky, her father and Theresa herself if not the grounds at the bottom of the cup), to have gone completely to hell. But things had not gone to hell.

"Ahem," said Ricky, as they walked together down the dirt road to check the mailbox. "You don't have to sound, you know, quite so astounded."

She didn't tell this part to her friends—what she did to Ricky after what her father did to her. They walked down the road together, Theresa still vibrating. She'd been mugged, once, in Miami while taking a smoke break outside the hotel where her conference was being held, and she'd vibrated like this, exactly like this, after having her bag wrenched out of her hands by a scabbed meth-head who'd called her cunt box. "Cunt box?" Theresa had repeated in disbelief, trying to catch the meth-head's eye as they struggled—and that's when she lost her bag, because she'd been more focused on trying to prompt the scabbed man to elaborate than on maintaining her grip.

She was forty-four. *I am forty-four!* she'd sputtered at her father. She had had babies. *I have had babies! Put on some pounds? I've put on some pounds?*

Theresa had jumped out of her chair so fast it fell over. Goosed by insult—the shock of the insult, the unexpectedness of the attack. Her father sat there looking affrontedly at the overturned chair as Ricky ran a hand over his bristled head, maybe wishing for his ball cap, wishing for a brim with which to fiddle. The truth is, Theresa wanted to run across the yard into the wall of pines at the edge of her father's property, there to hide and cry.

She was the Assistant Chair of her department. She had a paper coming out in *Hypatia*.[1] She was flying to Innsbruck, Austria, in the spring to deliver that very paper. There would be another conference in Santa Cruz a few months later where she was the keynote motherfucking speaker. She was being flown down there. *I am being flown down*, she'd hacked, asphyxiating on the rest of the sentence.

"However," Theresa narrated to her friends, "who gives a shit about any of that, right? The important thing I need to know is I'm a fat piece of crap."

"Don't say that," pleaded Ruth. "Don't say 'I'm fat,' because then it's like you're agreeing with him, you're affirming it on some level."

Dana leaned forward. "Did you have an eating disorder when you were a kid?"

*"Of course* I had an eating disorder," yelled Theresa. "Who didn't have an eating disorder?"

"They push our buttons," said Jenn. "The buttons are installed at puberty and they can push them whenever they want."

"I didn't think I had the buttons anymore," said Theresa.

"We always have the buttons," said Dana.

"*They fuck you up, your mom and dad*,"[2] quoted Jenn.

It was an obvious quote, there was no other quote in the world more appropriate to quote at that moment, but Ruth jerked around, frowning. Disappointed at Jenn, because feminists weren't supposed to quote the likes of

---

1    *Hypatia*  Prominent academic journal of feminist philosophy.
2    *They ... dad*  Opening line of Philip Larkin's 1971 poem "This Be the Verse."

Philip Larkin.[1] Theresa and Dana fired a secret *true-believer* grin at each other. Theresa was finally feeling like herself again.

She didn't tell her friends about anything else—the climax of the story had been told: *Put on a few pounds, didn't ya?* Ba dum *bump.* Punchline! She didn't tell them how she tried to offload her feelings onto Ricky as they walked the dirt road. He was only trying to make her feel better with the walk. But she kept jawing on about how great the house looked, how well their father seemed ("Same old Dad!"), how monumental it was that Ricky made him get up from in front of the TV and come to the table. And hiring a house-keeper—how had he known where to look? Then it just seemed natural that she move on to Ricky himself—he was looking great! He'd stopped smoking, she noticed. He seemed so fit, so together. She was getting personal now. Was he running? Going to the gym? He was dressing better, wasn't he—had that been, like, a conscious decision at some point? When had he ditched the ball cap—she had to be honest, that was a good call. Just shave the head, rock the bald-guy thing. Everyone was doing it these days. He was looking, she told him—forty-four-year-old divorcee sister to forty-three-year-old divorcee brother—very grown up.

Which was when he told her she did not have to sound quite so astounded by it all.

She used to do this to her mother, she remembered abruptly. Because she didn't have the nerve to retaliate against her father, she would torment her mother instead. Ricky had never done that, she was sure. He protected their mother. He absorbed things like a sponge, whereas Theresa had always needed someone to pay.

"Sorry," said Theresa.

"I was married for many years," said Ricky.

"Sure, I know," said Theresa.

"So I know how to run a home, is what I'm saying."

She realized she knew nothing about her brother's married life. The woman's name was June, they had eloped to Vegas (according to Theresa's mother, who'd told her over the phone) and so there wasn't even a wedding to attend, no in-laws to meet. June was a cashier at Ricky's pharmacy. Theresa had to admit she hadn't taken a huge interest in June. The last she heard about their activities as a couple, just before she heard about the divorce, was that they'd bought a speedboat.

"June," said Ricky, "struggled with depression."

He said it like an ad, a PSA. Like he had read many pamphlets, posters on a doctor's wall.

---

1    *feminists weren't ... Larkin* Some critics have condemned Larkin as a misogynist.

"Oh," said Theresa.

"Sometimes she would go to bed for weeks."

"Whoa," said Theresa. "Jeez."

"So that was shitty," he sighed.

And now you live with Dad? Theresa wanted to say. Now you reward yourself by moving in with Dad?

"It just made me see how easy it is for people to give up," said Ricky. "You have to be vigilant."

"Yeah," said Theresa. "Well—" She had nothing insightful to say to her brother. She'd spent her life being vigilant about other things. You can only be vigilant, she thought, about a few things at a time. Otherwise it's not vigilance anymore. It starts to be more like panic.

"Well, I just think it's great, Ricky. I mean—good for you. Really."

Ricky sighed again. They had arrived at the mailbox. As they were approaching it, Theresa could see the flag wasn't up. But they walked the rest of the distance anyway and Ricky rested his hand on the box like it was the head of a faithful dog.

"You wanna check?" he said.

This was sudden childhood. The walk to the mailbox. The peek inside for mail-treasure. Because sometimes, Theresa remembered, the postman just forgot to put the flag up. Or it fell down on its own, but the mail remained within. That was the earliest lesson, when it came to vigilance, the giddiest lesson. You flew to the end of the road no matter what the flag was doing, you didn't hesitate, you stood up on your toes and had a look either way. You could never trust the flag.

—2013

# Leanne Betasamosake Simpson
## b. 1971

"When I think about my life as an Indigenous woman, one of the things that I circle back to is this feeling of being lost or fragmented which, I think, comes from the experience of the violence of colonialism," says Leanne Betasamosake Simpson, a Michi Saagiig Nishnaabeg[1] writer, scholar, and musician. Simpson addresses Canadian colonialism not only in her nonfiction writing, teaching, and activism, but also in her fiction, music, and poetry. The power of the land, including urban landscapes, is a recurring motif in her work; Simpson has written on the importance of land as a form of pedagogy in Nishnaabeg education and epistemology. She positions her work in opposition to the racist narrative that justifies colonialism by suggesting that Indigenous thought "lack[s] theory, analysis, and intellect.... Naming our intelligence is important," she says, "because it is intervention, resistance and resurgence."

Simpson is a Distinguished Visiting Professor of Sociology at Ryerson University and has taught at the Dechinta Centre for Research and Learning, though she has conducted much of her academic work as an independent scholar. In *Dancing on Our Turtle's Back: Stories of Nishnaabeg Re-Creation, Resurgence, and a New Emergence* (2011), she examines how Nishnaabeg people "can re-establish the processes by which we live who we are within the current context," which she sees as "the first step in transforming our relationship with the state." In *As We Have Always Done: Indigenous Freedom through Radical Resistance* (2017), she goes further, envisioning possibilities for cultural and political resurgence that are not based on seeking recognition from the colonizing state but are instead founded in rebuilding Indigenous intellectual traditions and relationship to place.

Simpson published her first short story collection, *Islands of Decolonial Love*, in 2013. A major influence on her creative work is traditional Indigenous fiction;[2] its importance to her work is reflected in *The Gift Is in the Making* (2013), a collection of her retellings of Anishaabeg stories. In her next fiction book, *This Accident of Being Lost* (2017), songs appear alongside tightly constructed short stories, most only a few pages long; reviewer Melanie Lefebvre has praised these stories as "incredibly economical, with each word seemingly measured and weighed with great care, producing just the right balance of sarcasm and the sacred." Simpson is also a musician; her second album, *f(l)ight*, was released in 2016.

---

1   The Michi Saagiig Nishnaabeg are a traditionally Anishinaabe-speaking First Nations people whose territory, in southern Ontario, incorporates Toronto and Peterborough.

2   "Big Water," for example, references an Earth Diver origin story. See the first chapter of Thomas King's *The Truth about Stories*, in which he tells and discusses one version of this origin story.

# Big Water

I'm lying in bed with my legs entangled in Kwe's. My chest is against the precious thin skin on her back and my arms hold her warm brown. I'm imagining us lying in smoky calm on cedar boughs instead of in this damp on Oakwood Avenue. I wish I could fall asleep like this, with her so close, but I'm too nervous when nice happens; I get more anxious than normal. I'm shallow breathing at her atlas and I'm worrying that my breath is too moist on the back of her neck and that it feels gross for her, maybe so gross that it will wake her up. So I roll over and check my phone, just in case.

There are eight new notifications from Signal, all from Niibish. She just made me switch from imessage to threema to Signal because Edward Snowden[1] tweeted that Signal is the safest texting app, mostly because the code is open source and has been independently verified. I wonder if she knows what "code" and "open source" mean, but if anyone can be trusted about these things my money's on Snowden. Also I have no idea why she cares about internet security, but she clearly does. I have to look at my iphone every four minutes so I don't miss anything because I can't get the sound notifications to work on this app even though I've googled it. To be honest, this isn't actually that big of a problem because I look at my beloved screen every four minutes, whether or not the sound notifications are on anyway. We all do and we all lie about it.

Niibish wants to know where I am, why I'm not up yet, why I'm not texting her back, and she'd like my opinion on the stories in the *Toronto Star* and *Vice* this morning about the flood. "ARE THEY GETTING IT?" is the second-last text. The last text is another "Where are you? ffs."

Niibish is mad at me for making her text me instead of doing things the old way and she's right and I promised it's just a tool and that we'll still do things the right way once this crisis is over. She typed in "PROMISE" in all caps like she was yelling. I texted back "of course," like she was insane for thinking otherwise. Kwe texts me "of course" when she wants me to think I'm insane for thinking otherwise too.

I get dressed, take the bus and then the subway to headquarters. Headquarters is high up, like Nishnaabeg Mount Olympus,[2] so we can see Lake Ontario out of the window. Only I call it headquarters—really it's just a condo at Yonge and Dundas.

---

1    *Edward Snowden* American activist (b. 1983) who, when working for the CIA, copied a large number of classified government documents and released them to journalists in order to expose secret mass surveillance being conducted by the National Security Agency.
2    *Mount Olympus* The home of the gods in Greek mythology.

We call the lake Chi'Niibish, which means big water, and we share this brilliant peacemaker with the Mohawks. I call her Niibish for short and I'm the one that got her the iphone and taught her how to text. I look out the south-facing window of the condo and see her dense blue. She is full, too full, and she's tipsy from the birth control pills, the plastics, the sewage, and the contraband that washes into her no matter what. She is too full and overflowing and no one saw this coming like no one saw Calgary flooding, even though every single one of us should have.

Five days ago she spilled over the boardwalk and flooded the Power Plant and Queens Quay, and we all got into twitter fights about the waterfront. Six days ago, she crept over the Lakeshore and drank up Union Station,[1] and we called New York City because remember the hurricane. We found new places to charge our devices. She smothered the beach. She bathed the train tracks and Oshawa[2] carpooled. She's not angry even though she looks angry. She is full. She is full of sad. She wants us to see her, to see what we're doing to her, and change. That's the same thing that Kwe wants, so I know both the problem and the solution, and I know how much brave solutions like these require.

Niibish is just sitting and thinking and sporadically texting. They call it a crest, but not confidently because she should be receding by now. The math says receding and math is always confident, even when it's dead wrong. The weather is also confident when it is happening, and the predictors are being fed a string of variables in which they can only predict unpredictability. The public is not happy.

Niibish is reflecting and no one knows how long reflecting takes or what the outcome will be. She is wondering if this is enough for us to stay woke. She is wondering what will happen if she recedes—*Will they just build a big wall? Will they just breathe relief? Will they reflect on things?*

*Should this be a Braxton Hicks warning[3] or creation?*

While she's sitting and thinking she's also talking to Binesiwag. Those guys, hey. Only around in the summer, bringing big rains and big thunder and sometimes careless lightning and the fog that lets them do the things that need to get done and no one else wants to do. There's the crucial decision,

---

1   *Power Plant* Toronto art gallery on the shore of Lake Ontario; *Queens Quay* Road immediately adjacent to Toronto's lakefront; *Union Station* Toronto's train and bus transportation hub, less than a kilometre inland. All the locations named are in downtown Toronto.

2   *Oshawa* City about 60 kilometres east of Toronto.

3   *Braxton Hicks warning* Braxton Hicks contractions, sometimes called "false labour," are contractions felt during pregnancy that can be mistaken for actual labour.

which is always the same no matter what the question: Do we make the crisis bigger or smaller or keep it just the same?

I'm getting the log ready just in case. I've gathered my crew together and we're meeting where the nude beach used to be at Hanlan's Point[1] to practise holding our breath and diving. Everyone sat on a log during the last big flood, until we came up with a plan to create a new world. Muskrat got a handful of earth from the bottom of the lake like a rock star because everyone had already tried and failed. I breathed. Turtle shared her back, and we put her name on the place in return. We all danced a new world into reality. We made Turtle Island and it wasn't so bad for a while. For a while we all got lost in the beauty of things, and the intelligence of hopeless romantics won the day. We're not so confident in our making powers this time around though. Our false consciousness is large, our anxiety set to panic, our depression waiting just around the corner. We're in a mid-life crisis, out of shape and overcompensating because it's too late to change any of that. Beaver's doing push-ups on the soggy grass. Bear's doing power squats and bragging about his seven-minute workout app and the option of having a hippie with a whistle call out the next exercise. Muskrat is in his new wetsuit doing sit-ups, and not very good ones either. I'm wandering around the island instagramming pictures of big logs, deciding which one will be ours. And I'm texting Kwe, telling her that I love her, because she likes that, telling her to just stay in bed because I'll be back soon and we almost always survive.

—2017

---

1  *Hanlan's Point* Traditionally clothing-optional beach on an island near downtown Toronto.

# David Bezmozgis
b. 1973

David Bezmozgis was born in Riga, Latvia; in 1980, at the age of six, he emigrated with his family to Canada. Writing was not considered a proper profession by Bezmozgis's Russian-Jewish parents, who thought that their son's interest in filmmaking would result in a more suitable career. Bezmozgis has since pursued both activities, but in 2010, he was named to *The New Yorker*'s "20 Under 40" list of top young writers of contemporary fiction. His fiction is informed by his family's relocation from Europe to Toronto and, in his own words, describes "the experience of arriving and assimilating."

"Tapka" illustrates this focus. It first appeared in a 2003 issue of *The New Yorker* and later became the opening piece in *Natasha and Other Stories* (2004), a collection of seven linked short stories that span the life of their narrator Mark Berman from his childhood to early adulthood. Like Bezmozgis, Mark is a Jewish immigrant who grows up in Toronto. Describing his approach to autobiographical fiction, Bezmozgis says, "It's the game that the author plays and the purpose of the game is to establish a compelling intimacy between the story contained in the narrative and the reader's own life experiences and sensibility." This collection won the Commonwealth Writers Prize for First Book and was also nominated for a Governor General's Award. *The Calgary Herald*'s Meghan O'Rourke notes that Bezmozgis's strength is his "covert subtlety" and likens his immigrant stories to those of Jhumpa Lahiri, Nathan Englander, and Aleksandar Hemon.

Since *Natasha and Other Stories*, Bezmozgis has written his first novel, *The Free World* (2011), the story of a family fleeing the Soviet Union to Rome in 1978 to escape the Iron Curtain. His most recent novel is *The Betrayers* (2014).

# Tapka

Goldfinch was flapping clotheslines, a tenement delirious with striving. 6030 Bathurst: insomniac, scheming Odessa. Cedarcroft:[1] reeking borscht in the hallways. My parents, Soviet refugees but Baltic aristocrats,[2] took an apartment at 715 Finch, fronting a ravine and across from an elementary school—one respectable block away from the Russian swarm. We lived on the fifth floor, my cousin, aunt, and uncle directly below us on the fourth. Except for the Nahu-

---

1   *Goldfinch ... Cedarcroft* Streets in the Bathurst-Finch area of northern Toronto, the site of Toronto's largest community of Russian immigrants.

2   *Soviet ... aristocrats* The Soviet Union forcibly occupied the Baltic states—Estonia, Latvia, and Lithuania—from the 1940s until 1991.

movskys, a couple in their fifties, there were no other Russians in the building. For this privilege, my parents paid twenty extra dollars a month in rent.

In March of 1980, near the end of the school year but only three weeks after our arrival in Toronto, I was enrolled in Charles H. Best Elementary. Each morning, with our house key hanging from a brown shoelace around my neck, I kissed my parents goodbye and, along with my cousin Jana, tramped across the ravine—I to the first grade, she to the second. At three o'clock, bearing the germs of a new vocabulary, we tramped back home. Together, we then waited until six for our parents to return from George Brown City College, where they were taking an obligatory six-month course in English—a course that provided them with the rudiments of communication along with a modest government stipend.

In the evenings, we assembled and compiled our linguistic bounty.

Hello, havaryew?
Red, yellow, green, blue.
May I please go to the washroom?
Seventeen, eighteen, nineteen, twenny.

Joining us most nights were the Nahumovskys. They attended the same English classes and travelled with my parents on the same bus. Rita Nahumovsky was a beautician who wore layers of makeup, and Misha Nahumovsky was a tool-and-die maker.[1] They came from Minsk and didn't know a soul in Canada. With abounding enthusiasm, they incorporated themselves into our family. My parents were glad to have them. Our life was tough, we had it hard—but the Nahumovskys had it harder. They were alone, they were older, they were stupefied by the demands of language. Being essentially helpless themselves, my parents found it gratifying to help the more helpless Nahumovskys.

After dinner, with everyone gathered on cheap stools around our table, my mother repeated the day's lessons for the benefit of the Nahumovskys and, to a slightly lesser degree, for the benefit of my father. My mother had always been an exceptional and dedicated student, and she extended this dedication to George Brown City College. My father and the Nahumovskys came to rely on her detailed notes and her understanding of the curriculum. For as long as they could, they listened attentively and groped desperately toward comprehension. When this became too frustrating, my father put on the kettle, Rita painted my mother's nails, and Misha told Soviet *anekdoti*.[2]

---

1    *tool-and-die maker* Machinist who makes tools and moulds for use in manufacturing.
2    *anekdoti* Russian: anecdotes.

In a first-grade classroom a teacher calls on her students and inquires after their nationalities. "Sasha," she says. Sasha says, "Russian." "Very good," says the teacher. "Arnan," she says. Arnan says, "Armenian." "Very good," says the teacher. "Lyubka," she says. Lyubka says, "Ukrainian." "Very good," says the teacher. And then she asks Dima. Dima says, "Jewish." "What a shame," says the teacher. "So young and already a Jew."

The Nahumovskys had no children, only a white Lhasa Apso named Tapka. The dog had lived with them for years before they emigrated and then travelled with them from Minsk to Vienna, from Vienna to Rome, and from Rome to Toronto. During our first month in the building, Tapka was in quarantine, and I saw her only in photographs. Rita had dedicated an entire album to the dog, and, to dampen the pangs of separation, she consulted the album daily. There were shots of Tapka in the Nahumovskys' old Minsk apartment, seated on the cushions of faux-Louis XIV furniture; there was Tapka on the steps of a famous Viennese palace; Tapka at the Vatican, in front of the Colosseum, at the Sistine Chapel, and under the Leaning Tower of Pisa. My mother—despite having grown up with goats and chickens in her yard—didn't like animals and found it impossible to feign interest in Rita's dog. Shown a picture of Tapka, my mother wrinkled her nose and said, "Phoo." My father also couldn't be bothered. With no English, no money, no job, and only a murky conception of what the future held, he wasn't equipped to admire Tapka on the Italian Riviera. Only I cared. Through the photographs, I became attached to Tapka and projected upon her the ideal traits of the dog I did not have. Like Rita, I counted the days until Tapka's liberation.

The day Tapka was to be released from quarantine, Rita prepared an elaborate dinner. My family was invited to celebrate the dog's arrival. While Rita cooked, Misha was banished from their apartment. For distraction, he seated himself at our table with a deck of cards. As my mother reviewed sentence construction, Misha played hand after hand of *durak*[1] with me.

"The woman loves this dog more than me. A taxi to the customs facility is going to cost us ten, maybe fifteen dollars. But what can I do? The dog is truly a sweet little dog."

When it came time to collect the dog, my mother went with Misha and Rita to act as their interpreter. With my nose to the window, I watched the taxi take them away. Every few minutes, I reapplied my nose to the window. Three hours later, the taxi pulled into our parking lot, and Rita emerged from the back seat cradling animated fur. She set the fur down on the pavement where it assumed the shape of a dog. The length of its coat concealed its legs, and, as it hovered around Rita's ankles, it appeared to have either a thousand

---

1   *durak* A popular Russian card game.

tiny legs or none at all. My head ringing "Tapka, Tapka, Tapka," I raced into the hallway to meet the elevator.

That evening, Misha toasted the dog: "This last month, for the first time in years, I have enjoyed my wife's undivided attention. But I believe no man, not even one as perfect as me, can survive so much attention from his wife. So I say, with all my heart, thank God our Tapka is back home with us. Another day and I fear I may have requested a divorce."

Before he drank, Misha dipped his pinkie finger into his vodka glass and offered it to the dog. Obediently, Tapka gave Misha's finger a thorough licking. Impressed, my uncle declared her a good Russian dog. He also gave her a lick of his vodka. I gave her a piece of my chicken. Jana rolled her a pellet of bread. Misha taught us how to dangle food just out of Tapka's reach and thereby induce her to perform a charming little dance. Rita also produced Clonchik, a red-and-yellow rag clown. She tossed Clonchik under the table, onto the couch, down the hallway, and into the kitchen; over and over, Rita called, "Tapka, get Clonchik," and, without fail, Tapka got Clonchik. Everyone delighted in Tapka's antics except my mother, who sat stiffly in her chair, her feet slightly off the floor, as though preparing herself for a mild electric shock.

After the dinner, when we returned home, my mother announced that she would no longer set foot in the Nahumovskys' apartment. She liked Rita, she liked Misha, but she couldn't sympathize with their attachment to the dog. She understood that the attachment was a consequence of their lack of sophistication and also their childlessness. They were simple people. Rita had never attended university. She could derive contentment from talking to a dog, brushing its coat, putting ribbons in its hair, and repeatedly throwing a rag clown across the apartment. And Misha, although very lively and a genius with his hands, was also not an intellectual. They were good people, but a dog ruled their lives.

Rita and Misha were sensitive to my mother's attitude toward Tapka. As a result, and to the detriment of her progress with English, Rita stopped visiting our apartment. Nightly, Misha would arrive alone while Rita attended to the dog. Tapka never set foot in our home. This meant that, in order to see her, I spent more and more time at the Nahumovskys'. Each evening, after I had finished my homework, I went to play with Tapka. My heart soared every time Rita opened the door and Tapka raced to greet me. The dog knew no hierarchy of affection. Her excitement was infectious. In Tapka's presence, I resonated with doglike glee.

Because of my devotion to the dog, and their lack of an alternative, Misha and Rita added their house key to the shoelace hanging around my neck. During our lunch break and again after school, Jana and I were charged with caring for Tapka. Our task was simple: put Tapka on her leash, walk her to the ravine, release her to chase Clonchik, and then bring her home.

Every day, sitting in my classroom, understanding little, effectively friend-less, I counted down the minutes to lunchtime. When the bell rang, I met Jana on the playground and we sprinted across the grass toward our building. In the hall, our approaching footsteps elicited panting and scratching. When I inserted the key into the lock, I felt emanations of love through the door. And once the door was open Tapka hurled herself at us, her entire body consumed with an ecstasy of wagging. Jana and I took turns embracing her, petting her, covertly vying for her favour. Free of Rita's scrutiny, we also satisfied certain anatomical curiosities. We examined Tapka's ears, her paws, her teeth, the roots of her fur, and her doggy genitals. We poked and prodded her, we threw her up in the air, rolled her over and over, and swung her by her front legs. I felt such overwhelming love for Tapka that sometimes, when hugging her, I had to restrain myself from squeezing too hard and crushing her little bones.

It was April when we began to care for Tapka. Snow melted in the ravine; sometimes it rained. April became May. Grass absorbed the thaw, turned green; dandelions and wildflowers sprouted yellow and blue; birds and insects flew, crawled, and made their characteristic noises. Faithfully and reliably, Jana and I attended to Tapka. We walked her across the parking lot and down into the ravine. We threw Clonchik and said, "Tapka, get Clonchik." Tapka always got Clonchik. Everyone was proud of us. My mother and my aunt wiped tears from their eyes while talking about how responsible we were. Rita and Misha rewarded us with praise and chocolates. Jana was seven and I was six; much had been asked of us, but we had risen to the challenge.

Inspired by everyone's confidence, we grew confident. Whereas at first we made sure to walk thirty paces into the ravine before releasing Tapka, we gradually reduced that requirement to ten paces, then five paces, until finally we released her at the grassy border between the parking lot and the ravine. We did this not because of laziness or intentional recklessness but because we wanted proof of Tapka's love. That she came when we called was evidence of her love, that she didn't piss in the elevator was evidence of her love, that she offered up her belly for scratching was evidence of her love, that she licked our faces was evidence of her love. All of this was evidence, but it wasn't proof. Proof could come in only one form. We had intuited an elemental truth: love needs no leash.

That first spring, even though most of what was said around me remained a mystery, a thin rivulet of meaning trickled into my cerebral catch basin and collected into a little pool of knowledge. By the end of May, I could sing the ABC song. Television taught me to say "What's up, Doc?" and "super-duper."

The playground introduced me to "shithead," "mental case," and "gaylord." I seized upon every opportunity to apply my new knowledge.

One afternoon, after spending nearly an hour in the ravine throwing Clonchik in a thousand different directions, Jana and I lolled in sunlit pollen. I called her shithead, mental case, and gaylord, and she responded by calling me gaylord, shithead, and mental case.

"Shithead."

"Gaylord."

"Mental case."

"Tapka, get Clonchik."

"Shithead."

"Gaylord."

"Come, Tapka-lapka."

"Mental case."

We went on like this, over and over, until Jana threw the clown and said, "Shithead, get Clonchik." Initially, I couldn't tell if she had said this on purpose or if it had merely been a blip in her rhythm. But when I looked at Jana her smile was triumphant.

"Mental case, get Clonchik."

For the first time, as I watched Tapka bounding happily after Clonchik, the profanity sounded profane.

"Don't say that to the dog."

"Why not?"

"It's not right."

"But she doesn't understand."

"You shouldn't say it."

"Don't be a baby. Come, shithead, come my dear one."

Her tail wagging with accomplishment, Tapka dropped Clonchik at my feet.

"You see, she likes it."

I held Clonchik as Tapka pawed frantically at my shins.

"Call her shithead. Throw the clown."

"I'm not calling her shithead."

"What are you afraid of, shithead?"

I aimed the clown at Jana's head and missed.

"Shithead, get Clonchik."

As the clown left my hand, Tapka, a white shining blur, oblivious to insult, was already cutting through the grass. I wanted to believe that I had intended the "shithead" exclusively for Jana, but I knew it wasn't true.

"I told you, gaylord, she doesn't care."

I couldn't help thinking, Poor Tapka. I felt moral residue and looked around for some sign of recrimination. The day, however, persisted in unimpeachable brilliance: sparrows winged overhead; bumblebees levitated above flowers; beside a lilac shrub, Tapka clamped down on Clonchik. I was amazed at the absence of consequences.

Jana said, "I'm going home."

As she started for home, I saw that she was still holding Tapka's leash. It swung insouciantly from her hand. I called after her just as, once again, Tapka deposited Clonchik at my feet.

"I need the leash."

"Why?"

"Don't be stupid. I need the leash."

"No, you don't. She comes when we call her. Even shithead. She won't run away."

Jana turned her back on me and proceeded toward our building. I called her again, but she refused to turn around. Her receding back was a blatant provocation. Guided more by anger than by logic, I decided that if Tapka was closer to Jana then the onus of responsibility would be on her. I picked up the doll and threw it as far as I could into the parking lot.

"Tapka, get Clonchik."

Clonchik tumbled through the air. I had put everything in my six-year-old arm behind the throw, which still meant that the doll wasn't going very far. Its trajectory promised a drop no more than twenty feet from the edge of the ravine. Running, her head arched to the sky, Tapka tracked the flying clown. As the doll reached its apex, it crossed paths with a sparrow. The bird veered off toward Finch Avenue, and the clown plummeted to the asphalt. When the doll hit the ground, Tapka raced past it after the bird.

A thousand times we had thrown Clonchik and a thousand times Tapka had retrieved him. But who knows what passes for a thought in the mind of a dog? One moment a Clonchik is a Clonchik, and the next moment a sparrow is a Clonchik.

I shouted at Jana to catch Tapka and then watched in abject horror as the dog, her attention fixed on the sparrow, skirted past Jana and directly into traffic. From my vantage point on the slope of the ravine, I couldn't see what happened. I saw only that Jana broke into a sprint and I heard the caterwauling of tires, followed by Tapka's shrill fractured yip.

By the time I reached the street, a line of cars already stretched a block beyond Goldfinch. At the front of the line were a brown station wagon and a pale-blue sedan blistered with rust. As I neared, I noted the chrome letters on the back of the sedan: D-U-S-T-E-R. In front of the sedan, Jana kneeled in a tight semicircle with a pimply young man and an older woman with very large sunglasses. Tapka lay on her side at the centre of their circle. She panted in quick shallow bursts. She stared impassively at me, at Jana. Except for a hind leg twitching at the sky at an impossible angle, she seemed completely unharmed. She looked much as she did when she rested on the rug at the Nahumovskys' apartment after a vigorous romp in the ravine.

Seeing her this way, barely mangled, I felt a sense of relief. I started to convince myself that things weren't as bad as I had feared, and I tentatively edged forward to pet her. The woman in the sunglasses said something in a restrictive tone that I neither understood nor heeded. I placed my hand on Tapka's head, and she responded by opening her mouth and allowing a trickle of blood to escape onto the asphalt. This was the first time I had ever seen dog blood, and I was struck by the depth of its colour. I hadn't expected it to be red, although I also hadn't expected it to be not-red. Set against the grey asphalt and her white coat, Tapka's blood was the red I envisioned when I closed my eyes and thought: red.

I sat with Tapka until several dozen car horns demanded that we clear the way. The woman with the large sunglasses ran to her station wagon, returned with a blanket, and scooped Tapka off the street. The pimply young man stammered a few sentences, of which I understood nothing except the word "sorry." Then we were in the back seat of the station wagon with Tapka in Jana's lap. The woman kept talking until she finally realized that we couldn't understand her at all. As we started to drive off, Jana remembered something. I motioned for the woman to stop the car and scrambled out. Above the atonal chorus of car horns, I heard: "Mark, get Clonchik."

I ran and got Clonchik.

For two hours, Jana and I sat in the reception area of a small veterinary clinic in an unfamiliar part of town. In another room, with a menagerie of afflicted creatures, Tapka lay in traction, connected to a blinking machine by a series of tubes. Jana and I had been allowed to see her once but were rushed out when we both burst into tears. Tapka's doctor, a woman wearing a white coat and furry slippers resembling bear paws, tried to calm us down. Again, we could neither explain ourselves nor understand what she was saying. We managed only to establish that Tapka was not our dog. The doctor gave us colouring books, stickers, and access to the phone. Every fifteen minutes, we called home. Between phone calls, we absently flipped pages and sniffled for Tapka and for ourselves. We had no idea what would happen to Tapka; all we knew was that she wasn't dead. As for ourselves, we already felt punished and knew only that more punishment was to come.

"Why did you throw Clonchik?"

"Why didn't you give me the leash?"

"You could have held on to her collar."

"You shouldn't have called her shithead."

At six-thirty, my mother picked up the phone. I could hear the agitation in her voice. The ten minutes she had spent at home not knowing where I was had taken their toll. For ten minutes, she had been the mother of a dead child. I explained to her about the dog and felt a twinge of resentment when she said, "So it's only the dog?" Behind her I heard other voices. It sounded as though everyone were speaking at once, pursuing personal agendas, translating the phone conversation from Russian to Russian until one anguished voice separated itself: "My God, what happened?" Rita.

After getting the address from the veterinarian, my mother hung up and ordered another expensive taxi. Within a half hour, my parents, my aunt, and Misha and Rita pulled up at the clinic. Jana and I waited for them on the sidewalk. As soon as the taxi doors opened, we began to sob uncontrollably, partly out of relief but mainly in the hope of engendering sympathy. I ran to my mother and caught sight of Rita's face. Her face made me regret that I also hadn't been hit by a car.

As we clung to our mothers, Rita descended upon us.

"Children, what, oh, what have you done?"

She pinched compulsively at the loose skin of her neck, raising a cluster of pink marks.

While Misha methodically counted individual bills for the taxi-driver, we swore on our lives that Tapka had simply got away from us. That we had minded her as always but, inexplicably, she had seen a bird and bolted from the ravine and into the road. We had done everything in our power to catch her, but she had surprised us, eluded us, been too fast.

Rita considered our story.

"You are liars. Liars!"

She uttered the words with such hatred that we again burst into sobs.

My father spoke in our defence.

"Rita Borisovna, how can you say this? They are children."

"They are liars. I know my Tapka. Tapka never chased birds. Tapka never ran from the ravine."

"Maybe today she did?"

"Liars."

Having delivered her verdict, she had nothing more to say. She waited anxiously for Misha to finish paying the driver.

"Misha, enough already. Count it a hundred times, it will still be the same."

Inside the clinic, there was no longer anyone at the reception desk. During our time there, Jana and I had watched a procession of dyspeptic cats and lethargic parakeets disappear into the back rooms for examination and diagnosis. One after another they had come and gone until, by the time of our parents' arrival, the waiting area was entirely empty and the clinic officially closed. The only people remaining were a night nurse and the doctor in the bear-paw slippers, who had stayed expressly for our sake.

Looking desperately around the room, Rita screamed, "Doctor! Doctor!" But when the doctor appeared she was incapable of making herself understood. Haltingly, with my mother's help, it was communicated to the doctor that Rita wanted to see her dog. Pointing vigorously at herself, Rita asserted, "Tapka. Mine dog."

The doctor led Rita and Misha into the veterinary version of an intensive-care ward. Tapka lay on her little bed, Clonchik resting directly beside her. At the sight of Rita and Misha, Tapka weakly wagged her tail. Little more than an hour had elapsed since I had seen her last, but somehow over the course of that time Tapka had shrunk considerably. She had always been a small dog, but now she looked desiccated. She was the embodiment of defeat. Rita started to cry, grotesquely smearing her mascara. With trembling hands, and with sublime tenderness, she stroked Tapka's head.

"My God, my God, what has happened to you, my Tapkochka?"

Through my mother, and with the aid of pen and paper, the doctor provided the answer. Tapka required two operations. One for her leg. Another to stop internal bleeding. An organ had been damaged. For now, a machine was helping her, but without the machine she would die. On the paper, the doctor drew a picture of a scalpel, of a dog, of a leg, of an organ. She made an arrow pointing at the organ and drew a teardrop and coloured it in to represent blood. She also wrote down a number preceded by a dollar sign. The number was fifteen hundred.

At the sight of the number, Rita let out a low animal moan and steadied herself against Tapka's little bed. My parents exchanged a glance. I looked at the floor. Misha said, "My dear God." The Nahumovskys and my parents each took in less than five hundred dollars a month. We had arrived in Canada with almost nothing, a few hundred dollars, which had all but disappeared on furniture. There were no savings. Fifteen hundred dollars. The doctor could just as well have written a million.

In the middle of the intensive-care ward, Rita slid down to the floor and wailed. Her head thrown back, she appealed to the fluorescent lights: "*Nu, Tapkochka, what is going to become of us?*"

I looked up from my feet and saw horror and bewilderment on the doctor's face. She tried to put a hand on Rita's shoulder, but Rita violently shrugged it off.

My father attempted to intercede.

"Rita Borisovna, I understand that it is painful, but it is not the end of the world."

"And what do you know about it?"

"I know that it must be hard, but soon you will see.... Even tomorrow we could go and help you find a new one."

My father looked to my mother for approval, to insure that he had not promised too much. He needn't have worried.

"A new one? What do you mean, a new one? I don't want a new one. Why don't you get yourself a new son? A new little liar? How about that? New. Everything we have now is new. New everything."

On the linoleum floor, Rita keened, rocking back and forth. She hiccupped, as though hyperventilating. Pausing for a moment, she looked up at my mother and told her to translate for the doctor. To tell her that she would not let Tapka die.

"I will sit here on this floor forever. And if the police come to drag me out I will bite them."

"Ritochka, this is crazy."

"Why is it crazy? My Tapka's life is worth more than a thousand dollars. Because we don't have the money, she should die here? It's not her fault."

Seeking rationality, my mother turned to Misha—Misha who had said nothing all this time except "My dear God."

"Misha, do you want me to tell the doctor what Rita said?"

Misha shrugged philosophically.

"Tell her or don't tell her, you see my wife has made up her mind. The doctor will figure it out soon enough."

"And you think this is reasonable?"

"Sure. Why not? I'll sit on the floor, too. The police can take us both to jail. Besides Tapka, what else do we have?"

Misha sat on the floor beside his wife.

I watched as my mother struggled to explain to the doctor what was happening. With a mixture of words and gesticulations, she got the point across. The doctor, after considering her options, sat down on the floor beside Rita and Misha. Once again, she tried to put her hand on Rita's shoulder. This time, Rita, who was still rocking back and forth, allowed it. Misha rocked in time to his wife's rhythm. So did the doctor. The three of them sat in a line, swaying together, like campers at a campfire. Nobody said anything. We looked at each other. I watched Rita, Misha, and the doctor swaying and swaying. I became mesmerized by the swaying. I wanted to know what would happen to Tapka; the swaying answered me.

The swaying said: Listen, shithead, Tapka will live. The doctor will perform the operation. Either money will be found or money will not be necessary.

I said to the swaying: This is very good. I love Tapka. I meant her no harm. I want to be forgiven.

The swaying replied: There is reality and then there is truth. The reality is that Tapka will live. But, let's be honest, the truth is you killed Tapka. Look at Rita; look at Misha. You see, who are you kidding? You killed Tapka and you will never be forgiven.

—2003

# Hassan Blasim

b. 1973

Born in Iraq, Hassan Blasim is a filmmaker and the author of two acclaimed—and provocative—collections of Arabic short stories. While he tells the stories of Iraqis both in Iraq and abroad, Blasim's focus is not, he says, "the big events that lots of writers and journalists talk about; I'm more interested in the marginal events that don't get talked about." The resulting fiction is, in the words of the critic Boyd Tonkin, "[o]ften surreal in style and savage in detail, but always planted in heart-breaking reality."

Blasim studied filmmaking at the Academy of Cinematic Arts in Baghdad. After his politically subversive films began to draw the attention of government informants, he was urged by his instructors to leave the city. He lived for a period in Iraqi Kurdistan, where he shot the drama *Wounded Camera* (2004) under a pseudonym, but ultimately fled to Europe, settling in Finland. His first collection of short fiction, written in Arabic but published first in English as *The Madman of Freedom Square* (2009), offers dark, macabre, and surreal stories addressing matters of cultural integration, personal identity, trauma, refugee life, and madness. Blasim's second collection, *The Iraqi Christ* (2014), which won the Independent Foreign Fiction Prize, maintains his violently surreal style.

Though he still writes in his native Arabic, Blasim's taboo-breaking stories have been met with criticism and censorship in Arabic countries; his first collection, for example, was not published in the original language until 2012, with some of the most controversial content altered, and it was banned in Jordan upon its publication. English translations of his work, however, continue to be celebrated. The *Guardian* critic Robin Yassin-Kassab has described Blasim's writing as "tight, intelligent, urgent in each word," calling him "perhaps the best writer of Arabic fiction alive."

## The Nightmare of Carlos Fuentes[1]

In Iraq his name was Salim Abdul Husain and he worked for the municipality in the cleaning department, part of a group assigned by the manager to clear up in the aftermath of explosions.[2] He died in Holland in 2009 under another name: Carlos Fuentes.

---

1   *The Nightmare of Carlos Fuentes* Translated by Jonathan Wright; *Carlos Fuentes* Prominent Mexican author and political figure (1928–2012).

2   *aftermath of explosions* Iraq was invaded in 2003 by a group of countries led by the United States; the resulting war led to years of violence and political instability in the country.

Bored and disgusted as on every miserable day, Salim and his colleagues were sweeping a street market after a petrol tanker had exploded nearby, incinerating chickens, fruit and vegetables, and some people. They were sweeping the market slowly and cautiously for fear they might sweep up with the debris any human body parts left over. But they were always looking for an intact wallet or perhaps a gold chain, a ring or a watch which could still tell the time. Salim was not as lucky as his colleagues in finding the valuables left over from death. He needed money to buy a visa to go to Holland and escape this hell of fire and death. His only lucky find was a man's finger with a valuable silver ring of great beauty. Salim put his foot over the finger, bent down carefully, and with disgust pulled the silver ring off. He picked up the finger and put it in a black bag where they collected all the body parts. The ring ended up on Salim's finger and he would contemplate the gemstone in surprise and wonder, and in the end he abandoned the idea of selling it. Might one say that he felt a secret spiritual relationship with the ring?

When he applied for asylum in Holland he also applied to change his name: from Salim Abdul Husain to Carlos Fuentes. He explained his request to the official in the immigration department on the grounds that he was frightened of the fanatical Islamist groups, because his request for asylum was based on his work as a translator for the U.S. forces and his fear that someone might assassinate him as a traitor to his country. Salim had consulted his cousin who lived in France about changing his name. He called him on his mobile from the immigration department because Salim had no clear idea of a new foreign name that would suit him. In his flat in France his cousin was taking a deep drag on a joint when Salim called. Suppressing a laugh, his cousin said: "You're quite right. It's a hundred times better to be from Senegal or China than it is to have an Arab name in Europe. But you couldn't possibly have a name like Jack or Stephen, I mean a European name. Perhaps you should choose a brown name—a Cuban or Argentine name would suit your complexion, which is the colour of burnt barley bread." His cousin was looking through a pile of newspapers in the kitchen as he continued the conversation on the phone, and he remembered that two days earlier he had read a name, perhaps a Spanish name, in a literary article of which he did not understand much. Salim thanked his cousin warmly for the help he had given him and wished him a happy life in the great country of France.

Carlos Fuentes was very happy with his new name and the beauty of Amsterdam made him happy too. Fuentes wasted no time. He joined classes to learn Dutch and promised himself he would not speak Arabic from then on, or mix with Arabs or Iraqis, whatever happened in life. "Had enough of misery, backwardness, death, shit, piss, and camels," he said to himself. In the first year of his new life Fuentes let nothing pass without comparing it with the state of affairs in his original country, sometimes in the form of a question, sometimes as an exclamation. He would walk down the street muttering to himself sulkily and enviously: "Look how clean the streets are! Look at the toilet seat, it's sparkling clean! Why can't we eat like them? We gobble down our food as though it's about to disappear. If this girl wearing a short skirt and showing her legs were now walking across Eastern Gate Square,[1] she would disappear in an instant. She would only have to walk ten yards and the ground would swallow her up. Why are the trees so green and beautiful, as though they're washed with water every day? Why can't we be peaceful like them? We live in houses like pig sties while their houses are warm, safe, and colourful. Why do they respect dogs as much as humans? Why do we masturbate twenty-four hours a day? How can we get a decent government like theirs?" Everything Carlos Fuentes saw amazed him and humiliated him at the same time, from the softness of the toilet paper in Holland to the parliament building protected only by security cameras.

Carlos Fuentes's life went on as he had planned it. Every day he made progress in burying his identity and his past. He always scoffed at the immigrants and other foreigners who did not respect the rules of Dutch life and who complained all the time. He called them "retarded gerbils." They work in restaurants illegally, they don't pay taxes, and they don't respect any law. They are Stone Age savages. They hate the Dutch, who have fed and housed them. He felt he was the only one who deserved to be adopted by this compassionate and tolerant country, and that the Dutch government should expel all those who did not learn the language properly and anyone who committed the slightest misdemeanor, even crossing the street in violation of the safety code. Let them go shit there in their shitty countries.

After learning Dutch in record time, to the surprise of everyone who knew him, Carlos Fuentes worked non-stop, paid his taxes, and refused to live on welfare. The highlight of his efforts to integrate his mind and spirit into Dutch society came when he acquired a goodhearted Dutch girlfriend who loved and respected him. She weighed 90 kilos and had childlike features, like a cartoon character. Fuentes tried hard to treat her as a sensitive and liberated man would, like a Western man, in fact a little more so. Of course he always introduced himself as someone of Mexican origin whose father had left his country and settled in Iraq to work as an engineer with the oil companies. Carlos liked to describe the Iraqi people as an uncivilized and backward people who did not know what humanity means. "They are just savage clans," he would say.

Because of his marriage to a Dutch woman, his proficiency in Dutch, his enrolment in numerous courses on Dutch culture and history, and the fact

---

1    *Eastern Gate Square* Area in central Baghdad.

that he had no legal problems or criminal record in his file, he was able to obtain Dutch citizenship sooner than other immigrants could even dream of, and Carlos Fuentes decided to celebrate every year the anniversary of the day he became a Dutch national. Fuentes felt that his skin and blood had changed forever and that his lungs were now breathing real life. To strengthen his determination he would always repeat: "Yes, give me a country that treats me with respect, so that I can worship it all my life and pray for it." That's how things were until the dream problem began and everything fell to pieces, or as they say, proverbs and old adages do not wear out; it's only man that wears out. The wind did not blow fair for Fuentes. The first of the dreams was grim and distressing. In the dream he was unable to speak Dutch. He was standing in front of his Dutch boss and speaking to him in an Iraqi dialect, which caused him great concern and a horrible pain in his head. He would wake up soaked in sweat, then burst into tears. At first he thought they were just fleeting dreams that would inevitably pass. But the dreams continued to assail him without mercy. In his dreams he saw a group of children in the poor district where he was born, running after him and making fun of his new name. They were shouting after him and clapping: "Carlos the coward, Carlos the sissy, Carlos the silly billy." These irritating dreams evolved night after night into terrifying nightmares. One night he dreamt that he had planted a car bomb in the centre of Amsterdam. He was standing in the courtroom, ashamed and embarrassed. The judges were strict and would not let him speak Dutch, with the intent to humiliate and degrade him. They fetched him an Iraqi translator, who asked him not to speak in his incomprehensible rustic accent, which added to his agony and distress.

Fuentes began to sit in the library for hours looking through books about dreams. On his first visit he came across a book called *The Forgotten Language*, by Erich Fromm.[1] He did not understand much of it and he did not like the opinions of the writer, which he could not fully grasp because he had not even graduated from middle school. "This is pure bullshit," Fuentes said as he read Fromm's book: "We are free when we are asleep, in fact freer than we are when awake.... We may resemble angels in that we are not subject to the laws of reality. During sleep the realm of necessity recedes and gives way to the realm of freedom. The existence of the ego becomes the only reference point for thoughts and feelings."

Feeling a headache, Fuentes put the book back. How can we be free when we cannot control our dreams? What nonsense! Fuentes asked the librarian If

---

1    *Erich Fromm* German psychoanalyst and philosopher whose book *The Forgotten Language: An Introduction to the Understanding of Dreams, Fairytales, and Myths* (1951) argues that dreams and myths employ a universal language of symbols.

there were any simple books on dreams. The librarian did not understand his question properly, or else she wanted to show off how cultured and well-read she was on the subject. She told him of a book about the connection between dreams and food and how one sleeps, then she started to give him more information and advice. She also directed him to a library that had specialist magazines on the mysteries of the world of dreams.

Fuentes's wife had noticed her husband's strange behaviour, as well as the changes in his eating and sleeping habits and in when he went into and came out of the bathroom. Fuentes no longer, for example, ate sweet potato, having previously liked it in all its forms. He was always buying poultry meat, which was usually expensive. Of course his wife did not know he had read that eating any root vegetable would probably be the cause of dreams related to a person's past and roots. Eating the roots of plants has an effect different from that of eating fish, which live in water, or eating the fruits of trees. Fuentes would sit at the table chewing each piece of food like a camel, because he had read that chewing it well helps to get rid of nightmares. He had read nothing about poultry meat, for example, but he just guessed that eating the fowls of the air might bring about dreams that were happier and more liberated.

In all his attempts to better integrate his dreams with his new life, he would veer between what he imagined and the information he found in books. In the end he came to this idea: his ambition went beyond getting rid of troublesome dreams; he had to control the dreams, to modify them, purge them of all their foul air, and integrate them with the salubrious rules of life in Holland. The dreams must learn the new language of the country so that they could incorporate new images and ideas. All the old gloomy and miserable faces had to go. So Fuentes read more and more books and magazines about the mysteries of sleep and dreams according to a variety of approaches and philosophies. Fuentes also gave up sleeping naked and touching his wife's naked skin. In bed he began to wear a thick woolen overcoat, which gave rise to arguments with his wife, and so he had to go to the sitting room and sleep on the sofa. Nakedness attracts the sleeper to the zone of childhood, that's what he read too. Every day at 12:05 exactly he would go and have a bath and after coming out of the bathroom he would sit at the kitchen table and take some drops of jasmine oil. Before going to bed at night he would write down on a piece of paper the main calmative foodstuffs which he would buy the following day. This state of affairs went on for more than a month and Fuentes did not achieve good results. But he was patient and his will was invincible. As the days passed he started to perform mysterious secret rituals: He would dye his hair and his toenails green and sleep on his stomach repeating obscure words. One night he painted his face like an American Indian, slept wearing diaphanous orange pyjamas, and put under his pillow three feathers taken from various birds.

Fuentes's dignity did not permit him to tell his wife what was happening to him. He believed it was his problem and he could overcome it, since in the past he had survived the most trying and miserable conditions. In return his wife was more indulgent of his eccentric behaviour, because she had not forgotten how kind and generous he was. She decided to give him another chance before intervening and putting an end to what was happening. On one beautiful summer night Carlos Fuentes was sleeping in a military uniform with a toy plastic rifle by his side. As soon as he began to dream, a wish he had long awaited came true for the first time: he realized in his dream that he was dreaming. This was exactly what he had been seeking, to activate his conscious mind inside the dream so that he could sweep out all the rubbish of the unconscious. In the dream he was standing in front of the door to an old building that looked as though it had been ravaged by fire in its previous life. The building was in central Baghdad. What annoyed him was seeing things through the telescopic sights of the rifle he was holding in his hands. Fuentes broke through the door of the building and went into one flat after another, mercilessly wiping out everyone inside. Even the children did not survive the bursts of bullets. There was screaming, panic and chaos. But Fuentes had strong nerves and picked off his victims with skill and precision. He was worried he might wake up before he had completed his mission, and he thought, "If I had some hand grenades I could very soon finish the job in this building and move on to somewhere else." But on the sixth floor a surprise hit him when he stormed the first flat and found himself face to face with Salim Abdul Husain! Salim was standing naked next to the window, holding a broom stained with blood. With a trembling hand Fuentes aimed his rifle at Salim's head. Salim began to smile and repeated in derision: "Salim the Dutchman, Salim the Mexican, Salim the Iraqi, Salim the Frenchman, Salim the Indian, Salim the Pakistani, Salim the Nigerian ..."

Fuentes's nerves snapped and he panicked. He let out a resounding scream and started to spray Salim Abdul Husain with bullets, but Salim jumped out the window and not a single bullet hit him.

When Fuentes's wife woke up to the scream and stuck her head out the window, Carlos Fuentes was dead on the pavement and a pool of blood was spreading slowly under his head. Perhaps Fuentes would have forgiven the Dutch newspapers, which wrote that an Iraqi man had committed suicide at night by jumping from a sixth floor window, instead of writing that a Dutch national had committed suicide. But he will never forgive his brothers, who had his body taken back to Iraq and buried in the cemetery in Najaf. The most beautiful part of the Carlos Fuentes story, however, is the image captured by an amateur photographer who lived close to the scene of the incident. The young man took the picture from a low angle. The police had covered the body and the only part that protruded from under the blue sheet was his outstretched right hand. The picture was in black and white, but the stone in the ring on Carlos Fuentes's finger glowed red in the foreground, like a sun in hell.

—2009

# Anders Nilsen
b. 1973

American author and artist Anders Nilsen is known for comics that confront what he calls "big, complicated things"—the major philosophical issues underlying human existence. *Big Questions* (1999–2011) is the title of one of his most ambitious and acclaimed books: a 600-page illustrated fable that follows a community of birds and their interactions with a stranded pilot in the aftermath of a plane crash. Many of Nilsen's works, like *Big Questions*, adopt the tone of a parable set in bleak, abstracted landscapes reminiscent of absurdist theatre, and some draw their inspiration from religious or mythological figures. In other books, he has explored questions of life and death in a more directly personal way: *Don't Go Where I Can't Follow* (2006) recounts the death by cancer of his fiancée, Cheryl Weaver, and *The End* (2007–13) details his subsequent grief.

Nilsen was raised in Minneapolis and New Hampshire by "hippie" parents—his father was an artist and his mother, a librarian, gave him some of his first underground comics. He studied fine arts at the University of New Mexico and the Art Institute of Chicago, but cites as his main influences the cartoonist Chester Brown and Hergé, the creator of Tintin. In his own art style, Nilsen is best known for meticulous line drawing, though he has used a range of approaches to suit specific works; his "stream of consciousness" collection *Monologues for the Coming Plague* (2006), for example, employs a scribbling style, while *Don't Go Where I Can't Follow* makes use of collage materials from his life with Weaver.

*Big Questions* won the Lynd Ward Graphic Novel Prize and was a *New York Times* Notable Book for 2011, and Nilsen has also received three Ignatz Awards, which recognize excellence in comics or cartoons. In addition to his eight books, Nilsen has published shorter pieces in *Poetry* magazine, *Pitchfork Media*, *Medium*, and elsewhere. "Towards a Conceptual Framework ..." first appeared in the *New York Times*'s Opinionator section in 2014, as part of the paper's series of commissioned memoir comics. Nilsen classifies the piece as a "universal memoir," calling it "a slightly absurdist attempt to put one's own life into the largest of all possible contexts without losing sight of its deep personal meaning and importance."

## TOWARD A CONCEPTUAL FRAMEWORK FOR UNDERSTANDING YOUR INDIVIDUAL RELATIONSHIP TO THE TOTALITY OF THE UNIVERSE IN FOUR SIMPLE DIAGRAMS

### 1. THE PAST (COSMIC, NOT TO SCALE)

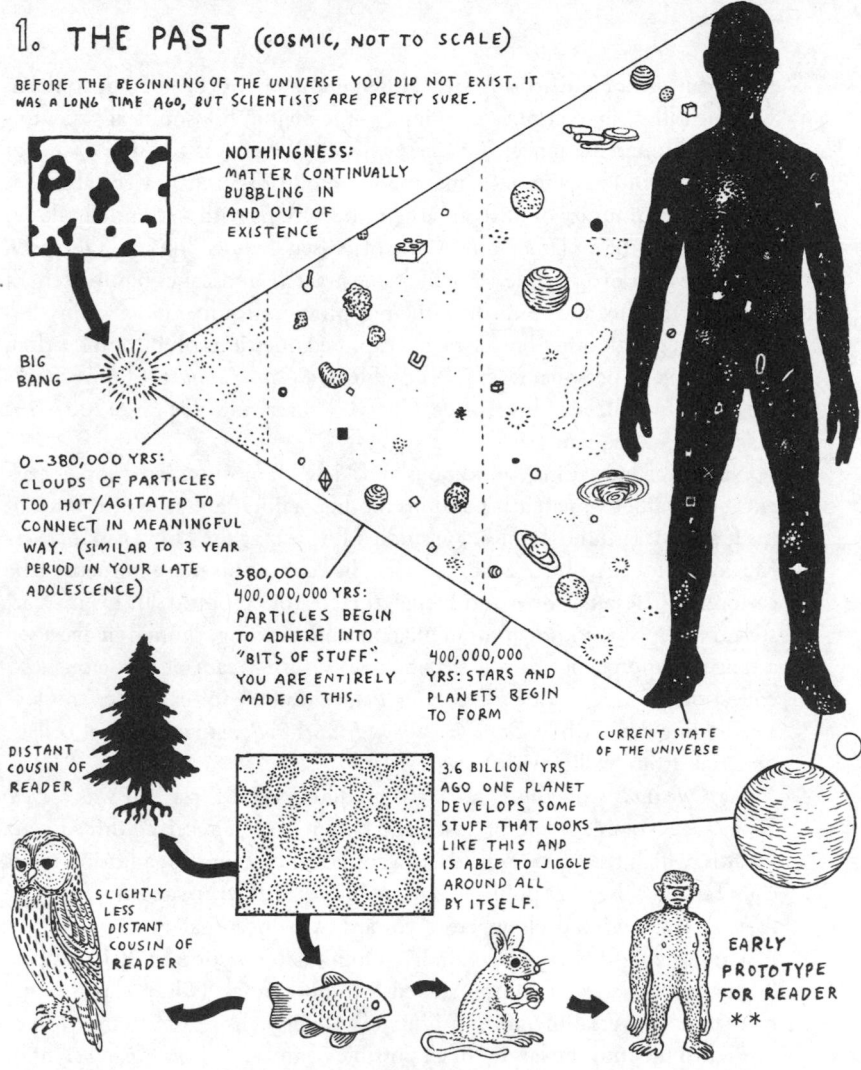

BEFORE THE BEGINNING OF THE UNIVERSE YOU DID NOT EXIST. IT WAS A LONG TIME AGO, BUT SCIENTISTS ARE PRETTY SURE.

NOTHINGNESS: MATTER CONTINUALLY BUBBLING IN AND OUT OF EXISTENCE

BIG BANG

0-380,000 YRS: CLOUDS OF PARTICLES TOO HOT/AGITATED TO CONNECT IN MEANINGFUL WAY. (SIMILAR TO 3 YEAR PERIOD IN YOUR LATE ADOLESCENCE)

380,000 400,000,000 YRS: PARTICLES BEGIN TO ADHERE INTO "BITS OF STUFF". YOU ARE ENTIRELY MADE OF THIS.

400,000,000 YRS: STARS AND PLANETS BEGIN TO FORM

CURRENT STATE OF THE UNIVERSE

DISTANT COUSIN OF READER

SLIGHTLY LESS DISTANT COUSIN OF READER

3.6 BILLION YRS AGO ONE PLANET DEVELOPS SOME STUFF THAT LOOKS LIKE THIS AND IS ABLE TO JIGGLE AROUND ALL BY ITSELF.

EARLY PROTOTYPE FOR READER **

# 2. THE PAST

GEOLOGICAL/ EVOLUTIONARY SCALE

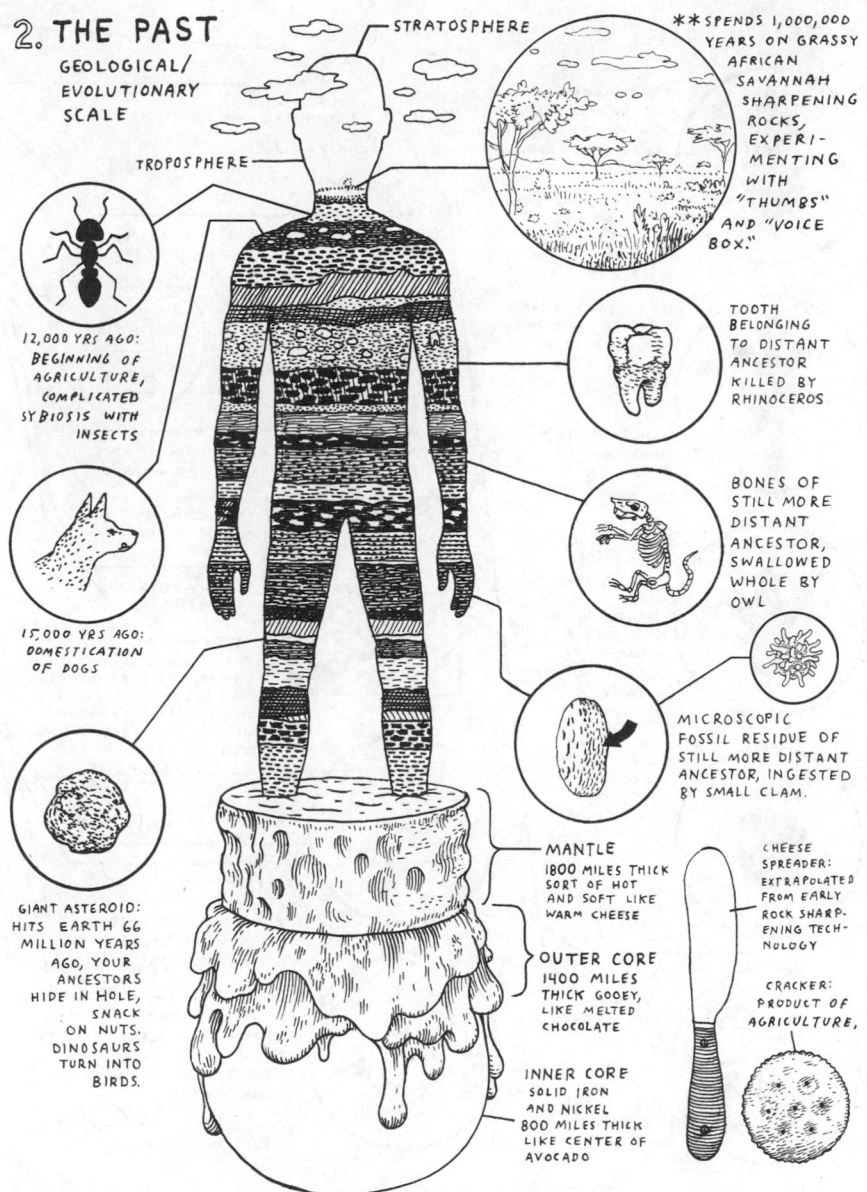

STRATOSPHERE

\*\* SPENDS 1,000,000 YEARS ON GRASSY AFRICAN SAVANNAH SHARPENING ROCKS, EXPERIMENTING WITH "THUMBS" AND "VOICE BOX."

TROPOSPHERE

12,000 YRS AGO: BEGINNING OF AGRICULTURE, COMPLICATED SYBIOSIS WITH INSECTS

TOOTH BELONGING TO DISTANT ANCESTOR KILLED BY RHINOCEROS

BONES OF STILL MORE DISTANT ANCESTOR, SWALLOWED WHOLE BY OWL

15,000 YRS AGO: DOMESTICATION OF DOGS

MICROSCOPIC FOSSIL RESIDUE OF STILL MORE DISTANT ANCESTOR, INGESTED BY SMALL CLAM.

GIANT ASTEROID: HITS EARTH 66 MILLION YEARS AGO, YOUR ANCESTORS HIDE IN HOLE, SNACK ON NUTS. DINOSAURS TURN INTO BIRDS.

MANTLE 1800 MILES THICK SORT OF HOT AND SOFT LIKE WARM CHEESE

OUTER CORE 1400 MILES THICK GOOEY, LIKE MELTED CHOCOLATE

INNER CORE SOLID IRON AND NICKEL 800 MILES THICK LIKE CENTER OF AVOCADO

CHEESE SPREADER: EXTRAPOLATED FROM EARLY ROCK SHARPENING TECHNOLOGY

CRACKER: PRODUCT OF AGRICULTURE,

# 3. THE PRESENT (MORE OR LESS)

1903 - ANNA BREKHUS, AGE 16, RECEIVES LETTER IN NORWAY FROM AMERICAN COUSIN: "MY HUSBAND HAS A BROTHER."

BECOMES YOUR GREAT-GRANDMOTHER.

1906 - ANNA NILSEN EXPELLED FROM CANADA FOR ASSAULTING POLICE OFFICER DURING STRIKE.

BECOMES YOUR OTHER GREAT-GRANDMOTHER.

1972 - EN ROUTE FROM SAN FRANCISCO TO ERIE, PENNSYLVANIA YOUR MOTHER TO YOUR FATHER: "I DON'T WANT TO BE IN THE COMMUNE ANYMORE."

1973 - YOU ARE CONCEIVED ON LONG, COLD WINTER NIGHT DURING SNOW STORM. CELLS BEGIN DIVIDING ACCORDING TO ANCIENT PATTERN.

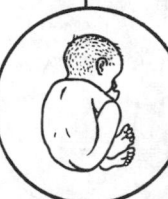

1973 - YOU ARE BORN.

U.S. PULLS OUT OF VIETNAM.

1977-1979 - YOU GRADUALLY BECOME SELF-AWARE.

PUNK ROCK INVENTED.

GENOCIDE IN CAMBODIA.

1981 - YOU PRACTICE DRAWING SPACESHIPS, DINOSAURS, GIANT DIAGRAMMATIC BATTLE SCENES.

RONALD REAGAN SHOT.

1983 - YOU ARE CAUGHT SHOP LIFTING LEGOS AT TARGET.

1984 - CLASSMATE PUNCHES YOU IN STOMACH FOLLOWING COMMENT RE: HIS MOTHER.

YOU GO THROUGH BRIEF CRIMINAL PHASE:

1986 - STEAL FIRST HOOD ORNAMENT.

1987 - STEAL SUNGLASSES, CANDY, CASSETTE TAPES, UMBRELLA. ALMOST CAUGHT STEALING EXPENSIVE CHOCOLATE, GIVE FALSE NAME TO MALL SECURITY WHEREUPON CRIMINAL PHASE MOSTLY ABATES UNTIL 2010 WHEN YOU FAIL TO FILE STATE INCOME TAX.

1987 - YOU EXPERIENCE MUTABILITY OF BRAIN CHEMISTRY VIA COMBUSTION/ INHALATION OF THC: STARE AT DOORKNOB FOR 138 MINUTES.

1990 - YOU HAVE SEX FOR THE FIRST TIME AFTER WATCHING MOVIE: THE ADVENTURES OF BARON MUNCHAUSEN.

SOVIET UNION COLLAPSES, COLD WAR ENDS.

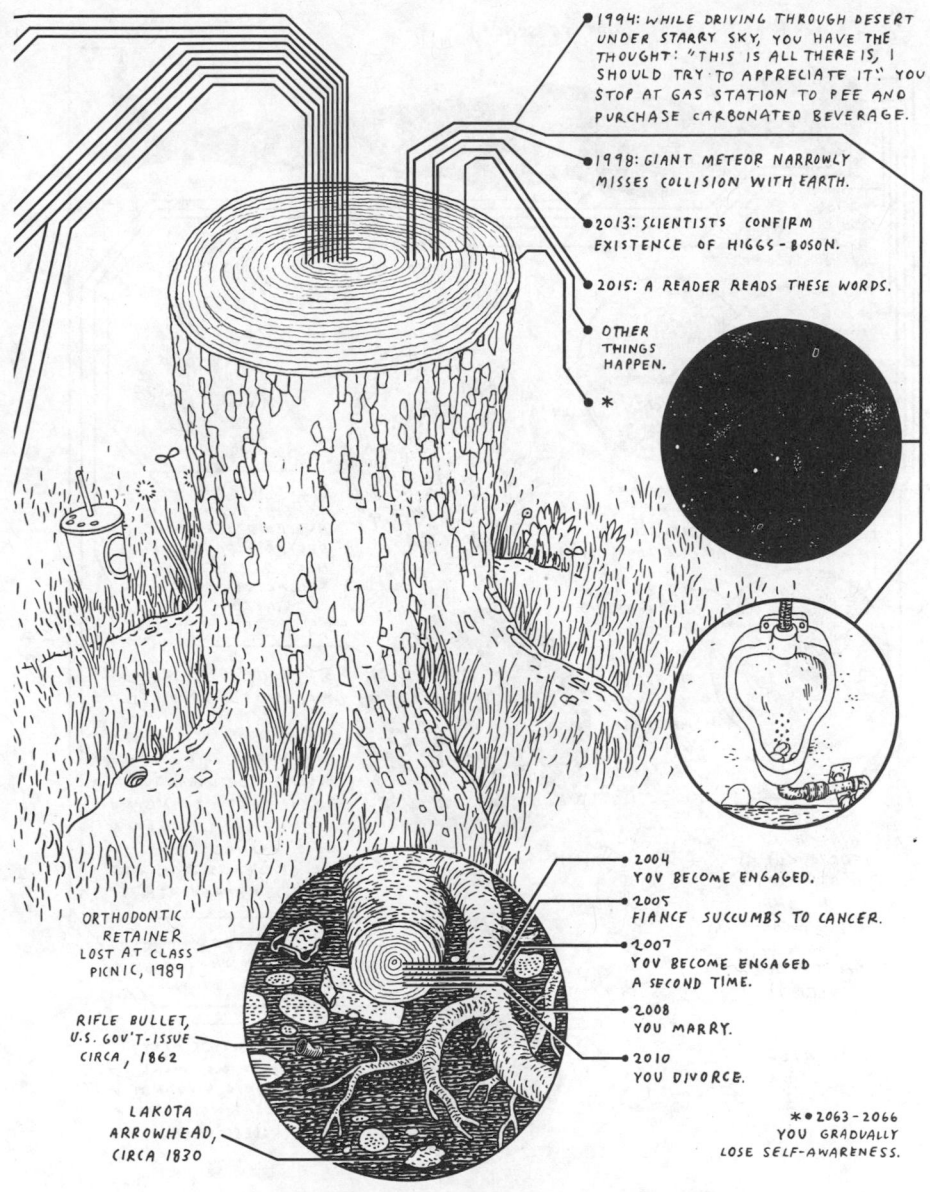

1994: WHILE DRIVING THROUGH DESERT UNDER STARRY SKY, YOU HAVE THE THOUGHT: "THIS IS ALL THERE IS, I SHOULD TRY TO APPRECIATE IT." YOU STOP AT GAS STATION TO PEE AND PURCHASE CARBONATED BEVERAGE.

1998: GIANT METEOR NARROWLY MISSES COLLISION WITH EARTH.

2013: SCIENTISTS CONFIRM EXISTENCE OF HIGGS-BOSON.

2015: A READER READS THESE WORDS.

OTHER THINGS HAPPEN.

*

ORTHODONTIC RETAINER LOST AT CLASS PICNIC, 1989

RIFLE BULLET, U.S. GOV'T-ISSUE CIRCA, 1862

LAKOTA ARROWHEAD, CIRCA 1830

2004 YOU BECOME ENGAGED.

2005 FIANCE SUCCUMBS TO CANCER.

2007 YOU BECOME ENGAGED A SECOND TIME.

2008 YOU MARRY.

2010 YOU DIVORCE.

* 2063-2066 YOU GRADUALLY LOSE SELF-AWARENESS.

# 3. THE FUTURE (NOT TO SCALE)

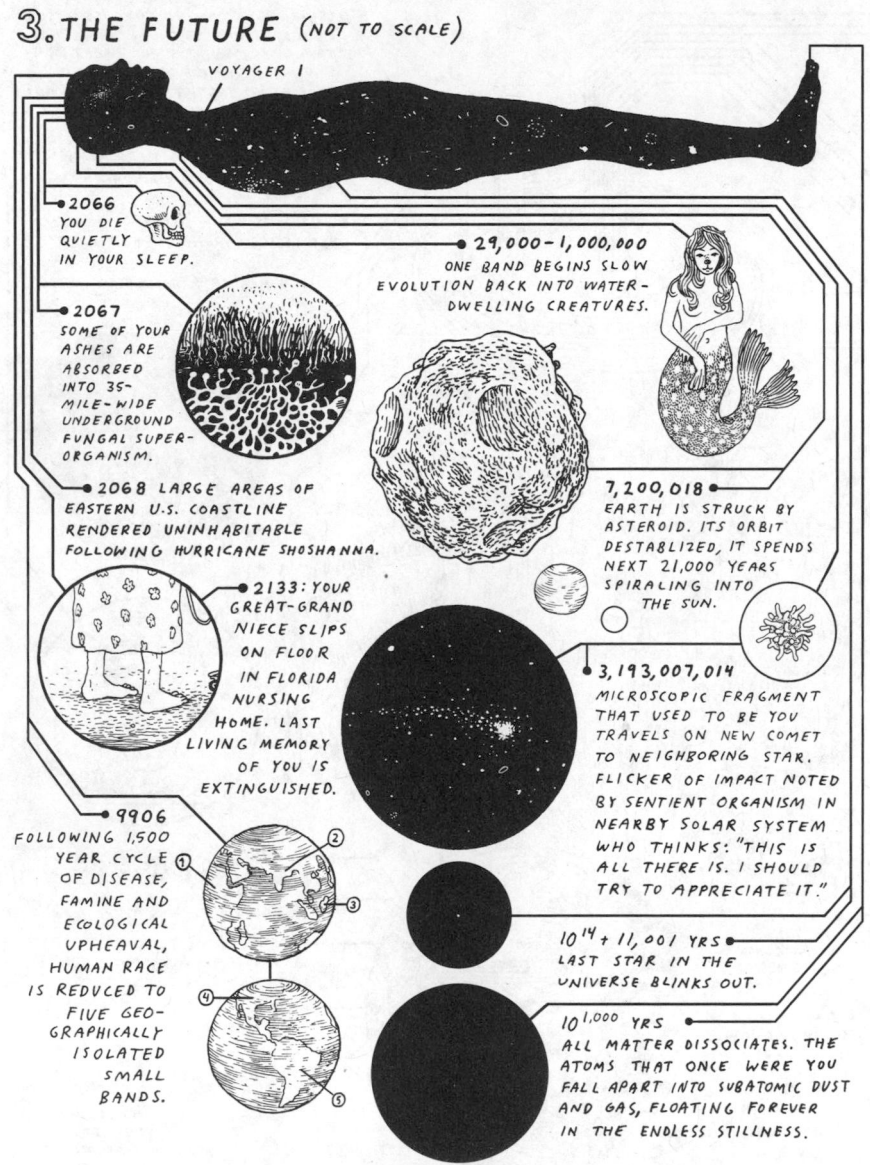

VOYAGER 1

**2066** YOU DIE QUIETLY IN YOUR SLEEP.

**2067** SOME OF YOUR ASHES ARE ABSORBED INTO 35-MILE-WIDE UNDERGROUND FUNGAL SUPER-ORGANISM.

**2068** LARGE AREAS OF EASTERN U.S. COASTLINE RENDERED UNINHABITABLE FOLLOWING HURRICANE SHOSHANNA.

**2133:** YOUR GREAT-GRAND NIECE SLIPS ON FLOOR IN FLORIDA NURSING HOME. LAST LIVING MEMORY OF YOU IS EXTINGUISHED.

**9906** FOLLOWING 1,500 YEAR CYCLE OF DISEASE, FAMINE AND ECOLOGICAL UPHEAVAL, HUMAN RACE IS REDUCED TO FIVE GEO-GRAPHICALLY ISOLATED SMALL BANDS.

**29,000-1,000,000** ONE BAND BEGINS SLOW EVOLUTION BACK INTO WATER-DWELLING CREATURES.

**7,200,018** EARTH IS STRUCK BY ASTEROID. ITS ORBIT DESTABILIZED, IT SPENDS NEXT 21,000 YEARS SPIRALING INTO THE SUN.

**3,193,007,014** MICROSCOPIC FRAGMENT THAT USED TO BE YOU TRAVELS ON NEW COMET TO NEIGHBORING STAR. FLICKER OF IMPACT NOTED BY SENTIENT ORGANISM IN NEARBY SOLAR SYSTEM WHO THINKS: "THIS IS ALL THERE IS. I SHOULD TRY TO APPRECIATE IT."

$10^{14} + 11,001$ YRS LAST STAR IN THE UNIVERSE BLINKS OUT.

$10^{1,000}$ YRS ALL MATTER DISSOCIATES. THE ATOMS THAT ONCE WERE YOU FALL APART INTO SUBATOMIC DUST AND GAS, FLOATING FOREVER IN THE ENDLESS STILLNESS.

—2014, revised 2016

# Madeleine Thien

b. 1974

The youngest of three children of Malaysian-Chinese parents—and the only child born in Canada—Madeleine Thien is a translator of cultural experiences. "I occupy a different kind of place," says Thien. "My sense of place is slightly different. I'm the child of immigrants without being an immigrant. I am the sister of immigrants without being an immigrant. It's a sense of occupying a new world, feeling I could embrace a new place right away, without hesitation." Her perspectives on family unity, immigration, and place inspire much of her fiction, and her stories of family dynamics and regional alliances have met with critical acclaim. She received the Canadian Author's Association award for most promising writer under 30 and the Ethel Wilson Fiction Prize for her first publication, a collection of short stories titled *Simple Recipes* (2001).

Thien was born and educated in Vancouver, British Columbia. She received a Master of Fine Arts in Creative Writing at the University of British Columbia, where she began work on the title story for *Simple Recipes*. Shortly after the success of her inaugural publication, Thien collaborated with Chinese-Canadian filmmaker and illustrator Joe Chang on a children's book adapted from his National Film Board short *The Chinese Violin* (2002). Thien's debut novel *Certainty* (2006), which addresses the complications of familial bonds, received international attention and has been translated into over 15 languages. Her 2016 novel *Do Not Say We Have Nothing* won the Scotiabank Giller Prize and was shortlisted for the Man Booker Prize.

Threads of her own family history and life experience are stitched throughout Thien's fiction; her stories are not, however, wholly autobiographical. Instead, Thien's real-life affinities serve as reminders of "what it is to write honestly."

# Simple Recipes

There is a simple recipe for making rice. My father taught it to me when I was a child. Back then, I used to sit up on the kitchen counter watching him, how he sifted the grains in his hands, sure and quick, removing pieces of dirt or sand, tiny imperfections. He swirled his hands through the water and it turned cloudy. When he scrubbed the grains clean, the sound was as big as a field of insects. Over and over, my father rinsed the rice, drained the water, then filled the pot again.

The instructions are simple. Once the washing is done, you measure the water this way—by resting the tip of your index finger on the surface of the rice. The water should reach the bend of your first knuckle. My father did not need instructions or measuring cups. He closed his eyes and felt for the waterline.

Sometimes I still dream of my father, his bare feet flat against the floor, standing in the middle of the kitchen. He wears old buttoned shirts and faded sweatpants drawn at the waist. Surrounded by the gloss of the kitchen counters, the sharp angles of the stove, the fridge, the shiny sink, he looks out of place. This memory of him is so strong, sometimes it stuns me, the detail with which I can see it.

Every night before dinner, my father would perform this ritual—rinsing and draining, then setting the pot in the cooker. When I was older, he passed this task on to me but I never did it with the same care. I went through the motions, splashing the water around, jabbing my finger down to measure the water level. Some nights the rice was a mushy gruel. I worried that I could not do so simple a task right. "Sorry," I would say to the table, my voice soft and embarrassed. In answer, my father would keep eating, pushing the rice into his mouth as if he never expected anything different, as if he noticed no difference between what he did so well and I so poorly. He would eat every last mouthful, his chopsticks walking quickly across the plate. Then he would rise, whistling, and clear the table, every motion so clean and sure, I would be convinced by him that all was well in the world.

• • •

My father is standing in the middle of the kitchen. In his right hand he holds a plastic bag filled with water. Caught inside the bag is a live fish.

The fish is barely breathing, though its mouth opens and closes. I reach up and touch it through the plastic bag, trailing my fingers along the gills, the soft, muscled body, pushing my finger overtop the eyeball. The fish looks straight at me, flopping sluggishly from side to side.

My father fills the kitchen sink. In one swift motion he overturns the bag and the fish comes sailing out with the water. It curls and jumps. We watch it closely, me on my tiptoes, chin propped up on the counter. The fish is the length of my arm from wrist to elbow. It floats in place, brushing up against the sides of the sink.

I keep watch over the fish while my father begins the preparations for dinner. The fish folds its body, trying to turn or swim, the water nudging overtop. Though I ripple tiny circles around it with my fingers, the fish stays still, bobbing side-to-side in the cold water.

For many hours at a time, it was just the two of us. While my mother worked and my older brother played outside, my father and I sat on the couch, flipping channels. He loved cooking shows. We watched *Wok with Yan*, my father passing judgment on Yan's methods. I was enthralled when Yan transformed orange peels into swans. My father sniffed. "I can do that," he said. "You don't have to be a genius to do that." He placed a sprig of green onion in water and showed me how it bloomed like a flower. "I know many tricks like this," he said. "Much more than Yan."

Still, my father made careful notes when Yan demonstrated Peking Duck. He chuckled heartily at Yan's punning. "Take a wok on the wild side!" Yan said, pointing his spatula at the camera.

"Ha ha!" my father laughed, his shoulders shaking. "*Wok* on the wild side!"

In the mornings, my father took me to school. At three o'clock, when we came home again, I would rattle off everything I learned that day. "The brachiosaurus," I informed him, "eats only soft vegetables."

My father nodded. "That is like me. Let me see your forehead." We stopped and faced each other in the road. "You have a high forehead," he said, leaning down to take a closer look. "All smart people do."

I walked proudly, stretching my legs to match his steps. I was overjoyed when my feet kept time with his, right, then left, then right, and we walked like a single unit. My father was the man of tricks, who sat for an hour mining a watermelon with a circular spoon, who carved the rind into a castle.

My father was born in Malaysia and he and my mother immigrated to Canada several years before I was born, first settling in Montreal, then finally in Vancouver. While I was born into the persistence of the Vancouver rain, my father was born in the wash of a monsoon country. When I was young, my parents tried to teach me their language but it never came easily to me. My father ran his thumb gently over my mouth, his face kind, as if trying to see what it was that made me different.

My brother was born in Malaysia but when he immigrated with my parents to Canada the language left him. Or he forgot it, or he refused it, which is also common, and this made my father angry. "How can a child forget a language?" he would ask my mother. "It is because the child is lazy. Because the child chooses not to remember." When he was twelve years old, my brother stayed away in the afternoons. He drummed the soccer ball up and down the back alley, returning home only at dinner time. During the day, my mother worked as a sales clerk at the Woodward's store downtown, in the building with the red revolving W on top.

In our house, the ceilings were yellowed with grease. Even the air was heavy with it. I remember that I loved the weight of it, the air that was dense with the smell of countless meals cooked in a tiny kitchen, all those good smells jostling for space.

The fish in the sink is dying slowly. It has a glossy sheen to it, as if its skin is made of shining minerals. I want to prod it with both hands, its body tense against the pressure of my fingers. If I hold it tightly, I imagine I will be able to feel its fluttering heart. Instead, I lock eyes with the fish. *You're feeling verrrry sleepy*, I tell it. *You're getting verrrry tired.*

Beside me, my father chops green onions quickly. He uses a cleaver that he says is older than I am by many years. The blade of the knife rolls forward and backward, loops of green onion gathering in a pyramid beside my father's wrist. When he is done, he rolls his sleeve back from his right hand, reaches in through the water and pulls the plug.

The fish in the sink floats and we watch it in silence. The water level falls beneath its gills, beneath its belly. It drains and leaves the sink dry. The fish is lying on its side, mouth open and its body heaving. It leaps sideways and hits the sink. Then up again. It curls and snaps, lunging for its own tail. The fish sails into the air, dropping hard. It twitches violently.

My father reaches in with his bare hands. He lifts the fish out by the tail and lays it gently on the counter. While holding it steady with one hand, he hits the head with the flat of the cleaver. The fish falls still, and he begins to clean it.

• • •

In my apartment, I keep the walls scrubbed clean. I open the windows and turn the fan on whenever I prepare a meal. My father bought me a rice cooker when I first moved into my own apartment, but I use it so rarely it stays in the back of the cupboard, the cord wrapped neatly around its belly. I have no longing for the meals themselves, but I miss the way we sat down together, our bodies leaning hungrily forward while my father, the magician, unveiled plate after plate. We laughed and ate, white steam fogging my mother's glasses until she had to take them off and lay them on the table. Eyes closed, she would eat, crunchy vegetables gripped in her chopsticks, the most vivid green.

• • •

My brother comes into the kitchen and his body is covered with dirt. He leaves a thin trail of it behind as he walks. The soccer ball, muddy from outside, is encircled in one arm. Brushing past my father, his face is tense.

Beside me, my mother sprinkles garlic onto the fish. She lets me slide one hand underneath the fish's head, cradling it, then bending it backwards so that she can fill the fish's insides with ginger. Very carefully, I turn the fish over. It is firm and slippery, and beaded with tiny, sharp scales.

At the stove, my father picks up an old teapot. It is full of oil and he pours the oil into the wok. It falls in a thin ribbon. After a moment, when the oil begins crackling, he lifts the fish up and drops it down into the wok. He adds water and the smoke billows up. The sound of the fish frying is like tires on gravel, a sound so loud it drowns out all other noises. Then my father steps out from the smoke. "Spoon out the rice," he says as he lifts me down from the counter.

My brother comes back into the room, his hands muddy and his knees the colour of dusty brick. His soccer shorts flutter against the backs of his legs. Sitting down, he makes an angry face. My father ignores him.

Inside the cooker, the rice is flat like a pie. I push the spoon in, turning the rice over, and the steam shoots up in a hot mist and condenses on my skin. While my father moves his arms delicately over the stove, I begin dishing the rice out: first for my father, then my mother, then my brother, then myself. Behind me the fish is cooking quickly. In a crockery pot, my father steams cauliflower, stirring it round and round.

My brother kicks at a table leg.

"What's the matter?" my father asks.

He is quiet for a moment, then he says, "Why do we have to eat fish?"

"You don't like it?"

My brother crosses his arms against his chest. I see the dirt lining his arms, dark and hardened. I imagine chipping it off his body with a small spoon.

"I don't like the eyeball there. It looks sick."

My mother tuts. Her nametag is still clipped to her blouse. It says *Woodward's*, and then, *Sales Clerk*. "Enough," she says, hanging her purse on the back of the chair. "Go wash your hands and get ready for supper."

My brother glares, just for a moment. Then he begins picking at the dirt on his arms. I bring plates of rice to the table. The dirt flies off his skin, speckling the tablecloth. "Stop it," I say crossly.

"*Stop it*," he says, mimicking me.

"Hey!" My father hits his spoon against the counter. It *pings*, high-pitched. He points at my brother. "No fighting in this house."

My brother looks at the floor, mumbles something, and then shuffles away from the table. As he moves farther away, he begins to stamp his feet.

Shaking her head, my mother takes her jacket off. It slides from her shoulders. She says something to my father in the language I can't understand. He merely shrugs his shoulders. And then he replies, and I think his words are so familiar, as if they are words I should know, as if maybe I did know them once but then I forgot them. The language that they speak is full of soft vowels, words running together so that I can't make out the gaps where they pause for breath.

My mother told me once about guilt. Her own guilt she held in the palm of her hands, like an offering. But your guilt is different, she said. You do not need to hold on to it. Imagine this, she said, her hands running along my forehead, then up into my hair. Imagine, she said. Picture it, and what do you see?

A bruise on the skin, wide and black.

A bruise, she said. Concentrate on it. Right now, it's a bruise. But if you concentrate, you can shrink it, compress it to the size of a pinpoint. And then, if you want to, if you see it, you can blow it off your body like a speck of dirt.

She moved her hands along my forehead.

I tried to picture what she said. I pictured blowing it away like so much nothing, just these little pieces that didn't mean anything, this complicity that I could magically walk away from. She made me believe in the strength of my own thoughts, as if I could make appear what had never existed. Or turn it around. Flip it over so many times you just lose sight of it, you lose the tail end and the whole thing disappears into smoke.

My father pushes at the fish with the edge of his spoon. Underneath, the meat is white and the juice runs down along the side. He lifts a piece and lowers it carefully onto my plate.

Once more, his spoon breaks skin. Gingerly, my father lifts another piece and moves it towards my brother.

"I don't want it," my brother says.

My father's hand wavers, "Try it," he says, smiling. "Take a wok on the wild side."

"No."

My father sighs and places the piece on my mother's plate. We eat in silence, scraping our spoons across the dishes. My parents use chopsticks, lifting their bowls and motioning the food into their mouths. The smell of food fills the room.

Savouring each mouthful, my father eats slowly, head tuned to the flavours in his mouth. My mother takes her glasses off, the lenses fogged, and lays them on the table. She eats with her head bowed down, as if in prayer.

Lifting a stem of cauliflower to his lips, my brother sighs deeply. He chews, and then his face changes. I have a sudden picture of him drowning, his hair waving like grass. He coughs, spitting the mouthful back onto his plate. Another cough. He reaches for his throat, choking.

My father slams his chopsticks down on the table. In a single movement, he reaches across, grabbing my brother by the shoulder. "I have tried," he is saying. "I don't know what kind of son you are. To be so ungrateful." His other hand sweeps by me and bruises into my brother's face.

My mother flinches. My brother's face is red and his mouth is open. His eyes are wet.

Still coughing, he grabs a fork, tines aimed at my father, and then in an unthinking moment, he heaves it at him. It strikes my father in the chest and drops.

"I hate you! You're just an asshole, you're just a fucking asshole chink!" My brother holds his plate in his hands. He smashes it down and his food scatters across the table. He is coughing and spitting. "I wish you weren't my father! I wish you were dead."

My father's hand falls again. This time pounding downwards. I close my eyes. All I can hear is someone screaming. There is a loud voice. I stand awkwardly, my hands covering my eyes.

"Go to your room," my father says, his voice shaking.

And I think he is talking to me so I remove my hands.

But he is looking at my brother. And my brother is looking at him, his small chest heaving.

A few minutes later, my mother begins clearing the table, face weary as she scrapes the dishes one by one over the garbage.

I move away from my chair, past my mother, onto the carpet and up the stairs.

Outside my brother's bedroom, I crouch against the wall. When I step forward and look, I see my father holding the bamboo pole between his hands. The pole is smooth. The long grains, fine as hair, are pulled together, at intervals, jointed. My brother is lying on the floor, as if thrown down and dragged there. My father raises the pole into the air.

I want to cry out. I want to move into the room between them, but I can't.

It is like a tree falling, beginning to move, a slow arc through the air.

The bamboo drops silently. It rips the skin on my brother's back. I cannot hear any sound. A line of blood edges quickly across his body.

The pole rises and again comes down. I am afraid of bones breaking.

My father lifts his arms once more.

On the floor, my brother cries into the carpet, pawing at the ground. His knees folded into his chest, the crown of his head burrowing down. His back is hunched over and I can see his spine, little bumps on his skin.

The bamboo smashes into bone and the scene in my mind bursts into a million white pieces.

My mother picks me up off the floor, pulling me across the hall, into my bedroom, into bed. Everything is wet, the sheets, my hands, her body, my face, and she soothes me with words I cannot understand because all I can hear is screaming. She rubs her cool hands against my forehead. "Stop," she says. "Please stop," but I feel loose, deranged, as if everything in the known world is ending right here.

In the morning, I wake up to the sound of oil in the pan and the smell of French toast. I can hear my mother bustling around, putting dishes in the cupboards.

No one says anything when my brother doesn't come down for breakfast. My father piles French toast and syrup onto a plate and my mother pours a glass of milk. She takes everything upstairs to my brother's bedroom.

As always, I follow my father around the kitchen. I track his footprints, follow behind him and hide in the shadow of his body. Every so often, he reaches down and ruffles my hair with his hands. We cast a spell, I think. The way we move in circles, how he cooks without thinking because this is the task that comes to him effortlessly. He smiles down at me, but when he does this, it somehow breaks the spell. My father stands in place, hands dropping to his sides as if he has forgotten what he was doing mid-motion. On the walls, the paint is peeling and the floor, unswept in days, leaves little pieces of dirt stuck to our feet.

My persistence, I think, my unadulterated love, confuse him. With each passing day, he knows I will find it harder to ignore what I can't comprehend, that I will be unable to separate one part of him from another. The unconditional quality of my love for him will not last forever, just as my brother's did not. My father stands in the middle of the kitchen, unsure. Eventually, my mother comes downstairs again and puts her arms around him and holds him, whispering something to him, words that to me are meaningless and incomprehensible. But she offers them to him, sound after sound, in a language that was stolen from some other place, until he drops his head and remembers where he is.

Later on, I lean against the door frame upstairs and listen to the sound of a metal fork scraping against a dish. My mother is already there, her voice rising and falling. She is moving the fork across the plate, offering my brother pieces of French toast.

I move towards the bed, the carpet scratchy, until I can touch the wooden bed-frame with my hands. My mother is seated there, and I go to her, reaching my fingers out to the buttons on her cuff and twisting them over to catch the light.

"Are you eating?" I ask my brother.

He starts to cry. I look at him, his face half hidden in the blankets.

"Try and eat," my mother says softly.

He only cries harder but there isn't any sound. The pattern of sunlight on his blanket moves with his body. His hair is pasted down with sweat and his head moves forward and backward like an old man's.

At some point I know my father is standing at the entrance of the room but I cannot turn to look at him. I want to stay where I am, facing the wall. I'm afraid that if I turn around and go to him, I will be complicit, accepting a portion of guilt, no matter how small that piece. I do not know how to prevent this from happening again, though now I know, in the end, it will break us apart. This violence will turn all my love to shame and grief. So I stand there, not looking at him or my brother. Even my father, the magician, who can make something beautiful out of nothing, he just stands and watches.

A face changes over time, it becomes clearer. In my father's face, I have seen everything pass. Anger that has stripped it of anything recognizable, so that it is only a face of bones and skin. And then, at other times, so much pain that it is unbearable, his face so full of grief it might dissolve. How to reconcile all that I know of him and still love him? For a long time, I thought it was not possible. When I was a child, I did not love my father because he was complicated, because he was human, because he needed me to. A child does not know yet how to love a person that way.

How simple it should be. Warm water running over, the feel of the grains between my hands, the sound of it like stones running along the pavement. My father would rinse the rice over and over, sifting it between his fingertips, searching for the impurities, pulling them out. A speck, barely visible, resting on the tip of his finger.

If there were some recourse, I would take it. A cupful of grains in my open hand, a smoothing out, finding the impurities, then removing them piece by piece. And then, to be satisfied with what remains.

Somewhere in my memory, a fish in the sink is dying slowly. My father and I watch as the water runs down.

—2001

# Michael Christie

b. 1976

Michael Christie arrived at his literary career via a somewhat unconventional path—through skateboarding. Prior to writing and publishing his first collection of short stories, *The Beggar's Garden* (2011), Christie was a professional skateboarder and writer for skateboarding magazines. Speaking of his former passion, Christie has described skateboarding culture as existing "completely outside the world of adults ... this arcane language and world that I shared with these other people." This sense of existing on the margins of society permeates much of Christie's fiction.

After growing up in Thunder Bay, Ontario, Christie worked for a time at a homeless shelter in Vancouver, an experience that informed much of the material for his debut collection. The characters at the heart of these stories, which are set in Vancouver and especially in its notoriously unstable Downtown Eastside neighbourhood, are largely people who could be considered outsiders: people facing such challenges as drug addiction, homelessness, and mental disabilities and illnesses. Christie later revisited his hometown experiences to write his first full-length novel, *If I Fall, If I Die* (2014). A coming-of-age story, the narrative centres on a sheltered young boy and his relationship with his agoraphobic mother, a dramatized version of his own childhood; the novel is dedicated to his late mother. Like Christie, the novel's young protagonist finds a kind of cathartic liberation in the world of skateboarding.

Steven W. Beattie, a critic for the *National Post*, has written that Christie's fiction "unsentimentally dramatiz[es] the way a certain segment of society lives now, and in doing so stands as a sympathetic and compassionate examination of modern urban loneliness and disaffection." Both *If I Fall, If I Die* and *The Beggar's Garden* were longlisted for the Giller Prize.

# The Extra

Me and Rick, we rent a basement suite at the bottom of Baldev's house. Actually, we only call it that to Welfare so they'll give us the most amount of money for rent, but really it's just a basement, no suite part. The walls are two-by-fours with cotton candy in between and there's no toilet or sink and it smells bad like your wrist when you leave your watch on too long. We sleep on hunks of foam beside the furnace between an orange lawnmower and used cans of paint that Baldev keeps down there. We take dumps at the gas station down the street and pee in plastic jugs we pour down a drain in the alley. Then at the tap on the side of the house, we rinse them and fill them for drinking and washing our pits and crotches. We used to have different jugs but then we got tired of remembering which was which.

When I say we rent, I really mean I do because my disability worker, Linda, sends a cheque for five hundred dollars a month to Baldev because she can't trust me with my money for the reason of my brain being disabled. But me and Rick and Baldev have this deal where Baldev gives us two hundred of the rent back in cash as long as we don't complain about the basement and how it's just a basement.

Rick needs my help. He can't get welfare because years ago he got kicked off for not telling them he had a job while he was still getting cheques. But Rick says we're lucky because I have a disabled brain and we get more money than the regular welfare pays anyway, so it works out, and we split the disabled money right down the middle. Without Rick I'd be starving with flies buzzing on my face or back in a group home. He says what we're going to do with our money because I'm bad at numbers, and also he cooks me dinners and lunches on his hot plate. He sometimes cooks spaghetti or mostly different stews he gets out of a can. He always makes me wait until the stew is hot before we eat because I eat things cold because I'm bad at waiting. It's just more proper, he says. Then he says it lasts longer in your belly if it's hot. When I ask why, he says because then your belly has to wait for it to get cool before it can soak it up.

Rick could have any job he wanted because he's sharp. He does our laundry and he made a copy of the key to the gas-station bathroom and he gives himself homemade tattoos with a guitar string and gets really mad whenever he thinks somebody is ripping us off. Rick is from Halifax but he never was a fisherman. He never set foot on a boat, he says, and besides there's more fish at your average pet store than in the whole goddamn ocean these days because of those big Japanese fish-vacuums he told me about. But he's not lazy. He's been a roofer, a car parker, a painter, a tree planter, and he once worked at night mopping at a big twenty-four-hour hardware store. But now he just goes to WorkPower with me, which I'll tell you about later. He even used to be married but his wife left him because she was a rotten witch. She got everything, he says. Everything was his house and his kids and all his stuff that he bought with hard-earned money. He even had one of those trucks with four tires on the back. He talks about it sometimes when he's falling asleep after he's had some cans of the beer with lots of X's all over it. Rick says I'm lucky I can't taste the beer. He named it swill, even though I can tell he likes it because it makes him a mix of confused and happy and tired.

Near the end of the month, when the disabled money and the money we get back from Baldev runs out, we get up at six in the morning. Then we put on our steeled-toe boots and bike to a place called WorkPower to stand in line to get jobs. Sometimes it's unloading boxes from trucks, or tearing copper wires out of buildings nobody wants. One time we had to carry blocks of ice from a truck to a freezer in a fish market and the gloves they gave us were thin as the butt of an old pair of underwear. Rick wanted to tell them where to stick it so bad but if one of the bosses complains to WorkPower they won't let us back. I like WorkPower because every time it's different but Rick doesn't like it because he thinks it's shit work. I ask him what shit work means and he says anything that makes you feel or look like shit.

One day after me and Rick got back from a whole day of picking up cigarette butts on a construction site, Baldev came down the stairs from his part of the house, where at the top there is a door that doesn't lock on our side but does on Baldev's side. It's always locked, I've checked.

Rick asked Baldev who the hell he thought he was. He said, You can't just come down here without properly notifying us, it ain't legal.

Baldev nodded like he thought so too and said he had a thing to tell us.

Rick stuck his hands in his armpits and told him to go on and say it.

I am changing, Baldev said. My friends I cannot be able to give you this money-back deal in the future.

Rick got the vein in his forehead that he gets when he thinks he's getting ripped off. It's shaped like one of those sticks that finds water.

So sorry, Baldev said. This is because the property taxes that we have, they are going up.

Well what if the city finds out this here ain't exactly a legal suite? Rick said. But I didn't want Baldev to get in trouble for the basement, he has three or maybe four kids who I hear stomping around upstairs and he has a wife who cooks food that smells good in a way like no food I've ever ate. I told Baldev we wouldn't tell on him.

You must vacate if you are wishing, my friends, Baldev said, ignoring me and what I said. Then he went up the stairs and I heard the door lock.

Rick kicked some of our stuff around for a while but he wasn't that mad because when I told him everything was going to be okay, we'd just work a little harder, he started laughing. Then he said we'd have to go back to Work-Power every day this week if we wanted to eat. I told him I didn't mind shit work as long as my disability worker didn't find out I wasn't as disabled as I was supposed to be, that I could carry boxes and pick up cigarette butts, and then stopped giving me my cheques. Rick said they wouldn't find out as long as I kept my mouth shut for the rest of the night. Then he rode his bike to go buy some beer with lots of X's on it because he can't go to sleep early without at least a few.

The next day, we were in our steeled-toe boots on our way back from cutting weeds as high as our heads at a place that sells motorhomes beside a highway. We had money in our pockets and we went to get some burgers because Rick said he was too damn tired to cook anything on the hot plate.

You eat your hamburgers too fast, Rick said, you can't even taste them. I told him I taste them good enough, but we both know I can't really taste anything too good because on account of my brain being disabled. But sometimes Rick acts like he's too much of the boss so I have to set him straight. If you're wondering why my brain is disabled it's because when I was born it didn't get enough air because there was some problem with my mom or the way I came out. My mom said they knew right after I came out because the doctor poked me on the feet with something sharp but I didn't care. Then he put lights in my eyes but my eyes didn't really care either. The doctor just frowned, she said. Most of the time I forget it's damaged. Maybe it's too damaged to know it's damaged. Or maybe it's not damaged enough for me to notice. Either way it's not very bad.

Rick always leaves his burger wrappers and his tray on the table. He says he doesn't want to take away the people's jobs who clean up, but I throw his out for him because I think they'd still have jobs but just do less if everybody pitched in more. While I was at the garbage, a guy was talking to Rick. He had nice clothes like a disability worker and had one of those pocket telephones in his hand. He talked the same as Rick. Because Rick's from Halifax, he says burr or guiturr when he tries to say bar or guitar, but he can turn it off when he wants. He's really good at being me too, which is funny for a while then makes me mad if he acts too much like a retard because I'm not. Rick told the guy we were working in construction but I could see the guy looking at the long pieces of yellow grass still stuck in my hair. I got bored of their talking so I went to the bathroom and drank out of the tap.

When we rode our bikes home Rick said him and the guy had gone to high school together back in Halifax and the guy had gave Rick a card with his name on it and said he should call him if our construction jobs slow down because now he was working for the movies and they needed some extra people for a movie that they were making. It'd be a lot easier than WorkPower believe me, Rick said, but I didn't believe him because bad things always happened whenever Rick got happy about something.

In our basement he said he always thought he might be in the movies then he asked me to grab him another of the beers that we keep in a bucket of water outside so they're more cold. The rest of the night I had to listen to him practise talking normal, like not saying burr or guiturr. Then he put on the classic rock station, which is music that is older and everybody agrees is pretty good, while he did the kind of push-ups where you do the clap in the middle or just go on your knuckles.

After waiting three days Rick called the guy from the pay phone at the gas station where we take dumps. Rick came back and hugged me and said we were going to have a party because he had just got us both jobs as extras.

I asked him what extras were.

He said they were the people in movies who stood around in the background and made everything seem more real just by being there.

It seemed like something we'd be good at, but I was still worried. I'll do it, I told Rick, as long as I don't have to say anything because I can't talk or remember very good because of my brain being disabled and Rick said no problemo.

That night, during our party, Rick drank lots of beers and threw our steeled-toe boots out on the lawn. Then he went up the stairs and pounded on Baldev's door yelling about room service. I told him to stop because it was three in the morning and he'd wake the kids and they probably had to get up early and go to school. He did what I said and came back downstairs. He looked at his pictures of the rotten witch for a few minutes, then started sleeping.

The next day Rick said we needed some nice clothes because they wouldn't want to film us if we looked like shit.

I don't think we look like shit, I said, and I stuffed my hands into the pockets of my favourite orange hoodie that I was wearing because there was white parts on the sleeves from me wiping my nose on them.

We just have to make sure they don't think we're bums who don't deserve the job, he said, but luckily we saved some money for just this kind of occasion. Close your eyes.

Why, I said.

I'm making a withdrawal from our emergency fund, he said.

I faked shutting my eyes and saw him reach for the pineapple can he'd hid behind an old dartboard, which I already knew was there. He pulled out some money and put some back.

Okay, he said.

We biked to five different second-hand stores to get some clothes for our new job as extra people. Rick got a white shirt that was only a little yellow around the collar, some black pants, some shoes he called loafers, and some shades. I just wanted another hoodie, but he made me get some nice jeans and a T-shirt with a collar on it that had a little picture of a guy on a horse holding a sword in the air like he was going to kill somebody. In the change room, Rick switched the tags on them so they were only two bucks each. But the old lady was nice and didn't make us pay for them anyway.

The day came, which was good because Rick said we were out of money and we had to eat some doughnuts out of a dumpster on our way downtown to the movie place. When we got there, a woman made us wait in a room with a whole lot of other extra people, who were either reading magazines about movie stars or had their ears to their pocket telephones. Some were making appointments to be extra people for other movies and some were talking more quiet to their families and friends.

After a while, they took us into a big room with lots of clothes on racks where we waited some more. Then they brought our costumes. I took mine out of the plastic bag and didn't understand it. One of the clothes ladies had to help me put it on and I was embarrassed because she saw my underwear. I put my golfing shirt on a hanger and she hung it up. The costume was just bits of fur glued to this dirty net made out of canvas that hung off me like a bathrobe made out of a chewed-up dog. I also got these leather boots that were like moccasins, except they had these little blinking lights on them.

What the hell is this? I heard Rick ask the clothes lady when he got his, which was like mine but he had a helmet and these big black plastic horns coming out of the shoulders.

She talked with pins in her mouth and said it was his costume.

What kind of person wears rags and furs and horns and shredded-up leather? Rick said.

She said this is a movie that takes place in the future.

Rick wanted to know how in the hell that explained anything.

I hadn't been working in movies very long but I had already learned that when a movie person doesn't like what someone else is saying they just walk away from them and that is exactly what the costume lady did, which made all shapes of veins bulge under Rick's helmet.

After everybody was dressed up they took us back to the waiting room.

How do you think they know what people are going to look like in the future? I asked Rick who was reading one of the movie-star magazines.

Maybe they're just taking a guess, Rick said.

I always thought the future would look like the Jetsons,[1] I said.

He turned a page and went humph.

Then we waited more in the waiting room.

Do you think we're getting filmed right now? I asked Rick.

No, they'll tell us when that happens.

---

1    *the Jetsons* Animated American sitcom (1962–63) set in a futuristic world.

Okay, good, I said, because I didn't feel like I was from the future yet. Actually I was too bored to feel anything. Plus I guess I was mad we had rode our bikes all day and spent our emergency fund on our party.

I think this is shit work, I told Rick an hour later. I'd rather carry ice blocks.

Then Rick told me to shut up so I kept talking about nothing really just to prove he wasn't the boss.

I felt better when it was time for lunch and we went outside to these big trucks that opened up and had kitchens inside. Us and the other extra people had to line up and wait which was okay because sometimes me and Rick waited for sandwiches at the Gospel Mission so I'm used to it. Rick said all the real actors had food brought to them in their trailers. I told him it was sad they had to live in trailers.

I asked the guy in the truck who had a beard and that knotted rope kind of hair to give me as much food as he could because I was starving. He laughed and piled my plate with all different colours of food. Can you believe this? I said to Rick when we sat down, but he was watching the star actor who was sitting with a pretty lady wearing sunglasses and an important-looking fat guy who had an old-fashioned hat on his head. Even with my disabled brain and my dead taste buds, I could tell this food had never even seen a can. There was lots of fish and different salads, which I don't like much but ate anyway because I didn't want to get fired. I went back up twice and ate so much my rag-and-fur future costume got tight and started to rip a little which was okay because you couldn't tell because it was already ripped.

After lunch, we went back and waited in the room for a long time. Then they said they were wrapping something up and I thought maybe we'd get a present but they just told us to come back tomorrow.

On the way home I asked Rick if he wanted to get some beers to celebrate.

Rick said this wasn't the kind of job where you get paid at the end of the day, we had to wait for our cheques.

How long will that take? I said. I was worried more about having money to eat than I was about drinking any beers.

Dunno, Rick said, could be a while.

Then I realized my disability worker would find out I wasn't disabled when I cashed my cheque.

Don't worry, Rick said, I gave them a fake name instead of your real one and we just sign it over to me and I'll cash it for you. Until then, we're gonna have to live off the lunch truck.

That's all right with me, I said.

We went back every day for a week. Then another week. Rick said we shouldn't ask about our cheques because they'd think we were desperate. I said, aren't we? and he said, not yet we aren't.

Our job was to wait in the room for them to call us. We got more used to our future costumes and didn't even bother wearing our nice clothes anymore because nobody really cared, we were all the same anyway once we got dressed up. And some of the other extra people had worse costumes than us like heavy fur robes, fake beards, hats made out of scratchy sticks. It made us feel grateful for ours. I was eating so much at lunch mine barely fit me anymore and I was scared to ask for a bigger one even though they had hundreds more in the other room.

Those nights in our basement Rick didn't talk, which was weird because before he was always putting different complicated plans together like a football coach. He didn't even want to play cards, and usually he hated it when he didn't have any beers to drink but now he didn't seem to care. He did lots of push-ups and went to bed early.

Then one day right after lunch the important fat guy with the hat who I found out was the Assisting Director came into our waiting room and told us finally that they needed us. This was how the movie people talked, they always said they needed something when from as far as I could tell they more just wanted it. He said they were going to need to have this big explosion in the middle of a street that they had closed down. Then he said he was going to need some people to lead our charge and he started looking around the room. Rick made himself taller and put on his helmet. You, the Assisting Director said to Rick, and you and you, to some other people. Come with me, he said, and they went to the other side of the room. I was happy he didn't pick me because I was worried about tripping over my rags and ruining the movie, but then I was scared I would do something even more stupid without Rick there to tell me it was stupid.

Then the Halifax guy came to the rest of us and told us our motivator which is like our reason for living. He said we were these hungry, starving people who were trying to get into where some space stuff was so we could take over the spaceships and get back to our planet where there was lots of food and it was also the place where our families lived. It made no sense to me but I looked over at Rick and now that he was one of the leaders he was taking it really serious. I need you to think starving, Halifax guy said to my group and I saw a lady suck in her cheeks. I'd been hungry lots of times in the past, like the time when Rick lost all our money on the way home from the bar or when we had to send money to Rick's dying sister in Halifax or when we had to buy extra things like our bikes, which Rick got off this guy he knew and were really expensive because they are some of the best racing bikes you can buy. So I just tried to focus on those times but it was hard to believe in my motivator and think starving right after three plates from the lunch truck.

After somebody came to make sure our costumes looked good enough, they took us through some hallways then outside to a street that they'd made to look all burned and wrecked like something really, really bad had happened. There were trucks and movie stuff everywhere. I could see five different cameras and there were tons of people standing around like on the edges of a football field.

They had us wait around more. Then the Director started talking into one of those loud-talking horns. Okay everybody we are only going to do this one time, he said. He was sitting up high on a crane. Someone came and told me to stand in a place. There were lots of us and everybody got their own place. I tried to see Rick but I couldn't see him.

Then all of a sudden I heard Action! and we were all running in a big pack and someone was yelling GoGoGoGo. I was trying not to fall down and my heart was beating like one of those loud things that breaks up the pavement and I started to get a cramp from all of the food that was bouncing around in my belly. A woman ahead of me screamed and tripped over her big stick that had a bird skull at the top and I had to jump over her because if helped her up I thought I would ruin the movie. Then there was this loud boom behind us and I felt heat go on my ears. I turned and saw the whole front of a building go on fire and there was little bits of stuff flying everywhere and all I could think was that I hoped Rick was okay.

It was the farthest I ever ran and I was almost passing out because my cramp hurt so bad when the Director said cut and they brought us back to the waiting room. Then they got us to take off our costumes and said thanks very much for your time and told us they didn't need us anymore. My legs were still shaking while I went looking for Rick. I walked around for an hour until I saw him still wearing his costume talking with the Halifax guy and the tall pretty lady and the fat Assisting Director over by the trailers.

You can't go in there, a guy with a clipboard said.

In where? I said. Over there, he said.

So I just biked home.

It had been a few days and I was waiting for the sound of the back gate when Baldev came down the stairs followed by the smell of his country's kind of food that Rick hates but as far as I can tell smells really good, like the lunch truck.

This has come for you, he said, holding out a letter with the government's picture on it.

I opened it but I didn't understand what it said because my disabled brain makes it so that I can't read.

Is this from girlfriend? Baldev said, making his big boobs. Let me tell you Baldev loves big boobs. He puts his hands out in front of his chest to show just how big of boobs he means, which is really, really big. Then he looks down at the boobs and squeezes them. He admires them like he would even settle for having big boobs himself if he ever got the chance. This is maybe the one thing him and Rick agree about.

No, I said, but louder so that he could understand. Baldev, can you read this for me?

Baldev dropped his boobs and took the letter. He saw the government picture at the top and said, no, no, this is not near to my business. Then he went back upstairs.

I sat on a chair trying to make myself read. Once I got a letter from them saying they were going to send somebody to check out whether I was still disabled and see if I could work. After Rick read it out loud, he ripped it up and said there was no way in hell me or my brain was ever going to get better and that they were the ones who needed their heads checked. Then he said something like he always says about how mean the whole world is. Then we sat down and drank beers and felt better. But nobody from Welfare ever came, which was good because we didn't want them to see the beers or that the basement was a basement. Now I was worried this letter was another one of those and that maybe this time they really were going to come. I stayed up all night listening to the furnace.

Rick didn't come back the next day or the next. I got hungry and couldn't stop my brain from thinking about the food truck. I wondered if it was still there, because if I could dress up in some old rags and furs again and sneak back, just once, I knew I could eat enough to last me at least a week. Or how maybe they moved the trucks to some other movie somewhere else, and I thought about riding my bike around looking for movie stuff, like cranes and things blowing up. But I was too tired. I could have got some emergency money from my worker, Linda, but the letter made me afraid they'd found out I was working as an extra person and they would kick me off like Rick or stick me in jail. I didn't even know where the good dumpster with the doughnuts in it was because I always just followed Rick.

Then early one morning I woke up to a noise I thought was rats. I turned the light on and saw Rick going through his boxes of stuff.

Oh. Hi, he said.

Where you been? I said.

He sat in a chair and leaned his head way back like somebody was washing his hair, and it sounded like he had a cold because he was sniffing lots. I saw he was wearing different shoes and a different coat. They looked new.

Then all of a sudden Rick started talking, not excited like he usually did but still staring up at the boards that I guess were actually holding up Baldev's floor, and even with my bad smell I noticed Rick smelled like lots of beers. He said that after they picked him to be a leader of the future, they gave him a laser rifle that he was supposed to fire at the star. What if you hit him? I asked, and he shut his eyes, blew air out his nose, and said they were going to add the laser beam later. Then Rick said when the Director yelled action and he started running, his helmet slipped over his eyes and he accidentally turned and crashed into the big star right before the huge explosion. He said he was in the only camera angle that they really needed so they had no choice, they had to give him a bigger part in the movie so it didn't seem weird that he was there.

Does that mean our cheques will be bigger? I said.

He said he guessed it did.

Then I asked when we'd get them because I was hungry.

Not yet, he said.

Oh, I said.

It's just like stew, he said. You have to wait. You get impatient.

I asked him if he had any money for us to go get burgers or make something on the hot plate.

No, he said, but there was food and beers at the wrap party. He took a half a sandwich out of his pocket and gave it to me.

Is that where you got those clothes? Were they presents from the wrap party? I asked. I was eating the sandwich as slow as I could, picking fluff from my mouth.

Yeah, he said. Then he got up and said he would go right then and find out where our cheques were.

I asked him if he could read my letter first.

He grabbed it out of my hand and read it really fast.

It's fine, he said, doesn't mean anything.

There's more on the back, I said.

He flipped it and read the back. It's still fine, he said.

Does it mean they know? I said. That I'm not disabled anymore?

No, he said, and started throwing his things into some grocery bags, but none of his important stuff. And you *are* still goddamn disabled, he said. It just means they don't know their ass from a hole in the ground.

Good, I said.

Then he dropped the bags and put his hands on his face.

You don't have to work anymore, it ain't right for you to, he said.

Especially if it's shit work, I said. Like being extra.

He stood there covering his face for a little bit, breathing weird, and I knew he was really angry because when he took his hands away his face was red and there were veins in it like a bunch of blue candy worms. But then he just gave me a long hug that squeezed my breath and left.

The good part about living with someone is you can sit there and look at their stuff and know they have to come back sometime to get it. He'd left the hot plate and his steeled-toe boots. Sure, he'd taken the pictures of the rotten witch, but he'd left most of his clothes and his favourite baseball cap. I checked outside and he'd left his racing bike, which made me feel even better.

After cleaning the place up a bit I sat for a while on my hunk of foam. I already forgave Rick for getting mad at me because I called his new extra job shit work. He liked to get mad sometimes for bad reasons, so I decided I'd just have to not talk about it ever again and it would be okay. Then I folded up the disabled letter as small as it would go and tried to throw it in the garbage bucket but I missed. I was thinking about how, after working as an extra person from the future for so long, it was like I was becoming a professional waiter, and how that now I could wait for pretty well anything as long as I knew it was coming. I thought about how long it would take for my belly to eat the sandwich Rick gave me, and about how long it would be before my disabled brain wouldn't be able to stop me from following the smell of Baldev's wife's food up the stairs and knocking on their door. I didn't know how long that would be.

—2011

# *Tom Gauld*
## b. 1976

Tom Gauld is a Scottish cartoonist and illustrator whose work is highly regarded for its minimalism, precision, and wit. Garnering praise as, in the words of reviewer Maria Popova, "an unparalleled visual satirist of the literary world," Gauld crafts comics that are at once wryly funny and heart-wrenchingly sad.

Gauld grew up in the countryside in Aberdeen, Scotland. Early on he became fascinated with drawing, and he attended the Edinburgh College of Art with the idea of becoming an illustrator; soon, however, he began to experiment with making comics. While completing an MA at the Royal College of Art, he met another artist, Simone Lia, with whom he started the independent comics publisher Cabanon Press. Gauld published several of his comics through Cabanon in the early 2000s, including *Guardians of the Kingdom* (2001) and *Robots, Monsters, etc.* (2005). He and Lia also published two volumes together, *First* (2001) and *Second* (2002).

In 2005, Gauld began drawing a weekly cartoon for *The Guardian* Arts and Books section, which led to a focus on literary topics, and consequently a reputation for "bookish" comics. *The Guardian* cartoons also led to increasing international recognition, and Gauld began contributing regularly to other magazines, including *New Scientist, The New Yorker,* and *Believer.* In 2012 he began publishing his longer-format books with Drawn & Quarterly press, beginning with *Goliath* (2012) and followed by *You're All Just Jealous of My Jetpack* (2013), *Mooncop* (2016), and *Baking with Kafka* (2017). These award-winning books combine elements of science fiction and fantasy, as well as drawing on historically significant texts such as the Bible and the Icelandic sagas. Combining pathos with farce, Gauld interweaves the languages of text, image, and space to make each strip, as a *Publishers' Weekly* review phrased it, "a carefully composed marvel."

—2015

# *Fiona McFarlane*
b. 1978

Hailed in 2017 as a "genius" by judges of the Dylan Thomas Prize for writers under 40, Fiona McFarlane is known for fiction that is often characterized by a tone of dread and of the surreal. As a writer McFarlane is, she says, "drawn to those moments when people do things that are mysterious even to themselves."

Born and raised in Sydney, Australia, McFarlane, like many of her characters, has lived abroad for much of her adult life. She holds a PhD from Cambridge University; she has also been a writer-in-residence at various American campuses, and earned her MFA from the University of Texas after submitting a thesis that would become her debut novel, *The Night Guest* (2013). The novel, about an elderly woman who becomes convinced that a tiger is stalking her home in the night, addresses subjects such as personal identity, death, and the effects of colonialism. McFarlane has said that *The Night Guest* is intended to convey the sense "[t]hat everything that was happening around you, no matter how mundane it was, had some larger significance, that there was this opportunity for transcendence in everything that you're doing."

In 2016, McFarlane published *The High Places*, a collection of short fiction. Many of these stories are, to use her words, about "Australianness and how it's been fashioned," although they also reflect her international experiences. She names Australian writers as a particularly strong influence, but has also been influenced by Flannery O'Connor and William Faulkner in her tendency to write narratives that move frequently between the realistic, the dreadful, and the mysterious. When *The High Places* was awarded the Dylan Thomas Prize, the judges praised its "mastery of form" and "characters, situations and places which were haunting in their oddity and moving in their human empathy."

# Exotic Animal Medicine

The wife was driving on the night they hit Mr. Ronald.

"My first drive since getting married," she said.

"First this, first that," said her husband. He looked at her, sitting high in the seat: her hair looked flimsy and blonde. It was ten o'clock and only just dark. These were the days for marrying—the long days, and the summer. It hadn't rained.

"You've got to be thankful for the weather," the registrar had said to the husband. The husband was thankful for the weather and for everything else.

He carried his shoulders inside a narrow suit and his wife wore a blue dress. They came out of the registry office into the pale summer and St. Mary's rang the hour.

"Listen!" said the wife. "Just like we've been married in a church."

It was midday, and because they were in Cambridge the college bells also rang.

"Like we've been married in every church," said the husband.

Their witnesses—two friends—took photographs. The four of them went to a pub on the river to celebrate among the tourists and the students who'd just finished exams. The tourists pressed around them, clumsy at the bar; the students slipped through and were served first. The bride and groom were rocked from side to side in the crush. They co-operated with the crowd and liquid spilled over their glasses.

They began to drink.

Their friend Robbie swayed above their table. He motioned over their heads with his benevolent arms.

"I suppose I'm best man," he said. "By default. So, a toast: to David and Sarah. To Sarah and David. I'll make a statement about love. I'll say a few words."

"You've already said more than enough," said the other witness, Clare.

"Not nearly enough," said Robbie, and sat down.

By now it was four in the afternoon and the June town was keeping quiet. The lawns maintained their perfect green. The river lay straight like a track for trains. David and Sarah and Clare and Robbie walked along it to find another pub, and beside them swans idled on the brown water, ducks chased punts[1] for food, geese slid against the wet banks. Tinfoil barbecues were lit on Jesus Green,[2] one by one, and the smoke hung in morose columns above each group, never thick enough to form a cloud. The husband and wife and their friends picked their way among the barbecues. They encountered dogs, friendly and wayward.

"Stay well today, canines," said David. "Stay happy and healthy."

Sarah was on call that night.

"I'm not worried about them," said Sarah. "It's the Queen of Sheba I'm worried about: But he'll be good."

(At the surgery, the Queen of Sheba lifted his haunches and lowered his head to stretch his grey back. He walked figure eights in his cage, the way a tiger would.)

"He'd better be good," said David.

"That bloody cat," said Sarah happily.

---

1   *punts*  Pole-propelled vessels commonly used as riverboats in Cambridge, England.

2   *Jesus Green*  Public park in Cambridge.

(The Queen of Sheba sat in his cage at the surgery and looked out at the ferrets and iguanas. He looked out at the tanks of scorpions and turtles. He settled, sphinx-like, and crossed his paws. The nurse poked her fingers through the grille as she passed Sheba's cage and Sheba, yawning, ignored them.)

The crowd at the pub seemed to part before the bridal party and they found an outdoor table, newly abandoned. Their happiness brought good luck. Sarah said, "I should stop drinking. I might have to work."

"You might," said Robbie, "and you might not."

"This is your wedding reception," said Clare, and she placed her arm around Sarah, coaxing.

"You need a gin and tonic," said Robbie.

"My first gin as a married woman," said Sarah. She sat beside David and felt the day carry them toward each other. The hours passed at the pub and they didn't go home, although this was what they looked forward to: the privacy of their bed below smudged windows, its view of small gardens, and the beat of trapped bees against glass that shook as the buses moved by. Their bed was a long way from the colleges and the river but the bells would still come over the roads and houses, and they would be alone, and married. The day moved them toward the moment in which they would face each other in their bed and see that despite their marriage there was no change, and that this was just what they wanted.

Sarah's phone rang at nine o'clock. She knew it would be work, and so did David. He creased his face at her, disbelieving, but found he wasn't disappointed. This way he would have her to himself. They would drive in the car and she would tell him her impressions of the day. He would imitate the mannerism he'd disliked in the registrar: a tendency to blink too often and too hard. He would rest his hand on her warm leg and watch the way her driving forced her to keep her usually animated hands still. This animation would pass instead into her face, where her eyebrows would knit and rise across her forehead. She would lean a long way forward to look left and right at intersections, as if she needed to see vast distances. Sarah drove as if she were landing an enormous plane full of porcelain children on a mountaintop.

"What a surprise," said Sarah. She placed her phone on the table. "The Queen of Sheba needs a catheter."

Clare said, "There must be someone else?"

"No one else," said Sarah, standing now, slightly unsteady on her feet, but graceful. "Sheba's all mine. He's a friend's cat."

"And does this friend know you got married today?" asked Clare.

Sarah laughed. No one knew they'd been married today.

"Your wedding night and you have to go stick something up a cat's dick," said Robbie.

(Sheba rolled in his cage. The pain felt familiar to him, but newly terrible, a hot pressure. He flicked his paws to shake it off. He couldn't.)

Sarah led David from the pub. He leaned against her the way he did when he was on the way to being very drunk. In fact, he was just perfectly, amiably, generously drunk, inclined to pause in order to kiss his new wife. He felt grateful when he looked at her. He felt an expansion in his brain that he enjoyed—a feeling that finally he had found his life, or was finding it, was on the verge of finding it, although he was still a graduate student and suspected he always would be. He said to himself, This is my youth, at this moment, right now, and because he was drunk, he also said it to Sarah.

The walk home wasn't far; still, they took their time doing it. Sarah felt a sense of urgency about Sheba but couldn't translate that urgency into hurry. She felt the way she did in those anxious dreams when she was due somewhere important and was unable to find the items she needed to bring with her. The light was lowering now. They spent whole minutes standing on the side of the road in order to watch a woman move around her lit basement kitchen, ironing. As they approached their flat, David said, "You know I'm coming with you," and she didn't argue. They changed their clothes and it felt to Sarah, briefly, as if it had been David's suit and her dress that had married each other earlier in the day. David followed her to the car. Before sitting in the driver's seat she shook her head from side to side as if she might clear it. She didn't feel drunk.

It was an old car, friendly but unreliable, that flew with dog hair when the windows were down. It required patience, particularly in the winter; even now, in June, it demonstrated a good-natured reluctance to start. Sarah turned the key; the engine kicked in and then out. David played with the radio to find a good song, and when there were no good songs, he turned it low. As if encouraged by this decrescendo, the car co-operated. Cambridge was lit with orange lights. They passed through the city with exaggerated care and were in the country very suddenly, with dark fields pressing round them and airplanes far overhead. England became a long dark road, then, with bright windows visible across fields, and trees against the sky.

"What's wrong with this cat?" said David.

"Urinary tract."

"I know that. But what's *wrong* with it?"

Sarah grew defensive on behalf of Sheba.

"He can't help it."

"Why call a tomcat Sheba?"

"They let their kid name it," said Sarah. "It's the name of a brand of cat food. It uses real cuts of meat rather than by-products."

"Crazy."

"Don't," said Sarah.

"It's crazy. It's like your mum naming your brother Leslie and your dad doing nothing to stop it."

"It's a family name. It's a boy's name! And I don't want to think about my mother. Right now I'm pretending she doesn't exist. I left my phone at home," said Sarah. "If she calls, I don't want to tell her we're married, and I don't want not to have told her."

"So just don't answer."

"I'd have to answer. I couldn't not answer. And then—you know." She spread her hands in order to indicate her predicament and returned them to the steering wheel.

"Then—disaster."

She hit at him with her left hand.

"Watch the road!" he said, laughing. She watched the road.

"My first drive since getting married," she said.

"First this, first that," he said.

A car pulled out of a dark side road and turned directly in front of them. Sarah veered to the left but still met the back corner of this car; trees moved in front of the windscreen, tires made a long noise against the road, Sarah and David jolted over the grass and stones of the verge, they hit a low wooden fence and felt the engine splutter and stall. And as this took place they were aware of something more urgent occurring behind them: the spin of the other car, its dive into a roadside tree. Sarah and David remained still for a moment, preparing for an impact that didn't come.

"Fuck," said Sarah, looking back down the dim road. The muted lights of tiny Cambridge hung orange at the bottom of the sky behind them. The car radio continued to play.

"You're all right?" asked David, but that was obvious. He opened his door and stepped out. The other car reminded him of a cartoon dog, excessively punched, whose nose has folded into its face for a brief and hilarious moment before relaxing out again, essentially unhurt. He watched Sarah run toward the car and ran after her. The driver's door had opened in the crash and the driver sat, his legs pinioned, his right arm hanging, and his head turned away as if he were embarrassed to have been found in this position. He wasn't moving.

"He's not dead," said Sarah, but couldn't have explained why she was so sure.

She knelt beside the car and held the man's wrist, and when she released it she wiped her fingers against her skirt. David leaned against the tree and passed his hand across his face. He felt the air press in around him and he wanted somehow to press it back. Sarah had found the man's wallet on the front passenger seat.

"His whole name is just three first names," she said, inspecting his licence. "Ralph Walter Ronald. He's eighty."

Sarah looked carefully at this Mr. Ronald, acknowledging his age and misfortune. She felt that his awkward name had lifted him out of a time in which she'd played no part and deposited him here, in his crushed car.

"We need to call someone," she said.

"No phone," said David.

"Where's yours?"

"In my suit, probably."

"Shit!"

"You left yours too," said David.

"Deliberately," said Sarah.

"Which way to the nearest house?"

"I don't know."

"Forward or back?"

"I don't know."

"This is your drive to work. You drive this way almost every day."

"It's dark. I haven't been paying attention."

"All right, all right," said David. He realized he was pulling at the roots of his hair. People really do that, then, he thought, in a crisis—pull their hair. "I'll try the car. It seems like ages since we saw a house."

"Nothing in England is ever far apart."

It began to rain, very lightly. The rain seemed to rise out of the ground and lift up into their faces, a cheerful mist.

"All right, try the car," said Sarah. "I'll sit with him. His car won't blow up, will it? Or is that just in movies?"

"It would have blown up by now. Wouldn't it?"

They stood helpless in their combined ignorance, considering Mr. Ronald's car and Mr. Ronald trapped within it. The passenger seat was whole and healthy, although the accordion fold of the front of the car left no leg room. Sarah brushed glass from the seat and slid in beside Mr. Ronald, tucking her legs beneath her.

David crossed to their car with mid-city caution. It wouldn't start; it would never start when he was late for a seminar or a critical train, it required tender solicitations after particularly steep hills. Of course it wouldn't start now, when his need was desperate. Perhaps it was finally beyond repair—and then there would be the panic of finding money for a new car. David tried again. It wouldn't start and wouldn't start. He ran back to Sarah.

"No good," he said. "Fuck it. I'll run. I'm sure I'll find someone. Another car."

"Go forward, not back," said Sarah. "I think there's a petrol station. God, I have no idea of distances on foot."

"Sweetheart," David said, leaning farther into Mr. Ronald's car, "it wasn't your fault."

"I know," she said. "It was his fucking fault. But, darling, I'm a little drunk."

She watched him comprehend this. He was drunker than she was. His eyes filled briefly. There was a scar above his right eye, half hidden in the eyebrow, left by childhood chickenpox. He often walked through their apartment on his toes, adding to his height, bending down over her as she lay on the couch. He would put his head on her stomach and look up at her face, and when he did this he reminded her of an ostrich.

"I'll be back soon," he said. "It's going to be all right, and I love you. Don't be scared."

He bent down to kiss her, bent his long, beautiful bird neck, then began to run.

Sarah looked at Mr. Ronald. He wore corduroy trousers and a neat shirt, a woolen vest, and bulky glasses over thick eyebrows. He lay with his head thrown back and to the side facing Sarah, and his facial expression was bemused and acquiescing. She felt again at his wrist. His legs were caught up with the buckled car and it was impossible to tell what damage had been done. She sat on her side, looking into his face, and felt the faint breath that hung around his mouth. It smelled like a doctor's waiting room: just-extinguished cigarettes and something human rising up through disinfectant. She heard David try the car again, and she heard the car fail. Then his footsteps on the road. Then nothing. Sarah felt loneliness fall over her, and fear.

"The Queen of Sheba," she said.

(Sheba paused in his tiger-walk, his head lifted toward the surgery door, waiting. No one came through the door, and he dropped his head again, letting out a low small sound that startled the macaws opposite into frantic cries.)

Sarah was married and no one knew but herself and David, Robbie and Clare. Her mother didn't know. She wondered now about the secrecy—how childish it seemed. They only wanted privacy. They wanted a new visa for Sarah, and they didn't want to bother about the fuss that went with weddings. The last of the gin wound itself up against the side of Sarah's head that tilted against the seat; it hung there in a vapour, then seemed to drain away. Mr. Ronald's burnt breath came in little gusts against her face. Was he breathing more, or less? Sarah pulled the door behind her as far as it would go in order to feel safe, and to guard against the slight chill in the wind. This is summer, she thought. You wait for it all year, shoulders pushed up against the cold and the dark, and this is your gift: the sun and the bells, the smoke over Jesus

Green, geese on the river. A midday wedding. A cat's catheter and Mr. Ronald by the side of the road.

Mr. Ronald's eyes opened and Sarah drew back from his face. They studied each other. His eyes were yellow at the edges. They were clever and lucid. They looked at Sarah with calm acceptance; they looked at the windscreen, shattered but half in place, and at the close proximity of the tree.

"I've had an accident," he said.

"Yes, you have. How do you feel? Stay still," said Sarah. She felt composed. Everything she did felt smooth and immediate.

"I'm all here," said Mr. Ronald. "Everything's attached, at least." He gave a small laugh. "It happened so fast, as they say. I see I've hit the tree." He said "the tree" as if there were only one tree in the whole country; as if he had always known he would hit it.

"Good of you to stop," he said.

"Of course!" cried Sarah.

"Plenty wouldn't. Decent of you. I don't suppose he even thought for a minute about stopping."

"Who?" asked Sarah. She looked into the back of the car in panic, as if there might be someone else crushed inside.

"The lout who swiped me."

Sarah remained quiet. Then she said, "My husband's gone to find help."

She had been waiting to use this phrase: "my husband." Her first time.

"Ah," said Mr. Ronald. "I don't suppose you happen to be a doctor. That would be convenient."

"Not a human doctor," said Sarah. "An animal doctor, though."

"My leg, you see," he said. "I think it should hurt, but at this moment it doesn't."

"You're probably in shock."

"You're not British, are you. Antipodean."[1]

"Australian."

"I thought so, but didn't venture it. From the first few sentences you might just as well be a New Zealander."

He pronounced it "New Zellander."

"No, no!" Sarah protested. "We sound completely different." She demonstrated the difference: "Fish and chips," she said. "That's us. This is a Kiwi: fush and chups."

"Nonsense," said Mr. Ronald. "No one speaks that way at all."

Sarah felt chastised. She didn't resent it—there was something pleasantly authoritarian about Mr. Ronald, who made her think of a school principal

---

1    *Antipodean*  From Australia or New Zealand.

driving home from church, or the father of a boyfriend, to whom she must be polite at all costs.

"A veterinarian," said Mr. Ronald. "Dogs and cats."

"Actually I specialize," said Sarah. "Exotic animal medicine. But dogs and cats too, sometimes. Mostly for friends."

"What counts as exotic these days?" asked Mr. Ronald. His right hand moved slowly over his chest and toward his legs, testing for pain and damage.

"Chinchillas," said Sarah. "Ferrets. Hermit crabs. Monkeys."

"Monkeys?" said Mr. Ronald. "Good god. Does anyone in England actually own a monkey?"

"You'd be surprised."

"And is it legal?"

"I'm afraid it is."

"And people will spend hundreds of pounds to cure a hermit crab?"

"People become very attached to their pets," said Sarah. She had defended her clients on this subject before, at parties and college dinners, and whenever she did she saw them all in the surgery waiting room, bundled against cold and worry, holding cages and carriers and shoeboxes with holes punched in them.

"Yes, you're right," said Mr. Ronald, and he thought about this for a moment. "Dogs I understand, and cats too, in their own way. I grew up with a bull-mastiff. He could knock me down until I was eleven, and then I could knock him. He ate the leg off a rabbit once."

The bull-mastiff walked through Sarah's mind: Hip dysplasia, she thought. Hypothyroidism. A heavy dog. She'd need help lifting it.

"And you've treated a monkey yourself? You seem very young."

"A capuchin once, with a broken leg."

This mention of a broken leg seemed to remind Mr. Ronald of his situation. His face altered in pain.

"Do you feel it now?" asked Sarah. The skin whitened around his mouth and he let out a sound that reminded her of a tiger, a long and drawn-out "ooow."

"It won't be long," she said. "My husband will be back soon."

She looked out of the window. The road was dark in both directions and overshadowed with trees. There were shapes in the trees. They looked like small crouching monkeys escaped with their rotten teeth and cataracts from back-yard sheds all over England. When she looked back at Mr. Ronald, he seemed to have recovered a little. He laid his head against the seat and breathed quietly. A band of sweat bound his forehead. She placed her fingers on his wrist: his heartbeat was steady now; and slow. She kept her hand where it was, despite feeling revolted by the dampness of his old skin. They sat together listening for cars. Someone will come in this minute, thought Sarah; but the minute passed.

"A capuchin, you say," said Mr. Ronald. "A kind of monk, isn't it?"

"Well, a monk, yes, I think so. But also a kind of monkey."

"I saw an orangutan in the Berlin Zoo once, painting on the wall with a dish brush. Looked just like my wife cleaning the shower. But here Douglas is, against primate testing. I can't go in for that. Douglas calls me species-ist." Sarah decided not to ask who Douglas was. "If they cure Parkinson's, then it's worth those gorillas, I think. Not a popular stance, I'm told. I myself can't stand vegetarians."

"I'm a vegetarian," said Sarah.

"Well, in the abstract. It makes sense for someone like you. A veterinarian. Why heal them and then eat them? But I always say vegetarians ought to eat meat when it's served to them. Imagine being a guest in someone's home and turning down food that's offered."

This reminded Sarah of her grandfather: perplexed and indignant, having survived a war, to find that people cared about other kinds of suffering. Food might run out—eat what you're given. Life might be lost—don't mind the monkeys. Sarah liked to argue on this topic, calmly maintaining her position, but in this case she would not.

"Oh, but I'm sure you're a charming guest," said Mr. Ronald. "And here you are, helping an old man in distress."

He chuckled and the pain came again—stronger, it seemed, this time. It lifted him from the seat a little, and the lifting caused more pain. He shut his eyes against it. Sarah waited for this to pass, as it had the last time, and when he was quiet she asked, "What can I do? Anything? Is it your legs?"

He laughed again, sucking in his cigarette breath, and moved his wrist away from her hand. The rain grew heavier and the trees on the road began to move their monkey arms. The damp fields gave up their deeper smells of mice and manure. No cars passed by. Sarah worried about David in the rain. He couldn't have been gone for longer than ten minutes, she reasoned; perhaps fifteen. She wondered briefly if the woman was still ironing in her house.

She asked again, "How are your legs?"

"Funny," said Mr. Ronald, and his breath was shorter now. It left his throat unwillingly. "Funny, but one of them's not even a leg. Left leg, below the knee. Plastic."

Sarah imagined him at other times rapping his fingers against the plastic of his leg, knocking it through his neat trousers while chatting on a bus. The war, she thought, he must have lost it in the war; she saw him and other men moving quickly over a French field. Poppies blew in the grass, and he was a young man, strong of limb, and the sea lay behind them all as they ran.

"Diabetes," said Mr. Ronald. "Didn't know, did you, that it could take your leg off?"

Sarah shook her head, but she did know. She'd seen diabetic dogs, cats too. She'd cut off their legs. The French field fell into the sea, and the rain still fell against the roof of the car.

"Started as a blister, then an ulcer," said Mr. Ronald. "Just a mishap. A blister from new shoes. No one tells the young: be careful of your feet. Feet should last a lifetime. What can be prevented? Everything, they say. No they don't. They say not everything."

He laughed harder now, in a thin straight line, and his cheeks drew in over the laugh so that Sarah could see the shape of his skull and the crowded teeth, nicotine-stained, that swarmed in his mouth. Perhaps this wasn't laughing, but breathing. The steady rain and wind moved the car slightly, back and forth. The branches of the tree against which the car was pressed were darting shapes at the corner of Sarah's eye, like Sheba at night, stalking rats with his stomach full of jellymeat.[1]

(Sheba lay panting in the corner of his cage, overwhelmed by the pain on which he concentrated with a careful doling out of attention. He kept himself steady but his small side rose and fell, rose and fell, higher and then deeper than it should. His eyes moved toward the door and his mouth sat open, showing pink.)

Mr. Ronald's laugh was a clatter behind his teeth. Sarah huddled close to him as he moved against his seat. She placed her arm around his shoulders, touched his damp forehead, and felt her hair lift away from her skin, all along her arms and the back of her neck. The summer passed through the car, windy and wet.

"Hold on," said Sarah. "Just hold on." Her mouth was close to his ear. David would come soon. You could swear at a cat that rocked this way, crowded close in pain and confusion; you could talk softly, not to the cat but to the idea of the cat, to the faces of the family to whom you must explain the cat's condition. You could sing to the cat and if you had forgotten its name you could call it "kitty"—you could say "Hold on, kitty" while your hands moved and your neck craned forward and the parts of you that understood the machinery of a cat, its secret places, worked despite the cat's terror. You could set the leg of a monkey and watch it, later, as it limped back and forward across the surgery floor, scowling and shaking its funny fist at you.

Noises came from Mr. Ronald's throat now, and these sounds seemed accidental, the by-product of something else. They continued past the point Sarah felt certain he had died; they rattled on in the can of his throat. After they had subsided—although this took time, and they came in unexpected spurts—she became aware of the sound of a radio playing. In her own car, or this one? Who could Douglas be? A son? A grandson?

---

1    *jellymeat* Type of wet cat food, set with gelatin.

Sarah was unsure how long she had been sitting beside Mr. Ronald and how long it had been since he stopped making any sound at all. His wife cleaned the walls of their shower and he had been to see orangutans in Berlin. He was too young to have been in that war.

Without warning, David filled up the space in the passenger door of Mr. Ronald's car. She had been so certain she would hear his footsteps on the road, but here he was in the doorway as if she'd summoned him out of the field.

"I'm sorry, I'm sorry, I didn't find anyone." He was wet and his breath came quickly. "I ran and finally found a house but there was no one home. I thought about breaking in. Kept going for a bit but no sign of life. No cars on the road, even. So I came back to try the car again."

He looked at the stillness of the man in the driver's seat. He saw the blood on Mr. Ronald's trousers and the way that it crept toward his belt and shirt, and he searched for blood on Sarah.

Sarah concentrated on David's face, which swam in the sound of the rain and the radio. My husband. She smiled because she was happy to see him. Then she placed the wallet in Mr. Ronald's lap. She moved to step out of the car and David made space for her.

"How is he? How does he seem?"

When a cat died during an operation, when a macaw was too sick, when a snake was past saving, then Sarah must tell its owners. It was difficult to tell them this true thing, and so along with it she added other, less true things: that the tumour caused no pain, that the animal hadn't been frightened to go under anaesthetic. Still, it was difficult. It made no difference to Sarah that words were inadequate to her enormous task. Of course they were. There might be a time when she would have to tell her friends, Sheba's owners, that he wouldn't survive his infection. Each loss of which she had been the herald seemed to have led to this new immensity: Mr. Ronald, dead in a car. But they didn't know Mr. Ronald. David had never even spoken to him. She had been married that midday, with no rain. There were only two witnesses.

"He's dead," said Sarah.

She stood and shut the door behind her. David fought the desire to lower his head and look through the window. It seemed necessary to make sure, but more necessary to trust Sarah. He held his hands out to her and she took them.

"My god," he said. She shook her head. He knew that when she shook her head in this way, it meant: I'm not angry with you, but I won't talk.

"What now?" he asked. "Should we take him somewhere?"

David felt that Sarah owned the wreck, owned the tree and piece of road on which Mr. Ronald had died, and that he need only wait for her instructions, having failed to find help. He thought of her sitting alone with the unconscious body of an old man, and he thought of the moment at which she must have realized that Mr. Ronald was no longer unconscious, but dead. David saw with certainty that Sarah was another person, completely separate from him, although he had married her today. His wife.

"We'll try the car again," said Sarah. "We just have to get to the surgery."

"We can use the phone there," said David.

Sarah crossed the road and he followed her. She didn't look back at the wreck. Waiting on its grassy rise slightly above the road, their car had a look of faithful service, of eagerness to assist. It started on the third try with a compliant hum. Sarah had always been better at coaxing it; even before trying the ignition she'd known it would work. She was unsure if this resurrection was good or bad luck, or beyond luck—simply inevitable. Now that she could see the rain in the headlights, she realized how soft it was, how English. She missed home, suddenly: the hard, bright days and the storms at the end of them, with rain that filled your shoes.

It grew bright and then dark in Mr. Ronald's car as their headlights passed over him, and it remained dark as they left that piece of road and that tree. David watched Sarah drive. They didn't speak. As the distance between their car and Mr. Ronald's grew, it seemed that the roads were all empty—that all of England was empty. It lay in its empty fields while the mice moved and the airplanes flew overhead to other places, nearby and far away.

They reached lit buildings and the surgery so quickly that David was embarrassed at having failed to find help. Sarah walked calmly, and she spoke calmly with the nurse about Sheba. She didn't look at the telephone. There was no blood on her clothes. David watched his wife as she made her way toward the cat, who rubbed his head against the bars of his cage. He was waiting for the pain to stop. And then he would be let out, healed, to hunt mice in the wet grass.

—2010

# Glossary

**Absurdist:** characterized by a minimalist style and bleak worldview. The term is most frequently used with reference to certain plays of the post-World-War-II period (notable examples include Samuel Beckett's *Waiting for Godot* and Tom Stoppard's *Rosencrantz and Guildenstern Are Dead*). Such works seem set in a world stripped of faith in god or a rational cosmos, in which idealism has been lost, and human action and communication are futile. Absurdist characters are often portrayed as trapped in a pointless round of trivial, self-defeating acts of comical repetitiveness. For this reason, absurdism can verge on *farce* or *black comedy*. See also *existentialism*.

**Aesthetes:** members of a late nineteenth-century movement that valued "art for art's sake"—for its purely aesthetic qualities, as opposed to valuing art for the moral content it may convey, for the intellectual stimulation it may provide, or for a range of other qualities.

**Allegory:** a narrative with both a literal meaning and secondary, often symbolic meaning or meanings. Allegory frequently employs personification to give concrete embodiment to abstract concepts or entities, such as feelings or personal qualities. It may also present one set of characters or events in the guise of another, using implied parallels for the purposes of satire or political comment.

**Alliteration:** the grouping of words with the same initial consonant (e.g., "break, blow, burn, and make me new"). See also *assonance*.

**Allusion:** a reference, often indirect or unidentified, to a person, thing, or event. A reference in one literary work to another literary work, whether to its content or its form, also constitutes an allusion.

**Ambiguity:** an "opening" of language created by the writer to allow for multiple meanings or differing interpretations. In literature, ambiguity may be deliberately employed by the writer to enrich meaning; this differs from any unintentional, unwanted ambiguity in non-literary prose.

**Anachronism:** accidentally or intentionally attributing people, things, ideas, and events to historical periods in which they do not and could not possibly belong.

**Analepsis:** see *flashback*.

**Analogy:** a broad term that refers to our processes of noting similarities among things or events. Specific forms of analogy in poetry include *simile* and *metaphor.*

**Apostrophe:** a figure of speech (a *trope*; see *figures of speech*) in which a writer directly addresses an object—or a dead or absent person—as if the imagined audience were actually listening.

**Archetype:** in literature and mythology, a recurring idea, symbol, motif, character, or place. To some scholars and psychologists, an archetype represents universal human thought-patterns or experiences.

**Assonance:** the repetition of identical or similar vowel sounds in stressed syllables in which the surrounding consonants are different: for example, "shame" and "fate"; "gale" and "cage"; or the long "i" sounds in "Beside the pumice isle...."

**Atmosphere:** see *tone.*

**Baroque:** powerful and heavily ornamented in style. "Baroque" is a term from the history of visual art and of music that is sometimes also used to describe certain literary styles.

**Bathos:** an anticlimactic effect brought about by a writer's descent from an elevated subject or tone to the ordinary or trivial.

**Black Comedy:** humour based on death, horror, or any incongruously macabre subject matter.

**Bombast:** inappropriately inflated or grandiose language.

**Burlesque:** satire of an exaggerated sort, particularly that which ridicules its subject by emphasizing its vulgar or ridiculous aspects.

**Canon:** in literature, those works that are commonly accepted as possessing authority or importance. In practice, "canonical" texts or authors are those that are discussed most frequently by scholars and taught most frequently in university courses.

**Caricature:** an exaggerated and simplified depiction of character; the reduction of a personality to one or two telling traits at the expense of all other nuances and contradictions.

**Carpe Diem:** Latin (from Horace) meaning "seize the day." The idea of enjoying the moment is a common one in Renaissance love poetry.

**Characterization:** the means by which an author develops and presents a character's personality qualities and distinguishing traits. A character may be established in the story by descriptive commentary or may be developed less directly—for example, through his or her words, actions, thoughts, and interactions with other characters.

**Chronology:** the way a story is organized in terms of time. Linear narratives run continuously from one point in time to a later point, while non-linear narratives are non-continuous and may jump forward and backward in time. A *flashback*, in which a story jumps to a scene previous in time, is an example of non-linearity.

**Classical:** originating in or relating to ancient Greek or Roman culture. As commonly conceived, *classical* implies a strong sense of formal order. The term *neoclassical* is often used with reference to literature of the Restoration and eighteenth century that was strongly influenced by ancient Greek and Roman models.

**Closure:** the sense of completion evoked at the end of a story when all or most aspects of the major conflicts have been resolved. An example of the resolution of an internal conflict in Charlotte Perkins Gilman's "The Yellow Wallpaper" is the narrator's "merging" with the woman behind the paper. Not every story has a strong sense of closure.

**Coloured Narrative:** alternative term for *free indirect discourse*.

**Comedy:** as a literary term, used originally to denote that class of ancient Greek drama in which the action ends happily. More broadly the term has been used to describe a wide variety of literary forms of a more or less light-hearted character.

**Conceit:** an unusually elaborate metaphor or simile that extends beyond its original tenor and vehicle, sometimes becoming a "master" analogy for the entire poem (see, for example, Donne's "The Flea"). Ingenious or fanciful images and comparisons were especially popular with the *metaphysical poets* of the seventeenth century, giving rise to the term "metaphysical conceit."

**Conflict:** struggles between characters and opposing forces. Conflict can be internal (psychological) or external (conflict with another character, for instance, or with society or nature).

**Connotation:** the implied, often unspoken meaning(s) of a given word, as distinct from its *denotation*, or literal meaning. Connotations may have highly emotional undertones and are usually culturally specific.

**Convention:** aesthetic approach, technique, or practice accepted as characteristic and appropriate for a particular form. It is a convention of certain sorts of plays, for example, that the characters speak in blank verse, of other sorts of plays that characters speak in rhymed couplets, and of still other sorts of dramatic performances that characters frequently break into song to express their feelings.

**Denotation:** see *connotation*.

**Dénouement:** that portion of a narrative that follows a dramatic climax, in which conflicts are resolved and the narrative is brought to a close. Traditional accounts of narrative structure often posit a triangle or arc, with rising action followed by a climax and then by a dénouement. (Such accounts bear little relation, however, to the ways in which most actual narratives are structured—particularly most twentieth- and twenty-first-century literary fictions.)

**Dialogue:** words spoken by characters to one another. (When a character is addressing him or her self or the audience directly, the words spoken are referred to as a *soliloquy*.)

**Diction:** word choice. Whether the diction of a literary work (or of a literary character) is colloquial, conversational, formal, or of some other type contributes significantly to the tone of the text as well as to characterization.

**Didacticism:** aesthetic approach emphasizing moral instruction.

**Dramatic Irony:** this form of *irony* occurs when an audience has access to information not available to the character.

**Ellipsis:** the omission of a word or words necessary for the complete grammatical construction of a sentence, but not necessary for our understanding of the sentence.

**Embedded Narrative:** a story contained within another story.

**Epigraph:** a quotation placed at the beginning of a work to indicate or foreshadow the theme.

**Epiphany:** a moment at which matters of significance are suddenly illuminated for a literary character (or for the reader), typically triggered by something small and seemingly of little import. The term first came into wide currency in connection with the fiction of James Joyce.

**Episodic Plot:** plot comprising a variety of episodes that are only loosely connected by threads of story material (as opposed to plots that present one or more continually unfolding narratives, in which successive episodes build one on another).

**Ethos:** the perceived character, trustworthiness, or credibility of a writer or narrator.

**Euphemism:** mode of expression through which aspects of reality considered to be vulgar, crudely physical, or unpleasant are referred to indirectly rather than named explicitly. A variety of euphemisms exist for the processes of urination and defecation; *passed away* is often used as a euphemism for *died*.

**Euphony:** pleasant, musical sounds or rhythms.

**Existentialism:** a philosophical approach according to which the meaning of human life is derived from the actual experience of the living individual. The existential worldview, in which life is assumed to have no essential or pre-existing meanings other than those we personally choose to endow it with, can produce an *absurdist* sensibility.

**Exposition:** the setting out of material in an ordered (and usually concise) form, either in speech or in writing. In a play those parts of the action that do not occur on stage but are rather recounted by the characters are frequently described as being presented in exposition. Similarly, when the background narrative is filled in near the beginning of a novel, such material is often described as having been presented in exposition.

**Fable:** a short *allegorical* tale that conveys an explicit moral lesson. The characters are often animals or objects with human speech and mannerisms. See *parable*.

**Fantasy:** in fiction, a sub-genre characterized by the presence of magical or miraculous elements—usually acknowledged as such by the characters and the narrative voice. In *magic realism*, by contrast, miraculous occurrences tend to be treated by the characters and/or the narrative voice as if they were entirely ordinary. In fantasy (also in contrast to magic realism), the fictional world generally has an internal consistency to it that precludes any sense of absurdity on the part of the reader; and the plot tends to build a strong sense of expectation in the reader.

**Farce:** sometimes classed as the "lowest" form of *comedy*. Its humour depends not on verbal wit, but on physicality and sight gags.

**Fiction:** imagined or invented narrative. In literature, the term is usually used to refer to prose narratives (such as novels and short stories).

**Figures of Speech:** deliberate, highly concentrated uses of language to achieve particular purposes or effects on an audience. There are two kinds of figures: schemes and *tropes*. Schemes involve changes in word-sound and word-order, such as *alliteration*. Tropes play on our understandings of words to extend, alter, or transform meaning, as in *metaphor* and *personification*.

**First-Person Narrative:** narrative recounted using *I* and *me*. See also *narrative perspective*.

**Flashback:** in fiction, the inclusion in the primary thread of a story's narrative of a scene (or scenes) from an earlier point in time. Flashbacks may be used to revisit from a different viewpoint events that have already been recounted in the main thread of narrative; to present material that has been left out in the initial recounting; or to present relevant material from a time before the beginning of the main thread of narrative. The use of flashbacks in fiction is sometimes referred to as *analepsis*.

**Flashforward:** the inclusion in the primary thread of a story's narrative of a scene (or scenes) from a later point in time. See also *prolepsis*.

**Flat Character:** the opposite of a *round character*, a flat character is defined by a small number of traits and does not possess enough complexity to be psychologically realistic. "Flat character" can be a disparaging term, but need not be; flat characters serve different purposes in a fiction than round characters, and are often better suited to some types of literature, such as allegory or farcical comedy.

**Foil:** in literature, a character whose behaviour and/or qualities set in relief for the reader or audience those of a strongly contrasting character who plays a more central part in the story.

**Foreshadowing:** the inclusion of elements in a story that hint at some later development(s) in the same story. For example, in Flannery O'Connor's "A Good Man Is Hard to Find," the old family burying ground that the family sees on their drive foreshadows the violence that follows.

**Free Indirect Discourse:** a style of third-person narration that takes on characteristics of first-person narration, thus making it difficult to discern whether the reader is receiving the impressions of the character, the narrator, or some combination of the two.

**Freytag's Pyramid:** a model of plot structure developed by the German novelist, playwright, and critic Gustav Freytag and introduced in his book *Die Technik des Dramas* (1863). In the pyramid, five stages of plot are identified as occurring in the following order: exposition, rising action, climax, falling action, and *dénouement*. Freytag intended his pyramid to diagram the structure of classical five-act plays, but it is also used as a tool to analyze other forms of fiction (even though many individual plays and stories do not follow the structure outlined in the pyramid).

**Genre:** a class or type of literary work. The concept of genre may be used with different levels of generality. At the most general, poetry, drama, and prose fiction are distinguished as separate genres. At a lower level of generality various sub-genres are frequently distinguished, such as (within the genre of prose fiction) the novel, the novella, and the short story; and, at a still lower level of generality, the mystery novel, the detective novel, the novel of manners, and so on.

**Gothic:** in architecture and the visual arts, a term used to describe styles prevalent from the twelfth to the fourteenth centuries, but in literature a term used to describe work with a sinister or grotesque tone that seeks to evoke a sense of terror on the part of the reader or audience. Gothic literature originated as a genre in the eighteenth century with works such as Horace Walpole's *The Castle of Otranto*. To some extent the notion of the medieval itself then carried with it associations of the dark and the grotesque, but from the beginning an element of intentional exaggeration (sometimes verging on self-parody) attached itself to the genre. The Gothic trend of youth culture that began in the late twentieth century is less clearly associated with the medieval, but shares with the various varieties of Gothic literature (from Walpole in the eighteenth century, to Bram Stoker in the early twentieth, to Stephen King and Anne Rice in the late twentieth) a fondness for the sensational and the grotesque, as well as a propensity to self-parody.

**Grotesque:** literature of the grotesque is characterized by a focus on extreme or distorted aspects of human characteristics. (The term can also refer particularly to a character who is odd or disturbing.) This focus can serve to comment on and challenge societal norms. The story "A Good Man Is Hard to Find" employs elements of the grotesque.

**Hyperbole:** a *figure of speech* (a *trope*) that deliberately exaggerates or inflates meaning to achieve particular effects, such as the irony in A.E. Housman's claim (from "Terence, This Is Stupid Stuff") that "malt does more than Milton can / To justify God's ways to man."

**Image:** a representation of a sensory experience or of an object that can be known by the senses.

**Imagery:** the range of images in a given work. We can gain much insight into works by looking for patterns of imagery. For example, the imagery of spring (budding trees, rain, singing birds) in Kate Chopin's "The Story of an Hour" reinforces the suggestions of death and rebirth in the plot and theme.

**Implied author:** see *narrator*.

**Incantation:** a chant or recitation of words that are believed to have magical power. A poem can achieve an "incantatory" effect through a compelling rhyme scheme and other repetitive patterns.

**Intertextuality:** the act of bringing one cultural text into relationship with another, as when a writer references a painting, a song title or lyric, another novel, poem, or play, a famous theoretical work, etc. A literary text may connect with other cultural texts via *allusion, parody,* or *satire,* or in a variety of other ways.

**Irony:** the use of irony draws attention to a gap between what is said and what is meant, or what appears to be true and what is true. Types of irony include verbal irony (which includes *hyberbole, litotes,* and *sarcasm*), *dramatic irony,* and structural irony (in which the gap between what is "said" and meant is sustained throughout an entire piece, as when an author makes use of an unreliable narrator or speaker).

**Litotes:** a *figure of speech* (a *trope*) in which a writer deliberately uses understatement to highlight the importance of an argument, or to convey an ironic attitude.

**Magic Realism:** a style of fiction in which miraculous or bizarre things often happen but are treated in a matter-of-fact fashion by the characters and/or the narrative voice. There is often an element of the absurd to magic realist narratives, and they tend not to have any strong plot structure generating expectations in the reader's mind. See also *fantasy.*

**Metafiction:** fiction that calls attention to itself as fiction. Metafiction is a means by which authors render us conscious of our status as readers, often in order to explore the relationships between fiction and reality.

**Metaphor:** a *figure of speech* (in this case, a *trope*) in which a comparison is made or identity is asserted between two unrelated things or actions without the use of "like" or "as."

**Metonymy:** a *figure of speech* (a *trope*), meaning "change of name," in which a writer refers to an object or idea by substituting the name of another object or idea closely associated with it: for example, the substitution of "crown" for monarchy, "the press" for journalism, or "the pen" for writing. *Synecdoche* is a kind of metonymy.

**Modernism:** in the history of literature, music, and the visual arts, a movement that began in the early twentieth century, characterized by a thoroughgoing rejection of the then-dominant conventions of literary plotting and characterization, of melody and harmony, and of perspective and other naturalistic forms of visual representation. In literature (as in music and the visual arts), modernists endeavoured to represent the complexity of what seemed to them to be an increasingly fragmented world by adopting techniques of presenting story material, illuminating character, and employing imagery that emphasized (in the words of Virginia Woolf) "the spasmodic, the obscure, the fragmentary."

**Mood:** this can describe the writer's attitude, implied or expressed, toward the subject (see *tone*); or it may refer to the atmosphere that a writer creates in a passage of description or narration.

**Motif:** pattern formed by the recurrence of an idea, image, action, or plot element throughout a literary work, creating new levels of meaning and strengthening structural coherence. The term is taken from music, where it describes recurring melodies or themes. See also *theme*.

**Motivation:** the forces that seem to cause characters to act, or reasons why characters do what they do.

**Narration:** the process of disclosing information, whether fictional or nonfictional.

**Narrative Perspective:** in fiction, the point of view from which a story is narrated. A first-person narrative is recounted using *I* and *me*, whereas a third-person narrative is recounted using *he*, *she*, *they*, and so on. When a narrative is written in the third person and the narrative voice evidently "knows" all that is being done and thought, the story is typically described as being recounted by an "omniscient narrator." Second-person narratives, in which the narrative is recounted using *you*, are very rare.

**Narrator:** the voice (or voices) disclosing information. In fiction, the narrator is distinguished from both the author (a real, historical person) and the implied author (whom the reader imagines the author to be). Narrators can also be distinguished according to the degree to which they share the reality of the other characters in the story and the extent to which they participate in the action; according to how much information they are privy to (and how much of that information they are willing to share with the reader); and according to whether or not they are perceived by the reader as reliable or unreliable sources of information. See also *narrative perspective*.

**Neoclassicism:** literally the "new classicism," the aesthetic style that dominated high culture in Europe through the seventeenth and eighteenth centuries, and in some places into the nineteenth century. Its subject matter was often taken from Greek and Roman myth and history; in *style*, it valued order, reason, clarity, and moderation.

**Omniscient Narrator:** see *narrative perspective*.

**Onomatopoeia:** a *figure of speech* (a scheme) in which a word "imitates" a sound, or in which the sound of a word seems to reflect its meaning.

**Oxymoron:** a *figure of speech* (a *trope*) in which two words whose meanings seem contradictory are placed together; we see an example in Shakespeare's *Twelfth Night*, when Orsino refers to the "sweet pangs" of love.

**Parable:** a story told to illustrate a moral principle. It differs from *allegory* in being shorter and simpler: parables do not generally function on two levels simultaneously.

**Parody:** a close, usually mocking imitation of a particular literary work, or of the well-known style of a particular author, in order to expose or magnify weaknesses. Parody is a form of *satire*—that is, humour that may ridicule and scorn its object.

**Pastiche:** a discourse that borrows or imitates other writers' characters, forms, style, or ideas, sometimes creating something of a literary patchwork. Unlike a parody, a pastiche can be intended as a compliment to the original writer.

**Pathetic Fallacy:** a form of *personification* in which inanimate objects are given human emotions: for example, rain clouds "weeping." The word "fallacy" in this connection is intended to suggest the distortion of reality or the false emotion that may result from an exaggerated use of personification.

**Pathos:** the emotional quality of a discourse; or the ability of a discourse to appeal to our emotions. It is usually applied to the mood conveyed by images of pain, suffering, or loss that arouse feelings of pity or sorrow in the reader.

**Persona:** the assumed identity or "speaking voice" that a writer projects in a discourse. The term "persona" literally means "mask."

**Personification:** a *figure of speech* (a *trope*), also known as "prosopopoeia," in which a writer refers to inanimate objects, ideas, or non-human animals as if they were human, or creates a human figure to represent an abstract entity such as Philosophy or Peace.

**Phoneme:** a linguistic term denoting the smallest unit of sound that it is possible to distinguish. The words *fun* and *phone* each have three phonemes, though one has three letters and one has five.

**Plot:** the organization of story materials within a literary work. Matters of plotting include the order in which story material is presented; the inclusion of elements that allow or encourage the reader or audience to form expectations as to what is likely to happen; and the decision to present some story material through exposition rather than present it directly to the reader as part of the narrative.

**Point of View:** see *narrative perspective.*

**Postmodernism:** in literature and the visual arts, a movement influential in the late twentieth and early twenty-first centuries. In some ways postmodernism represents a reaction to modernism, in others an extension of it. With roots in the work of French philosophers such as Jacques Derrida and Michel Foucault, it is deeply coloured by theory; indeed, it may be said to have begun at the "meta" level of theorizing rather than at the level of practice. Like modernism, postmodernism embraces difficulty and distrusts the simple and straightforward. More broadly, postmodernism is characterized by a rejection of absolute truth or value, of closed systems, of grand unified narratives.

Postmodernist fiction is characterized by a frequently ironic or playful tone in dealing with reality and illusion; by a willingness to combine different styles or forms in a single work (just as in architecture the postmodernist spirit embodies a willingness to borrow from seemingly disparate styles in designing a single structure); and by a highly attuned awareness of the problematized state of the writer, artist, or theorist as observer.

**Prolepsis:** originally a rhetorical term used to refer to the anticipation of possible objections by someone advancing an argument, prolepsis is used in discussions of fiction to refer to elements in a narrative that anticipate the future of the story. The *flashforward* technique of storytelling is often described as a form of prolepsis; the inclusion in a narrative of material that foreshadows future developments is also sometimes treated as a form of prolepsis.

**Protagonist:** the central character in a literary work.

**Pun:** a play on words, in which a word with two or more distinct meanings, or two words with similar sounds, may create humorous ambiguities. Also known as "paranomasia."

**Realism:** as a literary term, the presentation through literature of material closely resembling real life. As notions both of what constitutes "real life" and of how it may be most faithfully represented in literature have varied widely, "realism" has taken a variety of meanings. The term "naturalistic" has sometimes been used as a synonym for *realistic*; naturalism originated in the nineteenth century as a term denoting a form of realism focusing in particular on grim, unpleasant, or ugly aspects of the real.

**Romance:** a dreamlike genre of fiction or storytelling in which the ordinary laws of nature are suspended—in which, for example, statues come to life, or shipwrecked men emerge from the sea unharmed.

**Romanticism:** a major social and cultural movement, originating in Europe, that shaped much of Western artistic thought in the late eighteenth and nineteenth centuries. Opposing the ideal of controlled, rational order associated with the Enlightenment, Romanticism emphasizes the importance of spontaneous self-expression, emotion, and personal experience in producing art. In Romanticism, the "natural" is privileged over the conventional or the artificial.

**Round Character:** a complex and psychologically realistic character, often one who changes as a work progresses. The opposite of a round character is a *flat character*.

**Sarcasm:** a form of *irony* (usually spoken) in which the meaning is conveyed largely by the tone of voice adopted; something said sarcastically is meant to imply its opposite.

**Satire:** literary work designed to make fun of or seriously criticize its subject. According to many literary theories of the Renaissance and neoclassical periods, the ridicule through satire of a certain sort of behaviour may function for the reader or audience as a corrective of such behaviour.

**Setting:** the time, place, and cultural environment in which a story or work takes place.

**Simile:** a *figure of speech* (a *trope*) which makes an explicit comparison between a particular object and another object or idea that is similar in some (often unexpected) way. A simile always uses "like" or "as" to signal the connection. Compare with *metaphor*.

**Stock Character:** a character defined by a set of characteristics that are stereotypical and/or established by literary convention; examples include the "wicked stepmother" and the "absent-minded professor."

**Story:** narrative material, independent of the manner in which it may be presented or the ways in which the narrative material may be organized. Story is thus distinct from *plot*.

**Stream of Consciousness:** a narrative technique that conveys the inner workings of a character's mind, in which a character's thoughts, feelings, memories, and impressions are related in an unbroken flow, without concern for *chronology* or coherence.

**Style:** a distinctive or specific use of language and form.

**Sublime:** a concept, popular in eighteenth-century England, that sought to capture the qualities of grandeur, power, and awe that may be inherent in or produced by undomesticated nature or great art. The sublime was thought of as higher and loftier than something that is merely beautiful.

**Subplot:** a line of story that is subordinate to the main storyline of a narrative. (Note that properly speaking a subplot is a category of story material, not of plot.)

**Subtext:** implied or suggested meaning of a passage of text, or of an entire work.

**Surrealism:** Surrealism incorporates elements of the true appearance of life and nature, combining these elements according to a logic more typical of dreams than waking life. Isolated aspects of surrealist art may create powerful illusions of reality, but the effect of the whole is usually to disturb or question our sense of reality rather than to confirm it.

**Suspension of Disbelief:** a willingness on the part of the audience member or reader to temporarily accept the fictional world presented in a narrative.

**Syllable:** vocal sound or group of sounds forming a unit of speech; a syllable may be formed with a single effort of articulation. Some syllables consist of a single phoneme (e.g., the word *I*, or the first syllable in the word *u*-ni-ty) but others may be made up of several phonemes (as with one-syllable words such as *lengths*, *splurged*, and *through*). By contrast, the much shorter words *ago*, *any*, and *open* each have two syllables.

**Symbol:** something that represents itself but goes beyond this in suggesting other meanings. Like metaphor, the symbol extends meaning; but while the tenor and vehicle of metaphor are bound in a specific relationship, a symbol may have a range of connotations. For example, the image of a rose may call forth associations of love, passion, transience, fragility, youth, and beauty, among others. Depending upon the context, such an image could be interpreted in a variety of ways, as in Blake's lyric, "The Sick Rose."

**Synecdoche:** a kind of *metonymy* in which a writer substitutes the name of a part of something to signify the whole: for example, "sail" for ship or "hand" for a member of the ship's crew.

**Syntax:** the ordering of words in a sentence.

**Theme:** in general, an idea explored in a work through character, action, and/or image. To be fully developed, however, a theme must consist of more than a single concept or idea: it should also include an argument about the idea. Thus if a poem examines the topic of jealousy, we might say the theme is that jealousy undermines love or jealousy is a manifestation of insecurity. Few, if any, literary works have single themes.

**Third-Person Narrative:** see *narrative perspective*.

**Tone:** the writer's attitude toward a given subject or audience, as expressed through an authorial persona or "voice." Tone can be projected through particular choices of wording, imagery, figures of speech, and rhythmic devices. Compare *mood*.

**Tragedy:** in the traditional definition originating in discussions of ancient Greek drama, a serious narrative recounting the downfall of the protagonist, usually a person of high social standing. More loosely, the term has been applied to a wide variety of literary forms in which the tone is predominantly a dark one and the narrative does not end happily.

**Trope:** any figure of speech that plays on our understandings of words to extend, alter, or transform "literal" meaning. Common tropes include *metaphor, simile, personification, hyperbole, metonymy, oxymoron, synecdoche*, and *irony*. See also *figures of speech*.

**Unreliable Narrator:** a narrator whose reporting or understanding of events invites questioning from the reader. Narrators may be considered unreliable if they lack sufficient intelligence or experience to understand events, or if they have some reason to misrepresent events. See also *narrative perspective*.

**Acknowledgement:** The glossary for *The Broadview Introduction to Literature* incorporates some material initially prepared for the following Broadview anthologies: *The Broadview Anthology of Poetry*, edited by Herbert Rosengarten and Amanda Goldrick-Jones; *The Broadview Anthology of Drama*, edited by Jennifer Wise and Craig Walker; *The Broadview Anthology of Short Fiction*, edited by Julia Gaunce et al.; *The Broadview Anthology of British Literature*, edited by Joseph Black et al. The editors gratefully acknowledge the contributions of the editors of these other anthologies. Please note that all material in the glossary, whether initially published in another Broadview anthology or appearing here for the first time, is protected by copyright.

# Permissions Acknowledgements

# Index of Authors and Titles

## From the Publisher

A name never says it all, but the word "Broadview" expresses a good deal of the philosophy behind our company. We are open to a broad range of academic approaches and political viewpoints. We pay attention to the broad impact book publishing and book printing has in the wider world; we began using recycled stock more than a decade ago, and for some years now we have used 100% recycled paper for most titles. Our publishing program is internationally oriented and broad-ranging. Our individual titles often appeal to a broad readership too; many are of interest as much to general readers as to academics and students.

Founded in 1985, Broadview remains a fully independent company owned by its shareholders—not an imprint or subsidiary of a larger multinational.

For the most accurate information on our books (including information on pricing, editions, and formats) please visit our website at www.broadviewpress.com. Our print books and ebooks are also available for sale on our site.

broadview press

www.broadviewpress.com

This book is made of paper from well-managed FSC® - certified forests, recycled materials, and other controlled sources.